SOUNDS LIKE LIFE

OXFORD STUDIES IN ANTHROPOLOGICAL LINGUISTICS
William Bright, *General Editor*

1. *Classificatory Particles in Kilivila*
Gunter Senft

2. *Sounds Like Life*
Sound-Symbolic Grammar, Performance, and Cognition in Pastaza Quechua
Janis B. Nuckolls

SOUNDS LIKE LIFE

Sound-Symbolic Grammar, Performance, and Cognition in Pastaza Quechua

Janis B. Nuckolls

New York Oxford
OXFORD UNIVERSITY PRESS
1996

Oxford University Press

Oxford New York
Athens Auckland Bangkok
Calcutta Cape Town Dar es Salaam Delhi
Florence Hong Kong Istanbul Karachi
Kuala Lumpur Madras Madrid Melbourne
Mexico City Nairobi Paris Singapore
Taipei Tokyo Toronto

and associated companies in
Berlin Ibadan

Published by Oxford University Press, Inc.
198 Madison Avenue, New York, New York 10016

Oxford is a registered trademark of Oxford University Press, Inc.

Chapter 5, "Sound-Symbolic Involvement," which appeared in a different version in the *Journal of Linguistic Anthropology* 2:1 (June 1992), is reprinted by permission of the American Anthropological Association.

Library of Congress Cataloging-in-Publication Data
Nuckolls, Janis B.
Sounds like life: sound-symbolic grammar, performance, and cognition in Pastaza Quechua / Janis B. Nuckolls.
p. cm.—(Oxford studies in anthropological linguistics)
Includes bibliographical references and index.
ISBN 0-19-508985-5
1. Quechua language—Onomatopoeic words. 2. Quechua language—Aspect.
3. Quechua language—Ecuador—Pastaza (Province)
I. Title. II. Series.
PM6303.N78 1996
498'.323—dc20 94-48118

1 3 5 7 9 8 6 4 2

Printed in the United States of America
on acid-free paper

For Charles and Will

ACKNOWLEDGMENTS

While a graduate student at the University of Chicago, I wrote a dissertation that developed a preliminary formulation of the problems tackled by this book. My most important influences from this period are the members of my committee. I had the great fortune to work with Paul Friedrich, whose provocative intellect and luminary insights on the aesthetic dimensions of language structure and use provided a wealth of intellectual inspiration. The idea for this research was, in fact, catalyzed by a footnote in his article on Homeric aspect, which alluded to possible links between aspect grammar and cultural semantics. Howard Aronson's courses introduced me to the subtleties of Praguean structural analysis and have made a lasting impression on my thinking about grammatical categories. Bill Hanks influenced my thoughts on the important pragmatic dimensions of linguistic iconicity and was a most important sounding board throughout the writing process. Bruce Mannheim's clarion insights on iconicity in historical change deepened my understanding of its significance for this work. He also broadened my perspective on the family of Quechua languages and on a number of theoretical issues.

The field research for this book was conducted in Ecuador from January 1987 to June 1988. It was funded by the Joint Committee on Latin American Studies of the Social Science Research Council and the American Council of Learned Societies. The National Science Foundation provided funds for equipment, and the Wenner-Gren Foundation assisted with equipment and travel expenses. Funds from the American Association of University Women gave me an entire year of free time for writing. I am very grateful to all these institutions for their generous financial support. I would also like to express my gratitude to Norman and Sibby Whitten, whose own research overlapped with my fieldwork. They helped me in countless ways, both intellectual and practical. While in Ecuador, I was also greatly assisted by Dr. María del Carmen Molestina Zaldumbide of Los Museos del Banco Central, Quito, with whom I was affiliated; Dr. del Carmen very generously steered me through several difficult processes. I also thank Dr. Ruth Jaramillo of the Instituto Nacional de Patrimonio Cultural del Ecuador for making my relations with the institute so productive and pleasant.

To my Quechua-speaking friends in Puka yaku, Puyo, and Sara yaku, I extend my deepest and sincerest thanks. All of them put up with many kinds of interferences, impositions, and nuisances directly related to my presence in their homes. I am particularly indebted to Acevero, Alberto, Antonia, Camilla, David, Dilvia, Dina, Eloisa, Faviola, Irma, Malako, Manilla, Orlando, Rosa Elena, Salvadore, Theresa, and Ventura, all of Puka yaku. I would also like to thank Rebecca Hualinga and Armadora Aranda of Sara yaku for many hours of enjoyable conversation. My debt to Estella Dahua of Puyo is great. She was my first Quechua-speaking friend. She also taught me much about pottery making, from the initial mining of clay to the final stages of painting and glazing. It is difficult to adequately thank Eloisa Cadena of Puka yaku and Puyo: without her brilliant and creative assistance, I would not have been able to untangle the intricacies of sound-symbolic usage. Not only was she able to assist me with these specific grammatical problems, she also contributed immeasurably to my understanding of what Pastaza Quechua speakers consider interesting and important.

Sincerest thanks to Carlos Viteri of Sara yaku and Quito for many hours of enjoyable conversation and especially for the poster, included in chapter 6, which he provided. His perspectives on political and cultural issues have been incorporated into my ideas about the interrelations between sound, nature, and Pastaza Quechua culture. I hope he will find my interpretations interesting.

Many thanks to Fr. Elias Murguizu O.P., of the Vicariato Apostólico de Puyo, whose warm and generous hospitality enabled me to live far more comfortably in Puka yaku than circumstances would otherwise have allowed. I also owe a great debt to the many brave pilots who transported me between Shell and Montalvo. I am particularly grateful to a man named Mosquera who managed to guide myself, my *comadre*, and one very ill godchild through a big, awful rainstorm and safely into Shell, just before running out of fuel. Warmest thanks to Joe Brenner of Quito for his friendship and hospitality. I spent many enjoyable hours sitting in his kitchen and learning about his indigenous art collections.

In 1990 I joined the faculty of the Department of Anthropology and the Center for Latin American and Caribbean Studies at Indiana University where I enjoyed the collegial stimulation and encouragement of Dick Bauman, Michael Herzfeld, Michael Jackson, Bonnie Kendall, Ray de Mallie, Doug Parks, John McDowell, Russell Salmon, Carol Greenhouse, Joelle Bahloul, and Della Cook. I was particularly enriched in my thinking by Dick Bauman's ideas on verbal art and performance and on poetics and social life. The idea of performance has now become central to my thinking about sound symbolism. Thank you, also, to Jim Vaughan, Geoff Conrad, and Russell Salmon, who in their roles as chair very generously granted me leave time for turning a dissertation into a book.

In addition to collegial stimulation and time off, Indiana also gave the me the rare opportunity during 1992 to 1993 to work with a Quechua speaker for a year in Bloomington. Warmest thanks to Sergio Gualinga, of Sara yaku, Ecuador, for coming. Working with him has greatly enriched my perspective on sound-symbolic usage. I am particularly indebted to Russ Salmon for his help in arranging for Sergio's visit to the United States; he also helped Sergio in countless ways, once he arrived. I am also deeply grateful to Norman Whitten of the University of Illinois and his wife, Sibby, who took on the formidable task of facilitating Sergio's visit from Ecuador, as I was in the late stages of pregnancy and unable to travel. They arranged for his visa, passport, and plane tickets and practically delivered him to my doorstep.

Since joining the faculty of the Department of Anthropology at the University of Alabama at Birmingham, I have benefited greatly from the collegial atmosphere created by our chairman, Roger Nance, and my colleagues Brian Hesse, Bruce Wheatley, Chris Taylor, Tom McKenna, Barbara Michael, and Eileen Van Schaik.

I gratefully acknowledge the many helpful comments and suggestions of William Bright, Joel Sherzer, and an anonymus reviewer who read this book at the manuscript stage. I also thank Peter Ohlin, assistant editor, and Cynthia Garver, production editor, both of Oxford University Press, who have assisted in countless ways with the production process.

My greatest personal debts are to my son, Will, and my husband, Charles. Will was born between the penultimate draft and final revisions. He has been a constant source of inspiration and happiness throughout the upheavals and difficulties of living in a commuting marriage family. I hope he is, and will continue to be, as thrilled to be our child as we are to be his parents. Thank you also to the women who cared for him while I was working on this book: the late Petra Lorimer, Haihong Yang, Jhansi Akhinesi, and Padmalatha. My husband, Charles, of the Department of Anthropology at Emory University, is my closest colleague. His own interests in cognition and mind have deepened my theoretical perspectives on language. He has, in a way, helped to incubate every significant development in my thinking. To him and to our son I dedicate this effort.

Birmingham, Alabama
April 1995

J.B.N.

CONTENTS

Abbreviations and Symbols, xiii

I Sound-Symbolic Grammar and Performance

1 Introduction, 3
2 The Theoretical Dimensions of Aspect, 21
3 The Grammatical Ecology of Aspect in Pastaza Quechua, 40
4 The Performative Expression of Durativity and Perfectivity, 62
5 Sound-Symbolic Involvement, 79
6 Signs of Life in Sound, 101

II The Sound-Symbolic Construction of Spatiotemporal Experience

7 Sound-Symbolic Iconicity and Grammar, 137
8 Sound-Symbolic Contrasts of Sensible Experience, 145
9 Sound Symbols of Contact and Penetration, 178
10 Sound Symbols of Opening and Closing, 204
11 Sound Symbols of Falling, 219
12 Sound Symbols of Deformation, 232
13 Sound Symbols of Suddenness and Completiveness, 250
14 Conclusion, 276

Appendix: Conjugation of *rina*, 281
Notes, 283
Bibliography, 289
Index, 295

ABBREVIATIONS AND SYMBOLS USED IN TRANSLATIONS OF TEXTS

ACC	Accusative case
ADV	Adverb
AG	Agentive
CAUS	Causative
CIR	Circumventive
CIS	Cislocative
COMP	Comparative
CNDL	Conditional
COR	Coreference
DAT	Dative case
DUB	Dubitative
DUR	Durative aspect
EV	Evidential
EXCL	Exclamative
FUT	Future
FINF	Future infinitive
IMP	Imperative
ICH	Inchoative
INCL	Inclusive
INST	Instrumental case
LIM	Limitative
LOC	Locative case
NEG	Negative
NOM	Nominalizer
PERF	Perfect aspect/tense
PL	Plural
POSS	Possessive
QN	Question
RCP	Reciprocal
SUB	Subjunctive
SWRF	Switch reference
TOP	Topic
TRSLC	Translocative
XPRO	Exclusive pronoun
1	First person
2	Second person
3	Third person

Extended narrative texts that appear in these pages use structural principles of line and verse as outlined by Bright (1979), Hymes (1981), and Tedlock 1983. I follow Tedlock (1983) in using pause breaks to guide the division of narrative into lines. Pause breaks are used by Quechua speakers to mark off lines of varied structure and length. Lines indicated by pause breaks can be as lengthy as two or more predicates or as brief as a single word. If a pause after a line is much longer than usual, it will be indicated with the words "long pause" in parentheses. Otherwise ellipses will be used to indicate pauses of ordinary duration. Parentheses are also used to enclose any special moods that accompany an utterance. A bracket preceding an utterance ([ ) indicates that it is spoken simultaneously with the preceding utterance. I follow Hymes (1981) in using sentence-initial particles as a general guide for grouping lines into larger units of verse. There are several such particles in Pastaza Quechua, including *chiga* "and so, so then, here then"; *ña* "then"; and *chayga* "there then." However, these particles are not in and of themselves adequate predicators of verse change. *Chiga* "and so" is sometimes used to articulate a process of reasoned thought that is not meant to introduce a new verse structure. For example, one might hear it used as follows: "They want to catch a big turtle that night, and so right there on the beach they're going to sleep." Futhermore, a new verse can be indicated without the introduction of a new particle. A word that is highly foregrounded intonationally can serve as a conceptual and structural pivot, allowing both speaker and listener to switch their focus of attention to a new set of lines. Reported speech can have a similar funciton, particularly when it is presented as interruptive of the speaker's preoccupations and conscious concerns. Verses, then, are determined by both formal evidence from sentence-initial particles and semantic structural features of the narrative. Each line is numbered.

I

SOUND-SYMBOLIC GRAMMAR AND PERFORMANCE

1

Introduction

In her introduction to *Language the Unknown*, political theorist and linguist Julia Kristeva states the following: "The question *'what is language?'* could and should be replaced with another: *'How was it possible to conceive of language?'* (1989: 5)." This question assumes particular importance for the anthropologist investigating the language practices of speech communities unfamiliar with Western scientific culture. How can a scientific conception of language, which insists on its abstraction from the material world and from the body of the speaker, have any meaning for people who conceive language as a material force integrated with the natural and cosmic world? A scientific representation of language as an abstract, disembodied, and immaterial essence is ill equipped to understand, for example, magical practices that depend for their efficacy on the power of words. Nor can a scientific representation of language explain such practices as naming taboos, which are based on beliefs that link the uttering of a name to the bringing forth of a person's being.

This book takes the spirit of Kristeva's question and uses it to frame an analysis of sound symbolism in Pastaza Quechua. Quechua speakers' use of sound symbolism suggests an orientation to the world that unites the material with the conceptual and the natural with the cultural or conventional. For the lowland Ecuadorean Quechua, language use is modeled on sounds, patterns, movements, and rhythms of the natural world and of one's bodily experiences in it. The "sounds of sound" communicate not an abstract, detached meaning, but a concrete movement, rhythm, or process unfolding in time. Sound-symbolic utterances simulate the material qualities of the natural, sensible world and thereby articulate Quechua peoples' cultural constructions of it. They are productively examined here as a performative style of speaking that is consciously imitative and analogous to English speakers' use of onomatopoeic words such as "thump" and "whack."[1] Quechua speakers' sound symbolism, however, is quite varied in the range of sensations it imitates. Sounds, rhythms, visual patterns, and psychophysical sensations make up their repertoire of sound-symbolic forms. Another important difference is that English speakers' sound-symbolic style is highly restricted in its function, indicating affective tones of whimsy or childishness. Quechua sound symbolism, by contrast, is central to peoples' discursive practice. Its distinctive formal properties and grammatical functions pervade the architecture of the language, providing speakers with a rich inventory of expressive possibilities.

Sound symbolic words are incorporated into the grammatical system of Quechua in the form of schematic structures that are grounded in peoples' bodily and perceptual experience. The term *schemas* or *schemata*, is used by cognitive linguists, anthropologists, and psychologists to describe the basic kinds of knowledge structures that are required by our bodily experience: they are preconceptual structures that allow us to understand, for example, that some objects may contain others, that some objects may be linked with others, that some kinds of experiences are oriented in an upward rather than a downward direction, and so on. In Pastaza Quechua, sound-symbolic schemas mark grammatical aspect. Generally defined, *grammatical aspect* specifies the relative duration or nonduration of an action, event, or process. The image most commonly employed to conceptualize aspect is the contrast between a point and a line. A *line* represents an image of an action's duration, and a *point* represents an image of its momentaneousness. Sapir explained these images thus: "Aspect is the geometric form of time: all events [can be conceived of as either] a point or a line, and this [distinction] is formalized by certain languages. "She burst into tears" is a point, while "she lived happily ever after" is a line; and this in Nootka is more important than tense" (1994: 109). This book will demonstrate that the point-line contrast is only the most basic image of an event shape. An understanding of grammatical aspect in Pastaza Quechua requires more than the simple point-line contrast; Pastaza Quechua aspect expression draws on complex kinesthetic schemas encoded in sound-symbolic words. These schemas are based in cognitively salient experiences such as making contact with a surface, opening and closing, falling, deforming, experiencing sudden realizations, making abrupt movements, and moving through water or across space.[2]

Sound-symbolic utterances simulate such experiences through foregrounded moments of performance that communicate "through the present appreciation of the intrinsic qualities of the act of expression itself" (Bauman 1986: 3). The function of sound-symbolic utterances is at least as aesthetically significant as it is grammatically and cognitively significant. Sound-symbolic expression, therefore, represents an important area for investigating Quechua language and culture. The discourse-centered approach to language and culture, represented by Sherzer (1983, 1987), Urban (1991), and many others, considers discourse, especially aesthetic forms of discourse, to be the concrete expression of language and culture interrelations. This approach carries on a tradition of inquiry first established by Whorf, Sapir, and Jakobson and rearticulated by Friedrich (1979, 1986). Among the more provocative claims of the discourse-centered approach, and one that informs this book, is that speech styles are culturally constituted signals which bring one's world into emotional and intellectual focus (Urban 1985: 328). Speech styles are able to do this, it is hypothesized, because the stylistic message is indexical, pointing one's attention to contexts and cultural values. Speech styles call attention to what is felt, sensed, and embodied, in addition to what is referred to (Urban 1991: 139–145). Sound symbolism is a style of speaking that foregrounds or "marks" what is significant for the Pastaza Quechua. It uses the sound qualities of the sign to represent Quechua speakers' culturally constituted perceptions of the natural world. At the same time, sound-symbolic discourse embodies those perceptions because it is articulated by a speaker's conscious shaping of the vocal tract, movements of the mouth, and pitch fluctuations of the voice.

Its pervasiveness in Quechua speakers' discursive practice suggests that sound symbolism ramifies with their larger cultural concerns by pointing their attention to what is perceptually salient, affectively suggestive, and imaginatively engaging. For the Pastaza Quechua, sound is a modality for representing what is significant about human experience (cf. Feld 1982; Basso 1985; Mannheim 1988). Sound-symbolic impressions are part of the way they organize their memories and anchor their understandings of key life experiences. The most significant events of peoples' lives are interpreted against a backdrop of sound-symbolically rendered perceptions of natural phenomena, such as animals' sounds, atmospheric signs, and processes of growth and decay. Death, illness, and misfortune call for explanations that link perceptions of the natural world with the most significant events of human experience. Such explanations are part of Quechua cultural constructions of a manageable world. They also reveal a sense of what, for them is unnatural. Sound, then, is a modality for representing the naturalness or unnaturalness of perceptual experience. The movements of the mouth, the shaping of the vocal tract, and the fluctuating pitch of the voice are all uses of the body to imitate movements and processes of perceptual experience. By imitating these movements and processes, Quechua speakers achieve a sense of control over them. In this way, sound-symbolic language becomes a physiological force integrated with the natural and cosmological world, rather than an abstract, detached code of signification.

In searching for the deeper cultural significance of sound-symbolic style, this work draws on the insights of Urban, who states that speech styles are highly complex sign vehicles with multiple iconic, indexical, and referential functions, which "tend to occur in connection with contexts or subject matters that are areas of cultural emphasis" (1985:327). Speech styles call attention to areas of cultural emphasis, he hypothesizes, through their formal and functional markedness. *Markedness* is a concept employed by linguists and anthropologists to describe a semiotic situation whereby a sign exists in a normal, natural, or neutral form and also in a form that is interpreted as unusual or unexpected, hence "marked" (Kean 1992: 390). The concept of markedness will be employed in chapter 3 to discuss the aspectual oppositions of Quechua's verbal system. Although Quechua's verb roots are neutral or unmarked for aspect values, they exist in a form that is marked for aspectual durativity by suffixation with the durative morpheme *-u-*. Sound-symbolic adverbial modification of verb phrases adds an additional level of markedness for aspectual perfectivity. In addition to their grammatical markedness, moreover, sound-symbolic adverbs are stylistically marked.

Speech styles can be marked through formal amplification or embellishment of the sign vehicle or through their expressive restriction (Urban 1985). Formal amplification of the sign vehicle points attention to the subject matter of the discourse, alerting one to its significance. Chapter 4 will explain in detail the variety of techniques for formal amplification of sound-symbolic adverbs. Preliminary comparative observations, however, suggest that their markedness is not everywhere the same. Chapter 6 will address issues revolving around linguistic style and markedness, cultural values, and social change. What happens when the conceptual and social conditions congenial to sound-symbolic expression change? How do Quechua speakers retain, adapt, or reinterpret a style of expression that represents what is significant about their experience? These are urgent questions because forces of modernization are changing the nature of their experience, and many of these changes create experiential frameworks that are cognitively dissonant with sound-symbolic discourse. Literacy in conjunction with social, political, and economic change is affecting the sound-symbolic style of Quechua speakers in eastern Amazonian Ecuador. Preliminary comparative observations of sound-symbolic usage in another Quechua-peaking village suggest that it is becoming restricted to two interrelated functions and undergoing much less formal amplification.

Sound Symbolism and Linguistic Theory

The scientific representation of language as an abstract, disembodied, and immaterial essence was first articulated in the writings of Saussure, the conceptual architect of modern linguistic theory.[3] This paradigm has supplied formal linguistics with the conceptual tools of its trade. For the anthropologist working in another culture, however, certain aspects of the Saussurean paradigm have proven problematic, if not outright impossible to reconcile with the language practices and beliefs of nonscientific cultures. Motivated by the desire to establish language study as a science, Saussure insists that language is a system isolated from its social life. Besides isolating language from its social contexts of use, Saussurian structuralism has also considered language apart from the material properties of its medium—that is, its physical, acoustical properties. In Saussurean logic, a linguistic sign such as a word unites a *concept* (rather than a material object) with a *sound image* (rather than an actual sound). In conceiving language as an abstract, disembodied, and immaterial entity, Saussurean linguistics was motivated by the desire to establish language as a suitable object for scientific inquiry. In so doing, however, it adopted a stance that is fundamentally at odds with native speaker intuitions about language. In his recent sociohistorical study of southern Peruvian Quechua, Mannheim states that the importance of sound imagery for Quechua speakers reflects a particular orientation toward their language: for Quechua speakers, words are consubstantial with their objects: "Language is part and parcel of the natural world" (1991: 184).

For the lowland Ecuadorean speakers of Pastaza Quechua as well, linguistic sound is consubstantial with natural sound. For the Pastaza Quechua, the salient qualities of the natural world and their bodily experiences in it are, to a significant extent, rendered with sound-symbolic words. Sound-symbolic words are "physiognomic," to use Werner's (1948) term. They give an outward form to the inner movements, sensations, and awarenesses experienced through one's body. They represent, for example, all of the possible positions in which a body experiences unobstructed movement through space or water. They may describe different kinds of contact with another body, degrees of penetration through a medium, or various types of opening and closing. Substances and objects that fall are described with sounds that indicate whether their own bodies are reconfigured or left intact by a fall. And there are large numbers of sound-symbolic adverbs that describe processes enacted by one's body, such as tearing, fissuring, cutting, and bursting. Quechua speakers use the movements of the mouth, the vocal tract, and voice pitch to model and shape their perceptions of sounds, visual patterns, movements, and rhythms. The following example illustrates this claim. The sound-symbolic adverb *sa,* which describes a radial pattern of movement from a center, is performatively foregrounded to imitate the way turtle hatchlings emerge from a nest in the sand and go off in every direction.

1. Na $sa^{a^{a}}$ l^{y}ukshi-nga.
   then emerge-3FUT

   "Then $sa^{a^{a}}$, they'll emerge."

The pitch contour imposed on *sa* presents a sound image of the spatial pattern defined by the scattered turtles. By spanning the extent of the speaker's own voice range and gliding the pitch of *sa* upward, the speaker imitates the extent of the movement throughout a space. At the same time, the word *sa* by its own sound qualities communicates an image of this extended movement because the speaker's mouth moves during its pronunciation from a position of constriction to a position of openness. The contrast between the initially constricted and subsequently more open position of the mouth imitates the initial clustering and subsequent expansion outward of the movement described with *sa.*

The next example features the sound-symbolic adverb *patang*, which describes the way something heavy falls without losing its shape. Here it describes the force with which a snake flings its tail to the ground.

2. Pa-t^{h}anng! (pause) ima ismu kaspi-ta shina tuksi-g a-shka chupa-ta!
   what rot log-ACC like throw-AG be-PERF tail-ACC

   "He went *pa-t^{h}anng*! (pause), throwing his tail down as if it were some rotted log!"

By breaking up his pronunciation in a way that separates the first and second syllable, the speaker imitates the component movements described by this sound-symbolic adverb. The first syllable, *pa-*, imitates the throwing motion of the tail; the second syllable, *-t^{h}anng*, imitates the heaviness and forcefulness of the tail's impact with the ground. By breaking up his pronunciation of these two syllables, the speaker uses articulation to gesture the component movements described.

The foregoing examples make evident the imitative, or *iconic*, basis of sound-symbolic communication. An icon is defined by Peirce as "a sign that refers to the Object that it denotes merely by virtue of characters of its own, and which it possesses, just the same, whether any such Object actually exists or not" (1955: 102). Iconicity is problematic for classical Saussurean theory because the linguistic symbol is characterized by its fundamentally arbitrary nature. According to Saussure's views, as presented in the *Course in General Linguistics*, arbitrariness excludes iconic or onomatopoeic words in principle (1959: 69). Saussure's objections to onomatopoeia are essentially threefold: he states that "onomatopoeic formations are never organic elements of a linguistic system" (1959:69), they are numerically insignificant, and onomatopoeic forms are subject to change over time and are therefore not purely imitative.

His quantitative objection is easily refuted with evidence from non-Indo-European languages that have large inventories of onomatopoeic words (Diffloth 1976; Samarin 1971). Saussure's objection to onomatopoeic words on the basis of their diachronic change is not a valid objection either, because it is based on the assumption that a sign vehicle can only communicate in one semiotic modality. It is the fact that onomatopoeic words have some arbitrary, conventional aspects, evident by their ability to undergo diachronic change, which invalidates their iconicity for Saussure. But such an overly simplified view of onomatopoeia is not warranted by semiotic theory. The most widely cited semiotic taxonomy is the tripartite, Peircean classification of signs into iconic, indexical, and conventional symbols. However, Peirce did not intend these three semiotic categories to be literally understood as a typology of symbols themselves. He stated "a sign may represent its object mainly by its similarity, no matter what its mode of being" (1955: 105). In other words, a sign such as an onomatopoeic word may communicate partly by resemblance and partly by an arbitrary convention.

Saussure's third objection to onomatopoeia, that it is not "organic" to the linguistic system, is also dispensed with. It is not exactly clear what he meant by this statement. In any case, it would seem to be contradicted by his own observation that onomatopoeic words undergo some of the same kinds of diachronic changes that other words undergo. Their tendency to change over time in principled ways implies that sound-symbolic words have some systematic relationship with the structural principles of their language. Putting aside the issue of their change over time, there is another respect in which sound-symbolic words mesh with their grammar. Sound symbolism in Pastaza Quechua discourse is integrated with the grammatical system itself—specifically with the complex subsystem of aspect. Through their morphological shape and also by the intonational contours imposed on them in foregrounded moments of performance, sound-symbolic utterances embody aspect distinctions such as duration, perfectivity, and punctuality. The expressive force of sound-symbolic words is related to their vivid representations of an action's spatiotemporal unfolding, and it is because they concern the spatiotemporal qualities of an action's unfolding that sound-symbolic words are linked to grammatical aspect. The implications of this are important because such an integration reveals yet another area of the overlap between grammar and poetic language noticed by Friedrich (1979, 1986), Jakobson (1968), Sapir (1921), Sherzer (1987), and others.

To understand how sound symbolism intersects with Quechua grammar, it is necessary to consider a concept of grammatical organization that goes beyond the technical, formal systems approach. A formal systems grammar such as the transformational-generative model is represented with mathematically notated rules and is characterized by notions such as "generative power" that have no cognitive significance. However, many linguists have recently turned to a "cognitively salient" (Lakoff 1987) or "cognitively realistic" (Langacker 1991) conception of grammar. Lakoff (1987: 487-488), for example, considers grammar an ecological system, characterized by cognitively salient structures that have their own niche within the overall grammatical system. Lakoff's conception of cognitive salience draws on recent findings in cognitive research that place central importance on the gestalt-like properties of image schematic structures for communicating and understanding. At the same time, "cognitive salience" refers to the fact that image schematic structures are motivated rather than arbitrary in Saussurean terms. They are motivated insofar as they fit into their systems by complex relations of analogy, including metaphor and metonymy. Sound-symbolic words in Pastaza Quechua extend the concepts of cognitive salience and grammatical ecology by their link with the subsystem of aspect and also with the structuring of coreference clauses.

Sound-symbolic words occupy a definite niche in the grammatical structure of Pastaza Quechua. They allow Quechua speakers to tread their way through chained series of coreference clauses without losing their sense of communicative clarity and grammatical explicitness. To understand their grammatical function within the overall ecology of the grammar, it is necessary to explain some basic facts about Quechua clause construction. Briefly, the Quechua language has a way of combining clauses that is unlike the subordination and coordination employed by speakers of English. Quechua speakers *chain* clauses together. For example, an English speaker might say the following to describe the way a canoe is docked by stabbing a riverbank with a steering pole.

3. I stabbed the riverbank and brought the canoe to a standstill.

This sentence features a coordinate construction. A Quechua speaker, however, would use a chaining construction. In Pastaza Quechua, as in other dialects as well, a chained clause is evident by a word final suffix *-sha* which occurs word finally on a Quechua verb, just as the progressive suffix *-ing* occurs word finally on an English verb. A hypothetical translation of such a chaining construction follows. The -ing is underlined to indicate the chained status of its verb.

4. Stabbing the riverbank, I brought the canoe to a standstill.

Sometimes chaining constructions involve more than two verbs, as does the following hypothetical translation. The -ing of each verb is again underlined to indicate its status as a chained clause.

5. Stabbing the riverbank, bringing the canoe to a standstill, tying it to the pole, I headed for my uncle's house.

It is not difficult to understand how such a series of chained constructions might seem insufficiently differentiated from a cognitive point of view. According to their translations, each of the chained clauses would seem to indicate that its action is constantly unfolding and never coming to an end. Yet, the pragmatic semantics of this sentence indicate that each action is concluded before the next one takes place. The canoe has to be tied to the pole before the person can head for the house, and it must be brought to a standstill before it can be tied to the pole. Furthermore, the riverbank has to be stabbed with the pole before the canoe can be brought to a standstill.

Why then, do Quechua speakers use such chaining constructions? To understand this, it is necessary to clarify the difference between Quechua's chaining suffix and the English progressive *-ing* used in the translations. For Quechua speakers the suffix *-sha* which links or chains verbs can indicate that an action is in progress, as does the English progressive *-ing*. However, the main function of this suffix is to indicate that its chained verb refers to an action performed by the same agent as the finite verb. The chaining suffix links each of its verbs to the finite verb, telling a listener that all of these actions are performed by the same agent. Again, the chaining suffix can also indicate that its action is in progress with respect to another. However, Quechua speakers have a way of overriding that interpretation when it is not desired. And this is where sound-symbolic words enter the picture. Many sound-symbolic words function as adverbs to indicate completion, punctuality, or resultativity. When sound-symbolic adverbs modify a chained verb, they effectively establish that verb's temporal closure, despite the progressivity that is implied by the chaining suffix.

Consider, now, the following examples, which are translations of actual Quechua sentences. In the following example, the sound-symbolic adverb *tsak*, which is onomatopoeic of a puncturing or piercing, describes the stabbing of a riverbank with a steering pole to dock a canoe.

6. Chi-ga ña tsak shayari-k shamu-sha, 'maykan-da a-ngichi kay-bi guardia-ga
   that-TOP now stand-AG come-COR which-QN be-2PL here-LOC guard-TOP
   ni-ra-mi?'
   say-PAST-EV

   "So then, *tsak* as-a-stander coming, he said, 'Which of you is the guard here?'"

In this sentence, *tsak* modifies the chained construction "as-a-stander coming." It is the speaker's use of *tsak* that establishes for the listener a clear-cut, cognitively salient boundary between the action of the chained construction and that of the finite verb, "said." The speaker's use of *tsak* creates a vivid sound image of the punctual moment when the riverbank was stabbed and the canoe brought to a standstill.

In the next example, the sound-symbolic adverb *pak*, which describes a sound image of a liquid-like substance falling onto a surface, modifies a chained verb to describe the way tree sap falls onto a wooden bench.

7. Pak urma-sha banku-y chay-bi hapiri-ra shil^{y}kil^{y}u.
   fall-COR bench-LOC there-LOC catch-PAST shil^{y}kil^{y}u

   "Falling *pak* onto the bench, the *shil^{y}kil^{y}u* sap stuck there."

Pak modifies the chained verb "falling." The speaker's use of *pak* clearly delineates, by means of a sound image, the act of the sap's falling from the process of the sap's sticking.

These examples demonstrate that many sound-symbolic adverbs function within a grammatical niche created by chained-clause constructions. Sound-symbolic adverbs provide a cognitively salient boundary for the implied ongoingness of actions described by chained verbs. They are not limited to modifying chained verbs, nor is their occurrence with chained verbs obligatory. However, their frequent use with chained verbs attests to their grammatical and expressive significance. They function in a way that is simultaneously expressive and grammatically explicit by establishing a cognitively salient boundary for the action described by a chained verb. The cognitive salience of sound-symbolic adverbs derives from their expressive imitation of vivid sensations. The grammatical significance of such imitations is that they specify an action's temporal closure.

The Semiotic Significance of Sound-Symbolic Expression

Stankiewicz once observed that "there is an inverse relationship between degrees of emotive intensity and degrees of lexical and grammatical specificity" (1964: 242). However, the nature of the relationship between sound symbolism and grammatical aspect in Quechua renders this distinction suspect, at least for the Pastaza Quechua. Sound symbolism is at once highly expressive and grammatically explicit. Stankiewicz's polarization between grammaticality and expressivity suggests analogies with the Euro-American concern for objective truths on the one hand and aesthetically apperceived truths on the other. Lakoff and Johnson (1980: 186–189) refer to these two conceptual orientations, respectively, as the myth of objectivism and the myth of subjectivism. According to the myth of objectivism, there is a rational, objective, and correct reality, which is describable with clear and precise language. Among the more important tenets of the myth of subjectivism, by contrast, are the dependence on one's senses, intuitions, feelings, and aesthetic sensibilities and the belief that artistic achievements transcend rational or objective truths. Lakoff and Johnson state that both myths are inadequate and argue for "an experientialist synthesis" (1980: 192–193) which employs an imaginative rationality. Metaphor plays a key role in their synthesis because it is both imaginative and rational.

Sound symbolism embodies a type of imaginative rationality, although it is not a form of metaphor. Using Friedrich's (1991) theory of poetic tropes,[4] sound symbolism can be classified as an image trope, because sound-symbolic words "represent various kinds of perceptual images that 'stand for themselves'" (Friedrich 1991:27). Because sound-symbolic words communicate in an imageic or iconic mode, they are appropriate for a variety of affective, expressive, and epistemic functions. An iconic visual sign, such as a photograph of a person, is precise and explicit because, in Peircean terms, it establishes a direct connection between itself and the person it represents. This direct connection is constituted by a perceived resemblance between the sign vehicle—that is, the photograph—and the object, that is, the person. Iconic signs are also expressive, however, because they share their objects' sensory qualities. A photograph of a person, particularly one that focuses on facial features, does more than just provide an objective representation of that person. It also expresses something about that person's affective qualities. In the same way, sound-symbolic words are linguistic icons that communicate in a way that is simultaneously explicit and expressive.

Because sound symbolism cuts across the boundaries of objectivism and subjectivism, it is not surprising that it defies analysis with respect to other categorical distinctions as well. Sound-symbolic utterances are semiotically distinctive. Their semiotic distinctiveness is related, in part, to their iconically performative expression. An iconically performative statement has a different semiotic status than an assertative or referential statement. A prototypical assertion states something about an event, process, or action (Lyons 1983: 726) and is therefore grounded in the distinction made by Jakobson (1971c) between a speech event (E^s) and a narrated event (E^n). However, sound-symbolic performances communicate not by referring, but by iconically simulating the most salient features of an action, event, or process. When a Quechua speaker engages in a sound-symbolic performance, he or she is asking a listener to participate in imagining the action, event, or process being simulated. The distinction between a speech event and a narrated event is therefore blurred in sound-symbolic performance. The speech event *becomes* the narrated event. This is illustrated in the following example, which features a simulation of the sound of a tapir crying as it is being pursued by an anaconda.

8. Chuuuuuuu chu chu waka-sha uyari-mu-n hanag-manda.
   cry-COR sound-CIS-3 upriver-from

   "Crying *chuuuuuuu chu chu,* it is heard from upriver."

The first pronunciation of sound-symbolic *chu* is extended to simulate the sound of the tapir's crying. The two nonextended repetitions of *chu* that follow indicate that its crying was repeated over a space of time. The performative representation of its crying is intended by the narrator to collapse the distinction between the speech event and the narrated event. The narrator expects the listener to imaginatively project into this simulation, thereby experiencing the tapir's cry as if he or she were present as well.

Sound-symbolic words are also semiotically distinctive in their structure, which is schematic. Schemas, or schemata, describe knowledge structures "that constantly recur in our everyday bodily experience: containers, paths, links, forces, balance, and in various orientations and relations: up-down, front-back, part-whole, center-periphery, etc." (Lakoff 1987: 267). Casson (1983) traces the schema concept back to Kant; however, its current use by cognitive linguists and psychologists, he states, can be attributed to a reaction against associationist theories of cognitive processing which held that mental representations were mere recordings of the perceived world. Johnson (1987) states that schemas are not structured by any cognitive operations involving logic or abstract thought. In the following excerpt he clarifies the difference between a schematic structure and a logical, propositional structure.

> "Embodied schema[s]" . . . [are] structures that are constantly operating in our perception, bodily movement through space, and physical manipulation of objects. As embodied in this manner, therefore, *image schemata are not propositional* [emphasis his], in that they are not abstract subject-predicate structures (e.g., "The cat is on the mat") that specify truth conditions or other conditions of satisfaction (e.g., the cat's being on the mat). They exist, rather, in a continuous, analog fashion in our understanding. . . . [They] are abstract and not limited only to visual properties. . . . [They] transcend any specific sense modality, though they involve operations that are analogous to spatial manipulation, orientation, and movement. (1987: 23–25)

An important semiotic consequence of their basis in bodily experience is that schematic structures are directly meaningful. Evidence from their syntactic isolation in a number of contexts of use will confirm that sound-symbolic schemas are directly meaningful for Quechua speakers. When a sound-symbolic adverb is syntactically isolated, it occurs all by itself, without a verb or a sentence to frame it. In such usages, a listener must infer from the schematic structure of the adverb what course of action a narrative is following. What their syntactic isolation reveals is that the use of sound-symbolic schemas depends on a shared knowledge of the world and a common discursive practice.

Because of the configuration of properties that characterize sound-symbolic utterances, their function in discourse cannot be understood by comparison with the function of referential statements. Their iconic, performative, and schematic properties give sound-symbolic utterances unique discursive functions. In everyday contexts of discourse, sound-symbolic descriptions intensify the interactional involvement between interlocutors. A speaker's performative foregrounding of a sound-symbolic form simulates the salient qualities of an action, event, or process and thereby invites a listener to project into an experience. This projected involvement, then, acts as an index pointing the listener to deeper kinds of emotional, intellectual, and imaginative understanding of what is said. Such intersubjective involvement legitimizes a conversational ideal of amiability. Sound-symbolic discourse is not used by the Pastaza Quechua in situations of conflict; it is used by people who are relaxed and at ease. The use of sound symbolism by the Pastaza Quechua is comparable to the use of "bird sound words" for the Kaluli of Papua New Guinea in that the latter are "reflective and sentimental" (Feld 1982:131). Sound symbolism lends itself to contexts in which amicability and goodwill prevail. This is possible, in part, because sound-symbolic utterances simulate basic kinds of sensory experiences that everyone is capable of sharing.

To illustrate, consider the next example, from a short narrative account describing the pursuit of a tapir by an anaconda. The narrator and her companions are not immediately aware of the anaconda's presence. At first they assume the tapir is running from a jaguar. Jaguars frequently pursue tapirs, and tapirs often try to escape by running into a river where a jaguar will not go. The narrator and her companions very quickly realize that the tapir is in fact swimming away from an anaconda by listening to the sounds and movements coming from underwater, which are an index of its presence. Their first realization of the anaconda's presence underwater, even before they've seen it, is described here, with the sound symbolic adverb k^h*aw*.

9. So then, (pause) in that pond, k^h*awwwwwwwwww*! (pause)

By drawing out her pronunciation of k^h*aw*, the narrator engages in a moment of performance designed to simulate for the listener a direct experience of a thrashing sound. At the same time, this thrashing sound points the listener's attention to the anaconda's presence underwater and thereby draws the listener into a deeper level of involvement with the events being described, by evoking the complex of thoughts and feelings typically experienced when anacondas are encountered. This deeper level of involvement is pragmatically enhanced by the fact that k^h*aw* is syntactically isolated: it occurs all by itself, without a verb, or for that matter, a sentence, to frame it. By requiring the listener to fill in the missing sentence, the speaker encourages the listener to infer the anaconda's presence in the same way that the bystanders have, before it's actually seen. Significantly, the bystanders never actually saw the anaconda until just before it closed in on the tapir, so they really did rely on this sound-symbolic impression when they decided that it was an anaconda. By allowing the listener to participate in the same inferential process, the narrator intensifies the listener's involvement and imaginative participation.

In one final respect, sound-symbolic utterances must be considered semiotically distinctive. Their iconic, schematic, performative, and involvement properties are often best described from the perspective of their discourse function, with reference to other semiotic modalities such as gesture and cinema. Sound-symbolic utterances communicate iconically, as do the images of gesture and cinema. Because they are schematically structured, sound-symbolic utterances are directly meaningful, as are all icons, including gestures and cinematic images. By their performativity, sound-symbolic utterances simulate the salient qualities of an action as it unfolds in time. Again, gestures and cinematic images are comparable insofar as they also present an image of an action unfolding in time. Finally, the interlocutionary involvement created by sound-symbolic utterances is also created by gesture and cinema. Kristeva has characterized the quality of involvement created by cinema as follows:

> Cinema calls for the subject to project himself into what he sees; it is not presented as an evoking of a past reality, but as a fiction the subject is in the process of living. The reason for the impression of imaginary reality that cinema elicits has been seen in the possibility of representing *movement, time, the narrative*, etc. (1989: 315)

In representing the salient qualities of an action's spatiotemporal unfolding, sound-symbolic utterances are often describable by analogy with cinematic techniques such as close-up shot, wide angle shot, juxtaposition, montage, fast motion shot, and slow motion shot. These will be employed throughout the book to describe some of the performative functions of sound-symbolic use.

A conception of language as abstracted from the material world and from the body of the speaker cannot provide a framework for understanding the grammatical, discursive, or cognitive significance of sound-symbolic expression for its speakers. The intersections between sound symbolism and aspect grammar make it necessary to rethink the point line conception of aspect, which is not just inadequate but misleading. Sound-symbolic adverbs have considerable potential for filling out abstract grammatical concepts such as completiveness, momentaneousness, and durativity with spatiotemporally specific images of actions, events, and processes. By depicting aspect with points and lines on a two-dimensional plane, we're in danger of representing it as a grammatical cetgory that is isolated from our sensible experiences of the world. To counteract this distortion, I've supplied figures of sound-symbolic adverbs in Part II which clarify the links between aspect, sound symbolism, and spatiotemporal experience.

It must be emphasized, however, that the spatiotemporal world encoded in sound-symbolic utterances is also, necessarily, a socially constructed world. Sound-symbolic discourse aligns interlocutors not with a private kind of experience, but with socially shared perceptions that are cognitively salient. That Quechua speakers themselves are aware of their cognitive salience is evident by their performative elaborations which create a heightened sense of an action's spatiotemporal unfolding. Its fundamentally performative nature frames sound symbolism is an interactional style for articulating what is shared about perceptual experience. Sound symbolism, however, is more than a style of speaking. It's a style of thinking about one's perceptions, one's language, and one's alignment with the natural world. The multifunctionality of sound-symbolic discourse indicates a cluster of attitudes and beliefs about causation, nature, and, especially, how to communicate perceptions, which are fundamentally different from Euro-American conventions.

The Ethnographic Setting

The terms *lowland Quechua* and *lowland Ecuadorean Quechua* are used interchangeably to refer to a regional and ethnic group, while *Pastaza Quechua* refers to a linguistic dialect. The lowland Ecuadorean Quechua inhabit a large territory that begins at the eastern foothills of the Ecuadorean Andes and extends through the lowland rainforest as far east as Ecuador's disputed border with Peru. Although they speak a dialect that is clearly related to the Inca lingua franca, the lowland Quechua do not identify strongly with the highland Andean culture to the west. Their activities and interests, whether they involve trading, hunting, or engaging in organized conflict, invariably take them further downriver, that is, further eastward. Many lowland Quechua trace their origins to the easternmost frontiers, and some remember families trapped on the Peruvian side after Peru invaded and won half of eastern Ecuador in 1941. Whitten (1976, 1985) has conducted the most intensive ethnographic studies among Quechua speakers in the eastern lowlands of Ecuador. He considers the lowland Quechua to be culturally distinctive from both the highland Andean Quechua and the various lowland ethnic groups with which they have merged. Because of the historical importance of the Roman Catholic administrative center in Canelos, he refers to the lowland Quechua as "Canelos Quichua."[5] His hypothesis of their origin follows.

> The Canelos Quichua may well have "formed" out of an Achuara-Zaparoan merger, and expanded the emergent culture through increased use of the Quichua language. The process is apparent in recent history, and extends back in time to "early colonial"—presumably at least to the seventeenth century. In short, we are confronted with a *perpetuative formative process*. Travelers, explorers, and missionaries in this zone seem repeatedly to encounter Canelos Quichua forming out of Zaparoan and Jivaroan intermarriages and alliances, with a mediating Quichua language borne by people in contact with distant sources of valued goods. (1976: 7–8)

The village where I conducted most of my fieldwork is called Puka yaku, which, translated, means "red water" (see figure 1-1). Puka yaku is a loosely nucleated hamlet situated along the Bobonaza River. There are as yet no roads leading to Puka yaku; entry can be made by landing at an airstrip controlled by a military base about an hour and a half walk and a canoe ride across the river from Puka yaku itself. There is a Catholic church administered by the Dominican order, located in what might be considered the center of the village. There is also an unenclosed classroom adjacent to the church. However, the priest is not always in residence, and it is difficult to find

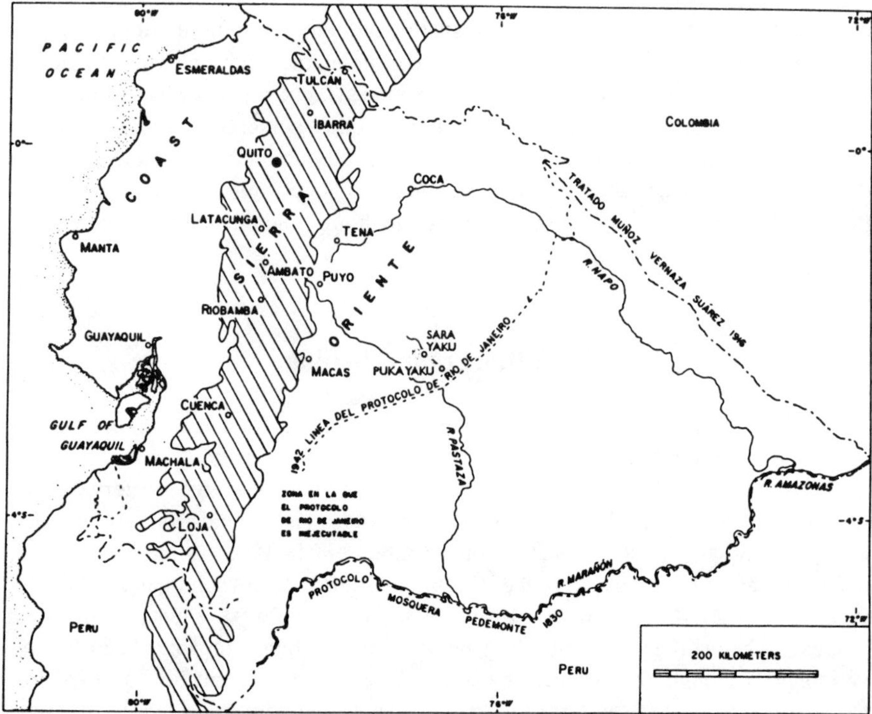

Figure 1-1 Map of Ecuador. From *Sicuanga Runa,* copyright 1985 by Norman Whitten, Jr. Used with permission of the author and the University of Illinois Press.

teachers willing to live in such a remote place without plumbing, electricity, and adequate medical facilities. The two institutional edifices of Puka yaku therefore remain unoccupied much of the time. The majority of adult Puka yakuans have had almost no formal education. Most families living in and around Puka yaku sustain themselves by hunting, gathering, fishing, and slash and burn agriculture, participating in the cash economy only to a very limited extent. There are a few supply stores owned by non-indigenous colonists from the western highlands, stocked with such items as soap, cigarettes, aluminum cooking pots, steel machetes, ammunition, batteries, and polyester clothing. People earn money to purchase these items in a variety of ways. The women tend to work for pay a day or two, every few months in the agricultural field of one of the highland families in the area. The men do odd jobs for the resident Catholic priest, or they work intermittently with the oil companies doing occasional exploratory work in the region. Some of them join the military and work at the nearby base. In fact, the two most sought after shamans in Puka yaku are both retired soldiers and draw monthly pensions from the Ecuadorean government.

The majority of people indigenous to Puka yaku and the surrounding territory speak Quechua. However, because Puka yaku overlaps with Achuar Jivaroan territory, it is populated by a few Achuara speakers as well. There was only one man living near Puka yaku who claimed to know Zaparoan. The relations between Quechua and Achuar, whom they refer to as *awka*, are complex and varied. There is a general feeling among Quechua speakers that the Achuar are culturally inferior. Yet, many of the same Quechua who profess disdain for the Achuar also give credence to their beliefs. Furthermore, there is a great deal of technology that is shared and practiced by Quechua and Achuar alike. This includes many items of domestic use, such as hexagonally woven baskets, pottery, hammocks, and even house construction; as well as hunting tools, such as blowguns, darts and quivers, fishing nets, and animal traps.

Fieldwork and Data Collection

The data for this research were collected by observation and elicitation. Although I had contact with many people in Puka yaku, I worked most closely with four interrelated households. During the first twelve months of fieldwork I acquired most of my data by listening to people, taking notes, and trying to ask questions, while also participating to the extent that was possible in their daily activities. I spent the first couple of months living with a family, which provided invaluable experience and helped pave the way for other friendships. During this first year I also recorded a lot of naturally occurring conversations and elicited many stories. The most difficult part of this initial phase was trying to understand what sound-symbolic adverbs meant. I had no idea at this time that they would be as significant to aspect expression as they were. My interest in understanding them was motivated by the belief that their frequency in everyday conversation, and the tremendous performative energy invested in their articulation, was evidence of their real significance for Quechua linguistic culture. However, my attempts to probe people about their meaning met with only limited success. It was hard for Quechua speakers to explain what they meant, unless they could somehow give a demonstration of their meaning. Often, however, they couldn't, and people seemed as frustrated by having to explain something so obvious as I was by my inability to understand what seemed so impenetrable.

Gradually, I was able to detect very general patterns of meaning by comparing the different contexts of their use. Attempts to ask people more specific questions about their connotative and affective meanings failed. Most people were not capable of, or perhaps just not interested in, talking about such things. I then attempted to find someone to help me on a regular basis, but this was problematic because no one was able to abandon the daily activities that sustained them. I finally did find a woman who, because of an illness was not able to lead a completely active life and was willing to work with me on a regular basis. During the final six months, then, I continued my observations, but I also began to conduct a series of structured interviews with this woman. In the first series of interviews I went through my list of the approximately 150 most commonly used sound-symbolic adverbs to elicit more contexts of use for each one and to clarify the meanings of the uses I had already noted. Although she wasn't familiar with every one of my sound-symbolic adverbs, she did know the great majority of them. Sometimes she disagreed about the form of a sound-symbolic adverb, giving it a different phonetic shape.

In the second series of interviews, I went through a list of about 275 of Quechua's most widely used verb roots and attempted to determine the cooccurrence possibilities for these verbs with each of the sound-symbolic adverbs. This was an extremely difficult task for both of us. Part of the problem was that it was very tedious for her to go through the lists of the possible combinations because it meant trying to imagine so many combinations that just were not possible. The result was that she very easily became distracted into relating memories or stories, which were extremely interesting, and which yielded more data on verbs and sound-symbolic adverbs, although it didn't always concern the sound-symbolic adverbs that had been the focus of my question. As long as I didn't try to press too many of these questions into one space of time, however, she was able to make judgments about the appropriateness of most of these combinations and also supply additional contexts of use. In the final series of interviews I asked her to tell me as much as possible about each of the verbs on my list, inviting her to free associate about the kinds of activities that each verb spontaneously called to mind. I was interested in determining which sound-symbolic adverbs would occur to her spontaneously in the process of describing a verb's activities. This was far easier and more enjoyable for her than the more structured framework of the previous series of questions, and it was also helpful to me because of the additional data it generated.

The Pastaza Quechua Language

Several sets of terms are now used for the classification of the family of languages known as Quechua. As outlined by Mannheim (1991: 11–16), all Quechua languages are divided into two groups. The dialects spoken in central Peru—specifically, the Departments of Ancash, Junin, Huaylas, Huánuco and Jauja—are variously called Quechua I, following Torero (1974); Quechua B, following Parker (1969, 1971); and Central Quechua, which is Mannheim's own terminology. The other group of Quechua languages includes those varieties spoken north of the first group, including the Peruvian dialects of Cajamarca, Lambayeque, and San Martín; all of the Quechua spoken in Ecuador; and the Inga language of southern Colombia. Also included in this second group are the southern Peruvian Quechua dialects, as well as those of Argentina and Bolivia. This second group of dialects is called, variously, Quechua II, after Torero; Quechua A, after Parker; and Peripheral Quechua, after Mannheim.

The origin of the Quechua language in Ecuador is a matter of controversy. In his discussion of the hypothesis of an Ecuadorean origin for Quechua, Cerrón-Palomino states that this hypothesis was partly fueled by the feeling that scarcely 100 years of Incaic conquest would not have been sufficient to impose this language throughout the Tahuantinsuyu territory (1987: 338). However, the arguments for the Ecuadorean origin of Quechua have not been widely accepted. Stark (1985) hypothesizes that Quechua originated in the eastern lowland region of Ecuador, the region that includes the Pastaza dialect on which this book is based, spread to the highlands, and then south to Peru. Her argument is based on the division of all Ecuadorean dialects into a Quechua A group, which is said to represent an older set of dialects, and a Quechua B group. Stark's argument is based on the internal reconstruction of a group of suffixes and archaeological evidence that is said to suggest the presence of Quechua speakers in the Ecuadorean Oriente who then moved westward into the Sierra as early as 600 A.D. Cerrón-Palomino disagrees, mostly on grounds stated by Hartmann (1979), that there is not enough evidence to assert the greater antiquity of Quechua A. Furthermore, regarding the archaeological evidence for expansion from the Oriente to the Ecuadorean Sierra and southward, Cerrón-Palomino reminds us that the lack of carbon 14 dating of the ceramics that are said to prove this expansion undermines the entire theoretical edifice (1987: 340).

Cerrón-Palomino (1987: 343–344) mentions a hypothesis originally formulated by Torero (1974), which has been favorably received by other scholars, that even if Quechua didn't originate in Ecuador, it may have been used in Ecuador as a trade language prior to its establishment there by the Incas. He cites evidence of a trade route between the coastal center of Chincha in Peru and Puerto Viejo and Quito in Ecuador. He speculates that it may have been diffused into eastern Ecuador and Colombia after the seventeenth century by the Dominican missions, although there would have been earlier incursions from the conquest. From eastern Ecuador, it may have then spread southward to eastern Peru by rubber traders.

Although her theory of the Ecuadorean origin of Quechua has not been widely accepted, Stark's (1985) division of all Ecuadorean dialects of Quechua into Ecuatoriano A and Ecuatoriano B has generally been adopted. Ecuatoriano A is spoken in the central Ecuadorean Andes, and Ecuatoriano B is spoken everywhere else, including the dialects of the eastern lowland rainforest. The dialects of the eastern rainforest have been classified by Orr (1978) into Pastaza, Tena, and Napo. The Pastaza dialect, which is the southernmost, is spoken in the town of Puyo and its surrounding villages and also in the settlements along the Bobonaza, Conambo, and Curaray Rivers. The Tena dialect, which is centrally located, is spoken in the towns of Tena, Archidona, and Arajuno and also in the area that extends from the lower Napo to Yurallpa. The Napo dialect, which is northernmost, is spoken in the towns of Loreto and Aquila and northward along the Payamino and Coca Rivers, and also by those living along the Napo River from Suno to Nuevo Rocafuerte.[6]

Although Stark (1985) states that there is some morphological evidence in support of these dialect divisions, she also suggests the likelihood that more dialects will be discovered in other remote regions of the Oriente. Further, given the great amount of present day migration and flux by Quechua-speaking people in the Oriente, she considers it unlikely that these dialects can still be considered discrete and reports that the varieties of Quechua spoken in the Oriente have been spread at several different time periods and through a number of channels. Prior to the arrival of the Spaniards, Quechua was used to facilitate trading between the highlands and lowlands. Quechua was also spread to the lowlands by migrations of highland Quechua speakers fleeing Spanish exploitation. Furthermore, until the borders between Peru and Ecuador were closed in 1941, there was a lot of movement between Peru and Ecuador by Quechua speakers, thus creating another channel for the spread of Quechua in eastern Ecuador. Finally, Quechua has also spread through the Ecuadorean lowlands by absorbing other indigenous languages. Stark states that Quechua has already absorbed the Zaparoan, Shimigae, and Andoan languages. Any Quechua speaker living in the Ecuadorean Oriente, therefore, could have an extremely mixed cultural background.

Tables 1-1 and 1-2 represent the phonemic consonants and vowels of Pastaza Quechua. I use a phonemic transcription throughout this book, except for the sound-symbolic adverbs, for which I have adopted a broad phonetic transcription, which includes noncontrastive features such as aspiration and allophonic variants such as [-ng] of the phoneme /n/ which are otherwise left unspecified in the rest of the text. The sounds of these adverbs are crucial in communicating their meaning, and a narrower representation of their sound shape is therefore pertinent to an understanding of their formal and semantic patterning. For a detailed study of Pastaza Quechua phonology, including a discussion of stress and juncture, syllable structure and patterns, morphophonemics, and a breakdown of the phonemes into distinctive features, the interested reader can consult Orr (1962).

Table 1-1 Pastaza Quechua Consonants

	Place of Articulation				
Manner of Articulation	Bilabial	Dental/alveolar	Alveolar	Alveo-palatal	Velar
Stop					
Voiceless	p	t			k
Voiced	b	d			g
Affricated voiceless			ts	ch	
Affricated voiced				dzh	
Palatalized	p^y	t^y			k^y
Fricative					
Voiceless			s	sh	
Voiced			z		
Tap			r		
Nasal	m		n	ñ	
Central approximant	w			y	h
Lateral approximant			l	l^y	

Table 1-2 Pastaza Quechua Vowels

	Front		Back
High	i		u
			o
Low		a	

2

The Theoretical Dimensions of Aspect

The grammatical category aspect concerns the ways in which abstract temporal concepts such as ongoingness or completion are encoded within an utterance. Such a minimal definition, however, suggests little of the deeper issues that have emerged in discussions of aspect grammar. It is sometimes difficult, for example, to isolate the temporal dimensions of an action's unfolding from the spatial frame in which that unfolding takes place. The sentence "He walked around the block" is aspectually perfective because the phrase "around the block" gives the action a definite *spatial*[1] and therefore *temporal* closure. Once the spatial framework of an action is allowed to enter into aspectual consideration, then other perceptual qualities become relevant as well. Movements, rhythms, and processes of sentient experience affect the encoding of aspect. Aspect expression is linked to the sensible world of spatiotemporal experience. In addition to the link between aspect and spatial, perceptual parameters, aspect is also, through its temporal dimension, linked to aesthetic expression. The "temporal contours" of one's experience, whether it is an experience of an unfolding rhythm in poetic verse or the salient rhythms of everyday sensations, are all built into the grammatical and expressive architecture of language and, therefore, of aspect.

This chapter surveys the literature on aspect, with special attention to the range of issues most relevant to the themes of this book. My aim is to formulate a theory of aspect that provides a basis for understanding how abstract notions such as relative duration and completion can be linked to the sound qualities of a sign vehicle. How, in other words, can physiologically produced sounds become representative of natural sounds that are grammatically encoded for aspect? An important component of this theory is the semiotic principle of iconicity. Aspect has a definite iconic dimension that is often evident in its morphological shape. In many languages, for example, aspectually durative forms have a greater number of phonemes than nondurative forms. The greater number of phonemes can be understood as iconic of durativity because they require more time for their articulation. Aspectual iconicity can be elaborated in performative expression as well. The repetition of sound-symbolic adverbs in Pastaza Quechua is one such performative technique that imitates the repeatedness of actions or processes. The iconicity of aspect is also embodied within the nature of linguistic communication. The sign vehicle is intrinsically durative since it consists of a spoken chain of significant differences; it is also intrinsically completive because of the limitations of the human breath which must spend itself at regular intervals of articulation. Iconicity, then, provides the link between abstract grammatical distinctions of aspect; the representation of natural sounds, rhythms, and processes; and the intrinsic qualities of embodied linguistic communication.

Theories of Aspect

Jakobson

One of the most streamlined conceptualizations of aspect is that offered by Jakobson (1971c), who considers aspect as a morphologically bound, invariant grammatical category. Jakobson states that aspect characterizes "the narrated event itself without involving its participants and without reference to the speech event" (1971ac: 134)." This entirely negative definition is part of a systematization of the logically possible relations between the variables that are relevant to linguistic communication. It is intended as part of a skeletal conceptualization of the verbal categories of Russian with a very limited set of variables, including the speech event, the narrated event, the participants in the speech event, and the participants in the narrated event. In contrast to grammatical categories such as person and number, aspect is exclusively concerned with the characterization of a narrated event. It encodes no information about the number of participants involved in that event, their gender, or person. The other part of Jakobson's definition—that aspect characterizes a narrated event without reference to a speech event—is meant to distinguish aspect analytically from tense. Tense places a narrated event within a temporal frame that shifts according to the time of the speech event. Aspect is at least analytically independent of this shift.

However, Jakobson's statement that grammatical aspect characterizes a narrated event without reference to a speech event is based on the assumption that aspect distinctions are only evident in referential statements and assertions. A prototypical assertion states something about an event, process, or action (Lyons 1983: 726) and is therefore grounded in Jakobson's distinction between a speech event (E^s) and a narrated event (E^n). Data from sound-symbolic performances, however, reveal that aspect distinctions are not always neatly sealed off from the speech event. This is because sound-symbolic performances are iconic: they communicate not by referring, but by simulating the most salient features of an action, event, or process. The distinction between a speech event and a narrated event is therefore collapsed in sound-symbolic performance: the speech event *becomes* the narrated event. A sound-symbolic performance uses the speech event to re-create the vivid features of the narrated event rather than to report it or refer to it. Yet, as will be shown throughout this book, sound-symbolic forms also encode aspect distinctions.

Although it is much less well known than Jakobson (1971c), Jakobson (1971b) also made an important contribution to aspect theory because it was the first acknowledgment that aspect morphology had an iconic dimension. There is often a perceived resemblance between the formal shape of a word and the aspectual distinction it expresses. In his comparison of both prefixed and prefixless Russian verbs, Jakobson found an overwhelmingly frequent correlation between the perfective and imperfective suffixes and lesser or greater numbers of phonemes. He linked the longer stem suffixes of the imperfective, indeterminate, and iterative aspects to an iconic expression of expansiveness and nonrestrictiveness, stating: "Whatever the historical background of the grammatical processes involved, the iconic character of the contemporary Russian aspectual design is patent" (1971b: 202). Data from Pastaza Quechua will reveal a number of features that contribute to aspectual iconicity, including the inherent features of a word's morphological shape, its suffixally derived forms, and its formal elaboration through performative foregrounding.

Finally, Jakobson (1985) made the significant discovery that a language's expressive resources are closely linked with its grammatical features, including its aspect categories. He became aware that the expressive power of Pushkin's poetry was so closely linked with the Russian language's morphological and syntactic resources that translation into Czech "produced the distressing impression of a complete rift with the original" (1985: 47). And grammatical aspect, along with tense, number, and voice, were important expressive resources, at times rivaling even "the artistic role of verbal tropes" (ibid). In particular, Jakobson noted the role of aspect in Pushkin's *The Bronze Horseman*: he noticed that the grammatical contrast between imperfective and perfective aspect forms was consistently used as an expressive symbol of two contrasting characters, Peter the Great and a clerk named Eugene. The imperfective forms were used to project the limitless and "seemingly eternal power of Peter the Great, ruler of half the world," while perfective forms described the "fatal limitedness of all the actions performed by the characterless clerk Eugene" (ibid.)[2] In Pastaza Quechua, durative and perfective aspect expression is closely linked with a concern on the part of Quechua speakers for expressively shaping and fixing their perceptions of the natural world. In performative sound-symbolic description, these perceptions are both explicit about their grammatical aspectuality and expressive of the vivid qualities of sensory experience.

Chung and Timberlake

Chung and Timberlake (1985) attempted a comprehensive typological outline of aspect that has universal relevance. Although their discussion contributes significant insights into aspect, it attempts generalizations that are too broad for the complex range of data they propose to acknowledge. They define aspect as follows: "Aspect characterizes the relationship of a predicate to the time interval over which it occurs" (1985: 213). This time interval, which is also termed the *event frame*, is crucial to their theory of aspect. The value of Chung and Timberlake's treatment is that it goes beyond morphologically bound invariant aspect categories and allows for a grammatical/semantic conception of aspect that is evident throughout the following four nested levels of structure: (1) a verb's inherent aspect, as well as the aspect encoded by morphological or thematic derivation; (2) a predicate consisting of a verb with its syntactic arguments; (3) a proposition consisting of a predicate in relation to a selected interval or frame; and (4) a narrative level encompassing the relations between a connected set of propositions. As examples of each of these levels, they offer the following.

6. verb: angry
7. predicate: John got angry at a stranger.
8. proposition: John got angry at a stranger on the bus today.
9. narrative: John got angry at a stranger on the bus today, and then apologized. (1985: 214)

Although aspectual values are encoded at each of these levels, Chung and Timberlake concern themselves primarily with the ways in which aspectual morphology is related to proposition-level parameters. Aspect parameters are the relatively autonomous semantic concepts that figure in all aspect systems and are therefore universally valid, although their configurations are specific to each language. They are, in principle, independent of morphology and are offered as an alternative to morphologically bound invariant aspect categories which are argued against elsewhere (Timberlake 1982). They are unlike semantic features insofar as they are extremely general in their specification. These parameters are considered of central importance in the organization of the aspect systems of all languages. They are characterized in two general categories as either topological or quantificational. This terminology is strongly suggestive of analogies with mathematics which are not acknowledged or explained.

Topological parameters are broadly defined by Chung and Timberlake as having to do with an event's dynamicity or closure. The essential distinction within the parameter of dynamicity is between a predicate describing a state of affairs that remains constant through time—that is, a "state"—and one that is dynamic, that is, a "process." In addition to their relevance for the encoding of aspect morphology, processuality and stativity are further linked to agency, modality, and morphosyntactic processes. For example, Chung and Timberlake state that agency is a commonly invoked criterion for distinguishing between states and processes (1985: 215) and give as examples of the difference a stative and a processual use of the verb "smell:" the sentence "I smelled the food" is processual because it is agentive, while "the food smells good" is stative. They also note that the difference between a state and a process is relevant to aspect encoding, specifically to the fact that the progressive cannot be used with states. However, they acknowledge that many stative verbs can be converted to processual verbs by adding an element of change, or an implication that the state is only temporary. The sentences "I understand this problem" and "I am understanding my problems more clearly every day" are, they claim, stative and processual, respectively, because the first sentence implies a permanent condition while the second implies a sense of change over time (216).

Their argument for the opposite phenomenon, whereby a process verb becomes a state, is less convincing, however, and it illustrates the fundamental problem with the different ways in which such "basic" terminology as "change," "constancy," and so on, are understood. What is particularly difficult to accept here is their assertion that a verb can be stativized by iterating it. They argue that an iterated verb can actually be considered, from the perspective of its macrolevel, as a state-like property: "Thus, in 'he occasionally worked/? was working overtime' the macroevent is a static property of John, even though the verb 'work' describes a process on any particular occasion" (Chung and Timberlake 1985: 215–216.) The problem with this is that it conflates two aspect categories, namely habituality and iterativity. Habituality attributes a characteristic quality to a form of behavior, action, or event that is repeated throughout a given period of time. As explained by Comrie, habituality is the more inclusive category: "The feature that is common to all habituals, whether or not they are also iterative, is that they describe a situation which is *characteristic* (emphasis mine) of an extended period of time" (1976: 27–28). The example offered by Chung and Timberlake would therefore have to be habitual rather than iterative because iteration implies mere repetition rather than repetition that is characteristic of a time interval. In Pastaza Quechua, the habitual aspect is used to describe considerable periods of time and could at the macrolevel be considered stative. However, iterative actions are typically very short term in duration and would not be compatible with the notion of stativity.

The second topological aspect parameter, closure, encompasses notions such as boundedness, limitation, holicity, and completion. Closure depends on the semantic properties of a verb—specifically, whether it encodes a process with a limit, that is, a telic verb, or a process without a limit, that is, an atelic verb. Chung and Timberlake note the important role of a predicate's arguments in determining the closure of a verb: specifically, whether a verb is telic or atelic can be determined by the presence or absence of a direct object, by the spatial limits specified within a complement, or by the degree to which a direct object is affected or changed by the action of a verb. At the propositional level, closure specifies that an event comes to an end within a designated interval.

In addition to the topological, there are quantificational parameters, which are subdivided into iteration and durativity. The discussion of iterativity acknowledges the complexity of this category, particularly with respect to its event frame. Chung and Timberlake make the important observation that an iterated action or event has a microlevel that refers to an individual subevent of the action, as well as a macrolevel that considers the individual subevents collectively. However, this discussion is flawed by the authors' assertion, both in this context and in the discussion of the Chamorro language, that iteratives are usually considered stative: "At the level of the macroevent, an iterative is usually stative" (1985: 221). As was pointed out earlier, they confuse iterativity with habituality. Their reason for doing this, I suggest, is that it is convenient to conflate the two because their distinction would make it necessary to consider the matter of their durativity: what is habitual is comparatively, at least, of longer duration than what is merely iterative. As the immediately following discussion reveals, they would like to consider aspect, in principle at least, independent of durativity.

The other quantificational parameter, durativity, is very briefly described as "the explicit measurement of the duration of the event frame" (Chung and Timberlake 1985: 222). This is the weakest section of their discussion because they attempt to claim that aspect is independent of durativity. This claim is not well argued. In comparing English, Mokilese, and Russian, they state: "Given that all three languages can measure duration whether the event is open or closed, aspect is apparently determined independently of duration" (1985: 222). They also argue that this is true for English with the two sentences "John read the book for an hour" (open) vs "John read the book in an hour" (closed). What they seem to have missed, however, is the fact that different aspect values can be simultaneously encoded at different levels of an utterance. In both sentences, the verb "read" is aspectually durative at the level of the predicate because it refers to an ongoing activity. However, the first sentence is durative at the level of the proposition, as is indicated by the phrase "for an hour" which indicates that during a particular temporal interval, the reading was ongoing. The second sentence, by contrast, is completive at the propositional level, as is indicated by the phrase "in an hour" which indicates that the book was completely read. A more accurate inference to draw from their observation would be that closure and duration can be simultaneously encoded at different levels of the same utterance. Rather than state as they have done, that aspect is independent of durativity, they should have said that predicate level aspect is sometimes independent and seemingly contradictory of propositional level aspect. The more general problem with the claim that aspect is independent of durativity is that it is counterintuitive. Duration is one of the fundamental properties of the linguistic sign vehicle, which is composed of components organized by their temporal succession (Jakobson 1971a). Durativity is embodied in the very act of articulation. It makes far more sense to assume that all languages are intrinsically designed to encode durativity as well as various types of closure.

The concluding generalization offered by Chung and Timberlake is that the aspect systems of languages have two alternative ways of dealing with the relationship between a predicate and its event frame: a predicate can occur within its frame, or the frame can be placed within the predicate. In a given language, one of these two possibilities will be defined in semantically narrow terms, while the other will be defined in semantically broad terms. What they mean by semantically narrow and semantically broad can be understood by analogy with the concepts of markedness. Semantically narrow and semantically broad correspond, respectively, to marked and unmarked categories. They offer the example of Russian to illustrate the first type of aspect system. In Russian the perfective is the narrowly defined category because it must be used for telic predicates that are closed within a frame. Perfectivity is therefore marked. The imperfective, by contrast, is the broadly defined category because it is used for states, iteratives, and events that are open at the predicate and propositional levels. Imperfectivity is therefore unmarked. Although this typology sounds simple, the authors admit that its application is complicated with some languages. They admit, for example, that in Mokilese, both dynamic and closed events are relatively narrowly defined. Mokilese, therefore, is both a dynamicity language and a closure language. The discussion of aspect in Quechua will demonstrate that Quechua is also, according to their typology, both a dynamicity and a closure language. Nevertheless, Chung and Timberlake have offered a useful framework for approaching aspect as a major grammatical subsystem relevant at several levels of structure. The multilevel dimensions of aspect have not received much attention from linguists.

Whorf

Chung and Timberlake attempted to pare aspect down into a minimal set of fairly abstract parameters that are valid for the aspect systems of all languages. Whorf, by contrast, offers a short treatment of the "rich and expressive" (1956: 51) aspect distinctions in one language. Whorf attempts to trace the connections between the grammatical and expressive properties of aspect and their dependence on various types of sensory experience and cognition. In a five-page article entitled "The Punctual and Segmentative Aspects of Verbs in Hopi," he links aspect categories to voice, transitivity, appearance, plasticity, torque, and a quasi-scientific classification of sensory experience. Whorf's analysis concerns only two of the nine categories expressed by the aspectual system of Hopi. These two categories, the punctual and segmentative, are evident as a morphologically realized contrast between a point-locus and an extent locus in time, in space, or in both, and are restricted to one class of verbs. Whorf demonstrates that the same morphological process, involving partial reduplication of a stem and suffixation with a durative morpheme, reveals sets of contrasts that depend on the physical properties of their referents.

For example, when this process takes place within a set of roots denoting rigid or semi-rigid substances, then the contrast can be described as the difference between a point-like configuration and a spatially extended configuration. The examples of this distinction are the differences between a root that describes an acute angle and its suffixed form that describes zigzags; a root describing a notch and its suffixed form describing serration; a root describing one inward slash versus its suffixed form describing a fringe, and so on. A few of the examples supplied by Whorf follow.

ho''ci it forms a sharp acute angle	*hoci'cita* it is zigzag
pa''ci it is notched	*paci'cita* it is serrated
ca'mi it is slashed inward from the edge	*cami'mita* it is fringed, it is slashed into a fringe along the edge

(1956: 52)

However, when the referents denoted by the roots are nonrigid or malleable substances, then the essential contrast captured by the same formal process of partial reduplication and suffixation is described as that between a pulse and a vibration. The examples of this contrast describe the difference between a single slosh of water and a tossing of waves, between one wavelike curve and an undulation, or between several agents versus a multitude of entities emerging. This set of contrasts is also distinguished from the the first set in that the segmentatively derived verbs describe both extension in space and in time, while the first set of segmentative verbs, above, are primarily spatial. A few of Whorf's examples follow.

wa'la it (e.g. a liquid) makes one wave, gives a slosh	*wala'lata* it is tossing in waves, it is kicking up a sea
nö'ŋa several come out (applied to objects or persons)	*nöŋa'ŋata* it is coming out in successive multitudes, it is gushing or spraying out (applied, e.g., to a fountain)

(1956: 53)

There is yet a third category of roots, describing actions characterized by rotation or torque which are performed by an agent that is both rigid and flexible. Within this contrastive set, a punctual verb will describe either one portion of this rotation or one complete rotating movement, while its derived segmentative will describe a continuous series of rotations that may or may not extend through space. Some examples of these contrasts include the distinction between making a complete sway from one side to another versus being in the act of swaying; between making a turn or a twist versus being in the process of rotating; and making a flap, for example of wings, versus being in the act of flapping. Examples follow.

ŋa'ya makes a sway from one side to the other	*ŋaya'yata* it is swaying
ro'ya makes a turn or twist	*roya'yata* it is rotating
pï·ya makes a flap like a pair of wings	*pï·ya'yata* it is flapping wings
	(1956: 53–54)

Several interesting issues are raised by these examples. For instance, an obvious iconic motivation underlies the morphological distinction between the punctual and segmentative aspects. Those forms denoting a point-like image, a punctual action or event, or a single complete movement of any kind are always disyllabic, while those describing a multiplicity of any of these phenomena have twice as many syllables. The longer formal shape of the segmentative aspects is imitative of longer duration or greater extension in space. Besides the fact that these examples illustrate the formal iconicity underlying this contrast, they also make evident the close interrelation between temporal and spatial description. The greater significance of Whorf's analysis for the present study is that it demonstrates a connection between the encoding of aspect and the description of perceptions and sensations. Whorf's work makes this connection explicit by demonstrating that the physical properties denoted by a verb root's referent affect the aspectual reading of its linguistic expression. Hopi aspect expression is not reducible to an abstract set of parameters. It is linked to a sensible world of spatiotemporal experience.

Friedrich

Beginning with an artfully simple definition, "Aspect . . . signifies the relative duration or punctuality along a time line that may inhere in words or constructions," Friedrich (1974: 1) then formulates a theory of aspect which considers its typologically universal characteristics while allowing for its language-specific organization and integration with other grammatical subsystems. He critiques a number of aspect studies for their lack of depth. With the notable exception of certain Indo-Europeanists and Slavists, aspect has frequently been ignored, confused with other grammatical categories such as tense, and underestimated in importance. He presents his own detailed analysis of aspect in Homeric Greek, arguing that durativity was the marked aspect value. He also makes a number of suggestive statements, including references to the role of aspect in poetic and affective messages, to the iconicity of aspect morphology, and to the overlap between the temporal, spatial, and shape-defined dimensions of aspect categories.

The advantage of Friedrich's theory of aspect is that it acknowledges and makes universal generalizations without compromising the complexity of this grammatical distinction. One of the strongest generalizations to emerge is his statement that "aspect to a greater extent than voice or mood is coded in terms of obligatory rules for verbal roots and themes" (1974: 5). Aspect, then, is one of language's most basic distinctions. It is not by any means a simple distinction, however, although it has often been treated as if it were. The approach criticized most by Friedrich is that which restricts consideration of aspect to its overt morphology: aspect is fundamentally not a problem of morphological form but of a theory of semantics and morphosyntax, where it deserves to play a central role" (1974: 37). His position is that aspect is composed of semantic features, including duration, completion, and totality, that are realized in a number of complex configurations. Aspect values depend on the inherent semantic features of a verb; derivational processes undergone by the verb; adverbial modification; and a verb's composition with other nonaspectual features such as plurality, performativity, and quantity.

The complexity of aspectual encoding makes it necessary to acknowledge structural relationships that are difficult to model within the two-dimensional confines of a piece of paper. Friedrich suggests a multidimensional network in the form of a categorial cube consisting of relatively independent and interconnecting systems and subsystems of features. There are, for example, the kinds of interconnections that link aspect features with other grammatical categories such as voice. This particular interconnection accounts for the high probability that an aspectually perfect verb will also be intransitive. There are also interconnections that define the structure of a feature which encodes an aspect distinction. The "perfect" for example, includes a feature "realized," which itself consists of the features "past tense" and "completed action." Finally, there are the logical taxonomic interconnections that relate aspect categories and subcategories. These interrelations are represented with a unidirectional tree diagram that branches out into increasingly marked distinctions of aspect.

Friedrich's treatment of aspect is thorough, and his willingness to confront its complex dimensions is admirable. In claiming that aspect is not a problem of morphological form but of semantics and morphosyntax, he challenges minimalist approaches to aspect which would undermine its significance because it is not morphologically encoded in a particular language. Yet his claim that aspect is fundamentally not a problem of morphological form should not prevent an appreciation of aspect's iconicity, which Friedrich recognizes, nor of its embodiment within the very act of linguistic expression. He cites evidence from his own studies of Tarascan where endings with durative meaning are longer than nondurative endings (1974: 17–18, note 61). He also refers to the work of Mutzbauer on Slavic, which found that perfectives were shorter in overt form than imperfectives, and featured shorter vowels, such as the high vowels i and u (ibid.). The iconicity of aspect expression, also acknowledged by Jakobson, is good reason for taking aspect morphology seriously, although not to the absolute exclusion of its morphosyntactic and semantic manifestations. Data from Pastaza Quechua will demonstrate that aspect is often completely dependent on the inherent iconic properties of sound-symbolic morphology and also on the performative elaborations of this morphology.

The final issue raised by Friedrich is the matter of the connection between aspect and poetic, emphatic, or intensified messages. He cites grammarians such as Mutzbauer, Kartsevsky, and Jakobson, all of whom have addressed this issue and a few of whom have claimed that aspect by its very nature implies immediacy, focus, and so on. Friedrich's position is cautious:

> But even where such emphatic functions of aspect can be demonstrated . . . I think that they have the status of tertiary implications of the primary implications such as "completive" and of secondary ones such as "momentaneous," which combine with contextual factors to connote emphasis on certain parts of the narrated event. It is important to properly locate such stylistic functions within the system of connotations where they operate as part of the subtle symbolism of poetry. (1974: 38)

Thus Friedrich does not wish to allocate an excessive amount of responsibility to aspect for the expression of poetic and affective messages because aspect is itself so complexly intermeshed with an utterance's compositional semantics and morphosyntax. The position of this book, on the other hand, is that it is possible to acknowledge that aspect has its own referential grammatical values, while also admitting that it becomes difficult, at times, to decide upon what is primarily or secondarily implied by such values. Why, for example, should abstract concepts such as completion and duration be any more primary than a vivid, rhythmic experience of duration or of the abrupt completion of an action?

In sound-symbolic performances, aspect becomes the only relevant grammatical dimension. The aspectual dimension of sound-symbolic performances is related to Friedrich's observation that aspect, to a greater extent than any other verbal category, is obligatorily encoded in verbal roots and themes. Yet, it can hardly be said that sound-symbolic performances are motivated by a speaker's desire to express grammatically aspectual concepts. Sound symbolic performances are aspectual because they obligatorily communicate information about the temporal unfolding of whatever they represent; however, this information is not an end in itself. It is the salient qualities of an action's spatiotemporal unfolding, heightened by their performative simulation, which are of primary concern in sound-symbolic communication.

Lakoff

To comprehend grammatical aspect's manifestation in sound symbols or sound images, it is necessary to discuss the concept of the image schema. As used here, the term *image schema* can be understood with reference to the work of Lakoff (1987). Lakoff's use of the schema as a structural principle of linguistic organization is part of a devastating critique against cognitive and linguistic theories that are based on scientific objectivism. Scientific objectivism is a complex set of ideas that have influenced Western science for centuries. Some of the fundamental premises of scientific objectivism include the idea that thought is a computational process involving the use of abstract symbols, that symbols such as words correspond to objects in the world, that thought about the world is logically structured and does not reflect the physical constitution of the organism doing the thinking, and, finally, that thought and language are atomistic and can be reduced to simple components (1987: xii–xiii). The last premise, that thought and language are atomistic, is quite evident in Hockett's theory of morphology and linguistic structure (to be discussed later in this chapter). Hockett conceptualizes the structuring of a grammatical theory as the construction of an edifice with building blocks, and he compares the violation of certain essential principles to removing the keystone of an arch.

Lakoff's alternative to scientific objectivism is "experiential realism", an approach that was first formulated in Lakoff and Johnson (1980). Lakoff and Johnson's experiential realism attempts to account for meaning, understanding, and reason while reflecting the way people actually categorize and communicate about the world. At the same time, experiential realism acknowledges several premises: "(a) the reality of a world existing independent of human beings, (b) constraints on our conceptual systems due to the nature of that reality, (c) a conception of truth that goes beyond mere internal coherence, (d) a commitment to objectivity, and (e) an account of how scientific knowledge can be stable" (Lakoff 1987: 266). In addition, experiential realism offers alternative models of cognitive and linguistic structure that are congenial with these ideals, as well as more explanatorily powerful than the atomistic, formal models of structure proposed by psychologists and linguists. The articulation of these models has been heavily influenced by the work of Rosch and others. Basic to categorization are preconceptual structures termed *kinesthetic image schemas*, generalized structures that are directly meaningful because they reflect our bodily experience. They include structures such as containers, paths, forces, and links, as well as orientations such as front-back, up-down, and source-path-goal. Central to the concept of schematic images is the idea of mapping: a schema maps a rough structural complex, "spelling out only the essentials or gross features" (Langacker 1991:103), which are then imposed onto more complex units of particular experiences.

The image schema most typically employed to understand grammatical aspect is that of the point and line, hereafter referred to as the *point-line schema*. The point-line schema can be understood as an idea of temporality; it is not meant to represent the arbitrary divisions of what is known as "real time." The point-line schema represents a graphic image of the contrast between ongoing duration and any moment of interruption in that duration. One can imagine ongoingness as a line or pulse that is constantly moving from left to right like the tracing defined by an an electrocardiograph. Any point along that line, then, stands for a moment which interrupts the flow of time. Both schemas in figure 2-1, for example, feature lines extending from left to right, indicating an idea of temporal flow. Schema (a) also features a bounded segment with definite endpoints to represent the boundedness of perfective aspect, while schema (b) is unspecified for boundedness, to represent the lack of boundedness for imperfective aspect.

The advantage of the point-line schema is that it provides a clear, precise, and cognitively salient image for some kinds of aspect distinctions. Its advantage, however, is also its liability: the clarity and precision of this schema propagates the implicit assumption that aspect categories are mappable and measureable in mathematically precise ways. In fact, aspect distinctions are not, by their nature precise designations, as Binnick has explained quite clearly; they often depend on one's subjective perception of an event's unfolding:

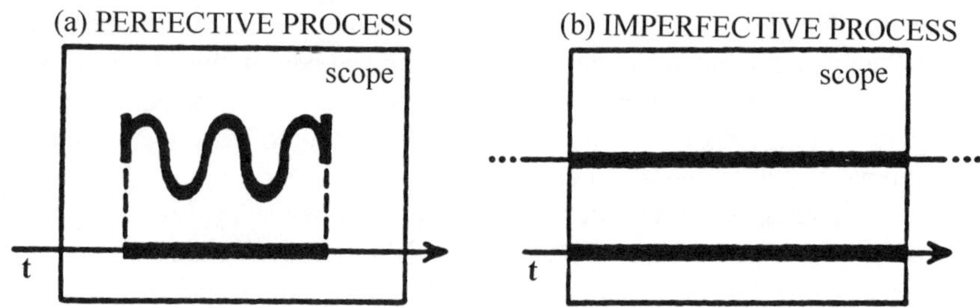

Figure 2-1 The English perfective and imperfective. From Ronald W. Langacker, *Concept, Image and Symbol* (Berlin: Mouton de Gruyter, 1991), p. 88. Used with permission of Mouton de Gruyter.

> The use of the term "aspect" (*vid*) proceeds from the fact that the very same situation (event or state of affairs) may be viewed either imperfectively or perfectively. In a given context one or the other aspect may be preferred or even obligatory, but often enough either could be used to describe precisely the same episode, just as in English we may say either *just the other day I visited Aunt Martha and saw your picture*, or *just the other day I was visiting Aunt Martha and saw your picture.* Both of these sentences describe the same event, although one views the visit as a completed whole, from the outside as it were, while the other views it as an ongoing, incomplete action, as if from the inside. (Binnick 1991: 136)

It is perhaps not accidental that Binnick uses the term "view" in the foregoing quote to describe the nature of aspect evaluation. He traces the root of the word "aspect" to the Russian *vid*, which is etymologically related to the words "view" and "vision" (ibid.). Aspect, then, has an imageic conceptual basis. This imageic basis is evident even in characterizations of specific aspect categories. Chatterjee (1988: 23) states that Poldauf and Sprunk define the Czech perfective and imperfective by noting that the perfective is comparable to a photograph of an action while the imperfective is comparable to a film. And within the last ten years, studies of aspect, for example, Hopper (1979), have used the visual/spatial metaphor of foreground/background as an organizing principle to understand the encoding of aspect in discourse.

The concept of image provides a suggestive basis for investigating Quechua speakers' sound-symbolic schemas. In sound-symbolic language use, the iconicity of sound-symbolic adverbs is used for grammatically aspectual purposes. Sound symbolic adverbs constitute an iconically expressive schematization of the perceptible world. In claiming they are schematic, it is claimed that sound symbolic adverbs have a gestalt-like structure. They cannot be understood with the traditional building-block principles of morphology, which will be discussed next: their meaning cannot be predicted or calculated as a sum of independently existing, abstract phonemic elements. Their structure makes sense only if one considers their physiological, embodied nature. The intrinsic durativity of the linguistic sign vehicle, which communicates as a spoken chain of significant differences, provides the articulatory basis for communicating aspectual durativity. The limitations of the human breath, which must spend itself at regular intervals of articulation, provide the articulatory basis for communicating aspectual completiveness. In Pastaza Quechua, schematizations of durativity and completiveness are particularly concentrated in sound-symbolic adverbs. The role of sound-symbolic adverbs in encoding aspect, particularly in the encoding of perfective aspect distinctions, makes sense with reference to Lakoff's concept of a grammar as an ecological system (1987). Sound-symbolic adverbs occupy a niche in Pastaza Quechua grammar, which allows their inherent iconic expressivity to function grammatically. The grammatical and expressive functions of sound-symbolic adverbs can be attributed to the inherent iconicity of their morphology, but their iconicity can also be elaborated by performative techniques that alter their syntactic position, their syllabic length, and their pitch qualities. All these performative elaborations enhance both their aspectual grammaticality and their imageic expressivity. To better appreciate the significance of these claims, it is necessary to understand the problematic role of iconicity in grammatical theory.

Iconicity and Grammatical Theory

Saussure and Benveniste

The concept of iconicity has always been at odds with the central premises of linguistic theory. The linguistic sign, described as a bond between a signifier and signified, which unites a concept (signified) and a sound image (signifier) is, stated Saussure (1959: 67), arbitrary. An excellent discussion of the subtle discrepancies between what Saussure says and how he actually considers the matter of arbitrariness is presented by Benveniste (1971). As Benveniste made clear, Saussure's claim that language is arbitrary is partly related to his desire to consider language as form rather than substance, and therefore fundamentally independent of the material world. The linguistic sign, states Saussure, unites "not a thing and a name, but a concept and a sound-image" (1959: 66). Saussure is then careful to add that by "sound-image" he means the psychological rather than the material sound image. However, in asserting that the nature of the linguistic sign is arbitrary, Saussure is forced to bring the reality itself into consideration: "When he spoke of the difference between *b -o -f* and *o -k -s* , he was referring, in spite of himself to the fact that these two terms applied to the same *reality* (emphasis his)" (Benveniste, 1971: 44). Benveniste then explains that, in fact, the bond between the signifier and signified is not arbitrary, but necessary. It is, rather, the relationship between the *reality* described by a signifier and the signifier itself which is arbitrary. The word "cow" is arbitrarily related to the reality that is a cow because other languages can and do use other terms. But the concept of a cow is necessary for the sound image "cow."

Hockett

Despite the subtle conceptual and philosophical problems in trying to delineate language as a structure from the social and physical world, the arbitrariness of the linguistic sign and the independance of language as a total system have remained central tenets of structural linguistics, including morphologically based theories. Since aspect is expressed at several levels of linguistic structure, it is relevant to syntax as well as morphology. However, because the *iconicity* of aspect is most relevant to the domain of morphology, in particular, the concept of iconicity to be developed here, I concentrate on the problematic posed by iconicity for morphological theory. As morphology was central to the postwar American descriptive approach, it is appropriate to discuss the work of one of "the most individually creative and wide-ranging" (Anderson 1985:278) of the American descriptivists, Charles Hockett. Hockett's work is particularly relevant here because he was one of the most ardent proponents of the principle of arbitrariness. In his "Two Models of Grammatical Description" (1957) he offers a detailed consideration of the advantages and disadvantages of two descriptive frameworks used by linguists. In the process of coming to the conclusion that neither framework is adequate in itself, he reveals important characteristic features of a grammatical/morphological theory that was professed for several decades. The most general assumption held by descriptivist theory is that language is an integrated structure of elements and their relations. The goal of the scientific linguist is to *discover* [emphasis mine] the structure used by speakers of a language, enabling the prediction and production of any utterances not part of the analysts' original corpus of data. For the postwar descriptivists, the analysis of language was comparable to "a logical calculus leading to the discovery of the basic units of language and their formal arrangement" (Kristeva 1989: 242).

For Hockett, the analysis of linguistic structure as it was typically conducted during the postwar period could be characterized with one of two approaches—"item and process," or IP, and "item and arrangement," or IA. The two terms "process" and "arrangement" can be understood by analogy with the logical, mathematical notions of operations and relations, respectively. The older of these two approaches, IP, assumed that if two forms were partly the same and partly different, they could be related to each other by a process of derivation. As Hockett notes, the notion of deriving one form from another through a "process" was borrowed from historical linguistics even though no historical chronology was assumed in such descriptions. Yet, he admits that the historical analogy is compelling in its logic and wonders what kind of logic can be assumed for a sychronic, structural notion of process:

> If it be said that the English past-tense form *baked* is 'formed' from *bake* by a 'process' of 'suffixation', then no matter what disclaimer of historicity is made, it is impossible not to conclude that some kind of priority is being assigned to *bake*, as against either *baked* or the suffix. And if this priority is not historical, then what is it?[2] (Hockett 1957: 386–87)

The kind of priority assumed by the IP model of description, to answer Hockett's question, is one based in atomism. The smaller unit or constituent, *bake*, is logically prior to the larger, *baked*. Atomism is a way of thinking about reality that is traceable at least as far back as Ancient Greece. Atomism is part of a scientific view of the world that contributed to linguistics a conception of language as a formal, logical system of units or elements and their relations (Kristeva 1989: 104–7).

The IP model assumes that in a given language there are atoms of meaning, or roots that undergo processes, the realizations of which are evident in a trace or marker of phonemic material not part of the original root. A grammar organized within an IP framework would feature a list of processes that specify the positions in which these processes could occur. Each of these positions would be characterized by a list of roots occurring in that position, as well as a list of processes that produce forms occurring in that position. There are, then, roots, markers, processes, and the tactical statements which list their positions of occurrence. These factors, however, are not always strictly separable. The arrangement of forms in a certain order, for example, can count as a grammatical process without an evident marker. One major problem with the IP approach acknowledged by Hockett is that the number of processes necessary to describe the intricacies of English morphology is excessive.

An alternative to the IP approach is the IA approach, which attempts an analysis of minimum units of meaning with distinctive patterns of arrangements and relations. All forms are either simple morphemes, composite constructions of morpheme constitutents, or markers of a construction. An IA grammar would include tactical statements that start with a list of constructions, each of which is specified as to its position of occurrence, and any of its identifying markers. Each position of occurrence would then be subspecified with a list of morphemes, constructions, or compoosite forms belonging to it. IA also provides for a distinctive set of morphophonemic statements that are included within the phonological components and the tactical statements. The major difficulty with IA is that arrangements of forms often involve "distinct internal chains of activity" (Hockett 1957: 390), or hierarchical structure. This means that a phrase such as "the old men and women" will have more than one logical interpretive structure. However, the major obstacle that impedes Hockett's acceptance of IA as a complete method of grammatical description is the problem proposed by an IA analysis of "took." To adopt the most attractive analysis, which is that there is a *process* of middle vowel replacement—/u/ < /ey/—would be equivalent, states Hockett, "to removing the keystone of the whole IA arch; the model begins to collapse" (1957: 394).

One important generalization that emerges from Hockett's analysis is that neither IP nor IA is adequate by itself. Each model draws from the other. The IP model makes use of tactical statements that specify the positions of occurrence for its processes. The IA model cannot efficiently account for all grammatical phenomena without using a notion of process. Hockett argues that just as mathematics involves both relations and operations, the description of grammatical structure also needs both constructions and processes. His solution, then, is to propose the use of IA along with his modified version of IP. Nevertheless, it is not difficult to understand why even the combination of these two approaches cannot achieve an adequate description of a grammar. Both approaches are essentially logical, formal, and atomistic in their conceptions of structure and therefore limited in their ability to capture the cognitive salience of linguistic patterning for a particular language's speakers. The most important critique of descriptivist approaches to morphology, however, is offered by Bolinger (1950), who argues that the principles of absolute sameness and absolute difference, which worked in the domain of phonology, are inappropriate for identifying morphemes. Bolinger argues that morphemes are not the same or different but, rather, similar or dissimiliar, and he offers a rich, psychologically salient treatment of English morphology that describes the aesthetically motivated, affective, and partially structured nature of morphemic networks.

Given the kind of approach taken by Hockett and others to morphology and grammatical theory, it is not difficult to understand why iconicity would have been problematic for such an approach. It is the arbitrariness of the linguistic sign that allows language the freedom to operate as a self-contained system, independent of "the positive facts of the external world" (DuBois, 1985: 343). Despite current work demonstrating that linguistic structure exhibits several types of schematic iconicity involving word order, for example (cf. Haiman 1985, Schachter 1985), the content of many grammatical concepts does not lend itself to iconic expression. This fact is related, then, to Hockett's belief that the arbitrariness of language also allows its speakers a greater freedom of expression. He believed that the arbitrariness of language was essential for its autonomous sytematicity, as well as for its freedom of expression. This relationship of resemblance between an iconic sign and its object is viewed by Hockett as limiting its possibilities for communication because its imitativeness restricts the ability of an icon to articulate abstract matters that have no corresponding objective or imitatable reality. The role of arbitrariness in the domain of morphology continues to be central in much of current work, particularly concerning the lexicon. However, morphology itself is no longer the center of grammar (cf. Anderson 1982: 571).

Mannheim and Waugh

Several important divergences exist in the approaches taken by Hockett and by Mannheim (1991) and Waugh (forthcoming). Waugh is concerned with the model of grammar that Hockett admits to neglecting in his own treatment, that of word and paradigm. Mannheim considers the patterns of sound change in Southern Peruvian Quechua and the sociopolitical forces that provided the contexts for those changes. In their conceptual orientation both Mannheim and Waugh are opposed to the principle of the arbitrariness of the sign in its strong form. Waugh states that iconicity is an important structural principle of human language; she conceives iconicity, broadly, as encompassing the kinds of recurrent correspondences between sound and meaning that make morphological analysis possible. Using Peirce's concept of diagrammatic icons, which "resemble their objects not at all in looks; . . . [but] only in respect to the relations of their parts (Peirce 1902: 105–107)," she cites patterns establishing parallel configurations of form and meaning throughout a language:

> Morphological analysis depends on diagrammatic parallelisms in concrete properties of form across words;. . . A simple example such as *dancer* has a diagrammatic relation with, on the one hand, *dance* and *dancing*, and, on the other hand, *worker, driver, speaker*, and so forth. The complex which means 'dancer' is motivated, not because its sounds have anything directly to do with 'dance' or 'agent of the action' (*-er*), but because they are tied by similarity to the sounds expressing these meanings elsewhere. That is, *dancer* is motivated relative to other words in the language, through a parallelism in the same form-meaning relation elsewhere. (forthcoming: 4–5)

Another type of iconicity discussed by Waugh that is important to the structuring of the lexicon is image iconicity, also known as sound symbolism or onomatopoeia. Evidence for the onomatopoeic basis of many lexical items, as well as the importance of submorphemic phonaesthemes, is used to question the primacy of the morpheme as an analytic lexical unit. And this is precisely where her approach to morphology contrasts most sharply with Hockett's. Hockett's structural models concern the arrangement and processing of elemental structures—that is, morphemes. Waugh states that the morpheme has for too long been considered the most important structural element. Citing evidence from the work of Bolinger (1940, 1950), Householder (1946), and Markel and Hamp (1960–61), she argues that structure is not always the result of integration of elements in a syntagmatic chain, but is often the result of sets of paradigmatic associations of submorphemes, phonaesthemes, and so on,which grade into, overlap with, and crosscut each other in complex semantic networks. She provides examples of synaesthetic associations that are apparent in the set of initial /fl-/ clusters in *flap, flare, flick,* and *fling*, all of which characterize movement, and also initial /gl-/ in *gleam, glow, glare, glitter,* and *gloat,* all of which characterize visual phenomena, and she then argues convincingly for the importance of elements other than morphemes. Even more significantly, she suggests a rethinking of the concept of a linguistic element. Word-initial clusters such as *fl-* and *gl-* do not lend themselves to a compositional morphemic analysis because once they are isolated, the rest of the word becomes semantically empty.

Submorphemic iconicity is of central importance also to the work of Mannheim (1991.) For Mannheim, it is significant because it challenges the traditional Neogrammarian view of historically exceptionless sound changes. He argues convincingly for submorphemic iconicity in the form of ejectives and aspirates as an explanation for otherwise unaccountable data. According to Mannheim, the ejectives and aspirates[3] in Southern Peruvian Quechua function as submorphemic sound images which constitute whole paradigms of sound/meaning correspondences. The aspirates for example are evident in *thuqay* "to spit," *khasay* "to belch," and *hach'iy* "to sneeze" (Mannheim 1991: 187–188). They are iconic of the expulsion of air in the various bodily processes they describe. The ejectives include *wikch'uy* "to expel violently, to vomit," *sik'iy* "to take or pull out violently," *hayt'ay* "to kick," and *hich'ay* "to throw out" (ibid.). In this set, the relatively great amount of energy of the ejectives is imitative of the sharpness or violence of the action so described. These sound images are significant for Southern Peruvian Quechua because they constitute evidence for a historical process of associative lexical influence. Mannheim argues that because ejectives and aspirates are rare in the Quechua languages, and because Southern Peruvian Quechua shares many ejective and aspirated words with Aymara, these features most likely were borrowed for aesthetic reasons, from Aymara stems. Ejectives and aspirates then spread through the lexicon through associative lexical influence—that is, through a process in which the features "spread from one lexical stem to other cognitively associated lexical stems" (201).

The results of associative lexical influence are elaborate lexical networks. Mannheim provides diagrams and verbal "roadmaps" through these networks to illustrate the ways in which sound imagery permeates the lexicon. In the following excerpt, he describes some lexical sets, one in which aspirated words are semantically associated with "fire" and another in which they are semantically linked by "air":

> Beginning at the left side of figure 8.11, stems (1–6) deal in a general way with 'fire': *rapha* 'flame', *ruphay* 'to be hot', to burn', *phuspuru* 'match', *rawray* ~ *yawray* 'to catch fire, to burn', *nina*[4] 'flame', *uspha* 'ash'. Mediated by *raphapapay* 'to flicker, to flutter', they give way to air movement and airborne motion: *phapapapay* 'to flap

> wings silently', *phararaaray* 'to flap wings violently' (7–8); and to the contiguous notions of 'wings, feathers, and flight', *pharpa* 'wing' (*phar* is the sound of flapping wings and the sound that announces the arrival of a mountain deity during a shaman's trance), *phuru* 'feather', *phaway* 'to take flight, escape, or leak out', *phawariy* 'to fly' (9–11); and 'noise': *wararaaray* 'to create a din', *aphan* 'noise, bustle' (12–13). The 'air' connection continues through *phusa* 'panpipe', *qhena* 'flute', *phullchu* 'puffed, puckered', *phukuy* 'to blow, to blow out' (14–17) and ties in with *phaskiy* 'to dry out' (18). (1991: 197–200)

Mannheim's work demonstrates that iconicity is both relevant to word structure and principled in its operation, although not in predictable ways. Evidence from extensive lexical networks suggests that sound imagery is a cognitively salient feature of Southern Peruvian Quechua. It ripples through semantically associated lexical items, thereby explaining certain facts of linguistic history, namely, the presence of ejectives and aspirates, which are otherwise quite uncommon to the family of Quechua languages. Submorphemic iconicity has also been discovered in the Quechua of Santiago del Estero. De Reuse (1986) noticed a pattern of sound symbolism in this dialect in which the phoneme /sh/, connoting diminutivization, had been frozen into word forms, thus providing an explanation for the irregularity of certain historical sound changes. All of this work demonstrates, then, that sound symbolism often operates outside the traditional analytical categories given by a "formal systems" approach to language.

Summary

The inherent durativity and completiveness of the physiologically produced sign vehicle provides an iconic basis for representing grammatical, aspectual concepts. The embodied nature of aspect is linked to deeper claims about the obligatory encoding of aspect distinctions within verbal roots and themes, the "nesting" of aspect throughout multiple levels of structure, and the close interrelations between aspect and other grammatical categories such as tense, mood, evidentiality, and status. Formal systems approaches to morphology and also to aspect grammar obscure the embodied nature of aspect and all of its complex ramifications. The inadequacy of formal systems approaches to morphology and aspect will become particularly apparent in chapter four, which illustrates the performative expression of durativity and perfectivity through sound-symbolic expression. When aspect distinctions become aesthetically salient in sound-symbolic utterances, they cannot be understood with the traditional building-block principles of grammatical form. Sound-symbolic communication is heavily dependent on performatively expressed intonational gestalts that cannot be predicted or calculated as sums of independently existing, abstract phonemic elements. Their structure makes sense with respect to their physiological, embodied nature. They are composed by articulatory and acoustical sound symbolism, which heightens one's experience of the natural, sensible qualities of spatiotemporal experience. In sound-symbolic expression, abstract aspectual distinctions such as duration and completiveness are physiologically simulated as the unfolding, ongoingness, becoming, completion, result, or final gesture of an action, event, process, or activity.

Chapter 3 will describe Pastaza Quechua's aspect system in detail, drawing out the ways in which aspect intersects with other features of the language such as tense, evidential mood, valency, and stativity. This detailed sketch of the aspectual subsystem will set the stage for showing how the schematic images encoded by sound-symbolic adverbs function within a niche and therefore have a role within, the overall ecology of Pastaza Quechua grammar.

3

The Grammatical Ecology of Aspect in Pastaza Quechua

Aspect expression is linked to the sensible world of spatiotemporal experience. In Pastaza Quechua this link is dramatically apparent in an elaborate subsystem of sound-symbolic adverbs that function within the grammatical and expressive architecture of the language. These adverbs operate beyond the stem-specific aspect distinctions of the verb, specifying discourse-level markedness values such as punctuality, completiveness, and resultativity. Sound-symbolic adverbs exploit grammatical aspect distinctions in order to allow speakers the use of various kinds of medial verbs and chained clause constructions without losing their sense of communicative clarity. They occupy an ecological niche within the overall structure of the language. This chapter lays the groundwork for understanding these claims with a detailed outline of the grammatical expression of aspect in Pastaza Quechua. The formal expression of aspect values through suffixation, periphrasis, and coreference is described, and paradigms for grammatical categories such as tense and evidential mood, which intersect with the aspectual subsystem are presented. The chapter is framed by a conceptual schema of markedness that divides all of Quechua's aspect expression into the privative oppositions of durativity and nondurativity. This analysis, then, supports a classification that defines Quechua for typological purposes as a dynamicity language according to the criteria set forth by Chung and Timberlake (1985.) In dynamicity languages, durativity is defined in semantically narrow terms. Quechua is a dynamicity language because the durative suffix *-u-* is used for verbs that are ongoing with respect to their event frames. To put it another way, durativity is the marked value. A verb stem suffixed with *-u-* specifies that its action is ongoing in its event frame. In accordance with the concept of markedness as it is extended to morphology, durativity is the marked category because the durative suffix "states the presence of a certain property A; the general meaning of the corresponding unmarked category states nothing about the presence of A and is used chiefly but not exclusively to indicate the absense of A" (Jakobson 1971c: 136).

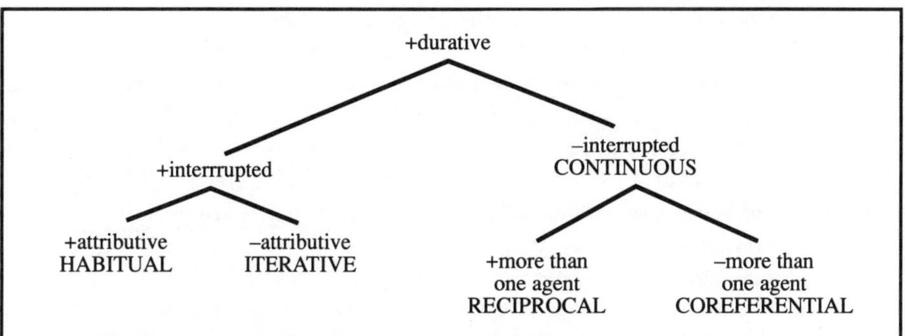

Figure 3-1 The durative aspects of Pastaza Quechua.

Figures 3-1 and 3-2 present the aspect values and categories to be discussed, in the form of a branching, implicational network of privative oppositions. The aspect categories appear in capital letters and may be realized lexically, morphologically, or, periphrastically. These diagrams are intended to represent the parameters that underlie aspect values in Pastaza Quechua. At the same time, they are meant to capture the interrelations between aspect values and other grammatical values. For example, among the nondurative categories, the perfect completive and perfect resultative are not exclusively aspectual; they intersect with mood and evidentiality. Within the durative aspects, the category coreferential establishes an agentive link between different verbs. These interrelations are specific to this language although they have also been noted in others. Some of the parameters used here to establish aspectual distinctions and categories for Quechua may have universal significance.

These figures are shown as branching taxonomic networks because their logic is implicational. For example, the durative aspects are subdivided into the features +interrupted and –interrupted. The –interrupted, or continuous, aspect is realized morphologically by the suffix *-u-*. The categories that are presented as subordinate to this node are all notionally continuous and therefore durative, although they do not ex-

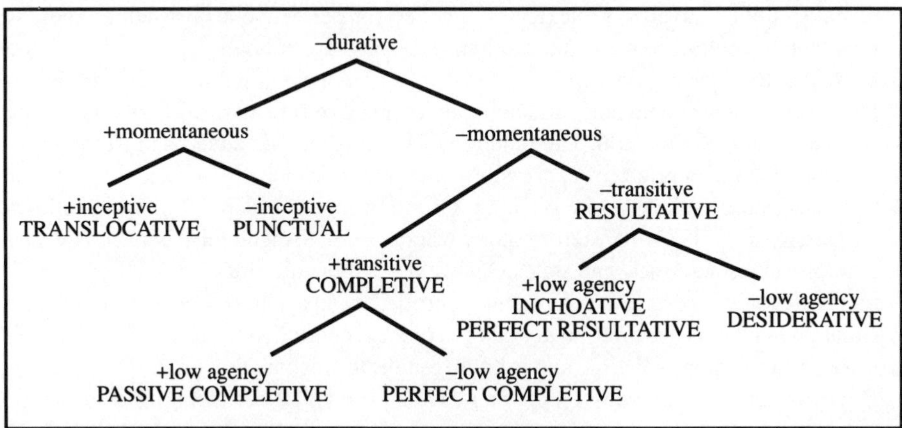

Figure 3-2 The nondurative aspects of Pastaza Quechua.

clusively concern duration. For example, the category labeled reciprocal is realized by a suffix which indicates that two or more agents are performing some action for or upon each other. The primary function of this suffix, then, is to indicate that the agent and the object of an action are interchangeable. However, aspectual durativity is implied by the reciprocal meaning of this suffix. The +interrupted subcategories are divided into +attributive, which is the habitual aspect realized by a periphrastic construction, and –attributive, which is the iterative aspect, realized by performative repetition. A habitual action is +attributive because it concerns a repeated action that is viewed "as a characteristic feature of a whole period" (Comrie 1976: 28). An iterative action, by contrast is –attributive, because it describes an action that is repetitive but is not characteristic of the agent doing the repeating.

In keeping with the tendency for unmarked categories to be more general in their meaning, and inclusive of more subcategories and distinctions, the –durative aspects are more numerous than the +durative. The first –durative distinction is between actions that are +momentaneous and those that are –momentaneous. The +momentaneous aspects are then further distinguished by the features +inception and –inception. The translocative, as its name implies, specifies that an action requires a change of location. The translocative is realized by a suffix translated "to go and do." It is +inceptive because it specifies the initiation of an action, and +momentaneous because it specifies the moment of the action's initiation. The punctual aspect, which is realized by a verb's modification with an adverb, is +momentaneous because it describes a quickly performed action, and -inception because it refers to the total accomplishment of the action rather than to its beginning. The –momentaneous categories are further distinguished by +transitive and –transitive: the +transitive feature includes the completive aspect, including the passive completive and perfect completive; the –transitive feature includes the resultative aspects, including the inchoative and desiderative constructions.

Although Quechua's aspect categories are initially framed with the privative oppositions of durativity and nondurativity, the final section of this chapter will demonstrate that when sound-symbolic adverbs are considered, Quechua can also be described with the privative oppositions of *perfective* and *imperfective*. A number of sound-symbolic adverbs are lexically encoded for perfective aspect values such as punctuality, completiveness, and resultativity. These are not pure aspect values in the sense that they specify only the closure of an action or event within its frame; rather, the adverbs as a set constitute an iconically expressive schematization of a Quechua speaker's perceptible world. The function of sound-symbolic adverbs must therefore be located at the interface of expressivity and grammaticality.

Before proceeding, a few working definitions are in order. All of what follows will use Lyons's (1983: 707) terminology where useful, to distinguish between events/acts, processes/activities, and states. An *event* is a dynamic situation that occurs momentarily; an *act*, or *action*, is an event controlled by an agent. A *process* is a dynamic situation that lasts over time; an *activity* is a process controlled by an agent, and a *state* is a situation that lasts in time and is homogenous throughout that time. Finally, *transitivity* is defined, following Hopper and Thompson (1980), as a conjunction of features that are more or less characteristic of a construction. The highest degree of transitivity is evident by the greatest number of the following features: two or more participants, kinesis or action, volitionality, agency, affectedness of object, individuation of object, and affirmation.

Organization of the Verb Stem

The following discussion of aspect follows a centrifugel logic. It will work from the inside out, starting with those suffixes closest to the root and proceeding outward into periphrastic and interclausally realized aspects. Table 3-1 represents the relative distribution of the Quechua verb's morphemes. A Quechua verb root is inherently transitive, intransitive, active, or passive. With respect to aspect, a root can be aspectually durative, nondurative, neither, or both. A root's reading as durative or nondurative depends on various factors, such as its inherent lexical semantics, its implied syntactic arguments, and the possibility of its modification by adverbs of quantification, degree, and manner. The factors affecting a verb's aspect reading have been clearly explicated by Friedrich.

> Aspectual meaning can result in many ways from the collaboration or "composition" of inherent nonaspectual categories of the verb and, on the other hand, of the features in prepositional phrases and similar structures. For example, a MOVEMENT feature (plus or minus) may combine with a phrase for SPECIFIED (or UNSPECIFIED) quantity to yield one aspect or the other (e.g., "he walked a mile" is aspectually COMPLETIVE). Similarly, a CONSTRUCT or CREATE verb can combine with an *accusativus effectivus* (of the thing created) to yield a –DURATIVE, +COMPLETIVE aspect (e.g., "he wrote a poem"). In other cases, aspect results from collaboration with an indirect object or from a singular as against a plural object (e.g., "he cobbled shoes" is +DURATIVE whereas "he cobbled a shoe" is –DURATIVE). Perhaps the most interesting of these "compositional aspects" involve PERFORMATIVE features (e.g., "he played a Bach concerto" is aspectually –DURATIVE, +COMPLETIVE if the verb is subcategorized for performative, with the sense that the actor performed a specific piece of music; otherwise it may be +DURATIVE and –COMPLETIVE and may be augmented, as in "he played a Bach concerto for hours"). All these cases involve a combination of verbal subcategorial nodes and a nominal node containing quantitative or quantificational information of some sort. (1974: 5–6).

Table 3-1 Verb Stem Composition in Pastaza Quechua

1	2	3	4	5	6	7	8
root	*-ri-* reflexive punctual inceptive resultative	*-naku-* reciprocal	*-chi-* causative	*-mu-* cislocative	*-wa-* first person object	*-gri-* translocative	-tense person number
	-ya- inchoative					*-u-*, *-hu-* durative	*-shka* perfect
	-naya- desiderative						*-sha*, *-shpa* coreference
							-kpi switch reference
							-k agentive

Completive, Resultative, and Durative Aspect Distinctions of the Root

The present and past indicative forms of roots, without any further affixal modification, are used by speakers to describe aspectually completive, resultative, or durative actions or events. Consider the following examples and their contexts. The following two sentences are aspectually completive because of their transitivity and because the contexts make it clear that they refer to telic actions. Although their translations use past tense forms, there are no past tense morphemes in the first three examples. The first was said by a boy after his unsuccessful attempt to grab a fish out of a stream:

1. Mana hapi-ni-chu!
   NEG catch-1-NEG
   "I didn't catch (it)!"

The next sentence was said by a woman upon seeing a finished clay pot.

2. Pi-ta awa-n?
   who-QN make-3
   "Who made (it)?"

The next example was stated in response to an inquiry about someone whose arrival was expected. Because the verb is lexically intransitive, and because the context makes it clear that the verb's action is telic rather than ongoing, the sentence is aspectually resultative.

3. Mana shamu-n-chu
   NEG come-3-NEG
   "He hasn't come."

Aspect Distinctions of the Stem

-ri-

The suffix *-ri-* in slot 2 (table 3-1) encodes a complex of interrelated values and functions. Its scope is lexical. Although in the great majority of examples that follow it intersects with nondurative aspect values, a root affixed with *-ri-* can usually be further modified with durative morphemes such as the continuous *-u-*. It affects the semantics of a verb root, often by a contrastive relation with a nonderived base form. Its semantic functions will be discussed in four overlapping sets. The first group of *-ri-* verbs exemplifies its reflexivizing function. In this set of verbs the relevant contrast is between an action performed by an agent upon him/herself and an action directed toward an object other than the agent. In this function *-ri-* often contrasts with the causative morpheme *-chi-*, which augments a verb's valency. It is therefore very rare for a stem to have both *-ri-* and *-chi-* suffixes. The reflexivizing function of *-ri-* is one of its most productive.

4.	*aspina*	to scrape any surface, e.g., tree bark, skin of fruit
	aspi-ri-na	to scratch one's skin
5.	*apana*	to take or buy something
	apa-ri-na	to carry something on one's back; to bear fruit
6.	*pil^{y}u-chi-na*	to wrap something, e.g., a belt around a newborn, raw meat with leaves
	pil^{y}u-ri-na	to wrap oneself, e.g., strands of beads around a wrist, coils of hair around head
7.	*pakana*	to hide or store something away
	paka-ri-na	to hide oneself
8.	*takana*	to touch, tap, pound, peck at something; to have sex with someone
	taka-ri-na	to touch, scrape oneself; to knock against something, e.g., the way a bowgun and dart quiver and knock against one's body while walking
9.	*il^{y}apana*	to shoot something or someone with a rifle
	il^{y}apa-ri-na	to shoot oneself with a rifle
10.	*mikuna*	to eat food
	miku-ri-na	to eat oneself, e.g., the way a mythic bat ate its own flesh
11.	*sakina*	to leave, abandon something or someone; to give up a habitual activity
	saki-ri-na	to stay in a place; to be left in a certain condition, e.g., the way water is left calm after waves have died down
12.	*anchu-chi-na*	to remove something, e.g., sap from a tree, or weeds, manioc, or potatoes from the ground
	anchu-ri-na	to remove oneself,; to withdraw from a place, move away from a person or an animal
13.	*al^{y}sana*	to pull or lift something
	al^{y}sa-ri-na	to pull oneself, e.g., to lift one's foot out of a muddy hole
14.	*tandana*	to gather something together, e.g., grains of rice to clean them
	tanda-ri-na	to gather together in a group, e.g., people, wasps, birds
15.	*warkuna*	to hang anything, e.g., clothes to dry them
	warku-ri-na	to hang, e.g., a loose tooth from gums, a sloth from a vine
16.	*awirina*	to paint oneself, e.g., with *genipa* juice or cosmetics[1]

Most of the *-ri*-derived verbs in this list are simply reflexive without being overtly aspectual. That is to say, most of these verbs would lend themselves to either a durative or nondurative aspectual use. Only two of the derived *-ri-* verbs are strongly aspectual. One verb, *sakirina* "to stay in a place; to be left in a certain condition," is lexically resultative, as is *tandarina* "to gather together in a group."

In the next set, *-ri-* distinguishes cognitive processess and emotions rather than typically reflexive actions. In the base forms there is an implied object of affection, knowledge, attention, or consideration. The verbs derived with *-ri-*, by contrast, focus on the processes themselves.

17.	*l^{y}akina*	to love, have affection for someone
	l^{y}aki-ri-na	to be sad, melancholy

18.	*yachana*	to know something
	yacha-chi-na	to teach, tell, inform someone about something
	yacha-ri-na	to be or become accustomed to something
19.	*musiana*	to notice something, e.g., an animal in the forest, ripe fruit on a tree
	musia-ri-na	to think to oneself; to mull something over
20.	*yuyana*	to be careful, cautious, or heedful, especially of some danger
	yuya-ri-na	to consider, remember, realize something
21.	*mandzha-chi-na*	to cause a scare or a bad fright
	mandzhana	to be afraid of something
	mandzha-ri-na	to be frightened or surprised
22.	*piñana*	to speak or act angrily to someone
	piña-ri-na	to feel angry
23.	*kungarina*	to forget

Many of the *-ri-* verbs in this set are aspectual. *Yacharina* "to become accustomed" and *kungarina* "to forget" are lexically resultative. *Yuyarina* "to realize something" is lexically punctual, as is *mandzharina* "to be surprised, startled."

The next set includes many *-ri-* verbs that have no base forms. All of these *-ri-* verbs are quite high in agentivity, and all describe configurational movements of the body. Most are lexically resultative.

24.	*tiyana*	to settle, to be in a place
	tiya-ri-na	to sit down
25.	*shayana*	to stand, be standing
	shaya-ri-na	to stand up or come to a halt
26.	*sirina*	to lie down
27.	*siririna*	to lie down
28.	*hatarina*	to get up
29.	*kungurina*	to kneel down
30.	*kaparina*	to call out, to shout
31.	*likcharina*	to wake up
32.	*kumurina*	to bend over
33.	*kushparina*	to shake, thrash, move back and forth
34.	*l^{y}ushkarina*	to slip, slide

From the foregoing set, the following *-ri-* verbs are lexically resultative: *hatarina* "to get up," *shayarina* "to stand up, come to a halt," *likcharina* "to wake up," *tiyarina* "to sit down," *sirina, siririna* "to lie down," *kungurina* "to kneel down," and *kumurina* "to bend over." The only verb in this set that is lexically durative (because it refers to a continuous activity) is *kushparina* "to shake, thrash."

The final group of *-ri-* verbs contrasts with their base forms by describing actions or processes in which agentivity is relatively low. These verbs are lexically resultative because they describe the outcome of a process.

35.	*wiñana*	to grow, thrive, e.g., babies, children
	wiña-ri-na	to sprout, e.g., plants, hair
36.	*wañuna*	to die, e.g., people, animals
	wañu-ri-na	to die out, e.g., a fire; to lie dormant, e.g., a plant

37.	*samana*	to rest
	sama-ri-na	to subside, e.g., any pain, sore, or infection
38.	*hambina*	to treat a river or pond with venom in order to catch fish.; to repair something.
	hambi-ri-na	to heal, e.g., an infection; to let up, e.g., an illness
39.	*al^{y}sana*	to pull or lift something
	al^{y}sa-ri-na	to be pulled, lifted, or configured in a certain way, e.g., the way the cusps of a new moon appear to be pulled in opposite directions
40.	*chupana*	to suck, e.g., on a piece of candy or on a cigarette while drawing on it
	chupa-ri-na	to be sucked, e.g., a foot into muddy ground
41.	*rikuna*	to look at or watch someone or something
	riku-ri-na	to appear, show up
42.	*uyana*	to listen
	uya-ri-na	to sound; to be heard
43.	*likina*	to tear something
	liki-ri-na	to tear, be torn
44.	*chaki-chi-na*	to dry something, e.g., by placing it in the sun
	chaki-ri-na	to dry up, e.g., a river when it lowers
45.	*chinga-chi-na*	to lose or misplace something
	chinga-ri-na	to be lost, scattered, spent (money)
46.	*tukuna*	to become; to be subjected to something
	tuku-ri-na	to be used up, finished, depleted
47.	*l^{y}uta-chi-na*	to attach something, e.g., a button to clothing
	l^{y}uta-ri-na	to stick, cling to, e.g., sticky substances, mites, chiggers, a star to the sky (myth), lovers devoted to each other
48.	*l^{y}uchuna*	to peel something, e.g., fruits, vegetables; to flay the skin of an animal; to strip bark from a tree
	l^{y}uchu-ri-n	to molt, peel off, e.g. scabs, scales, dry skin
49.	*kachana*	to send something to someone, e.g. food, news; to fling, throw something
	kacha-ri-na	to release, let go of something

To summarize, the functions of *-ri-* fall into four identifiable sets. Only one of these sets, the first one, in which the *-ri-* verbs are reflexive, is relatively insignificant for aspect. In the second group, which describes inwardly directed cognitive processes, most of the *-ri-* verbs have at least one nondurative interpretation. The third group, which describes bodily configurations and movements, is overwhelmingly nondurative. The fourth group of *-ri-* verbs, which describes agentively low processes, is also overwhelmingly nondurative. Their division into four distinctive sets does not preclude overlap between them. The verb *al^{y}sarina*, by one of its definitions, "to pull oneself from something" e.g., a muddy hole, belongs to the first group of reflexive *-ri-* verbs, but I have included it in the fourth set as well because it is used to describe an aspectually resultative event, which is the pulling of a new moon's cusps in opposite directions. Moreover, when it describes the pulling of one's foot out of a hole, this verb could also be included in the third set of resultative bodily configurations.

-ya-

The next aspectually relevant suffix, the inchoative *-ya-*, also in slot 2, describes the result of a change which in the overwhelming majority of cases is a perceptible change. This is a very productive process that usually involves what is notionally a noun, adjective, or adverb. Without any further modification, an inchoative verb is usually nondurative. However, inchoative verbs can be further suffixed with the continuous durative *-u-*. The following are just a few of the most commonly used nondurative verbs suffixed with inchoative *-ya-*.

50. *pundzha*	day	*pundzhayana*	to become daylight
51. *tuta*	night	*tutayana*	to become night
52. *puka*	red	*pukayana*	to become red
53. *wira*	fat	*wirayana*	to become fat
54. *kuska*	straight	*kuskayana*	to become straight
55. *chuya*	clear	*chuyayana*	to become clear
56. *wiksa*	stomach	*wiksayana*	to become pregnant
57. *wawa*	baby	*wawayana*	to give birth
58. *al^{y}u*	mold	*al^{y}uyana*	to become moldy
59. *kaspi*	stick	*kaspiyana*	to become rigid
60. *kuru*	short	*kuruyana*	to become short
61. *witu*	weed	*wituyana*	to become weedy
62. *chunl^{y}a*	quietly	*chunl^{y}ayana*	to become quiet
63. *agl^{y}u*	blister	*agl^{y}uyana*	to become blistered
64. *chul^{y}a*	uneven	*chul^{y}ayana*	to become uneven
65. *wistu*	crooked	*wistuyana*	to become crooked
66. *ichil^{y}a*	little	*ichil^{y}ayana*	to become small
67. *kushi*	happy	*kushiyana*	to become happy

-naya-

The desiderative suffix *-naya-*, also in slot 2, describes a typically nonperceptible state resulting from a desire that usually involves food, drink, or sleep. This suffix is not as productive as the inchoative *-ya-*. However, it is aspectually relevant because it describes a state which, depending on the contextual factors of its use and whether it undergoes further modification with the continuous durative *-u-*, can be either durative or nondurative. Some of the most commonly used verbs that take *-naya-* follow.

68. *upina*	to drink	*upinayana*	to be thirsty
69. *puñuna*	to sleep	*puñunayana*	to want to sleep
70. *mikuna*	to eat	*mikunayana*	to be hungry
71. *mandzhana*	to be afraid	*mandzhanayana*	to feel like being afraid

-naku-

Reciprocal *-naku-*, in slot 3 (table 3-1), describes actions shared by two or more usually human agents. It is often used to describe fighting and angry verbal exchanges between people. Durativity is implied in *-naku-* by the ongoingness of reciprocal actions.

72.	*tandana*	to gather something together, e.g., grains of rice to clean them
	tanda-ri-na	to gather in a group, e.g., wasps, birds, or people
	tanda-ri-naku-na	to be gathering together, e.g. for a work party, drinking party, fight
73.	*makana*	to hit someone
	makanakuna	to be engaged in fighting, e.g., of two or more people
74.	*piñana*	to speak angrily to someone
	piñanakuna	to be exchanging angry words
75.	*kipina*	to hug someone
	kipinakuna	to be engaged in hugging, e.g., two people

-gri-

The suffix *-gri-*, slot 7 (table 3-1), is nondurative as a consequence of its translocative function. It indicates that an action has to be performed or accomplished in another location and can be paraphrased as "to go and do." Because Quechua speakers understand translocative verbs as +momentaneous, they are aspectually punctual. Their aspectual punctuality is evident by the frequent cooccurrence of translocatives with degree adverbs such as *ukta* "quickly," comparatives such as *wayra shina* "like the wind," and the sound-symbolic *dzas*, which describes an immediate action. The momentaneousness of translocative verbs is also evident by the impossibility of their cooccurrence with the continuous durative *-u-*. Some examples of typical translocative verbs follow.

76.	*apagrina*	to go and take
77.	*tiyarigrina*	to go and sit down
78.	*pushagrina*	to go and fetch
79.	*rikugrina*	to go and see

-u -

The suffix *-u-* and its variant *-hu-*, also slot 7, are the only purely aspectual suffixes in Quechua. They describe the continuous duration of an action, state, or process, with respect to some point of reference or event frame. Older speakers tended to use *-hu-* far more frequently than their adult children. Overall, however, *-u-* is far more common regardless of age.[2] *-U-* and *-hu-* are always suffixed next to the final vowel of a verb root. When it is suffixed next to the high front vowel *-i-*, as in the verb *rina* "to go," the resulting derived form has one syllable more than its underived base. This is exemplified by the following sentence, which is the typical informal way for a guest to leave a house by simply announcing his or her departure while getting up to leave.

80. Ri-u-ni-mi kachun!
go-DUR-1-EV sister-in-law
"I'm going, sister-in-law!"

When a speaker wants to specify the continuous aspect of a verb which has this high back vowel *-u-* in the position next to the slot where continuous *-u-* would be suffixed, then that vowel is pronounced with a slight lengthening, as the next sentence with the verb *wañuna* "to die" demonstrates.

81. Wañu-u-ra-shi.
    die-DUR-PAST-EV
    "He was dying."

When *-u-* is suffixed next to a low back vowel -a- as in *rana* "to do, make," then it is pronounced like the central approximant *w*.

82. Ri-nga-mi ra-w-ni.
    go-FINF-EV make-DUR-1
    "I'm going to go"; lit.: "I'm making to go."

-shka

The final suffix to be discussed in this section combines distinctions of aspect, tense, and evidential modality. The perfect suffix *-shka*, slot 8 (table 3-1), is most saliently aspectual insofar as it encodes resultative or completive values. However, as has been noted by Comrie (1976: 52) and others, the perfect is a different kind of aspect. For this reason, I will not refer to it as aspectual unless it is used in a specifically indicated aspectual function, such as resultative perfect or completive perfect. A *-shka* suffixed root can function in several grammatical roles. It is commonly used as an adjective.

83. ismu-shka l^{y}achapa
    rot-PERF clothes
    "rotten clothes"

84. ñuka wañu-shka hachi
    I die-PERF uncle
    "my deceased uncle"

85. ungu-shka wawa
    be ill-PERF child
    "(the) sick child"

A *-shka* suffixed root also functions as a predicate adjective.

86. Kunan manga al^{y}pa chaki-ri-shka ma-w-n.
    now pot earth dry up-PERF be-DUR-3
    "Now the clay is dry."

Finally, a *-shka* suffixed root can take the accusative suffix *-ta* and function as an object complement:

87. Ukwi tiyari-shka-ta tupa-ra-ni.
ant be located-PERF-ACC find-PAST-1
"I found the location of some *ukwi* ants."

When used with a verb root, *-shka* combines past tense, perfect tense/aspect, and evidential modality in a way that is strikingly similar to Turkish, as described by Slobin and Aksu:

> The particle encoding indirect experience is related historically and ontogenetically to the perfect, and, in its participial form, functions to describe resultant states. In its use as a past tense morpheme, the particle carries modal functions of inference and hearsay, and is pragmatically extended to expressions of surprise, irony, and compliments. (1982: 185)

In narratives of myths and legends, *-shka* is used as a past tense form to defer the authority of what is asserted. When speakers use *-shka* in mythic or legendary narratives, they are also making an evidential distinction between a statement based on personal knowledge and one based on some other authority. A speaker's use of *-shka* indicates that a narrative is based on traditional authority. The appendix to this volume illustrates the paradigms for the present indicative, past tense, and narrative past tense forms.

In common with its validational use in mythic narrative, *-shka* can be used in everyday conversations to refer to the result of a nonwitnessed action or event.

88. Ima uras-ta wañu-shka, ushushi?
what time-ADV die-PERF daughter
"When did it (a baby chick) die, daughter?"

As was also noted for Turkish, the perfect function of *-shka* is extended to compliments and expressions of surprise. Quechua speakers often praise things with a simple statement:

89. Al^{y}i ma-shka.
good be-PERF
"It's good!" (of: a story, food that is being consumed, something repaired, an unfolded Swiss army knife, etc.)

-Shka also forms part of an exclamation used to express amazement, surprise, or awe, particularly when looking at something very nice, such as well-made, finely painted pottery. This expression is not easily translatable. The closest analogue from English would be something like "Wow!" This expression consists simply of the verb root *ushana* "to be able" suffixed with *-shka*:

90. Usha-shka!
be able-PERF
"Enabled!"

Finally, *-shka* is used in a typically perfect manner, to express the present relevance of an already accomplished action, event, process, or activity.

91. Ñuka mana wituk-ta yapa awiri-shka-ni-chu.
    I NEG genipa- ACC a lot paint-PERF-1-NEG
    "I haven't painted (myself) much with *genipa* dye."

A subtype of the present perfect occurs only in the second person. This construction is used to promise something to someone by assuring them that what is being promised is so certain to happen (or not to happen) to or for them, that it's as good as accomplished.

92. Ashka-ta pal^{y}a-kbi-ga monton-da ku-shka-ngi.
    much-ACC harvest-SWRF-TOP mountain-ACC give-PERF-2
    "If they harvest a lot, I'm going to give you a mountain of them"; lit.: "If they harvest a lot, you are given a mountain of them."

Or, as a mother once said to a child:

93. Masna-ta waka-kpi-s, mana apari-shka-ngi-chu!
    how much-ADV cry-SWRF-INCL NEG carry-PERF-2-NEG
    "No matter how much you cry, I'm not going to carry you"; lit.: "No matter how much you cry, you are not carried!"

All of *-shka*'s functions which have just been discussed, including the nonwitnessed resultative, the perfect, compliments, and exclamations, are part of the present perfect paradigm represented in the appendix to this volume.

The last function of *-shka* to be mentioned is its use as a past perfect, which is similar to a pluperfect because it places an action in an earlier time frame with relation to another action or event:

94. Ishkay-ta upi-chi-shka washa, ñuka wañu-shkara-ni shungu-wan.
    two-ACC drink-CAUS-PERF after I die-PERFPAST-1 heart-INST
    "After being made to drink two of them, I had died in my heart (i.e., lost consciousness)."

The past perfect paradigm is represented in the appendix to this volume.

Although the grammatical constructions and functions of *-shka* are many, intersecting with past tense and evidential modality, they can be divided into two aspectual categories of use. Any verb root suffixed with *-shka* is either resultative or completive. When a *-shka*-suffixed root functions as an adjective or predicate adjective, it tends to be resultative, because it usually describes a state or condition resulting from an accomplished event or process. When a *-shka* verb is used in the present or past perfect, however, it can be either resultative or completive, depending on a variety of factors, including the transitivity of its verb, the arguments of its predicate, and so on. Consider the aspectual difference between the following two examples. In the first, the verb *pukuna* "to ripen" functions as a predicate adjective in a perfect resultative construction, which describes the condition resulting from a process.

95. Kunan palanda puku-shka ma-w-n.
now plaintain paint-PERF be-DUR-1
"Now the plaintains are ripened."

In the next example, by contrast, a *-shka*-suffixed verb is used as a perfect completive to describe a completed action. The speaker is saying that she has had the experience of using a certain type of vegetable dye to paint herself.

96. Ñuka wituk-wan awiri-shka-ni.
I wituk-INST paint-PERF-1
"I've painted myself with *wituk* (dye)."

Periphrastic Aspects

The remainder of this chapter will concern aspect distinctions that depend upon combinations of a finite verb with other structures, including coreference, agentive, and nominalized verb roots.

The Periphrastic Completive, Resultative

The periphrastic completive construction is formed with a nominalized verb root that functions along with a past tense form of the verb *pasana* "to pass" to describe an action's accomplishment.

97. Mikw-i pasa-ra-ngi-chu?
eat-NOM finish-PAST-2-NEG
"Did you finish eating?"

Speakers also use a present tense form of the verb *pasana* in this construction. There is no discernible distinction of anteriority between the present and past periphrastic completive forms. The preceding example could have been said in the following way, using a present tense form of *pasana*, without affecting the meaning.

98. Mikw-i pasa-ngi-chu?
eat-NOM finish-2-NEG
"Have you finished eating?"

The periphrastic resultative is used in the next example featuring the intransitive verb *rina* "to go."

99. Ña ri pasa-n.
now go pass-3
"He's already gone."

The Passive Completive

The passive completive describes the result of an action performed or enacted for, upon, or against, another. It is formed with a nominalized verb root and a finite form of the verb *tukuna* "to become." The following example demonstrates its use.

100. Iminata kara-y tuku-ra-nchi, Ulpiano urku-y?
COMP give food-NOM become-PAST-1PL Ulpiano hill-LOC
"(Do you remember) how we were given food on Ulpiano's hill?;" lit.: "Do you remember how we became fed?"

The Habitual

Another aspect distinction formed by periphrasis is the habitual, which is a durative aspect. It is formed with the agentivizing suffix *-k,* slot 8 (table 3-1). A verb root that is suffixed with agentive *-k* becomes incapable of further inflection with tense-person-number markers and of further modification with any of the other morphemes of the base form. Verb roots suffixed with *-k* usually occur with another finite verb, often a form of the verb *mana* "to be,"[3] and they attribute a certain role, activity, or trait to the subject of the finite verb, as the following examples demonstrate.

101. Kawsa-k ma-n.
live-AG be-3
"It's alive!" (about a snake lying belly up in a pond)

102. Macha-k ma-n.
become drunk-AG be-3
"He's a drunk."

It is not difficult to understand how aspectual durativity can intersect logically with the kind of attribution expressed by the above sentences. The attribution is based on knowledge of past actions, and it implies that the behavior is characterized by a regular recurrence, which is a durational property. However, attribution can be a separate matter from durativity. The following sentence is ambiguous because it can be interpreted in two ways: the subject doesn't sing either because she lacks the intrinsic ability or because she has given it up (upon the death of a child or other close relation).

103. Ñuka mana kanta-k-chu a-ni.
I NEG sing-AG-NEG be-1
"I'm not a singer." Or: "I'm not in the habit of singing (anymore)."

Durative habitual aspect is most salient when a verb occurs in the past tense or when it is modified by an adverb that quantifies the action. The following sentence meets both of these specifications.

104. Ñuka yaya yapa puri-k ma-ra Marañon-gama.
my father much travel-AG be-PAST Maranon-until
"My father used to travel a lot, as far as the Marañon (River)."

Coreference Verbs and Durative Aspect

Many languages, typically non-Indo-European ones, use a type of clause structure called a "chaining" construction. Languages such as Quechua which use chaining structures, explains Longacre (1985: 238), have one verb that can be called the "dominating verb" because it is fully inflected for tense, mood, person, number, and so on. Besides this full-form verb there will be another "medial" verb that is less marked, formally, than the finite verb. This medial verb, however, might formally indicate whether its subject is the same or different from that of the finite verb, that is to say, whether it is "coreferential." The term *chaining* is used because there may be several medial verbs within the same sentence, although there will never be more than one finite verb. Because of the variety of structural and semantic relations that are possible between a coreference verb and a finite verb, and because of their relevance to aspect, they are here discussed as an entire section.

The suffix *-sha*, slot 8, functions to correlate the actions of verbs. The suffixation of *-sha* to a verb root is similar in consequence to agentive *-k* suffixation because the suffixed verb root becomes incapable of any further modification. More specifically, *-sha* indicates that the action of its verb root is performed by the same subject as the finite verb. The suffixation of *-sha* on a verb root indicates that it is a chaining verb. *-Sha* contrasts with the switch reference suffix *-kpi*, which, if substituted for *-sha* would indicate that the actions of the *-kpi* verb and of the finite verb were performed by two different agents. As an example of the way these two suffixes function, consider the difference between the next two examples.

105. Yaku-manda *l^{y}ukshi-sha* hanag-ma ri-ra.
water-from emerge-COR upriver-DAT go-PAST
"*Emerging* from the water, it went upriver."

106. Yaku-manda *l^{y}ukshi-kpi* tuksi-ra.
water-from emerge-SWRF pierce-PAST
"*(As it) emerged* from the water, he speared (it)."

In the first example *-sha* relates the action of "emerging" to the same agent that did the "going" referred to by the finite verb. The coreferentiality of these two verbs encourages one to interpret the two actions as ongoing with respect to each other. Therefore, even though the finite verb is not suffixed with the continuous *-u-*, the coreference verb "emerging" creates an ongoing event frame which is itself aspectually continuous. By contrast, the switch reference suffix *-kpi* creates a clause-like structure with a different agent. Aspectual ongoingness is not implied by *-kpi* as it is by *-sha*-suffixed verbs. A switch referenced *-kpi* verb does not, by itself, imply aspectual durativity or nondurativity. The preceding example sentence has been translated in a way that makes the *-kpi* clause seem aspectually durative:

> "*As it emerged* from the water, he speared it."

However, it could also have been translated with a nondurative *-kpi* clause:

> "*When it emerged* from the water, he speared it."

Switch reference *-kpi*, then, does not intersect with aspect as does coreference *-sha*.

Durative aspect is encoded by coreferential structures in several semantically distinctive ways. First, actions performed by the same subject are often temporally simultaneous with respect to each other, as example 105 demonstrated. Consider the following example.

107. *Riku-sha-mi* shaya-w-ra-nchi.
watch-COR-EV stand-DUR-PAST-1PL
"We were standing there *watching (it)*."

Here the act of watching and the act of standing are temporally simultaneous and virtually inseparable, although they could in principle be separate actions. It is possible to be standing without looking, and it is also possible to be looking without standing. In the following example, it is difficult to cleanly divide the act of stumbling from the act of falling, although there is some sense of their separability.

108. *Mikt'ya-sha* urma-ra.
stumble-COR fall-PAST
"*Stumbling*, he fell down."

When it relates the actions described by two verbs that are not easily analyzed as separate, the *-sha* verb often carries more semantic information about the action than the finite verb and can therefore be considered logically simultaneous because it is semantically fused with the finite verb. However, a *-sha* verb can also be fully separable from a finite verb in the sense that it describes a completely separate action that preceded the action of the finite verb. In such uses, there is always a close thematic continuity or simultaneity between the separate actions. The fact that the relations between chaining structures involve both chronological overlap and succession, states Longacre, means that they also "shade off into logical relations such as cause and effect, result, and so forth" (1985: 264). In the following subsections, I will discuss the most important kinds of interclausal-like relations which may be expressed by coreferential *-sha* verbs. Specifically, I will illustrate examples in which a condition, action, or process leads to, and may overlap with, the action of the finite verb.

-sha as a Circumstantial Clause

A *-sha* verb is often used to describe a circumstance that makes possible another action. In each of the next two examples, the *-sha* verb functions in this way as a circumstantial clause.

109. Pay-guna-ta *uma-sha,* kishpiri-ra.
he-PL-ACC deceive-COR escape-PAST
"*Deceiving* them he escaped."

110. *Chasna a-sha-shi* chasna kasa-k a-n.
like that be-DUR-EV like that hunt-AG be-3
"*Being like that* is how he's a hunter."

In both of the foregoing examples, the *-sha* clause is aspectually continuous because it describes a condition or state which makes the action of the finite verb possible. In the first sentence, it is the creation of an ongoing state of deception that makes an escape possible; in the second sentence, it is an animal's habit of watching from underwater, whatever passes above him, that defines his ability to hunt.

-sha as Clause of Reason or Purpose

There is no sharp categorial distinction between the circumstantial *-sha* clause just discussed and the *-sha* clause that describes a causal relation between two actions. When it functions causally, the verb suffixed with *-sha* typically describes an action or process that transparently leads to the action of the finite verb. Consider the following sentence. The coreference verb describes a way of thinking that led to the action, or, rather, the nonaction, of the finite verb. This sentence is taken from an account. It states that a group of people restrained themselves from shooting a tapir because they wanted the hide of the jaguar which they believed to be pursuing the tapir.

111. *Chi-ta ni-sha* pay-guna wagra-ta mana il^{y}apa-naw-ra.
that-ACC want-COR he-PL tapir-ACC NEG shoot-3PL-PAST
"*(Because) they were wanting that,* they didn't shoot the tapir."

In this sentence the aspectual value of the *-sha* clause is continuous because it describes an ongoing preference which led to but also overlapped with the action of the finite verb.

-sha as a Clause of Hypothetical Condition

The next example illustrates another type of *-sha* clause expressing a hypothethetical condition. The sentence was uttered by a man who expressed regret at not having known about the medicinal value of the teeth of a poisonous snake he had just killed.

112. *Yacha-chi-shka a-sha,* apa-y-ma ma-ra-ni.
know-CAUS-PERF be-COR take-NOM-CON be-PAST
"*If I had been informed,* I would have taken (them)"; lit.: "*It being the case that I had been informed,* I would have taken them."

The hypothetical condition described by the *-sha* clause is aspectually continuous because it describes an ongoing state of knowledge which, if it had existed, would have influenced the action of the finite verb.

Narrative Level Durativity of *-sha* Clauses

When two or more *-sha* verbs are juxtaposed in a sentence, each describing a different action, the result is a narrative-level durativity, which is concerned not simply with the relative temporal duration of a chain of actions, but with their thematic continuity as well. By way of illustration, the next example describes the efforts of an ant attempting to lift and carry off the stem of a leaf. The speaker begins and ends the description with the finite verbs *pitina* "to cut" and *rina* "to go." Occurring in between the first and last verbs, however, are coreference *-sha* forms of the verbs *urmana* "to fall," *hatarina* "to get up," *shayarina* "to stand up," and *ushana* "to be able." All of these *-sha* verbs are thematically unified as a series by the coreference suffix. Besides their formal status as coreference verbs, they have in common their semantic reference to the ant's unsuccessful attempts to lift up the leaf stem and carry it off.

113. Lomo panga-ta piti-n; chi-wan-ga urma-sha, hatari-sha, shayari-sha, mana
manioc leaf-ACC cut-3 that-INCL-TOP fall-COR rise-COR standup-COR NEG
usha-sha-chu ri-n.
be able-COR-NEG go-3
"(First) he cuts off the manioc leaf; (then) falling down with it, getting up, (trying to) stand up; (but), not being able to, he goes off."

In the above description, the narrator's use of the coreferential *-sha* verbs creates a narrative level durativity that conflicts with the nondurative aspect encoded at the level of the proposition. The verb *urmana* "to fall" is aspectually resultative at the propositional level. By suffixing this verb with *-sha*, the speaker links the act of falling with the subsequent attempts to rise and stand up, thus creating an ongoing, narrative-level durativity.

Sound-Symbolic Adverbs and Perfective Aspect

It would seem, then, that descriptions of actions or activities conducted by the same agent are overdetermined by the system of coreference for aspectual durativity; however, this is not the case. Speakers of Pastaza Quechua can use sound-symbolic adverbs to specify perfective aspect values. The following sentences show how a coreference *-sha* verb, when modified by a sound-symbolic adverb, becomes clearly specified for aspectual perfectivity. Since the entire second part of this book will concentrate on sound-symbolic adverbs, I will limit my discussion of them here to a few examples.

In the following, the sound-symbolic adverb *tsak,* which is sound symbolic of a puncturing or piercing, describes the stabbing of a riverbank with a steering pole to dock a canoe.

114. Chi-ga ña tsak shayari-k shamu-sha, 'maykan-da a-ngichi kay-bi guardia-ga
that-TOP now stand-AG come-COR which-QN be-2PL here-LOC guard-TOP
ni-ra-mi?'
say-PAST-EV

"So then, now *tsak* as-a-stander coming, he said 'Which of you is the guard here?'"

In this sentence *tsak* modifies the coreference verb phrase "as-a-stander coming," making it clear that there was a definite point in time when the action of coming to a standstill took place.

In the next example, the sound-symbolic adverb *ang*, which presents an image of a wide open mouth, describes the feeding of a baby bird with balls of masticated food.

115. Bul^{y}us-l^{y}a ra-sha ang paska-sha, uku-y uku-y sati-k a-ra-ni.
ball-LIM do-COR open-COR inside-LOC inside-LOC insert-AG be-PAST-1

"Making little balls, opening its mouth up *ang*, inside inside I would put them."

In this sentence *ang* modifies the coreference verb *paskasha*, making it clear that at a certain point, the opening of the bird's mouth was definitively accomplished.

The final example of this chapter uses the sound-symbolic adverb *tsuk*, which is sound symbolic of plucking a piece of something from its mass. In this example *tsuk* describes plucking out the heart of a palm tree.

116. Tsuk aysa-sha pal^{y}a-nchi lisan yuyu-ta.
pull-COR harvest-1PL lisan heart-ACC

Tsuk pulling it out, we harvest the heart of the *lisan* palm tree.

In this sentence *tsuk* modifies the coreference verb *paskasha* "pulling," making it clear for a listener that the act of pulling out the heart of the palm tree was accomplished at a certain point, rather than ongoing, as an unmodified coreference verb would have suggested.

Although the coreference *-sha* suffix functions to link its verb to the finite verb, telling a listener that all of these actions are performed by the same agent, it can also imply that its action is ongoing with respect to the action of the main verb. However, Quechua speakers have a way of overriding that interpretation when it is not desired. And this is where sound-symbolic adverbs enter the picture. Many sound-symbolic adverbs specify completion, punctuality, or resultativity. When sound-symbolic adverbs modify a coreference verb, they effectively establish that verb's temporal closure, despite the ongoingness that is implied by the coreference suffix. These examples demonstrate,then, that sound-symbolic adverbs function grammatically within an ecological niche created by coreference constructions. Without modification by a sound-symbolic adverb, coreference verbs are aspectually imperfective because they allow for the possibility that an action or event is ongoing throughout its event frame (Chung and Timberlake 1985: 236). When they are modified by perfective sound-symbolic adverbs, coreference structures become aspectually perfective because such adverbs provide a cognitively salient boundary for the implied ongoingness of actions described by chained verbs. To understand sound symbolism's aspectual significance it is instructive to try to image speaking English without using particles and prepositions like *up*, *down*, *over*, *across*, and *in*. These particles and prepositions function, in part, to indicate the completiveness of their verbs' actions. To *eat up* means to have eaten everything. To *sit down* means to have completed the action of sitting in a certain place. The construction *grab on* indicates the moment when something is touched. In Pastaza Quechua many sound-symbolic words function like particles and prepositions in English. They specify completive aspect through their sound simulation of basic kinds of sensory images.

Summary

Aspect in Pastaza Quechua is encoded within a finite verb by the inherent semantic properties of its root and by suffixation. Only one suffix, *-u-*, is purely aspectual in function; the rest combine distinctions of valency, stativity, evidentiality, and tense along with their continuous, punctual, completive, and resultative aspects. Other aspect distinctions depend on combinations of a finite verb with a variety of structures, including agentive, nominalized, and coreference verbs. Finally, even these compound verb structures can be further modified aspectually, with sound-symbolic adverbs. Sound-symbolic adverbs occupy an ecological niche within the overall structure of the language. They allow speakers to use various kinds of medial verbs and chained clause constructions without losing their sense of aspectual explicitness and communicative clarity.

The chapter began by stating that the aspect system of Quechua can be described fairly neatly with the binary, privative oppositions of durativity and nondurativity. Durativity is the marked value. The fact that there is no specifically nondurative suffix conforms to the generalization that the unmarked value is realized by "zero expression." However, if one considers sound-symbolic adverb/verb constructions, then the aspectual picture of Pastaza Quechua is further complicated. Many sound symbolic adverbs specify that an action's limit is reached within an event frame. And this is how Chung and Timberlake define the category they call *perfective* (1985: 219), except that they limit this term to morphological categories of the verb base. Sound-symbolic adverbs provide another set of oppositions operating beyond the structure of the finite verb. Quechua's aspect system is best described, therefore, as two equipollent sets of oppositions, consisting, on the one hand, of the durative/nondurative aspect categories of a verb stem and of compound verb constructions, and on the other hand, of the perfective/imperfective aspect categories that are schematically encoded by sound-symbolic adverbs. However, as part 2 will demonstrate, sound-symbolic adverbs can only be partly understood within a binary framework of aspectual perfectivity; they do not lend themselves to finer classification within an implicational hierarchical taxonomy of grammatical features. The next chapter concerns the ways in which sound symbolic adverbs become formally and expressively elaborated through performative foregrounding.

4

The Performative Expression of Durativity and Perfectivity

The concept of markedness was used in chapter 3 to analyze the Quechua verb's grammatical aspectual structure. Urban (1985: 314), following Hymes (1974) and Silverstein (1976) has shown that markedness can also clarify the complex multifunctionality of speech styles. As stylistic types, sound-symbolic adverbs have both marked and unmarked tokens. This chapter examines the expressive possibilities for stylistically marking sound-symbolic utterances. In general, sound-symbolic utterances are stylistically marked by their formal amplification through such performative features as intonational elaboration, repetition, syllabic extension, and syntactic isolation, all of which create a heightened sense of an action's spatiotemporal unfolding. Performative features enhance Pastaza Quechua's grammatical resources for the expression of aspect. In addition, there are more subtle, nuanced specifications of tempo, rhythm, process, and movement. The existence of performative aspect suggests yet another area of dynamic interconnection between grammar and poetry that has concerned scholars such as Friedrich (1979, 1986), Jakobson (1968), Mannheim (1986), Sapir (1921), and Sherzer (1987, 1990). More generally, performative aspect illustrates a fundamental characteristic of Pastaza Quechua language use. For the Pastaza Quechua, language use is modeled on sounds, patterns, movements, and rhythms of the natural world and of one's bodily experiences in it. The movements of the mouth, the shaping of the vocal tract, and the fluctuating pitch of the voice are all uses of the body to imitate movements and processes of perceptual experience. The sounds of sound communicate not an abstract, detached meaning, but a concrete movement, rhythm, or process unfolding in time.

That there is a phenomenon identifiable as "performative aspect" supports Hopper's (1979) assertion that aspect makes best sense from a functional narrative point of view, as a mechanism for the foregrounding and backgrounding of certain parts of a narrative. Aspectual durativity lends itself to performative foregrounding because of the temporal successivity of the linguistic sign vehicle. Aspectual perfectivity is also congenial with performative foregrounding because linguistic expression is subject to the limitations of the human breath, which must spend itself at regular intervals of articulation. The qualities of ongoingness and termination that are embodied in the linguistic sign vehicle are embellished through performance for a variety of iconically expressive aspectual effects. This chapter, then, will describe the performative techniques that enhance aspect expression in Pastaza Quechua. The transcription of these techniques draws from the work of a number of scholars, including Bolinger (1986), Sherzer (1990), and Tedlock (1983). This chapter will also suggest some functional similarities between performative foregrounding techniques and other communicative modalities. The performative expression of aspect distinctions is often best understood with reference to other semiotic modalities, such as the gestural and the cinematic. The following discussion divides performative aspect into the general categories of durativity and perfectivity.

Durativity

Quechua speakers make frequent use of the intrinsic duration of the linguistic sign vehicle for the performative expression of aspectual durativity. In conjunction with prosodic and rhythmic features, repetition expresses various kinds of iteration and spatial distribution. Besides repetition, speakers also use syllabic lengthening in performative utterances. The lengthening of a syllable expresses ongoing duration, movement across space, the totality of a dispersed image, or focus upon an image. All of these performative features assist in the expression of aspect. However, an otherwise unmarked utterance may be totally dependant on performative features for the expression of aspectual durativity.

Reduplication

Reduplication is a morphological process occurring in many languages; it involves copying part or all of a stem. Since reduplication affects the aspectual value of a predicate, it could have been discussed in the preceding chapter. However, because of its affinity with multiple repetition, which is broader in its structural scope, it is illustrated in this section. As noted by Moravcsik (1978) in her cross-linguistic survey, reduplication expresses plurality, the repeated occurrence of an event or action, and various kinds of intensification, including both increased quantity and diminution. The following data from Quechua will show that reduplication also expresses spatial distribution. For the purposes of this discussion, reduplication will be defined as a construction featuring a single, complete copying of a form. In other words, there will only be two copies of a form.

In Pastaza Quechua, reduplication is a common device for indicating the repetition of an action over a time frame. It therefore communicates iterative aspect. Reduplication is the most minimally performative technique for expressing iteration because a reduplicated form is usually incorporated within the intonational contours of the utterance as a whole. It is not typically foregrounded by variations in pitch or by syllabic extensions. The following examples illustrate the semantic consequences of reduplication and the range of structures it encompasses. In the following sentence the reduplicated form is a verb root that functions as an adverb and modifies a finite verb. It describes the repeatedness of dogs' sniffing.

1. Al^{y}ku-guna *mukti mukti ri-naw-ra* armadizhu-ta maska-sha.
dog-PL smell smell go-3-PAST armadillo-ACC search-COR
"The dogs *went sniffing and sniffing*, looking for the armadillo."

A nonperformative version of the preceding sentence would simply use a coreference verb in place of the reduplicated root, as in the following.

Al^{y}ku-guna *mukti-sha ri-naw-ra* armadizhu-ta maska-sha.
dog-PL smell-COR go-3PL-PAST armadillo-ACC search-COR
"The dogs *went sniffing*, looking for the armadillo."

In the next example, the reduplicated verb root occurs within a relative clause structure, to describe repeated crying.

2. Ñuka *waka waka* pasa-shka-ta, kan mana yacha-ngi-chu.
I cry cry pass-PERF-ACC you NEG know-2-NEG
"You don't know what I've been through, *crying and crying*."

Nouns and adjectives can also be reduplicated.[1] A reduplicated noun can be used to describe the appearance of a repeated movement, in addition to the fact of its iteration. The next sentence repeats the Spanish *barbas* "whiskers" to describe the way the long barbels on the mouth of a catfish move when it eats.

3. *Barbas barbas* miku-n bagri-ga.
whiskers whiskers eat-3 catfish-TOP
"The catfish eats *whiskers whiskers* (i.e., moving its whiskers).

Finally, a reduplicated noun or adjective can simply describe the spatial distribution of its referent. In the next sentence the Quechua noun *tuyaka* "pit" functions as an adverb to describe the gullies and depressions of water scattered throughout a dried up riverbed.

4. Chakiri-shka-y *tuyaka tuyaka* sakiri-n yaku.
dry up-PERF-LOC pit pit remain-3 water
"When the river dries up, *gullies and gullies* of water remain.

The next example also uses reduplication to describe the spatial distribution of its referent. It describes the speed with which small stumps of fungi growing all over a rotting log become mushrooms.

5. Ala-guna, shuk pundzha *muku muku*; kayandi pal^{y}a-y-bak.
   fungus-PL one day stump stump following harvest-NOM-able
   "One day the fungi (are nothing but) *stumps stumps (all over)*; the next day they're harvestable."

Multiple Repetition

The repetition of any part of an utterance three or more times is considered multiple repetition. In principle there is no upward limit to the number of repetitions a speaker will give a form. Some speakers even draw an extra breath during a repeated series, to keep it going. However I've never heard a speaker repeat a form for more than the time that it takes to run out of one breath and inhale a fresh one. Multiple repetitions have in common with reduplication the performative expression of the iterative duration of an action, process, or activity. The temporal relationship between the multiple repetitions of a form can, as Moravcsik states, involve "all the logically possible temporal relations that any event can bear to any other, including: simultaneity, immediate precedence, non-immediate precedence, overlap, inclusion, and interlocking" (1978: 305). Pastaza Quechua speakers also use multiple repetition to enumerate objects distributed throughout a space.

The principal difference between reduplication and multiple repetition, besides quantity, has to do with with their relative pragmatic importance within their respective utterances. Reduplicated forms usually function as adverbs or predicate adjectives. They typically require a finite verb, which may not be overtly expressed, to complete a predication. Furthermore, reduplicated forms are typically assimilated into an utterance's intonational contour. They are usually not highly foregrounded. By contrast, a form that undergoes multiple repetition, particularly when it is quantitatively large, assumes a pragmatic importance that is typical of a verb. Even though a form is syntactically and morphologically an adverb which modifies a finite verb, its multiple repetition often confers upon it a notionally predicative value. The multiple repetition of a form is also more performative of an action's durativity than simple reduplication. This is because it is relatively more foregrounded by expressive prosodic devices, including pitch variation, metrical stress patterns, and even paralinguistic signals, which subcategorize aspectual iterativity into finer specifications of tempo and rhythm. When a form undergoes multiple repetition, it can often be understood as an expressive gesture of what a verb would merely refer to.

The following discussion will briefly survey the variety of syntactic structures that undergo multiple repetition and at the same time call attention to the finer semantic nuances suggested by prosodic and rhythmic variations in these performative repetitions. In the following sentence the finite verb *aysara* "he pulled" is repeated to describe the attempts to pull in a large turtle which had just been speared. Each repetition is given a forceful and energetic emphasis, which can't be conveyed orthographically. By giving each element of the repeated series equal intonational emphasis, the speaker eloquently expresses the repeated effort to capture the turtle.

6. Pay aysa-shka-ta muyuri-ra-nchi sambayachi-sha, *aysa-ra aysa-ra aysa-ra*
he pull-PERF-ACC circle-PAST-1PL make tired-COR pull-PAST pull-PAST pull-PAST
aysa-ra puya-ta-ga aysa-shka, ña shamu-kpi shuk-wan randi tuksi-ra.
pull-PAST lance-ACC-TOP pull-PERF then come-SWRF one-INST instead spear-PAST

   "(While) we circled around what he'd pulled, (trying to) tire it out, *he pulled and pulled and pulled and pulled on the lance*; the next time it came (up), he speared it with another (one)."

In addition to finite verbs, coreference *-sha* verbs can also undergo multiple repetition to expressively gesture iteration. The next sentence can be understood as iterative in two dimensions. The repetition of the coreference verb *alʸasha* "digging" describes both the iterativity of the act of digging in the sand for turtle eggs and the repetition of that activity over a block of narrative time.

7. *Lulun-da alʸa-sha alʸa-sha alʸa-sha* shamu-ra-nchi kanoa-wan.
egg-ACC dig-COR dig-COR dig-COR come-PAST-1PL canoe-IN

   "*Eggs digging, digging, digging* we came, by canoe."

It is sometimes the case that nouns suffixed with case markers undergo multiple repetition and serve as an index to an action that is not explicitly stated with a finite verb. The next sentence serves as an illustration. Taken from a description of a salt mining expedition, it describes the way salt was broken off from boulders and then put into numerous baskets.

8. Hacha-ng paki-sha-ga *ashanga-ma ashanga-ma ashanga-ma ashanga-ma.*
ax-INST break-COR-TOP basket-DAT basket-DAT basket-DAT basket-DAT

   "Breaking it up with an ax, (they put it) *in one basket and in another and in another and in another.*"

In the foregoing example the multiple repetitions of a case-suffixed noun stand for a covertly understood verb. In the next example, a series of multiple repetitions function as the subject of a sentence. The Spanish word *olas* "waves" is repeated over and over to describe the appearance of crests of waves moving across water. These repetitions are additionally configured by a pitch contour that rises and then falls back down.

9. Olas olas olas olas olas olas olas olas olas olas olas-shi rikuri-ra ni-ra.
waves-EV appear-PAST say-PAST

   "Waves waves waves waves waves waves waves waves waves waves waves appeared, he said."

The repetitions of *olas* are not simply iterative along a temporal axis; they are meant to express the spatial distribution of their referents as well. The circumscribing pitch rise and fall enhances the image of the waves' movement in space. This enhancement is effected by the series of incrementally ordered pitch variations. These variations are iconic of an idea of spatial distribution because they define a range of possible "places" marked by the speaker's voice pitch.

A series of multiple repetitions may also be framed by a pitch rise and fall, the function of which is not to express spatial distribution but simply to break the monotony of the series of repetitions. In the following sentence the word *chaki-n* "with foot" is repeated in fast motion to illustrate the kind of quick walk that a mother expects from her child when they go to their agricultural field.

10. Shina a-sha haku-ngi, sindzhi-ta puri-wa-ngi, kunan
like that be-COR come-2 strong-ADV walk-1ACC-2 now foot-ADV

chaki-n chaki-n chaki-n chaki-n chaki-n chaki-n chaki-n chaki-n.

"O.K., then, come along and walk with me strongly now (going)

foot foot foot foot foot foot foot foot."

In this example a series of repetitions expresses relatively distinctive subactions. The distinctness of each footstep is enhanced by the speaker's use of pitch variation. Each repeated instance of *chakin* "with foot" can be understood as an iconic gesture of a single footstep in a rapid walk. The speaker's use of extremely fast paced multiple repetitions is comparable to the cinematic technique which presents an action in accelerated motion by projecting the film at a faster speed than that at which it was shot.

In the next example, however, a series of multiple repetitions is performed in a way that diminishes the distinctiveness of its subactions. The sentence is taken from a myth. It describes a lengthy journey made by a girl who is anxious to get as far away as possible from the jaguars that ate her brother. The speaker describes her journey through the forest with multiple repetitions of the narrative past tense form *rishka* "she went."

11. Turi-ta miku-nawn ni-sha, *ri-shka ri-shka ri-shka ri-shka ri-shka ri-shka.*
brother-ACC eat-3PL say-COR go-PAST

"Thinking 'they ate my brother,' *she went and went and went and went and went and went."*

Here multiple repetitions are used to emphasize the consistent ongoingness of the girl's repeated movement through space. It is the consistency of her movement that is important because it indicates her determination to get as far away as possible from the jaguars. To emphasize this continuity, the speaker leaves no pauses between any of the verb's repetitions. It sounds to a listener as if she is saying one long repetitive word.

The final example contrasts strikingly with the preceding insofar as it presents a series of multiple repetitions, emphasizing as much as possible the intermittency and interruptedness rather than the continuity of each subaction. This sentence uses the locational/temporal adverb *washa* "behind, after" to describe the way a woman secretly followed her husband through the forest. While following him she allowed herself to lose sight of him now and then so that she wouldn't be discovered. Each of the repetitions of *washa*, then, stands for his reappearance within her view. The interruptedness of this activity is emphasized by two performative features. First, the speaker uses a marked stress pattern on *washa*. In its citation form, *washa* is always stressed on its penultimate syllable; however, in the following example, it is stressed on its final syllable. This marked stress foregrounds each individual instance of catching up with and catching sight of the husband from behind. The other performative feature that emphasizes the intermittency of the action is the pause which follows each repetition.

12. Ima-manda-shi ni-sha, *washa (pause) washa (pause) washa (pause) washa (pause)*
    what-from-EV say-COR behind
    washa (pause) washa (pause) washa (pause) ña chagra-y pundzha-l^{y}a-shi
    then chagra-LOC day-just-EV
    pakta-gri-ra.
    arrive-TRSLC-PAST

    "Wondering what (he was doing), *(she followed) behind (pause), behind (pause) behind (pause) behind (pause) behind (pause) behind (pause) behind (pause)*, then, when it was just becoming daylight, he went and arrived at the *chagra*."

The comparison of this example with sentence 11, which repeats the verb *rishka* "went" to describe a girl's journey through the forest, strengthens the claim about the iconicity expressed by multiple repetition when combined with tempo and stress. The repetitions of *rishka* are regularly stressed and pronounced with almost no pause or interval between them; this repeated series communicates the continuity of the girl's journey through the forest. Sentence 12, by contrast, describes a very segmented, individuated series of actions, consisting of the wife following her husband to catch up with him, reaching sight of him, dropping back behind him so as not to be discovered, and then starting again in her efforts to catch up with him. The segmented, individuated quality of this series is conveyed by the marked word-final stress and slight pause after each repetition of *washa*.

Lengthening

Lengthening is a very common performative technique for the expression of durativity. In this section I will discuss the range of grammatical structures with which it is used and its consequences for aspectual expression. The preceding discussion demonstrated that multiple repetition expresses both aspectual iterativity as well as spatial distribution; the following discussion will present examples demonstrating that lengthening also expresses both temporal and spatial descriptions. That lengthened pronunciation can be iconic of duration was noted by Bolinger in his study of English prosody:

> Inherent length . . . adheres to words as a form of sound symbolism. Except for their initial consonants, *ball* and *drawl* contain the same distinctive sounds, but whereas in a sentence like *He's playing with a ball* we can shorten *ball* to the point of almost eliminating the pitch drop at the end, a similar treatment of *He's talking with a drawl* would probably be misunderstood—*drawl* is lengthened approximately as much as

-drawal in *withdrawal*. Similarly, *dawn* and *yawn* as in *It dawned on me* and *He yawned at me*. And similarly *side—sighed. Take the pine away* and *She'll just pine away* reveal additional length in the verb *pine*. (1986: 43)

Although Bolinger's statement doesn't mention aspect specifically, it implies the relevance for aspect of syllable length because it is the inherent aspect, specifically, the lexical durativity of the verbs "drawl," "yawn," and "sigh" that makes the lengthening of their vowels appropriate.

The range of grammatical structures that can be lengthened in Quechua is extensive.[2] The following example demonstrates that a verb root need not be suffixed with the continuous morpheme *-u-* to express durativity. The root vowel of the verb *rina* "to go" is lengthened to describe the continuous, unbroken movement of a plane's flight path as it moves across the sky. The person who said this was actually watching the plane's movement as she commented on the fact that her uncle was inside it. In this example the lengthening alone expresses durativity since there is no other grammatical expression of it.

13. Rik-i hachi Cervantes *riiiiiiiiiiiii-n* hawa l^{y}akta-ta.
look-IMP uncle Cervantes go-3 high land-ACC
"Look, there *goooooo-es* uncle Cervantes to the highland."

Interestingly, I have heard the same verb used with an identical extension of its root vowel to describe the path of movement defined by a tarantula walking across the upper support beams of a house, as observed by people watching it from below.

In the next sentence, by contrast, durativity is maximally expressed by a combination of the coreference suffix *-sha*, the continuous *-u-* suffix, and lengthening. The narrator lengthens the portion of the coreference verb *kalpawsha* "running," which is suffixed with the continuous *-u-*. The sentence is taken from a fable about a race between a deer and a tortoise.

14. Sambaya-sha *yapa kalpa-wwww-sha* wañu-shka taruga.
become tired-COR much run-DUR-COR die-PAST deer
"Tiring (because he was) *ruuuun-ning so much*, the deer died."

In the next sentence the final syllable of an adjective is lengthened, to describe the duration of a state of being alone.

15. Kan-guna chasna *sapal^{y}aaaaaa* a-kbi-mi shamu-ra-nchi.
you-PL like that alone be-SWRF-EV come-PAST-3PL
"Because you-all are *alooooone* like that, we came."

To focus on the continuous durativity of an action referred to with a coreference *-sha* verb, speakers frequently lengthen just the *-sha* portion of a verb. The following example taken from a myth describes the way two children stared as their relatives who had just jumped into a river all turned into dolphins. The lengthening of the final *-sha* on *rikusha* "staring" expresses the duration of the staring.

16. Chi wawa-guna *riku-shaaaaa* shaya-naw-ra ishka-ndi-guna payna win bugyu
    that child-PL look-COR stand-3PL-PAST two-INCL-PL XPRO all dolphin
    tuku-shka-y.
    become-PERF-NOM
    "Both of those children stood *stare-iiinnng* as all of them had become dolphins."

The next example also uses a coreference form of the verb *rikuna* "to see." In this sentence, however, the narrator extends the final syllable of the object that is being watched, rather than of the verb that refers to the watching. The sentence, taken from a myth, describes two brothers looking up at the sky and watching the stars they will eventually marry. In this sentence the lengthened syllable is actually the accusative case marker *-ta*. The lengthening of *-ta* expresses both the durativity of the looking and it also focuses a listener's attention on the image of the stars as a total spatial expanse.[3]

17. Ishka-ndi wawki *istileres-taaaaa* riku-sha siri-shk-awna.
    two-INCL brother stars-ACC look-COR lie-PERF-3PL
    "Both of the brothers laid there looking *at the starrrrrs."*

Lengthening can also take place on a noun functioning as an adverb. The next example, taken from a myth, illustrates this with the noun *pundzha* "day," which, in this context refers to the daylight-like brightness of a star. It describes a star's ascent back to the sky after having spent time on the earth. The lengthening on the adverbial form *pundzha-n* "with brightness" is iconically performative of the continuous streak of brightness blazed by the star as it shoots upward.

18. *Pundzhaaaaaaa-n-shi* ri-ra hawa-y.
    bright-ADV-EV go-PAST up-LOC
    "With a streaaaaaaak she went upwards."

The lengthened adverb *pundzhan* is used in the preceding example to describe both the duration and the spatial expanse of the star's movement through the sky. However, it can also be used by a narrator to focus on a specific image in a narrative description. Consider the next sentence, which describes the image of an alligator as revealed at night by a flashlight. The flashlight's illumination is described with lengthening on the same syllable of *pundzhan* as the preceding sentence. In the following sentence, however, the duration of *pundzhan*'s lengthening serves to focus on the presentation of an image, rather than to express relative duration.

19. Kucha sapi-ta ri-u-ra-nchi; *pundzhaaaa-n!* Lagarto-ta riku-ngi-ma!
    pond end-ACC go-DUR-PAST-1PL bright-ADV alligator-ACC look-2-CON
    "We were heading for the end of the pond, (then) *with the brightnessssss*, you would see (such) an alligator!"

Finally, a lengthened form can also undergo multiple repetition. The next sentence repeats the adverb *kushnin* "with smoke" to describe the way vapor is repeatedly expelled from the smokestack of a steamboat. The lengthening of each repetition represents the duration of the narrator's focus on the individual images of expelled smoke.

20. Riku-kbi *kushniiiiii-n kushniiiiii-n kushniiiiii-n kushni-n,* tobo ruku-manda
look-SWRF smoke-ADV smoke-ADV smoke-ADV smoke-ADV pipe big-from
l^{y}ukshi-k a-n.
emerge-AG be-3
"Upon looking (I saw) *ssssssmoke ssssssmoke ssssssmoke smoke* emerge from that big pipe."

Although the form *kushnin* is morphologically an adverb, it is also the notional subject of its sentence. It both modifies the verb *l^{y}ukshina* "to emerge" and is the subject because of its pragmatic focus on the presentation of the image.

Perfectivity

Performative perfectivity is usually expressed with sound-symbolic adverbs. Sound-symbolic adverbs are not limited to the performative expression of perfectivity. Many can undergo lengthening and multiple repetition to express durativity. However, their perfectivity is what links them to the grammatical architecture of the language. Their perfectivity affects the lexical and predicate-level aspect values of verbs, and it also affects a variety of coreference structures, thereby allowing speakers to communicate with optimal clarity and expressivity. This discussion will therefore focus on the ways in which all of this is accomplished through performance. In the preceding chapter, the examples supplied to illustrate the aspectual perfectivity of sound-symbolic adverbs were very neat and unproblematic. In this chapter, some of the more complex examples of performatively foregrounded sound-symbolic adverbs will be discussed. The following discussion will divide foregrounding techniques into the syntactic and intonational, and then it will show how these two are combined.

Syntactic Foregrounding

Before embarking on the discussion of sound-symbolic adverbs' syntactic foregrounding, it is necessary to comment briefly on the inherent foregroundedness of sound-symbolic adverbs. A Quechua speaker's use of a sound-symbolic adverb, whether it is performatively foregrounded or relatively unforegrounded, as were the examples in the previous chapter, can usefully be compared with the close-up shot used by cinematographers. A close-up shot enlarges some detail which is a characteristic feature of the image as a whole (Arnheim 1957: 79). The function of the close-up shot is to guide a viewer's attention to the relevant features of the narrative's unfolding and, at the same time, communicate expressive subtleties that would not be evident from long-range shots. In the same way, sound-symbolic adverbs take the most vivid feature of an action and focus a listener's attention upon it. The function of the perfective sound-symbolic adverb in discourse is to mark off the closure of one narrative action from another and, at the same time, to express that closure with the most cognitively salient details. It is its similarity to the close-up shot that accounts for the inherent foregroundedness of sound-symbolic adverbs.

To understand how the inherent foregroundedness of sound-symbolic adverbs can be performatively foregrounded, it will be useful to consider performativity as a matter of degree rather than an absolute phenomenon. I will consider performative foregrounding to be representable along a continuum of syntactic and intonational features. The most minimally performative utterances featuring sound-symbolic adverbs are those exemplified by sentences 114, 115, and 116 in chapter 3. In all of these example sentences, the sound symbolic adverbs occur to the left of their verb or verb phrase. This is the unmarked order for adverbs and verbs. These examples are also minimally performative because they are relatively assimilated into the intonational contours of their respective utterances. For example, consider sentence 111 from the last chapter, which describes the way a canoe was brought to a standstill by stabbing a riverbank with a steering pole. The sentence is reproduced here as the next example. The sound-symbolic adverb *tsak*, which is onomatopoeic for the sound of piercing or stabbing something, occurs to the left of its verb phrase "as-a-stander coming." It is therefore unforegrounded syntactically because it occurs in the unmarked position. Furthermore, it is pronounced at the same level of pitch as its utterance, making it unforegrounded intonationally, as well.

21. Chi-ga ña tsak shayari-k shamu-sha, 'maykan-da a-ngichi kay-bi guardia-ga'
 that-TOP then stand-AG come-COR which-QN be-2PL here-LOC guard-TOP
 ni-ra-mi
 say-PAST-EV
 "So then, now *tsak* as-a-stander coming, he said, 'Which of you is the guard here?'"

Consider how this same sentence could be transformed in ways that increase its performativity. There could be a change in its syntactic position. For example, the speaker could move *tsak* so that it did not immediately precede its verb or verb phrase. I will refer to this movement as *syntactic displacement.*

22. Chi-ga ña shayari-k shamu-sha tsak (pause), 'maykan-da a-ngichi . . .'
 that-TOP then stand-AG come-COR which-QN be-2PL
 "So then, now, as-a-stander coming *tsak* (pause), he said, 'Which of you . . .'"

By uttering *tsak* after its verb phrase, the speaker calls attention to it and thereby increases its semantic importance. In addition, syntactic displacements are often accompanied by pause breaks that disrupt the sentence's rhythmic flow. Sentence 21 would be uttered with no discernible break between the sound-symbolic adverb and what follows it. However, sentence 22 features a pause break after the syntactically displaced sound-symbolic adverb. The syntactic displacement, together with the pause, adds greater foregrounding to the already inherently foregrounded *tsak.*

The most syntactically foregrounded version of sentence 21 would involve yet another focusing technique which I will refer to as *syntactic isolation*. It involves the use of a sound-symbolic adverb without a finite verb to stand for an action or event.

23. Chi-ga ña tawna-wan tsak (pause) 'maykan-da a-ngichi . . .'
    that-TOP then pole-INST which-QN be-2PL
    "So then, now, with the pole *tsak* (pause), 'Which of you . . .'"

This is an extremely common focusing technique. In this sentence *tsak* stands for an unstated verb phrase "as-a-stander-coming." The ability of sound-symbolic adverbs to substitute for verbs and verb phrases suggests that they are directly meaningful, gestalt-like structures of the kind referred to by Lakoff (1987) as kineasthetic image schemas. Sound-symbolic adverbs can undergo syntactic isolation because they are iconic schemas of a particular action or event. However, when their iconicity points to an action or event, it is also indexical. By pointing to an action or event, this indexicality ensures that there is no rupture in a listener's comprehension, due to the lack of a finite verb or verb phrase. That syntactic isolation does not present Quechua speakers with ambiguities or problems of comprehension is evident by the often observed tendancy of Quechua listeners to participate in someone else's narrative by supplying a verb or verb phrase that was only suggested but not stated, by a sound-symbolic adverb. I infer from this practice that an understanding of sound-symbolic adverbs is part of every Quechua speaker's linguistic competence.

Intonational Foregrounding

A number of other focusing techniques depend on intonational variations. A sound-symbolic adverb can be pronounced more loudly, more forcefully, and with a higher pitch. The following sentence 24 illustrates this, again, with a variant of sentence 21.

24. Chi-ga na tsak shayari-k shamu-sha . . .
    that-TOP then stand-AG come-COR
    "So then, now *tsak* as-a-stander coming . . ."

This sentence features an example of a *level pitch rise*. Level pitch rises are so called to distinguish them from upjumps and upglides, the discussion of which follows. Level pitch rises are used only with monosyllabic rather than disyllabic sound-symbolic adverbs. Level pitch rises foreground an action or event by interrupting the pitch of the surrounding utterance with a distinct moment of higher pitch. By doing this, a speaker calls a listener's attention to the foregroundedness of the image described by a sound-symbolic adverb.

Another example of a level pitch rise is the next sentence, featuring *ping*, a sound-symbolic adverb that describes a sudden or complete change from light to darkness. In this sentence *ping* undergoes a level pitch rise to describe the sudden darkness that results when a flashlight goes out.

25. Linterna ping wañu-ra.
flashlight die-PAST

"The flashlight *ping* died out."

By raising the pitch of *ping* above the utterance's baseline, the speaker fixes the listener's attention on the complete and sudden darkness that occurred when the flashlight died.

Monosyllabic sound-symbolic adverbs can also undergo a *gliding pitch rise*. I will adopt Bolinger's (1986: 29) term *upglide* to refer to this phenomenon. The upglide emphasizes the component parts of a monosyllable. If we divide a monosyllabic sound-symbolic adverb into a beginning onset, a middle peak, and an ending coda, then the upglide takes place over the middle peak and is highest over the coda. Upglides are consistently correlated with aspectually perfective uses of sound-symbolic adverbs. This correlation can be attributed to the iconicity of a gliding pitch rise. When a speaker's voice becomes quite high at the end of an upglide, there is a suggestion that a scale of possibility is reached and therefore completed at the termination of the rise.

The following sentence illustrates an upglide. It features the sound-symbolic adverb *ling*, which describes an insertion into a bounded space. In this sentence it describes an image that requires one to imagine a very thin woman as analogous to a stick being "inserted" into a dress. The upglide on *ling* enacts this "inserting," which is completed at its termination

26. Chi uras-ga tulʸu ma-k a-ra tulʸu, bata-ta, imashti kaspi l^i^ng (pause)
that time-TOP bone be-AG be-PAST bone dress-ACC what stick
churari-shka-gama rikuri-k ma-k a-ra.
put on-PERF-until appear-AG be-AG be-PAST

"At that time she was a bony thing, bony. She looked like, what would you say, a stick *l^i^ng* (pause) with a dress put on."

By gliding the pitch of *ling*'s pronunciation upward, the speaker performatively gestures the act of inserting. At the termination of the upglide, the insertion has been completed, and the listener's attention is fixed on an image of the woman-as-bony-figure, with a dress inserted over her body.

Not all examples of upglides enact gestures. The next example illustrates an upglide that is imitative of a process. The image is described with an upglide over the sound-symbolic adverb *tak*. In one of its senses *tak* describes an expanse of contact between surfaces. This particular example expands this sense to refer to a painful pressure resulting from a swelling of lymph nodes as a result of walking an extremely long distance.

27. Ishka-ndi changa-ma papa muyu t^a^k tiyari-wa-shka-ra, pungi-wa-shka-ra.
two-INCL leg-DAT father seed sit-1ACC-PERF-PAST swell-1ACC-PERF-PAST

"The big nodes in both of my legs had sat up in me, *t^a^k* they had swelled up in me."

The speaker's upglide over *tak* can be understood as a performative enactment of the process of swelling. At the same time, the upglide focuses on the state resulting from this swelling.

Thus far, the discussion has concerned the possibilities for intonational foregrounding on monosyllabic sound-symbolic adverbs. I will now describe the intonational foregrounding of disyllables and discuss the ways in which their foregrounding enhances expression. In Pastaza Quechua, the performative foregrounding of a disyllabic sound-symbolic adverb is characterized by an *upjump* rather than an upglide. I follow Bolinger (1986: 29) in characterizing this difference as that between the continuous, transitional, pitch rise of an upglide and the relatively sharper, skipped jump from a low pitch to a higher pitch. An upjump presents a listener with a sharper rise in pitch than an upglide. This evident distinction between the low-pitched initial syllable and the higher pitched final syllable lends itself to different expressive purposes.

When an upjump is used over certain sound-symbolic adverbs, the initial low-pitched syllable and the higher pitched final syllable function as intonationally performative gestures of the component parts of an action or event. In such utterances, the initial, lower pitched syllable is analogous to the inception or initial movement, while the final higher pitched syllable is analogous to the final realization of the action. The following sentence serves as an example. It features the sound-symbolic adverb *polang*, which describes the moment of emergence from underwater to the surface. In this sentence *polang* is used to describe the way a canoe which was passed underneath a fallen tree, reemerged on the water's surface. The high jump in pitch over the second syllable of *polang* imitates the canoe's jump from underwater to the surface.

28. Yaku uray-ma pasa-chi-ra-nchi, yaku uku-ta, kanoa-ga po^{lang}!
water downriver-DAT pass-CAUS-PAST-1PL water under-ACC canoe-TOP

"We passed it (in the direction of) downriver, under the water, and the canoe (went) *po*^{lang}!"

The pronunciational shape of *polang* is an iconic gesture of the event it describes. The first syllable, *po*-, describes the canoe's position underwater; the second syllable, *-lang,* describes its punctual reemergence to the water's surface. The iconicity of *polang*'s sound shape is related to the low/high contrast provided by the upjump. The contrast provides a neat conceptual division between the component movements of this event. Furthermore, the low/high pitch contrast is also iconic of the initially low position of the canoe, followed by its final, higher position on the water's surface.

The following sentence features another example of an upjump functioning as an intonationally performative gesture. The sound-symbolic adverb *polo*, which describes the act of passing through a barrier, is upjumped to describe the way a type of leaf can be funneled into a cup for catching rainwater and then secured by poking a stick through it.

29. Kay-ta kaspi-ta po^{lo} pasa-chi-naun.
here-ACC stick-ACC pass-CAUS-3PL

"They pass the stick right through here *po*^{lo}."

The first syllable, *po-*, can be understood as that part of the movement which precedes the penetration; the second syllable, *-lo,* describes the punctual moment when the stick passes through the funneled leaf. Again, the pitch contrast provided by the upjump provides a neat bifurcation for the components of this action.

However, not every use of an upjump can be interpreted as a performative gesture of an action or event. In many of its uses, the upjump simply provides a pitch contrast that iconifies a conceptual contrast, which enhances the description of a resultant state. In such uses, the initial and final syllable can be said to correspond to a before/after contrast. For example, the following sentence is taken from a myth. It describes the way a forest was decimated by a type of spirit that ate all the leaves from the trees, leaving only the trunks and bare branches. In this example, the upjump occurs over the sound-symbolic adverb *waling*, which describes a pattern of positive/negative space created by an eating or burning away of something. The resultant state in which the forest was left is performatively foregrounded by the upjump over *waling*.

30. Ranchu panga-ga wa^{ling}! (pause) Puñuna panga-s wa^{ling}!
    small house leaf-TOP sleep leaf-INCL
    "The hut leaves *wa*^{ling} (were gone); and the leaves for the sleeping (house) too, *wa*^{ling} (were gone)!"

The pitch contrast provided by the upjump over *waling* provides a before/after conceptual contrast. The initial low-pitched syllable, *wa-*, by its contrast with the final high pitched syllable, *-ling,* provides a frame for the expression of a difference, which in this example, is the difference described by the forest's absence of leaves.

Another example of an upjump functioning to foreground a before/after contrast comes from a description of clearing land for planting. This example features *tsuping*, a sound-symbolic adverb used to describe a complete, stark, bareness. In this example *tsuping* describes the way land is completely cleared before it is planted.

31. Kimi-shka washa, wakta-nga kal^{y}ari-ra-ni, ñuka, win tsu^{ping} (pause) hatun-da
    circumscribe-PERF after hit-FINF begin-PAST-1 I all big-ACC
    chagrari-ra-ni.
    make chagra-PAST-1
    "After outlining (an area), I began to chop, all of it, *tsu*^{ping} (pause), I made a big *chagra.*"

Again, the pitch contrast provided by the upjump over *tsuping* provides a before/after conceptual contrast. The initial low-pitched syllable, *tsu-*, by its contrast with the final high-pitched syllable, *-ping,* provides a frame for the expression of a difference, which in this example, is the difference described by an area of land's absence of growth.

There is one more intonational technique to discuss for its assistance in the performative expression of aspectual perfectivity. This technique involves the repetition of a series of sound symbolic adverbs that increase gradually in pitch. This will be called a *telic pitch progression*. The performativity of such progressions is characterizable by the same iconic logic as that of an upglide or upjump. The higher pitched termination of an upglide or upjump suggests that a range of possibilities has been reached or completed. In the same way, the end of a telic pitch progression is iconic of a logical endpoint. The difference between an upglide or upjump and a telic pitch progression can be characterized by what they choose to foreground. Upglides and upjumps minimize the internal complexity of an action, activity, or process and focus on its completion or resultant state. A telic pitch progression, by contrast, presents this complexity by enumerating the component subevents leading up to the completion or result of an action or state.

The following sentence uses the sound-symbolic adverb *saw* in a telic pitch progression. *Saw* describes the pouring movement of a fluid, or an idea of the sound made by such a pouring. This example is taken from the star woman myth. The repetitions of *saw* present the star woman's repeated acts of vomiting into a jar until it was full. Each repetition of *saw*, then, is an act of pouring forth her vomit into the jar. To understand why she does this, it is necessary to consider the idea of mythic reversal, where the normal course of things is turned upside down. In this case, the normal way of processing manioc is reversed. Rather than masticating cooked manioc and then allowing it to ferment in a clay jar, she eats it raw and ferments it inside of her stomach and then vomits it back out into a jar, much to the horror of her human mother-in-law.

32. Ña pay miku-shka-ta, il^{y}a-kta tinaha-y-ga saw$^{\text{saw}^{\text{saw}}}$ hunda-kta-shi pusku-xxl^{y}a-shi
then she eat-PERF-ACC lack-until jar-LOC-TOP full-until-EV foam-ADV-EV
kwina-k a-ra.
vomit-AG be-PAST

"Then she would vomit into the jar *saw*$^{\textit{saw}^{\textit{saw}}}$, until there was nothing left of what she had eaten, until the jar was foaming full."

In this sentence each repetition of *saw* is a subevent of a telic activity, that of filling the jar. The assertion that each repetition of *saw* is an increment of progression toward the action's achievement is evident by the narrator's use of the adverb *hundakta,* literally, "full-until," in the description. The narrator's repetitions of *saw* can also be understood with an analogy from cinema. When an editor wants to present the time spanned by a process or activity, he or she juxtaposes a series of shots, each representing a subevent of that process or activity. Such cinematic juxtapositions communicate the same message as a telic pitch progression. Both techniques present a process or activity taking place before they present its completion or result.

One more example featuring a telic pitch progression will be discussed. The preceding sentence used a telic pitch progression over repeated instances of an activity, in a way that is analogous to a film editor's use of juxtaposed shots. This is, in fact, the most common use for a telic pitch progression—to compress, and at the same time foreground the passage of time, by presenting the successive stages of an activity or process leading to its conclusion. There is another kind of image expressed by a telic pitch progression, however. Speakers may use such a progression to present the complete extent of a spatial expanse. The next sentence exemplifies this use. It features the sound symbolic adverb *tak*, which in this sense describes any feature or quality as extended in space. In the following example the repetition of *tak* describes how, when one reaches the Marañon River, it appears to be so wide—its opposite shore to be so far away—that there doesn't appear to be any more forest. The river itself seems to blend into the sky, making the sky look as if it extends as far as the eye can see.

33.	Sacha-ga	il^{y}a-k	il^{y}a-k	il^{y}a-k,	cielo	tak$^{tak^{tak}}$	cielo-l^{y}a-shi	rikuri-k	a-n	chay-bi.
	forest-TOP	lack-AG	lack-AG	lack-AG	sky		sky-just-EV	appear-AG	be-3	there-LOC

"The forest is gone, gone, gone; only the sky appears there *tak*$^{tak^{tak}}$."

In this example, each repetition of *tak* progressively widens the view of the expansive sky. With its last repetition at the highest pitch, the speaker has spanned the entire expanse of sky. This particular use of a telic pitch progression is analogous to a cinematic wide-angle shot which gradually increases its angle to allow for an increase in the viewer's range of vision. Both techniques span the extent of a space by increasingly widening their field of vision.

Summary

Performative aspect provides a definitive link between grammar and perceptual experience. It rides along the intrinsic durativity and perfectivity of the linguistic sign vehicle, using these properties for grammatical clarity and expressive resonance. Reduplication and multiple repetition in conjunction with intonational elaboration are expressive gestures of actions; their repeatedness; their distribution throughout a space; and their quickness, interruptedness, or consistency. The lengthening of a syllable or part of a syllable communicates duration, unbroken movement across space, and an existential state with affective overtones of sadness; it also focuses attention on an image for its own sake. Syntactic foregrounding and isolation, when combined with upjumps, upglides, and level pitch rises, call attention to images and also gesture the completion or result of an action or process. Such gestures may break an action or process into an inception and a final realization, or an initial "before" and a resultant "after." Finally, telic pitch progressions present the complete extent of a spatial expanse or the subevents that lead up to the completion or result of an action or state. The role of these various foregrounding techniques can be understood by analogy with other semiotic modalities such as gesture and cinematic techniques, including close-up shots, wide angle shots, accelerated motion shots, and juxtaposition and montage. Chapter 5 will examine the use of sound symbolism in an extended stretch of discourse, with the goal of demonstrating that its semiotic distinctiveness ramifies with deeper consequences for Quechua cultural values.

5

Sound-Symbolic Involvement

Examples of sound symbolism from preceding chapters have consisted of isolated utterances. This chapter illustrates sound-symbolic communication in a sustained stretch of discourse. I will adapt the sociolinguistic concept of "involvement" to an examination of the multiple functions of sound symbolism in a narrative of personal experience. I will argue that sound-symbolic utterances are used by the Pastaza Quechua to create a particular kind of interlocutionary involvement. Quechua speakers' sound-symbolic performances present perceptual images that enhance an understanding of and involvement in a communicative interaction. A speaker's performative foregrounding of a sound-symbolic form simulates the salient qualities of an action, event, or process and thereby invites a listener to project into an experience. A listener projects into a sound-symbolic performance in a way that is analogous to a viewer's projection into a cinematic image. A cinematic image "is not presented as an evoking of a past reality, but as a fiction the subject is in the process of living" (Kristeva 1989: 315).

Sound-symbolic descriptions give both speaker and listener alike an opportunity to share, even if only for a moment, their cognitive focus on the sensory qualities of an action, event, or process. Such interfocusing is distinctive from the kind of independent tracking that typically occurs between speakers during non-sound-symbolic discourse. During discourse that is not sound-symbolically performative, the interlocutors' attention may follow distinctive trains of thought and paths of ideas while simultaneously attending to a narrative. However, sound-symbolic performances, by their very nature, invite interlocutors to mingle their attention momentarily on the simulated reality of an action, event, or process. It is this interfocusing of attention that leads to various kinds of imaginative, intellectual, and cognitive engagement with the narrative. Further, this interfocusing of attention legitimizes a conversational ideal of amiability. Sound-symbolic discourse is not used by the Pastaza Quechua in conflict-ridden discourse, nor have I observed its use in political debates. Typically, its use reveals that interlocutors are relaxed, congenial, and at ease.[1] For the Pastaza Quechua, sound-symbolic discourse is comparable to "bird sound words" for the Kaluli in that the latter are "reflective and sentimental, ideally causing a listener to empathize with a speaker's message without responding to it verbally" (Feld 1982: 131). My argument here is based on analysis of a conversational narrative translated from Quechua. Before proceeding with the argument itself, I will discuss the significance of involvement for discourse studies and its theoretical implications for sound-symbolic discourse.

Involvement, Sound Symbolism, and Iconicity

Involvement can be understood, most generally as any of the efforts made by interlocutors, whether spoken, gestural, or cognitive, to participate in a conversation. As used by sociolinguists (Chafe 1982; Tannen 1982a, 1982b, 1989), however, the term refers to a style of speaking and an attitudinal alignment or footing (Goffman 1979) that manifests oral rather than literate values. Tannen (1982b) suggests that oral and literate values can be characterized, respectively, as either involved in the communicative interaction or detached from the interaction and focused on message content. Involvement as an attitudinal alignment implies all of the ways that one communicates an empathetic, cooperative, and personal message. A detached attitudinal alignment, by contrast, is characteristically more focused on message content and concerned with maximally coherent, and explicit communication. The assumption underlying this scheme is that certain properties intrinsic to oral and written media came to be associated with a dichotomous set of values. Oral communication has been associated with *involvement* values such as affectivity, expressivity, and fragmentation. Literate communication has been associated with *detachment* values such as explicitness, rationality, and complexity. In other words, literate communication is most autonomous, to use Kay's (1977) term, because its understanding is least dependent upon interpersonal negotiations of meaning. These values, in turn, have taken on a life of their own insofar as they are no longer restricted to spoken and written media (Chafe 1982; Tannen 1982a).

The use of the terms *oral* and *literate* is not intended to invoke an oversimplified or essentializing dichotomy. Many are familiar with McLuhan's suggestion that literacy has produced a visual bias in our own culture which is in conflict with the auditory proclivities of tribal cultures. Well known also are the critiques of his and others' more specific claims that literacy has produced a "great cognitive divide" that underlies the development of civilization and typifies its various stages. This work follows the suggestion of Howes and others who believe that literacy encourages "littler divides" of perceptual and speaking styles and knowledge modalities, and that these "littler divides" ramify with potentially great implications (1991: 173) . Sound symbolism has been associated with peoples and cultures that are oral. This association may be well grounded. It is possible that literacy and its technologies diminish the functional importance of sound-symbolic discourse. However, an empirically grounded, comparative investigation of peoples' sound-symbolic discourse at varying stages in their journey toward literacy has never been conducted. Furthermore, literacy is not a strictly isolable feature or skill. It links up with social, political, and economic parameters, all of which have their own potentially momentous effects on a peoples' language use.

For the purposes of this analysis, the terms oral and literate are prototypical designations with concomitant implications for linguistic style. A prototypically literate individual would be someone who not only reads and writes but also makes frequent use of those skills in a variety of social, political, and economic contexts. The stylistic implications of literate, or "detached," and oral, or "involved," modes of communication are also complex. Detached and involved styles are not restricted to respectively literate and oral individuals. They can be adopted and adapted by speakers in a constant, shifting interplay of stylistic and strategic choice. The significance of involvement and detachment as styles or communicative strategies is that they can be related to perceptions of ethnic and socioeconomic differences. The negative evaluation of involved styles of communication is often linked to negative stereotyping of entire subcultures and ethnic groups. Such negative perceptions can be traced in part to a particular view of literacy in which detachment, maximal explicitness, and the "essential" content of a message are highly valued (cf. Heath 1983; Labov 1972; and Tannen 1980, 1984).[2]

The contribution of sociolinguists has been to clarify the aesthetic and emotional logic by which involved styles of communication frame a social interaction and thereby articulate messages that are simultaneously affective, explicit, rational, and expressive. I build on this work by analyzing the ways in which complex messages are framed by sound-symbolic discourse. What appears to be an overwhelmingly affective, expressive, and involved conversational style is also communicative of precise and explicit information. A speaker's performative foregrounding of a sound-symbolic form through morphological, syntactic, or intonational features makes explicit the salient features of an action's spatiotemporal unfolding, and through this such performances simultaneously point one's attention to a deeper awareness and understanding of the action itself and of its significance for the narrative. Sound-symbolic forms, then, are not simply iconic and imitative. They are complex signs with multiple functions. In order to understand the specific ways that sound-symbolic discourse creates involvement, it is necessary to identify the qualities of sound symbolism that lend themselves to involvement. Because of its imitativeness, sound-symbolic expression communicates in an iconic mode. Iconicity is a particular type of imagery, and imagery is central to theories of involvement. Iconic imagery is particularly suited to create involvement, I suggest, because it establishes a direct connection between a sign and an object. This direct connection is constituted by a perception of resemblance between the sign vehicle and an object.

Quechua speakers' sound-symbolic iconicity will be analyzed with semiotic concepts articulated by Peirce, who distinguished between three kinds of iconicity. An image icon stands for an object by what Pierce called its "simple qualities" or "First Firstnesses" (1955: 105); a photograph of a person is an image icon or First Firstness of that person. The second type, a diagrammatic icon, communicates by resembling in some way, the configuration of an object's component parts: a map of the United States is a diagrammatic icon of the territory known as the United States. The third type of icon, the metaphor, signifies by establishing a parallel relationship between different objects. Of these three iconic types, metaphor has been given the most detailed attention (Friedrich 1991: 48; Jakobson 1960: 375), and it continues to engage scholars, not only for its use in myth, poetry, and discourse (Fernandez 1991), but also for its role in deeper cognitive processes (Lakoff and Johnson 1980; Lakoff 1987). The narrative to be analyzed features only a couple of metaphors; however, it makes prodigious use of imageic and diagrammatic icons. Sound-symbolic words are image icons because they imitate the sensuous qualities or First Firstnesses of an action's spatiotemporal unfolding. When they are performatively foregrounded, many sound-symbolic words are also diagrams of an action's component movements or gestures.

Conversational Narrative: What an Anaconda Caught

The following conversational narrative emerged during a series of interviews with a woman from Puka yaku. The goal of these interviews was to understand the meaning of sound-symbolic adverbs and to discover their cooccurrence possibilities with Quechua verbs. However, the format of the interviews seemed at times tediously difficult for my friend. She frequently became distracted by a memory of an event that she thought important and instructive enough to relate. And so, except for the interruptions, my interview changed into her narrative account. Although I welcomed these digressions, I also felt the need to participate in them by asking questions whenever they occurred to me. Looking back on these questions, I realize that many of them were fairly trivial and were motivated more by a need to be involved than by a burning curiosity. Nevertheless, her answers to my better questions often revealed crucial insights on sound-symbolic adverbs. Moreover, I consider these interviews to be a first step toward a more dialogue-based (cf. Tedlock 1979) anthropological linguistics. I determined the overall framework of the interviews, but my friend frequently transformed the situation by breaking out of this format and into a narrative performance of a myth or memory (cf. Hymes 1975). Although these narratives were not generally directly pertinent to my questions, they were always interesting in themselves and they usually provided me with more valuable data on sound-symbolic adverb usage.

The following narrative describes the pursuit and capture of a tapir by an anaconda. It would be difficult to overemphasize the significance of the *amarun,* a term designating both anacondas and boas, for the Pastaza Quechua. References to these animals are pervasive in mythology and cosmological beliefs. The patterns on their skin are studied and copied for the decoration of drinking bowls. Shamans work their sorcery with the help of the *amarun*. Some families even feel a particular affinity for the *amarun,* considering themselves kindred. The narrator, for example, once told me that she considered herself of the same flesh as the *amarun*. Besides their significance for the lowland-dwelling Pastaza Quechua, there is evidence for the symbolic importance of the *amarun* in highland Quechua cosmology as well. Salomon and Urioste's recent translation of the early seventeenth-century *Huarochirí* manuscript includes a reference to a two-headed *amaru* that turns into a vein of white marble. They consider this *amaru* to be "symbolic of disorder erupting in the transition to a new order" (1991: 93). The early seventeenth-century manuscript by Santacruz Pachacuti Yamqui, *Relación de las antigüedades deste reyno del Piru* includes a description of the *amaru* as a "very fierce beast . . . with ears and fangs and beards" (Harrison 1989: 70–71). Synthesizing the exegetical work of Earls and Silverblatt (1976) and Sharon (1978), Harrison relates the *amaru* to a cluster of symbols, including lightening, rainbows, the stellar cycles, and the upward-to-downward flowing of water. The image of the *amaru* as an upward-to-downward flowing movement may also indicate its importance as a symbolic link between highland and lowland Quechua culture.

In everyday life these animals are greatly feared for their ability to kill humans. I heard stories about anacondas swallowing humans whole, and also about boas strangling them. Besides their often stated fear of the *amarun,* Quechua speakers also express feelings of awe and respect for its ability to hunt down and subdue its prey. These sentiments are evident in the following narrative. It relates a process of discovery which is said to be facilitated by impressions described with sound-symbolic words. The narrator describes the pursuit and capture of a tapir by an *amarun* or anaconda; however, the presence of the anaconda is not immediately known to the narrator and her companions. At first they assume that the tapir is running from a jaguar. Jaguars frequently pursue tapirs, and tapirs often try to escape by running into a river or pond where a jaguar will not go. The bystanders therefore assume, at first, that there is a jaguar somewhere nearby. Their attention quickly becomes focused on the sounds and movements of the water, however, which signal to them the anaconda's presence. Although the anaconda is eventually seen on the water's surface, much of what takes place in this narrative is not actually witnessed. It has to be inferred by observing the visible movements of the water and listening to its sounds.[3]

Returning from a Hunt

1. Riku-ngui, ñukanchi-ga mashti-manda shamu-ra-nchi, kay . . . chapa-ngi kay
look-2 we-TOP where-from come-PAST-1PL this wait-2 this
Tigri-manda!
Tigri-from

"Look, we were coming from, where was it, wait . . . from this river called Tigre."

2. Lulun-da al^{y}a-sha al^{y}a-sha al^{y}a-sha shamu-ra-nchi kanoa-wan.
egg-ACC dig-COR dig-COR dig-COR come-PAST-1PL canoe-INST

"Eggs digging, digging, digging, we came by canoe."

Q: [Maykan? Charapa lulun?
which turtle egg

"What kind? Turtle eggs?"

3. Charapa lulun-da wacha-y uras ma-ra; chi raygu-mi chi kucha-y puñu-ra-nchi.
turtle egg-ACC hatch-NOM time be-PAST that reason-EV that pond-LOC sleep-PAST-1PL

(nods assent) "It was turtle egg hatching time; that's why we were sleeping beside that pond."

Settling Down for the Night

4. Pl^{h}aaaaaaya ma-ra! Chi-bi, hatun charapa wacha-k a-ra.
beach be-PAST that-LOC big turtle hatch-AG be-PAST

"It was a beaaaaaach! That's where big turtles would be hatchers."

5. Chi-mi chi puñu-sha wañuchi-naw-ra payna, paba-ta; sukta-ta wañuchi-mu-nawn.
there-EV that sleep-COR kill-3PL-PAST XPRO turkey-ACC six-ACC kill-CIS-3PL
"Because we were sleeping there, they killed turkeys; six of them they killed and brought back."

6. Chi yanu-nga ñuka yanda-ta ra-w-ra-ni.
that cook-FINF I wood-ACC do-DUR-PAST-1
"I was gathering wood to cook them."

7. Payna wasi-u-ra-wna,
XPRO house-DUR-PAST-PL
"They were putting up a hut (for us to sleep),"

8. panga-ta pal^{y}a-ni, yanda-ta apamu-sha ñuka ña
leaf-ACC harvest-1 wood-ACC bring-COR I now
"and I'm picking the leaves and bringing the wood."

9. Listo apamu-ni, piti-sha ña kanoa ukw-i ñuka yanga tiya-sha shamu-ni, ñuka-ga.
ready bring-1 cut-COR now canoe in-LOC I useless be-COR come-1 I-TOP
"Readily cutting them, I bring them; sitting uselessly inside the canoe I've come.

10. Mana siki-ta-s ra-sha.
NEG rear-ACC-INCL do-COR
"Not even working the rear."

11. Chi-ga ñuka sumak pila-ni sumak piti-sha, manga-y chura-sha, ña arros-ta-s
so-TOP I nice pluck-1 nice cut-COR pot-LOC put-COR then rice-ACC-INCL
chura-sha palanda-ta-s l^{y}uchu-sha, sumak ra-sha.
put-COR plaintain-ACC-INCL peel-COR nice make-COR
"So I pluck (the turkeys) clean, cutting them up nicely and putting them in a pot, along with rice, and peeling plaintains, too, fixing them nicely.

12. Shayachi-na-l^{y}a.
stand-INF-LIM
"I had only to set them on the fire."

13. Ñuka yanda-ta apamu-ni, nina-ta hapichi-ni,
I wood-ACC bring-1 fire-ACC light-1
"I bring the wood, light the fire,"

14. shayachi pasa-ni ishka-ndi irmanga-ta ^{tak}
stand pass-1 two-both pot-ACC
"and finish setting them on the fire, both of the pots $^{\textit{tak}}$."

15. Mashtisha raw-shka-y yanda rama-ta apa-ngaw ri-ni
whatcha-ma-callit do-PERF-NOM wood branch-ACC take-FINF go-1
"Um, let's see, having done that, I go to get branches of wood."

A Tapir in Distress

16. 'Wagra-mi! Wagra-mi!' Chuuuuuu chu chu waka-sha uyari-mu-n
    cow-EV cow-EV cry-COR sound-CIS-3

    "'A tapir ! It's a tapir !' Crying *chuuuuuu chu chu* it sounds"

17. hanag-manda.
    upriver-from

    "from upriver."

18. 'Wagra-mi! Chay-ga! Chay-ga! Il^{y}apa-y-chi! Il^{y}apa-y-chi!' uyari-u-nguna.
    cow-EV there-TOP there-TOP shoot-2IMP-PL shoot-2IMP-PL sound-DUR-3PL

    "'It's a tapir! There! There! Shoot it! Shoot it!', they are heard saying."

19. Chiga "mana! Puma chari apamu-n; puma-mi urma-chi-n wagra-ta;" 'puma-ta
    so NEG jaguar perhaps bring-3 jaguar-EV fall-CAUS-3 tapir-ACC jaguar-ACC
    wañuchi-shun-chi!'
    kill-1-IMP-PL

    "So then,' no! Jaguar maybe brings it; a jaguar's made the tapir fall in the water. 'Let's kill the jaguar!'"

To Kill the Jaguar or the Tapir; and What to Do with All the Meat?

20. Puma kara vali-k ma-ra; chi uras-ga vali-ra puma kara.
    jaguar skin value-AG be-PAST that time-TOP value-PAST jaguar skin

    "Jaguar hide used to be valuable; at that time jaguar's hide was valuable."

    Q: Kunan-ga?
    now-top

    "What about now?"

21. Kunan, hm hm? . . . pi-ta yachan?
    now hm hm who-QN know-3

    "Now, hm hm . . . who knows?"

22. Chi-ga chi-ta ni-sha pay-guna wagra-ta mana il^{y}apa-naw-ra.
    So-TOP that-ACC say-COR he-PL cow-ACC NEG shoot-3-PAST

    "Because they were wanting that, they didn't shoot the tapir."

23. Ñuka mana-shi wanuchi-nawn-ma-chu ni-u-ra-ni.
    I NEG-EV kill-3PL-CNDL-NEG say-DUR-PAST-1

    "I was thinking 'they shouldn't kill it.'"

24. 'Ima-manda chakichi-sha' ni-sha, piñari-u-ni, kil^{y}a-w-ni-mi, ñuka.
    what-from dry-1FUT say-COR be angry-DUR-1 be lazy-DUR-1-EV I

    "Wondering how I will dry all of it, I'm getting angry, feeling lazy."

25. Ña chishi ma-ra indi-s. (laughter)
then afternoon be-past sun-INCL

"It was already an afternoon sun." (laughter)

26. Ña basta aycha-ta apa-sha ri-u-nchi riku-ngi-ma.
now enough meat-ACC take-COR go-DUR-1PL look-2-CNDL

"We're already carrying enough meat, you would see."

27. Kushil^y^u aycha chari, pawa pawshi!
spider monkey meat perhaps curassow

"Spider monkey meat and curassow! Every kind of meat."

28. Tuk^w^i aycha-mi ri-u-n riku-ngi-ma chakichi-shka-ga.
every meat-EV go-DUR-3 look-2-CNDL dry-PERF-TOP

"Every meat goes, you would just see the dried meat."

29. Asta charapa aycha-mi chakichi-shka ri-u-n.
even turtle meat-EV dry-PERF go-DUR-3

"Even dried turtle meat goes with us."

30. Maytu! Riku-ngi-ma maytu-ta!
roast look-2-CNDL roast-ACC

"And the leaf-wrapped roasted meat! You would see such roasted meat!"

Not a Jaguar, an Anaconda

31. Chi ñuka-wan ri-k Lusawra ni-n 'mikya, riku-k shamu-y'; mashti
that I-INST go-AG Lusaura say-3 aunt look-AG come-2IMP whatch-a-macallit
'wagra-mi wayta-w-n' ni-wa-n.
cow-EV swim-DUR-3 say-1ACC-3

"Then Lusawra, the one traveling with me, says, 'Come and look, aunt; there's a tapir swimming,' she tells me."

32. 'May?' ni-ni; ñuka ña yanda-ta apamu-u-ra-ni.
where say-1 I then wood-ACC bring-DUR-PAST-1

"'Where?' I ask; I was bringing wood then."

33. Riku-kbi wagra rigriii-ng, chuuuuuuu chu chu waka-sha ri-u-n.
look-SWRF cow ear-INST cry-COR go-DUR-3

"I look and see the tapir's earrrs moving across the water, crying *chuuuuuuu chu chu,* it is going."

34. Ña kucha-y
then pond-LOC

"Then in that pond"

35. Loriana Pitishka ni-nawn chi kucha-ta—
Loriana Pitishka say-3PL that pond-ACC—

"Loriana Pitishka they call that pond—"

Q: [Loriana?
Loriana?

36. um um Loriana Pitishka kucha ni-nawn chi-ta—
um um Loriana Pitishka pond say-3PL that-ACC
"um hm, Loriana Pitishka pond they call that —"

Q: [Pi-ta Loriana?
who-QN Loriana
"But who was Loriana?"

37. Pay-guna shutichi-shka ma-n, chi kucha ña chasna shuti-yuk.
he-PL give name-PERF be-3 that pond now like that name-POSS
"That's how they've named that pond, now that's its name."

38. Chiga ña chay
so then that
"So then"

39. kucha-y
pond-LOC
"in that pond"

40. kʰawwwwwww
"*kʰawwwwwww*!"

41. Chay-ga! Amarun-mi hapi-n! ni-naw-ra-mi.
that-TOP anaconda-EV catch-3 say-3PL-PAST-EV
"'There! An anaconda's got it,' they said."

42. Ña runa-s mandzha-w-shka, chimba-pura-y nuspa, ima-cha a-ra-nchi?
now people-INCL be afraid-DUR-PERF across-purely-LOC crazy what-EV be-PAST-1PL
Puñu-u-ra-nchi kay-ma rik-i!
sleep-DUR-PAST-3PL this-DAT look-2IMP
"Now we people are also frightened, being right across from it; were we crazy or what? Look, we're going to sleep here!"

43. Hatun charapa-ta-shi hapi-na-ta muna-nawn, payna tuta.
big turtle-ACC-EV catch-INF-ACC want-3PL XPRO night
"They want to catch a big turtle that night."

44. Chiga ña chi-lʸa-y puñu-chi-wa-w-n-guna ñuka mandzha-w-ni kucha-ta
so then there-LIM-LOC sleep-CAUS-1ACC-DUR-3-PL I be afraid-DUR-1 pond-ACC
riku-sha.
look-COR
"And so, right there they are making me sleep; I'm frightened just looking at that pond."

Q: Pay-guna polaya-y puñuna-ta muna-naw-ra-chu?
he-PL beach-LOC sleep-ACC want-3PL-PAST-NEG
"They wanted to sleep on the beach?"

45. Ña polaya-y puñu-nga ra-w-nchi, ña polaya-y puñu-nchi!
now beach-LOC sleep-FINF do-DUR-1PL now beach-LOC sleep-1PL
"Now on the beach we're going to sleep, on the beach we'll sleep!"

46. Ñuka mandzha-w-ni puma-ta, tukwi-ta—
I fear-DUR-1 jaguar-ACC everything-ACC
"I'm afraid of jaguars and everything—"

Q: [um hm

47. Ah ow, yapa mandzha-k ma-ni, ñuka pumata.
ah hah a lot fear-AG be-1 I jaguar-ACC
"Ah hah, I'm very afraid of jaguars."

48. Chiga pay-ga ni-u— chi-mi shina kwinta-w-n-guna runa-guna-ga.
So he-TOP say-DUR this-EV like talk-DUR-3-PL people-PL-TOP
"So then, he is say—like this they are talking, the others."

An Anaconda's Eye View

49. Pay-ga imayna-ta ñukanchi kay riku-nchi, ni-n, kasna
he-TOP COMP-ADV we here look-1PL say-3 like this
"In the same way that we watch from here like this."

50. pay chasna-shi kanoa-ta-s riku-k a-n.
he like that-EV canoe-ACC-INCL look-AG be-3
"like that he also is a watcher of canoes."

51. Polaaaang ri-uuuuu ima wayta-w-n tuk^{w}i-ta-shi riku-n.
go-DUR what swim-DUR-3 everything-ACC-EV look-3
That are *polaaaang* going byyyyy, whatever is swimming."

52. Tuk^{w}i-ta-shi riku-n chasna a-sha-shi chasna kasa-k a-n
everything-ACC-EV look-3 like that be-DUR-EV like that hunt-AG be-3
"He sees everything; that's how he's able to hunt."

53. Dinu mana riku-sha-s tiya-w-sha ima shina-ta kasa-nga-ya?
otherwise NEG see-COR-INCL dwell-DUR-COR what how-INT hunt-3FUT-TOP
"Otherwise, being there, not watching, how will he hunt?"

54. Pi-ta pay-ta rima-gri-nga?
who-INT he-ACC speak-TRNSL-3FUT
"Who will go and tell him that there's something to catch?"

Back to the Surface

55. Chi-ga, 'kishpichi-n-mi' ni-naw-ra riku-kbi, wagra chay intiru-wan p^huyyyyyy
    this-top let free-3-EV say-3PL-PAST look-SWRF tapir that entire-INST
    -l^ya l^yukshi-gri-ra!
    -LIM emerge-TNSL-PAST

    "So then, 'he's let go,' they said, and I looked and saw the tapir go and emerge with all of a *p^huyyyyyyl^ya*!"

56. Chi-bi: chuuuuuu kishpichi-shka wagra-ga, riku-ngi-ma pay wayta-ta!
    this-LOC let free-PERF tapir-TOP look-2-CNDL he swim-ACC

    "And there it cried *chuuuuuu;* you should see a runaway tapir swim!"

57. Ña riku-sha, 'kasil^ya a-ngi-chi! pi-ta chakichi-nga kay tukwi?'
    now look-COR quiet be-2-PL who-QN dry-3FUT this all

    "As we were watching, I said, 'Be still! who's going to dry all of this?'"

58. Ña tutaya-w-n—
    now become night-DUR-3

    "It was already nightening—"

    Q: [Pay-guna wagra-ta il^yapana-ta muna-naw-ra-chu?
    he-PL cow-ACC rifle-ACC want-3PL-PAST-NEG

    "They wanted to shoot the cow?"

59. Ña il^yapana-ta, wañuchina-ta muna-w-n-guna pay-guna!
    now rifle-ACC kill-ACC want-DUR-3-PL he-PL

    "They want to shoot and kill it."

    Q: Dinu amo-ga-ya?
    but owner-TOP-TOP

    "But what about the owner?"

60. Imay chi amo, chi amarun?
    which this owner this anaconda

    "Whose owner? The anaconda's?"[4]

    Q: Mana, chi wagra amo! Ah ah amarun-da wanuchina-ta muna-nawn?
    no that tapir owner ah hah anaconda-ACC kill-ACC want-3PL

    "No, the cow's owner! Ah hah (so) it's the anaconda they want to kill?"

61. Mana! Wagra kikin-da mikun-ga wañuchinata muna-w-ra-wna, sacha wagra-ta!
    no tapir actual-ACC eat-FINF kill-ACC want-DUR-PAST-PL forest cow-ACC

    "No! It's the actual cow that they want to kill and eat, the forest cow!"

    Q: Ahhh! Sacha wagra, mana wiba-shka wagra!
    ahhhh forest cow no raise-PERF cow

    "Ohh! A forest cow (i.e., tapir), not a domesticated cow!"

62. Mana! Sacha wagra!
no forest cow
"Yes! A forest cow!"

63. Chiga, chasna-y, ña, chi, chi-mi shina riku-nchi.
so like that-LOC then that that-EV like see-1PL
"So, like that, then, this is like what we see.

64. Ña chi k^hawww ra-k-ga,
then that do-AG-TOP
"Then, making (the sound) *k^hawww*,"

65. muliiiii-ng ima shina-cha churu siki-ta shina ra-ra.
whirl-INST what like-EV snail ass-ACC like do-PAST
"the water goes whirliiiiing; how like a snail's ass he made the water (look)."

Q: [Ima-ta k^haw?
what-QN
"What is '*k^haw*'?"

66. K^hawwwwwwww yaku uyari-k a-n k^hawwwwwwww kucha-y chi mulinu-y
water sound-AG be-3 pond-LOC this whirlpool-LOC
uyari-k a-n
sound-AG be-3
"*K^hawwwwwwww*. The water sounds *k^hawwwwwwww* in the pond, inside of that whirlpool it sounds"

67. Chiga, chasna uyari-k
so like that sound-AG
"So then, as it sounded like that,"

68. riku-u-ra-nchi, riku-shaaaa-mi shaya-w-ra-nchi wagra ri-u-k
look-DUR-PAST-1PL look-COR-EV stand-DUR-PAST-1PL tapir go-DUR-SWRF
imayna-shi ra-nga ra-w-n?
COMP-EV do-FINF do-DUR-3
"we were watching, standing there watching; the tapir was getting away; what was he going to do?"

The Anaconda Emerges

69. Pollll^{h}ang!
"*Pollll^{h}ang*!"

70. Wamburi-n, ri-ki!
float-3 look-2IMP
"Well, he rises to the water's surface; look!"

Q: Ima-ta?
what-QN
"What (rises)?"

71. Amarun ni-ni, kay yana amarun ruku-ga, ña yana yana shinki ma-ra!

anaconda say-1 this black anaconda big-TOP now black black shiny be-PAST

Riku-ngi-ma uma-ta!

look 2IMP-CNDL head-ACC

(impatient) "I'm talking about the anaconda, this great big black anaconda! He was so black, pitch black; you would see how big his head was!" (makes a large encompassing gesture with both arms)

Q: Chi tupu pay uma-chu a-ra?

that size he head-NEG be-PAST

(incredulous) "His head was that big?"

72. Yari wagra intiru pay nil^{y}puna-ta yari! Ima shina-ta ichil^{y}a shimi-manda wagra-ta

think tapir entire he swallow-ACC think what how-QN little mouth-from tapir-ACC

nil^{y}pu-nga? Kay sacha wagra ña laro ma-n, riksi-ngi chari kan.

swallow-1FUT this forest cow now big be-3 know-2 perhaps you

"Think about it! He's going to swallow an entire tapir; think about it! How, with a little mouth, is he going to swallow a tapir? These tapirs are large; maybe you're familiar with them."

73. Chiga, chasna

so like that

"So, like that,"

74. polang riku-n ña

look-3 then

"he rises *polang* and looks and"

75. ña wagra-ga ichu-u-ra-mi riku-ngi-ma wayta-sha.

then tapir-TOP swim-COR look-2-CNDL swim-COR

"then you would see the tapir swimming and leaving him behind."

76. Tupu$^{u^u}$ (long pause).

"*Tupu*$^{u^u}$ (long pause), he drops back into the water."

77. May-cha wagra ri-u-ra, ña chay-bi l^{y}ukshi-gri-ra, rik-i!

where-EV tapir go-DUR-PAST now there-LOC emerge-TNSL-PAST look-2

"Wherever the tapir was going, now there he went to emerge, look!"

78. Wagra-ga

tapir-ACC

"As for the tapir,"

79. ña ma-ra pay hapiri-na-ga.

now be-PAST he catch-INF-TOP

"now was its time to be caught."

80. 'Sindzhi ri-ngi-mi!' ñukanchi kapari-u-nchi pobre wagra-ta.

strong go-2-EV we shout-DUR-1PL poor tapir-ACC

"'Go faster!' We're shouting to the poor tapir."

81. L^yaki-u-nchi-mi.
empathize-DUR-1PL-EV

"We're feeling sorry for it. (laughs)

The Tapir Is Caught

82. Chiga ña chi riku-k polang wamburi-n riku-k-a, yanga kingu kingu kingu kingu
so then that look-AG float-3 look-SWRF-TOP just bend bend bend bend
olas-ta riku-ngi-ma motor olas shina-mi tuku-ra.
waves-ACC look-2-CNDL motor waves like-EV become-PAST

"So then he looks, he rises *polang* and looks, and the water just undu-undu-undu-undulates; you would see such waves, like motor waves it became."

83. Riku-l^yayta wagra-ta kanira.
look-ADV tapir-ACC bite-PAST

"Zeroing right in on him, he bit the tapir."

84. Kani-k-shi a-gk a-shka chi washa-shi pil^{y}u-k a-shka, ni-nawn runa-gunaga.
bite-AG-EV be-AG be-PERF that after-EV wrap-AG be-PERF say-3PL person-PL-TOP

"He bites and after that, they say, he strangles."

85. T^{o^n} wagra-ga (long pause)
tapir-TOP

"Now the tapir is completely swallowed t^{o^n} (long pause)."

86. Mana kuti rikuri-nga pobre wagra-ga.
NEG again appear-3FUT poor tapir-TOP

"The poor tapir is not going to appear again."

Q: Ton nil^{y}pu-ra?
swallow-PAST

"He swallowed the tapir *ton* (i.e., completely)?"

87. Nda, ña chi-l^ya-ng ma-ra turu; ña ichil^{y}a yaku ma-n, Puka yaku shina.
yes now that-LIM-INST be-PAST mud now little water be-3 water like

"Yes, and with that there was just mud; it's only a little pond, like Red water."

88. Chiga ña kasna-mi tuku-ra, turu-ta riku-ngi-ma, yanga
so now like this-EV become-PAST mud-ACC look-2-CNDL just

pus pus pus pus pus pus pus pus pus pus pus pus tsap^{h}aak tsap^{h}aak.

"And this is how it became; you would see the mud just (bubbling)
pus pus pus pus pus pus pus pus pus pus pus pus. And the water slapped the shore *tsap^{h}aak tsap^{h}aak*."

89. Ñuka mandzhari-ni, "hak^{w}-i-chi! Hanag-ma punu-gri-shun-chi hak^{w}-i-chi! Ima-ta
I be afraid-1 go-2IMP-PL upriver-DAT sleep-TRNSL-1IMP-PL go-2IMP-PL what-ACC
ni-sha kay kucha-guna-y puñu-chi-wa-ngi-chi?', ñuka piña-ra-ni.
want-COR this pond-PL-LOC' sleep-CAUS-1ACC-2-PL I be angry-PAST-1

"I felt so afraid. 'Let's go! Let's go upriver and sleep! Let's go! I angered: what can you be thinking to make me sleep beside ponds?'"

90. 'Ña kunan mana miku-y tuku-shun-chi-chu; wagra-ta miku-n,' ni-u-n-guna.
then now no eat-NOM become-1IMP-PL-NEG tapir-ACC eat-3 say-DUR-PL

"'Now we won't be eaten; he's had the tapir,' they are saying." (both of us laugh)

Q: Chi amarun al^{y}pa-y puri-k-chu a-n?
this anaconda ground-LOC travel-AG-INT be-3

"This anaconda, does it travel by land?"

91. Mana-ya, yaku-y; ñuka mandzha-w-ni de repente sika-mu-sha miku-nga ni-sha,
no-TOP water-LOC I fear-DUR-1 suddenly climb-CIS-COR eat-3FUT want-COR
chi raygu mandzha-w-ni, ñuka!
that reason fear-DUR-1 I

"No, in the water; but I'm afraid that, wanting to eat, it might suddenly climb out; that's why I'm afraid."

Q: [Um um! polaya-y.
um um beach-LOC

"Um hm, on the beach!"

92. Chiga ña pobre wagra-ga, ñaaa chari nil^{y}pu-y pasa-ra; ña miku-y pasa-n.
so then poor tapir-TOP then perhaps swallow-NOM pass-PAST then eat-NOM pass-3

"The poor tapir! By then maybe its swallowing had passed; by then its eating had passed."

93. Chi-bi ñuka kay-wan riku-shka-ni pay amarun hapi-shka-ta.
that-LOC I this-INST see-PERF-1 he anaconda catch-PERF-ACC

"And that's how I've seen with these (eyes), what he—an anaconda—caught."

Sound Images of Sounds

The narrator uses sound to present images of sounds, movements, states, and lexical referents. The first sound image to be used in this narrative is *tak* in line 14. *Tak* imitates a punctual sound created by placing a pot full of water on the logs that make up the cooking fire. Her use of *tak* is redundant insofar as it restates what she already said in line 14, about having finished setting the pots in place.[5] By using *tak*, however, she presents the listener with a sound-simulated experience of the same action. She foregrounds this action intonationally, by pronouncing *tak* with a level pitch rise and also by pausing afterward. The pause, together with the punctual quality of the sound image *tak,* establish a definitive conclusion to the series of tasks she elaborated in lines 11, 12, and 13. Upon hearing the imitated sound of this definitive conclusion, the listener anticipates the next set of events.

That expectation is met by the narrator's repetitions of *chu*. These repetitions of the tapir's crying, which occur in lines 16, 33, and 56 are an index of its presence. They are morphologically foregrounded by the fact of their repetition and also by the narrator's lengthening of the first *chu*. This initial lengthened *chu* imitates a "real time" sound image of the animal's crying, which makes the narrative all the more vivid for the listener. Its two shorter pronunciations indicate that this crying was iterated over a space of time. Although it is impossible to convey orthographically, the narrator's simulations of the tapir's crying sounds have an unmistakably mournful quality. This mournful quality involves the listener in a sense of the animal's pathetic helplessness, thereby sending the listener a larger message about its ultimate fate.

Just as the tapir is indicated by its cries, the anaconda is also represented by a distinctive sound, k^h*aw*, in lines 40 and 64. K^h*aw* simulates the thrashing sound created by the anaconda underwater. It functions as an index for the anaconda's presence underwater. It is this sound that allows the bystanders to say with certainty "An anaconda's got it" in line 41, even before they have seen it. The first time she uses k^h*aw* in line 40 she foregrounds it by lengthening its pronunciation. K^h*aw* is also foregrounded in line 40 by the fact that it is syntactically isolated. It alone stands for an unstated proposition of the form "It thrashed k^h*aw*" or "It sounded k^h*aw*", which the listener must "fill in." The morphological foregroundedness of k^h*aw* invites a listener to project him or herself into the experience it simulates. Its syntactic foregrounding creates further involvement because it encourages the listener to infer the anaconda's presence, in the same way that the bystanders have, before it is actually seen.

Sound Images of Movements and States

The preceding section discussed sound symbolic adverbs that principally communicate the sound qualities of actions. This section discusses sound-symbolic adverbs that are principally about movements (although they may also describe sounds made by those movements) and one sound image of a state. The most important, because it is most often used in this narrative, is *polang*. This sound-symbolic adverb presents two kinds of movement in water. *Polang* represents a continuous, gliding, floating movement across the surface of water, as in line 51. *Polang* also represents the moment of emergence from underwater to the surface, as in lines 69, 74, and 82.

In line 51 a morphologically foregrounded *polang* is used to simulate a direct experience of a movement across water. The narrator lengthens *polang*'s second syllable to imitate the smooth gliding motion of a canoe passing by. This image is then echoed by her extension of the durative verb *riu* "going" which occurs immediately after *polang*. Her extension of these two words invites the listener to project into the experience of movement. At the same time that one is involved in the simulation of this experience, one is involved at another level, in imagining how this movement looks from the anaconda's underwater perspective.

In another highly foregrounded use, *polang*, line 69, simulates the anaconda's rising movement from underwater to the surface. This is a very dramatic moment because it marks the anaconda's first visible appearance. Her pronunciation enhances the drama by dwelling on the medial *-l-*, and then forcefully aspirating the final syllable, which effectively imitates the force of its surge to the surface. This morphological and intonational foregrounding is further framed by her exhortation to "Look!" at what she is describing. This description also includes evidence for the narrator's expectation of my involvement. Her own involvement in articulating this image was based on the assumption that the image itself would facilitate and enhance my understanding of this dramatic moment. However, when my failure to be engaged in the image was apparent to her by my question "What rises?" she became noticeably impatient.

The sound-symbolic adverb *tupu*, line 76 contrasts semantically with *polang*. It represents an extended movement underwater and it also represents the moment of a fall into water. *Tupu* may have been, at one time, exclusively a sound image depicting the sound of a splash. Now it functions both as a sound and a movement image. In line 76 *tupu* simulates the anaconda's drop back down into the water. *Tupu* is syntactically foregrounded because it alone indicates this movement by the anaconda. There is no surrounding utterance to help a listener contextualize the image. The narrator also foregrounds *tupu* by gliding the pitch of its pronunciation upward. This foregrounded upglide is then enhanced by an immediately following pause, the longest pause of the entire narrative, lasting a full four seconds. This pause encourages further involvement because it causes the listener to ponder the unseen movement of the anaconda below the water's surface.

The sound-symbolic adverb *p^{h}uy* in line 55 simulates the tapir's bursting out of water. Its foregrounding is created first of all by what precedes it. The narrator introduces it by saying "and I looked and saw that," which in effect, creates a frame for the image of the tapir's bursting out, at the same time that it encourages the listener to "watch" this bursting. She then lengthens it, to describe the quality of the bursting sound as it unfolds in time. Her pronunciation is also strongly aspirated and devoiced to simulate the force of the burst. At the same time that it involves the listener in a direct experience of the tapir's bursting out of water, *p^{h}uy* effectively shifts the listener's involvement, which had been focused underwater in the immediately preceding episode, back to the water's surface.

What is perhaps the most abstract sound-symbolic adverb of the narrative occurs in line 85. *Ton* is a conceptual image rather than a sensorily grounded image. It is used when speakers want to emphasize that something is filled to utmost capacity, covered or drenched completely, or otherwise characterizeable by some attribute as completely as is possible. It is most commonly used to describe the complete filling up of a canoe with any kind of cargo. *Ton* is a sound-symbolic adverb that depicts an idea of a completely realized state. Speakers typically foreground their pronunciation of this adverb, as the narrator does in line 85, with an upwardly gliding pitch. One can speculate on the iconicity of this pitch rise and note that it communicates an idea of completiveness by going as far as the limits of the speaker's own voice range. *Ton* is also foregrounded by its syntactic isolation. It is the only vehicle for an underlying verb phrase of the form "was swallowed completely." That this is in fact the image she had in mind is evident by her affirmative response to my question "He swallowed the tapir *ton* (i.e., completely)?" In any case, the intonational and syntactic foregrounding of this image make similar involvement demands on a listener as her earlier use of *tupu*. The listener is invited to ponder what is believed to have taken place underwater: an image of the tapir's complete swallowing by the anaconda.

Lexical Images

In his recent sociohistorical study of southern Peruvian Quechua, Mannheim states that the importance of sound imagery for Quechua speakers reflects a particular orientation toward their language. For Quechua speakers words are consubstantial with their objects: "Language is part and parcel of the natural world (1991: 184). That this orientation applies to Pastaza Quechua speakers as well is evident not only by their use of sound-symbolic imagery but also by their imageic use of lexical items. The belief that words and objects have a natural connection accounts for the tendancy of Quechua speakers to focus their foregrounding on a non-sound-symbolic word to create lexical images. When Quechua speakers foreground their pronunciation of lexical items, they are asking their listeners to involve themselves in an imaginative apprehension of the salient qualities denoted by that lexical item. For example, the first lexical image of the narrative occurs in line 4. The narrator foregrounds the word *playa* "beach" by extending its first syllable at the same time that she aspirates and devoices it. Her intent is to communicate an image of the salient visual attributes of the beach. From personal experience of many canoe rides along rivers in this area, I can vouch for the striking appearance of any stretch of white sandiness against the muddy brown of the river's water and the green of the surrounding forest. It is this kind of image that she intends the listener to imagine.

The remaining lexical images in this narrative are parts of composite images. A composite image is used by the narrator when she wants to consider a single action, event, or process with more than one image. One such composite image in line 51, consisting of *polang* and *riu* "going" was already discussed. Another composite image occurs in line 33. She foregrounds the word *rigring*, literally "with ear," by extending its second syllable slightly and lowering her voice pitch to a murmur. She then "splices" onto this lexical image, the sound image of the tapir's cry *chu*, making the description a composite of the visual and auditory. The lexical portion of this image relates her first visual impression of the tapir. With the lexical part of this image, she is asking me to participate in imagining the appearance of the tapir's ears poking out of the water as it tries to flee from the anaconda. Moreover, by framing the image as a whole with the phrase "I look and see" she makes this expectation explicit.

Lines 64 and 65 feature another example of a lexical image combined with a sound-symbolic image. The narrator imitates the sound of the anaconda's thrashing below the surface with *k^haw* and then presents an image of the visible swirling movement of that thrashing with *muling* literally "with whirl." Her foregrounding of *muling* is identical to that of *rigring,* line 33. She extends the second syllable of *muling* at the same time that she lowers her voice pitch to a murmur. The entire composite is further foregrounded by the way it is introduced. She introduces it with "This is like what we see," which encourages the listener to actively imagine this image.

All of the lexical images discussed so far have been foregrounded by lengthening rather than repetition. However, the last two lexical images of the narrative undergo multiple repetition. In line 82 there is a composite image featuring the sound-symbolic adverb *polang*, describing the anaconda's rise to the surface, and the word *kingu* "bend," which is repeated four times to describe the undulations on the water's surface resulting from this rise. With each repetition the narrator simulates a wave movement, which she invites the listener to imagine when she says "you would see such waves."

The final lexical image occurs in line 88. It is a composite image consisting of multiple repetitions of *pus,* the first syllable of *pusku* "bubbles, foam," and one repetition of *tsapak*, a sound-symbolic image of water slapping the shore.[6] This is possibly the most foregrounded moment of the entire narrative. Both *pus* and *tsapak* create for the listener a general involvement in the images resulting from the underwater battle which is imagined to be taking place. The composite as a whole is framed by the narrator's introductory phrase "you would see." She then launches into multiple repetitions of *pus*. The multiple repetitions are foregrounded by their syntactic isolation, by the fact of their repetition, and also by the rise and fall of her voice pitch over the repetitions. This rise and fall of pitch conveys an image of spatial distribution. By using a series of pitch variations that go up and then back down a range of possible "places," she is presenting an image of a phenomenon that is distributed all over a circumscribed space. This rise and fall of pitch can also be considered aesthetic in function because it reduces the monotony of the multiple repetitions. Overall, this image of bubbles invites the listener to ponder what is happening below the water's surface.

The second portion of this composite image is the narrator's single repetition of *tsapak*, which presents a sound image of water slapping the shore. Just as *pus* is foregrounded in part by the fact that it occurs without a discursive proposition, so is *tsapak*. However, while the image of the bubbles encourages one to imagine the underwater battle between the anaconda and the tapir, the sound image of the water slapping the shore suggests a shift in focus to the bystanders themselves. By moving her attention to the water's edge with repetitions of *tsapak*, the narrator effectively shifts the focus of involvement to herself. She is now concerned about their proximity to the events taking place underwater, and their own vulnerability to attack. There is, after all, very little separating them from the water. That she expresses her fear of sleeping on the beach in the very next line, saying "I felt so afraid. 'Let's go! Let's go upriver and sleep! Let's go!' etc. is evidence for this shift in focus.

Other Iconicities

This chapter has concentrated on one particular kind of iconicity, the iconic image or First Firstness, as manifested in sound symbolic language use. I would now like to turn my attention to the narrator's use of metaphorical and diagrammatic iconicity. There are only two moments in this narrative when metaphors are used to promote involvement. In line 65, the narrator compares the whirlpool created on the water's surface to the shell of a snail. However, there is another metaphor embedded within this one: the snail's shell is itself referred to with the word *siki* "ass, rear." This metaphorical reference to its shell makes sense if one considers that Quechua speakers typically experience not simply the shell of a snail, but the living animal, with a shell perched on its back. The other metaphor, which occurs in line 82, compares the waves created by the anaconda to waves created by a canoe with an outboard motor attached. Both of these metaphors are secondary enhancements of sound-symbolic and lexical images. They enhance the listener's simulated experience of an action or process unfolding in time, by comparing these images to more commonly observed phenomena.

I now turn to a discussion of the diagrammatic iconic structures used by the narrator. The discussion will show that there is overlap rather than a radical break between linguistic diagrams and images. Although Peirce undoubtedly would have agreed with this, the fact is somewhat obscured by the examples of ideal images and diagrams offered in his discussion. All of his examples of image icons and diagrammatic icons are two dimensional. Image icons are exemplified by a lead pencil streak (1955: 104), a representational painting (105), and photographs (106). Diagrammatic icons include an architectural drawing (106), an equational brace showing a relation among different elements (107), and a set of algebraic equations arranged to highlight their correspondences (107). The essential difference that these examples are meant to capture is that diagrams resemble by the analogous relations of their parts, while images are perceived to share their objects' sensuous qualities. However this essential difference is somewhat problematic when a linguistic sign vehicle is considered. The difficulty arises because the linguistic sign vehicle is composed of components that are organized by their temporal succession (Jakobson 1971a). A linguistic sign vehicle is therefore susceptible to analysis of its constituent parts and relations, even if it communicates chiefly by resembling an action's sensuous qualities.

Consider, for example, the sound-symbolic adverb *tsapak* in line 88, which shares features of both an image and a diagram. It is a sound image of water slapping the shore. However its disyllabic structure can also be interpreted as a diagram of the movement, *tsa-*, and subsequent contact, *-pak,* of water with land. As an image, *tsapak* resembles by its suggestion of a similarity of sound. As a diagram, *tsapak* resembles by an analogous relation between its component syllables and the component parts of a movement. The other disyllabic adverbs, *polang* and *tupu,* are further examples of sound symbolism that are both imageic and diagrammatic: both imitate the sensuous qualities of various kinds of movement through water. However, their disyllabic structures also diagram these movements into component parts that distinguish between the portions of movement above, and those below the water's surface. Even clearer examples of the mingling of images and diagrams are the forms that use repetition: the tapir's crying, lines 16 and 33, is an image of a sound and also a diagram of its temporal intermittence. The repetitions of *kingu*, line 82, are both images of movement[7] and diagrams of the wave movements' spreading through space. Similarly, the repetitions of *pus*, line 88, feature individual lexical images of bubbles and also a diagrammatic presentation of their distribution in space.

The purest image icon of the narrative is *tak*, in line 14. *Tak* is relatively nondiagrammatic because it imitates the sensuous quality of a punctual sound. Since punctuality is defined in principle by its nondurativity, *tak* is least susceptible to an analysis of its component sounds. The purest diagrammatic icon, by contrast, is in line 2. The narrator repeats the verb *alʸasha* "digging" three times. This repetition diagrams not only the action of repeatedly digging in the sand for eggs but also the repetition of that action over an extended period of time. However, this is not a performative repetition because it is not presented by the narrator in a highly foregrounded manner. Her pronounciation of each of these verbs is intonationally unmarked. She is not asking the listener to imagine the salient, sensuous qualities denoted by the verb. The iconicity of these repetitions is a function, rather, of their analogous relations, which diagram the repeated action of digging.

Of the repeated elements and structures that create various kinds of parallel relations throughout this narrative, one recurrent theme deserves particular attention for its role in complementing and strengthening the involvement created by the sound symbolic images. The narrator repeatedly uses some form of the verb *rikuna* "to look, watch, see." Her use of this verb falls into two general categories. On the one hand, she repeatedly uses this verb in the form of metanarrative exhortations. Metanarration is defined by Bauman (1986: 98-99) as any shift out of narrative time and into the circumstances of the narrative's telling. Her frequent use of phrases such as "Look!" in lines 1, 42, 70, and 77, and "You would (or should) see" in lines 28, 30, 56, 70, 75, and 88, are metanarrative because they call attention to my presence as a listener. At the same time that these metanarrative comments shift attention away from the story and to myself, they refer back to the narrative by directing my attention to it. In this way, they help cement my involvement in the narration.

In addition to its use in metanarrative statements, the verb *rikuna* defines, in a sense, the primary activity of every actor in this narrative. The narrator and her companions watch. They tell each other to look. They speculate about what the anaconda sees. And the anaconda watches for the tapir. Putting aside its use in metanarrative statements, this verb is used in some form in lines 31, 33, 44, 49, 50, 51, 52, 53, 55, 57, 63, 68, 86, and 93. There is a direct link, then, between the repeated occurrence of this verb and my own involvement in the narrative. The verb itself defines the main preoccupation of the narrative. By repeatedly exhorting me to look and see, the narrator is encouraging me to participate as well in the narrative's main activity.

Summary

Chapter 2 called attention to the role of sound-symbolic adverbs in the grammatical system of aspect. Perfective sound-symbolic adverbs occupy a niche in Pastaza Quechua's grammar. They specify the perfectivity of coreference verbs, which are otherwise overdetermined for aspectual durativity. For switch reference and agentive verb structures, which are otherwise aspectually unspecified, sound-symbolic adverbs supply perfective or durative aspect values. Chapter 3 explored the range of techniques for the performative expression of durative and perfective aspect values. Many performative expressions of aspect are best understood in their discourse function, with concepts from other semiotic modalities, such as gesture and cinema. This chapter has concerned the use of sound-symbolic adverbs, both durative and perfective, in an extended narrative account. Sound-symbolic adverbs are an important feature of Quechua verbal art. They encourage interlocutionary involvement by iconic imitation of the salient qualities of an action's spatiotemporal unfolding. These simulations are created by performative foregrounding of intonational, morphological, or syntactic features. Sound symbolic forms focus on perceptually salient features of a narrative by simulating a direct experience of an action, event, or process. A listener projects into this simulation and is thereby involved. The greater significance of sound-symbolic involvement can be understood with reference to Urban's statement that speech styles call attention to what is felt, sensed, and embodied, in addition to what is referred to (1991: 145). Sound-symbolic style enhances the potential for involvement and empathy because it puts into relief the kinds of perceptions and feelings that everyone is capable of sharing.

The following chapter will examine the functional significance of sound-symbolic style for the Pastaza Quechua. By means of linguistic and nonlinguistic evidence, their conversational ideal of amiability with its emphasis on the sharedness of basic perceptual experience will be linked to an encompassing view in which sound, the body, and the perceptions it simulates are related to Quechua cultural constructions of the natural world. Furthermore, because sound-symbolic style is so enmeshed within the linguisticocultural matrix, it is also sensitive to the changing social conditions of its use. I offer some preliminary comparative observations of changes in its stylistic markedness that are related to shifting experiential frameworks of social, political, and economic forces.

6

Signs of Life in Sound

Sound-symbolic images allow the Pastaza Quechua to share moments of focused attention on the salient qualities of an action, event, or process as it unfolds in time. The use of sound-symbolic imagery contributes to an involved conversational style that legitimizes Quechua speakers' conversational ideal of amiability. This chapter concerns the deeper cultural significance of sound in daily life. It links the conversational ideal of amiability with its emphasis on the sharedness of basic perceptual experience, to an encompassing view in which sound, the body, and the perceptions it simulates are tied to an ideology of unity with the natural world. Sound resonates through one's body during verbal articulation. Sound-symbolic impressions reverberate through one's consciousness, organizing memories and anchoring understandings of key life experiences. The most significant events of peoples' lives are interpreted against a backdrop of sound-symbolically rendered perceptions of natural phenomena, such as bird sounds, atmospheric signs, and processes of growth and decay. Death, illness, and misfortune call for explanations that link perceptions of the natural world with the most significant events of human experience. Such explanations are part of Quechua cultural constructions of an orderly, manageable world. They also reveal a sense of what, for them is, unnatural. Their conceptions of naturalness and unnaturalness are based in their bodily capacities and perceptual experiences. For Puka yakuans, sound is a modality for representing the naturalness or unnaturalness of perceptual experience. It is so integral to their experience of the world that its linguistic expression in sound symbolism assumes multiple rhetorical functions. These claims will be substantiated with examples of sound-symbolic style from a wide variety of contexts, with nonlinguistic evidence from Quechua speakers' visual representations of themselves and with comparative observations of sound-symbolic style in two Quechua villages.

In searching for the deeper cultural significance of sound-symbolic style, this work draws on the insights of Urban, who suggests that speech styles are highly complex sign vehicles with mutiple iconic, indexical, and referential functions and which "tend to occur in connection with contexts or subject matters that are areas of cultural emphasis" (1985: 327). Speech styles call attention to areas of cultural emphasis, he hypothesizes, through their formal and functional markedness. The concept of markedness was employed in chapter 2 to discuss the aspectual oppositions of Quechua's verbal system. Quechua's verb roots are neutral or unmarked with respect to aspect values; however, they also exist in a form that is marked for aspectual durativity by suffixation with the morpheme *-u-*. Sound-symbolic adverbial modification of many verb phrases adds an additional level of markedness for aspectual perfectivity. Urban has shown that speech styles can also be productively examined with the concept of markedness. Speech styles can be marked by their expressive restriction or through formal amplification or embellishment of the sign vehicle. Formal amplifications of the sign vehicle point attention to the subject matter of the discourse, alerting one to its significance.

Although chapter 4 stated that sound-symbolic utterances were stylistically marked by formal amplication with a range of performative techniques, preliminary comparative observations suggest that sound-symbolic markedness is not everywhere the same. The final section of this chapter will address issues revolving around linguistic style and markedness, cultural values, and social change. What happens when the conceptual and social conditions congenial to sound-symbolic expression change? How do Quechua speakers retain, adapt, or reinterpret a style of expression that represents what is significant about their experience? These are urgent questions because forces of modernization are changing the nature of their experience, and many of these changes create experiential frameworks that are cognitively dissonant with sound-symbolic discourse. Literacy, in conjunction with social, political, and economic change, is affecting the sound-symbolic style of Quechua speakers in eastern Amazonian Ecuador. Preliminary comparative observations of sound-symbolic usage in another Quechua-speaking village, Sara yaku, suggest that it has become expressively restricted to two specialized and interrelated functions: it has become associated with a complex of features that mark women's speech from men's, and it has become an emblem of authenticity, of something distinctively "Quechua" that has no equivalent in the literate, Spanish-speaking world. In Puka yaku, by contrast, the use of sound symbolism is far more diffuse. It is woven into the fabric of Quechua speakers' daily life. Its functions are relatively unrestricted, cutting across context, gender, and social role.

Sound-Symbolic Functions

For Jakobson (1960), linguistic functions are linked to various factors of a communicative event. In isolating these factors and functions, Jakobson does not mean to suggest that communicative events are ever singular in their function. Rather, he sees these functions as interlocking into relations of dominance and subordination in any given speech event. Jakobson outlines six possible functions: referential, emotive, conative, metalingual, phatic, and poetic. Each function is linked to one of a set of six logically possible dimensions of the communicative event. When the orientation, or *Einstellung,* is focused on a contextually specified referent, the function of the message is referential. An orientation toward the addresser is emotive in function because it serves to express that person's feelings. An orientation toward the addressee, as in vocatives or imperatives, is considered conative. When the message is oriented toward the linguistic code itself, then the function is metalingual. A message that serves to retain the conditions congenial for communication, including the varieties of backchanneling devices such as "uh huh," "um hm," etc., is called phatic in function, a term Jakobson borrows from Malinowski. And when the message serves to highlight the message itself, for its own sake, then the function is considered poetic. Four of Jakobson's six functions—the poetic, referential, emotive, and metalingual—are relevant to sound-symbolic use among the Pastaza Quechua. In addition, a number of other functions—including the didactic, inferential, identificational, and epistemic—will also be discussed here.

Poetic

Jakobson's belief in the interconnectedness of poetics with all forms of expression is axiomatic to his thoughts on language and linguistics. The delineation of the "poetic" function of language into a separate category, therefore, is artificial at best. Rather than attempting to isolate poetic functions from other kinds of functions, this discussion will outline some of the most general poetic features of sound-symbolic language, with the goal of illuminating the ways in which these features can be appropriated for a multiplicity of subfunctions and nuances of expression. Poetic language, states Jakobson, is constituted by the projection of "the principle of equivalence from the axis of selection into the axis of combination" (1960: 358). Poetic effects or "equivalences" are achieved through parallelism, whether of sound qualities, morphologic shape, syntactic arrangement, or semantic association. In foregrounding parallelism as *the* poetic technique, Jakobson focuses on the infinite possibilities for sensible experiences of linguistic symmetry, whether of sounds, syllables, stresses and rhythms, or semantic associations. Jakobson noticed these symmetries in all kinds of language use, including the most hackneyed phrases and political slogans. The repetition of sound-symbolic adverbs is a type of parallelism because it establishes an equivalence or symmetry by use of the same form. In the following example, there are several kinds of equivalences that are simultaneously at work in a series of sound-symbolic repetitions. The speaker is describing the sounds and movements of walking through deep mud. She repeats the sound-symbolic *tupun* four times with a word final stress on each adverb. She then makes a parallel series of repetitions with the deictic adverb *chil^{y}ay* "right there," each of which also has word-final stress. Finally, after focusing on the rhythmicity of walking through mud, she presents another series of repetitions which alternates the two verbs *aysarina* "to lift oneself out" and *chuparina* "to be sucked in."

1. Turu-y-mi tupun tupun tupun tupun.
   mud-LOC-EV

   "In the mud we go *tupun tupun tupun tupun.*

2. Pambari-sha chil^{y}a-y chilya-y chilya-y rina a-n
   bury-COR there-LOC there-LOC there-LOC go be-3

   "Burying ourselves right there, right there, right there, right there,"

3. turu-ta!
   mud-ADV
   "in the mud!"

4. Mana dzas rina a-n.
   NEG go be-3
   "We can't go fast."

5. Chupari-nchi aysari-nchi chupari-nchi aysari-nchi.
   be sucked-1PL pull self-1PL be sucked-1PL pull self-1PL
   "We're sucked in, we pull out, we're sucked in, we pull out."

The repetition of sound-symbolic adverbs, deictic adverbs, and verbs establishes an equivalence and therefore a kind of parallelism which recreates the sounds, rhythms, and movements of walking through muddy ground.

In the spirit of Jakobson, who emphasized the pervasiveness of poetic language in the everyday, Friedrich (1991) offers an encompassing classification of poetic language that seems implicitly modeled on the design features of language itself. He suggests that all poetic language communicates by means of five general types and many subtypes of tropes or figures. Image tropes are figures that are primary or irreducible, in the way that roots are the basic, irreducible forms for other kinds of linguistic processes. Formal tropes involve operations such as addition, commutation, and ellipsis, and are comparable to phonological and morphological processes such as suffixation, deletion, and metathesis. Modal tropes are underlying moods or sentiments such as irony and shame, which tinge an expressive message and have their grammatical counterparts in modal and status categories such as the subjunctive, assertive, and conditional. Contiguity tropes are defined as "aesthetically effective juxtapositions" (1991: 34) and are analogous to the many kinds of syntagmatic associations and syntactic processes of language. Finally, analogical tropes such as metaphor and synechdoche reflect associational processes that are increasingly recognized in current research by cognitive linguists as basic to the construction of meaning.

Sound-symbolic adverbs are fundamentally image tropes because they communicate vivid perceptions that stand for themselves, as they simulate sensory qualities that are experientially basic to everyone. Sound-symbolic images are comparable to close-up shots which frame a viewer's attention on the most salient features of an action, event, or process. The imageic qualities of sound-symbolic adverbs are particularly salient in performative discourse, where their aesthetic function supersedes others. Sound-symbolic adverbs are comparable to images or figures against a background when they are performatively foregrounded by repetition, extended lengthening of a syllable, or higher pitched pronunciation over part or all of a sound-symbolic word. When their function is primarily aesthetic, many of the tropic devices outlined by Friedrich enhance their imageability.

Formal amplification of sound-symbolic adverbs through intonational foregrounding is one kind of formal device or trope which adds on to or elaborates the sounds of a word. The syntactic isolation of sound-symbolic adverbs from their underlying verbs is another kind of formal trope which, by deleting a finite verb, places primary expressive responsibility on a sound-symbolic adverb. Both of these tropic techniques are evident in the following example. The sound-symbolic adverb *polang*, which describes an image of something emerging from underwater, is intonationally foregrounded with a higher pitch on its second syllable. It is also syntactically isolated because its underlying verb *l^{y}ukshina* "to emerge" has not been used. The example describes the way a canoe which is blocked from passage by a fallen tree trunk is passed underneath the tree trunk and on to the other side of the river.

6. Yaku uray-ma pasa-chi-ra-nchi, yaku uku-ta, kanoa-ga po^{lang}!
water downriver-DAT pass-CAUS-PAST-1PL water under-ACC canoe-TOP

"We passed it (in the direction of) downriver, under the water, and the canoe (went) *po^{lang}*!"

By foregrounding the second syllable of *polang* with a higher pitched pronunciation, the speaker creates a vocal gesture of the movement of the canoe from below the water's surface as it is passed under the trunk to above the water's surface as it emerges. The syntactic isolation of *polang* from its underlying verb foregrounds it further by placing exclusive responsibility on this sound-symbolic adverb for communicating information about what the canoe did.

The syntactic foregrounding of sound-symbolic adverbs through marked word order, i.e. *syntactic displacement*, is a type of contiguity trope frequently used in sound-symbolic utterances. In the next example the adverb *patang* describes the way a large snake flung its tail to the ground in an effort to grab a dog. Although it modifies the verb *tuksina* "to throw," it does not occur immediately to the left of it. There is an intervening phrase *ima ismu kaspita shina* "as if it were some rotted log" that interrupts its modification of the verb.

7. Yanga dz^{h}iririri uyari-k-a, pa -t^{h}anng! (pause) ima ismu kaspi-ta shina
just sound-AG-TOP what rot log-ACC like
tuksi-k a-shka chupa-ta!
throw-AG be-PERF tail-ACC

"Just sounding *dz^{h}iririri*, (he went) *pa-t^{h}anng*! As if it were some rotted log he threw his tail down!"

By syntactically displacing *patang* from its verb *tuksina* "to throw," the speaker gives it a more important expressive function than an adverb ordinarily would have. The displacement of *patang* from its verb foregrounds the sound image of the snake flinging its tail to the ground. More important, this displacement tells a listener that *patang* does not simply modify its verb. It is expressively important in and of itself, as a sound image that stands for itself.

The perceptual images simulated by sound-symbolic adverbs can be used metaphorically, as analogical tropes in Friedrich's classification. In the next example the sound-symbolic *t^{y}api*, which describes the moment of contact made by two surfaces that stick to each other, describes the way love magic can affect a person.

8. Pay-ba simayuka-l^ya-wan kan-ga t^yapi (pause) pay-ma tuku-nga ra-w-ngi
   he-POSS love charm-LIM-INST you-TOP he-DAT become-FINF do-DUR-2
   pay-ta riku-sha.
   he-ACC see-COR

   "With just his love charm *t^yapi* (pause) toward him you'll become drawn, seeing him."

The use of *t^yapi* creates an analogy or metaphor between a physical and emotional experience: a strong emotional attachment is compared to the way two surfaces come together and stick to each other.

In general, the poetic uses of sound-symbolic expression capture the "what" of experience. The everyday sensations and perceptions that are shared by all are translated into a verbal medium and elaborated with a variety of performative devices. All of the poetic techniques just described are used in a number of contexts and genres. Although the examples here were drawn from narratives of everyday experience, there are abundant examples of poetic sound-symbolic usage in mythic and legendary narratives as well. When they occur in mythic narratives, sound-symbolic utterances have the effect of making the often bizarre and surrealistic occurrences they describe more accessible to listeners. The magical is made a little ordinary through sound-symbolic descriptions such as the following. Taken from a myth about the freshwater dolphin, it describes the moment when evil parents who have just had their eyes pecked out by hawks, as punishment for failing to feed their children, fall into the river and turn into dolphins. The force of their leaping in and out of the river is dramatically described with sound symbolism.

9. Bugyu tuku-sha b^huxxx b^huxxxx l^yukshi-sha ri-u-naw-ra.
   dolphin become-COR emerge-COR go-DUR-3PL-PAST

   "Becoming dolphins, emerging *b^huxxx b^huxxxx* they were going."

By repeating sound-symbolic *b^hux,* the narrator simulates a visual and auditory experience that is accessible and aesthetically pleasing to all. Moreover, this image has the effect of introducing normality and beauty into a narrative that has thus far concerned bizarre and unnatural events, such as the starving of children by parents, the pecking out of eyes by birds, and the transformation of humans into dolphins.

Referential

Sound-symbolic utterances are often used to focus on a contextually specified referent. In the next example, two sound-symbolic adverbs are used to refer to a sound image and a visual image. The example is taken from a discussion I overheard and managed to record, about techniques for repairing pottery. Speaker C states that when clay jars break apart in a certain way they have to be thrown out; speaker F advocates repair. In order to verify that speaker F understands the situation in the same way she does, speaker C uses two sound-symbolic adverbs, *taw* and *ing*. She uses *taw* to imitate a sound made by a clay jar when it explodes during firing. She uses *ing* to describe an image of the jar's fissuring as a result of the explosion.

10. C: Chasna-tas ichu-k ma-k a-ni, man-cha ñukanchi?
like that-INCL abandon-AG be-AG be-1 NEG-INT we
"I throw something like that out, don't we?"

11. Kayta paki-shka, ima-ta, ichu-k ma-ra-nchi.
here break-COR what-INT abandon-AG be-PAST-1PL
"If it's broken here what else can we do? We would have tossed it out."

12. F: [Chasnama hambi-k a-shka-wna-ra.
like that-DAT repair-AG be-PERF-3PL-PAST
"They would have repaired something like that."

13. C: Kay ima taw tuvya-sha, kuti, mana-chu ing ra?
here what burst-COR well NEG-INT go
"If it bursts apart here *taw*, well, isn't it true that it then goes (i.e., splits) *ing*?"

14. F: Ah ow.
"Um hm."

15. C: Ichu-k-l^ya ma-nchi.
abandon-AG-LIM be-1PL
"We can only toss it out."

That *taw* and *ing* are in fact referring to images, rather than simulating them, is evident by their lack of formal amplification. Their lack of performative foregrounding means that they are used in this context to exchange information and to verify understanding.

Metalinguistic

The semiotic distinctiveness of sound-symbolic utterances is evident in Quechua speakers' metalinguistic reflections and explanations of their own sound-symbolic use. These explanations and commentary reveal that sound-symbolic discourse provides them with another form of reflexivity, which can be characterized as *imageic*, not in a narrowly visual denotation but in a wider sense that includes all perceptual domains. If the meanings of sound-symbolic images are self-evident, as any image by definition should be, then people should try to explain them by simply repeating the sound-symbolic utterance in question. On the other hand, sound-symbolic words are also linguistic forms, and one of the design features of language is that it is reflexive and can be used in metalanguage, to refer to itself. The data reveal both tendencies. When asked for explanations of their meaning, people repeated and elaborated their sound-symbolic performances in order to explain them, and they also reflected on these words by paraphrasis and elaboration of the situational contexts of their use.

The next example is taken from an account of a child's disappearance. The sound-symbolic adverb *dzing* is used to describe a sudden start that the speaker felt when she realized that her child was missing. She explains the meaning of *dzing* through formal amplification and also metalinguistically, by rephrasing the description of the feeling through a comparison with another kind of feeling.

16. Ima shina ra-sha chari ^{dzing} yari-ra-ni wawa-ta?
what like do-COR perhaps remember-PAST-1 baby-ACC
"What perhaps was I doing (that caused me to), ^{dzing} remember (my) child?"

Q: [Dzing?
"*Dzing*?"

17. Nda ^{dzing} -mi yuyari-ra-ni, 'wawa-gaya? Luzawra' ni-ra-ni.' Hah? Kay-bi
yes -EV remember-PAST-1 child-TOP Luzawra say-PAST-1 huh here-LOC
ma-w-ra'—
be-DUR-PAST
"Yes, it was a ^{dzing} that made me say to Rosa Elena, 'What about the child?' 'Hah? (she answered me) he was right here'—"

Q: [Ima shinata dzing yuyari-u-ngi?
what how remember-DUR-2
"How are you thinking 'dzing'?"

18. Ña ^{dziinnnng} yuyari-ra-ni ñuka; aycha dzinng-l^{y}a tuku a-ra-ya.
now remember-PAST-1 I flesh -LIM become be-PAST-TOP
"Now ^{dziiiiing} I remembered; my flesh just became *dziiing*."

Q: [Ima shinata 'dzing' tuku-n aycha?
what how become-3 flesh
"How does flesh become *dzing*?"

19. Ima shina chari, ma-ra, ^{dzinng,} salta-shka shina tuku-k ma-ni, ñuka, yari-sha.
what like maybe be-PAST leap-PERF like become-AG be-1 I remember-COR
"In the way that I become when thinking, as if maybe, ^{dziiing} I've leaped."

The speaker's explanation makes it obvious that the sound-symbolic adverb *dzing* stands for itself. She explains its meaning by repeating it, with variations in its loudness, pitch, forcefulness, and length. Her performative foregrounding of *dzing* is explanatorily salient because it is the way this feeling stands out from her ordinary state of mind that makes it distinctive. She also explains it metalinguistically, by providing me with a phrase that equates *dzing* with a sudden start or leap.

The next example is taken from a myth. I was questioning speaker M about her multiple repetitions of *pa,* which she uses to describe the flapping of a condor's wings as it flies away.

20. Chuuuuuuuuuuuuuuu! P^{h}aa pa pa pa misha wawa-ta chay-l^{y}a-y k^{h}iiiii-shi
misha baby-ACC there-LIM-LOC -EV
ichu-sha ri-shka.
abandon-COR go-PERF
"*Chuuuuuuuuuuuuuuu* (they shrieked)! (And then) *p^{h}aa pa pa pa,* (the condor) went off, abandoning the baby misha hawks right there *k^{h}iiiii.*"

Q: [‘Pa pa pa ima-ta?
what-INT
“*Pa pa pa*, what is that?”

21. Nda, p^{h}aa pa pa pa pa pa pa pa pawa-sha ri-k, kuti mandzhari-ra-cha.
yes fly-COR go-AG well be afraid-PAST-EV
“Yes, flying *p^{h}aa pa pa pa pa pa pa pa*, it went off because it was frightened.”

The speaker’s explanation is metalinguistic because it supplies a paraphrase of *pa* in the form of the verb *pawasha* “flying.” Her explanation is also imageic, however, because she uses a more elaborate performance of *pa* to simulate the action it describes. In her explanation she uses a longer and more complex series of repetitions: the first few pronunciations of *pa* are more forceful and are pronounced separately, while the last few are not as forceful, are more rapid, and diminish in their intensity. This formal technique heightens the temporal and spatial unfolding of the action. The flapping begins more forcefully and then seems to fade in intensity as the birds themselves become more distant in space. By diminishing the force of her repetitions, the speaker simulates the experience of watching something appear to grow smaller as it moves away from a fixed vantage point.

Didactic/Explanatory

Sound-symbolic forms can be used to convey information of an explanatory nature, often involving fine points of detail. The following description contains several instances of sound-symbolic explanation. It was elicited during a series of interviews about verbs. The topic of this description is the verb *karana* “to give food; to fortify clay.” My friend’s description of this verb’s meaning focussed on its second, less common usage. She provides, with the help of sound-symbolic adverbs, a detailed portrait of techniques for fortifying raw clay with a type of tree bark to prevent it from breaking during firing. The following example well illustrates its instructional function because the narrator uses sound-symbolic adverbs in response to my requests for clarification.

22. Shuk-a karana ninchi, karana al^{y}pa.
one-TOP fortify say-1PL fortify clay
“About one type we say, ‘It has to be fortified; it’s fortifiable clay.’”

23. Chi-ta-ga apacharana-ta kutanchi.
that-ACC-TOP apacharan-ACC grind-1PL
“For that we grind *apacharana*.”

24. Kuta-shka washa
grind-PERF after
“After grinding it,”

25. Ima, mashti, cedazo il^{y}a-kpi-ga laranka panga?
what whachamacallit filter lack-SWRF-TOP orange leaf
“What do you call it—a filter—if there is no filter than an orange leaf?”

26. Kay laranka shayawn?
this orange stand-DUR-3
"You know how orange trees are standing?"

27. Chi panga-y shushunchi ñukanchi mukahata awa-ngaw
that leaf-LOC filter-1PL we mukaha-ACC make-FINF
"Over those leaves we filter it to make a *mukaha* (drinking bowl)"

28. sumak!
beautiful
"nicely!"

Q: Charak mana intindi-ni-chu karana, shuk sami al^{y}pa-chu a-n?
yet NEG understand-1-NEG fortify one type clay-INT be-3
"I don't yet understand 'to fortify'; is it for a type of clay?"

29. L^{y}ambu al^{y}pa ni-nchi.
all clay say-1PL
"We say this about all clay."

30. Mukaha awana l^{y}ambu al^{y}pa ni-nchi.
mukaha make all clay say-1PL
"About all *mukaha* making clay we say this."

31. Chi-ta-mi ñukanchi-ga apacharana-ta sumak rumi-wan kuta-nchi.
that-ACC-EV we-TOP apacharana-ACC nicely stone-INST grind-1PL
"That *apacharana* we grind nicely with a stone."

32. Kuta-shka washa kay shaya-w laranka panga Chi-bi-mi sa sa sa sa sa sa shita-kpi
grind-PERF after this stand-DUR orange leaf that-LOC-EV throw-SWRF
"After grinding it, this orange leaf,"

33. chi pay-ba paki-ga win urman, ñutu—
that it's break-TOP all fall-3 finely
"upon it, having thrown *sa sa sa sa sa sa* its small pieces all fall finely—

The sound-symbolic description is catalyzed by my question. The narrator answers the question by rephrasing her earlier description with more explanatorily transparent images. She uses sound-symbolic *sa* to describe the random sprinkling of the *apacharana* pieces in order to filter them. Her depiction is rendered performatively with multiple repetitions of *sa,* which imitate the repeatedness of the sprinkling, and with a pitch contour that mimics an idea of spatial distribution. She then proceeds with a description of the testing of the raw fortified clay. This testing involves biting into the clay, which should be gritty, or as the narrator states "like sand." She describes this testing process again with sound symbolism, using multiple repetitions of k^h*yu,* which imitate the sound of biting into properly fortified clay.

34. Kama-nchi kiru-wan kasna
    test-1PL teeth-INST like this
    "We test with teeth like this."

35. Kama-kpi-ga,
    test-SWRF-TOP
    "Having tested it,"

36. k^hyu k^hyu k^hyu k^hyu k^hyu k^hyu-mi uyari-n
    -EV sound-3
    "k^hyu k^hyu k^hyu k^hyu k^hyu k^hyu, it sounds"

37. tiyu shina.
    sand like
    "like sand."

Having clarified this point, she then proceeds with more sound-symbolic descriptions of the making of a small container with the fortified clay for a test firing. She describes the process of making the test pot with sound images of movements and lexical referents. The rolling of the clay into a ball is described with repetitions of the lexical item *bola* "ball." The fashioning of the ball into a container is then described with a composite image which consists of repetitions of sound-symbolic *tyak* and a single instance of the lexical item *purungun* "containment," which is performatively upjumped on its final syllable.

38. Chi-mi
    that-EV
    "Then,"

39. bola bola bola rik-i, kasna bola bola ra-sha tyak tyak tyak purun$^{\text{gu-n}}$ ra-sha.
    ball ball ball look-IMP like this ball ball make-COR container-ADV make-COR
    "Rolling rolling rolling, like this, rolling rolling, going *tyak tyak tyak* contain^{ment}."

The performative repetitions of *bola* "ball" imitate the repeatedness of the rolling action, while the repetitions of sound-symbolic *tyak* describe the process of molding the ball into a container by a series of quick movements of the fingers. The performative upjump over *purungun* "containment" provides a pitch contrast that emphasizes a resultant product, in this case, the containment provided by the test pot. When I asked for a clarification of this image she simply repeated it as if to say that its meaning was self-evident.

Q: Tyak tyak tyak?
"Tyak tyak tyak?"

40. Tyak tyak tyak tyak purun$^{\text{gu-n}}$ ra-nchi.
    container-ADV make-1PL
    "We go *tyak tyak tyak* contain^{ment}."

Q: Purungu-n?
contain-ADV
"Containment?"

41. Ah ow al^{y}pata.
ah hah clay-ACC
"Ah hah, of the clay."

Q: Puru-ta ra-sha?
container-ACC make-COR
"Making a container?"

42. Puru wawa-ta ra-nchi yanga tyak tyak ra-sha kasna purun^{gu-n} ra-sha.
container baby-ACC make-1PL just make-COR like this container-ADV make-COR
"A small container we make, just going *tyak tyak*, like this, making contain^{ment}."

Finally, in her description of the test pot's firing, she also makes use of sound symbolism. The exploding of a test pot which has not been adequately fortified is described with repetitions of *taw*.

43. Tosta-sha
toast-COR
"Firing it,"

44. nina-y sati-nchi
fire-LOC insert-1PL
"in the fire we stick it,"

45. nina-ta montona-sha.
fire-ACC pile-COR
"piling up the fire."

46. Chi-ga chasna montona-sha-ga kusa-nchi chi kasna wawa-ta kama—chi-ta
that-TOP like that pile-COR-TOP roast-1PL that like this baby-ACC test that-ACC
ni-nawn 'shañaku'
say-3PL shañaku
"Then, piling the fire like that we cook it, a small one like this we test—they call that a 'shañaku.'"

Q: Shañaku?
"A *shañaku*?"

47. 'Shañaku' ni-nawn chi, kasna puru wawa-ta shina ra-sha kusa-shka-ta.
shañaku say-3PL that like this container baby-ACC like make-COR cook-PERF-ACC
"Making a little container like this, they call what is cooked a *shañaku*."

48. Chi-ga al^{y}i kara-shka a-kpi chi shañaku mana tuvya-n-chu mana tuvya-n-chu.
that-TOP well fortify-PERF be-SWRF that shañaku NEG explode-3-NEG NEG explode-3-NEG
"Then if it's been well fortified, that *shañaku* doesn't explode; it doesn't explode."

49. Chi-mi awa-nchi.
that-EV make-1PL
"That's what we make."

50. Chi shañaku taw taw taw taw taw taw taw taw $w^{i^{n}}$ tuvya-n chi-ga charak pishi-n
that shanaku all explode-3 that-TOP yet lack-3
karana.
fortify
"But if that shañaku *taw taw taw taw taw taw taw taw* $a^{l^{l}}$ explodes, then it still lacks fortifying."

51. Charak pishi-n.
yet lack-3
"It is still lacking."

Every important aspect of the preceding set of instructions features sound-symbolic description: the way the ground-up tree bark is scattered *sa* over the orange leaf, the gritty sound *k^{h}yu* made by fortified clay when bitten, the movements of rolling the clay *bola* and fashioning it *t^{y}ak* into a small test pot, and the sound of an incompletely fortified test pot when it explodes *taw* during firing. That sound symbolism can be called upon to illustrate and explain such detailed processes is a testament to its integration with Puka yakuans' experience and knowledge of the world.

Inferential

Sound-symbolic utterances are often part of peoples' representations of their inference making. In the following example, repetitions of *how*, the sound symbol of a barking dog, are part of a description of just such a process. One night I left the household in which I was staying to visit another. When it became dark, my friend and her daughter, whose guest I was, began to wonder if I would return or spend the night where I'd been visiting. They inferred correctly that I was in fact returning when they heard the sound of barking dogs coming from a household located midway between their own house and the one I was visiting. In the example below, my friend explains how she came to this realization.

52. Chi-ga how how how how.
that-TOP
"So then the dogs go *how how how how*."

53. Chay!
there
"There!"

54. Shamu-n-mi ni-ni!
come-3-EV say-1
"'She's come!' I said."

Another example illustrating the inferential function of sound symbolism is taken from the narrative in the preceding chapter describing the pursuit of a tapir by an anaconda. The bystanders at first assume that the tapir is running from a jaguar. When they hear the sounds made by the water's movement, however, they infer that an anaconda is in fact chasing the tapir. The narrator's representation of the making of that inference is represented here.

55. Chiga ña
    so then
    "So then"

56. chay kucha-y
    that pond-LOC
    "in that pond"

57. k^{h}awwwwwww!
    "k^{h}awwwwwww!"

58. 'Chay-ga! Amarun-mi hapi-n!' ni-naw-ra-mi.
    that-TOP anaconda-EV catch-3 say-3PL-PAST-EV
    "'There! An anaconda's got it,' they said."

In claiming that sound-symbolic utterances are part of peoples' inference making, I do not wish to state that sound is the only medium relevant to the making of such inferences. I only suggest that in their representations of how they come to know or believe certain facts, sound symbolism is often foregrounded in Quechua speakers' descriptions.

Because sound symbolism is part of peoples' inference making, it is appropriate to discuss the evidential and validational status of sound-symbolic utterances. Pastaza Quechua does employ a set of suffixes to indicate assertion from the speaker's point of view, assertion from someone other than the speaker's point of view, and doubt. The assertative suffixes also function to focus a portion of an utterance, to indicate primary versus secondary focus, and to mark the rheme or new information as distinct from the theme or old information (Nuckolls 1993). Given the subtle possibilities for evidential specification and the inferential significance of sound-symbolic utterances, it would be reasonable to expect some overlap between evidentiality and sound symbolism, yet the overwhelming majority of sound-symbolic utterances lack evidential specification. This apparent anomaly can be understood, I suggest, in light of the semiotic singularity of sound symbolism. Most sound-symbolic utterances are performative simulations of an action, event, or process. The distinction between a speech event and a narrated event is therefore collapsed in sound-symbolic performance, which uses the speech event to recreate the salient features of the narrated event rather than to report it or refer to it. Sound-symbolic performances, therefore, are typically exempt from the usual requirements of assertion making. Such performances are also, by their nature, already highly foregrounded or focused. For these reasons, sound-symbolic expression largely escapes the necessity for evidential and validational specification.

Modal/Emotive

The experientially basic perceptions simulated by sound-symbolic adverbs are not in and of themselves emotionally charged. Rather, they are like rough sketches that are filled in with various kinds of affect by the contextual factors of their use. Factors that affect their emotive power include degree of formal amplification through performative foregrounding; semantic associations, and immediate linguistic environment. In the following narrative, sound symbolism is used to invoke a feeling of fear. The fear is of darkness, which seems to arrive too quickly, without warning, on a cloudy day. In this context the darkness is threatening because it begins to arrive when the narrator is in the forest, far from home, working her agricultural field. The darkness is signaled by the sound-symbolically rendered cry of the *dzhuluy* bird. Each time the narrator repeats this bird's cry, she also uses the sound-symbolic adverb *ping*, which describes a sudden change from light to darkness, to describe the speed with which nightfall seems to happen when one is unprepared for it. Together, the sound-symbolic renderings of the bird's cry and the darkening sky communicate a feeling of panic, which is further enhanced by the narrator's description of the speed with which she ran each time she heard the bird.

59. Ñuka kal^{y}pa-shka-l^{y}a shamu-ra-ni, ña tutaya-w-sha ñambi-manda, chagra
I run-PERF-LIM come-PAST-1 then night-DUR-COR path-from field
ñambi-manda.
path-from

"I came just running from the path, the *chagra* path, then when it was nightening"

60. Tamya tuta—
rain night

"A rainy night—"

61. kasna tamya pundzha.
like this rain day

"on a rainy day like this."

62. Mana ñukanchi indi-ta acerta-k-chu a-nchi al^{y}ma-w-sha o tarpu-sha.
NEG we sun-ACC ascertain-AG-NEG be-1PL weed-DUR-COR or plant-COR

"We can't be sure of where the sun is, when we're weeding or planting."

63. Mana al^{y}ma-k-chu a-nchi.
NEG weed-AG-NEG be-1PL

"But we don't weed if it's a rainy day like this."

64. Peru kasna tamya pundzha
but like this rain day

"If it's a rainy day like this,"

65. tarpu-k ma-nchi tola-sha.
plant-AG be-1PL dig-COR

"we plant, making holes in the ground."

66. Arroz-ta tarpu-nchi dinu-ga lomo kaspi dinu-ga kay palanda mal^{y}ki,
rice-ACC plant-1PL otherwise-TOP manioc stick or-TOP this plaintain shoot

"We plant rice or manioc cuttings or plaintain shoots,"

67. o papachina papa, lomo kaspi, barbasco, tarpu-nchi ñukanchi.
or taro potato manioc stick barbasco plant-1PL we

or taro root, potato, manioc cuttings, *barbasco*, we plant."

68. Al^{y}mana-ta mana al^{y}ma-nchi-chu ñukanchi kasna tamya-y.
weed-ACC NEG weed-1PL-NEG we like this rain-LOC

"Weeding we won't do, in rain like this."

69. Chi-ga ñukanchi tarpuu tukuchinagama, ña ura-ta ku-n: dzhaas dzhaas
that-TOP we plant-DUR finish-until then hour-ACC give-3
dzhaas dzhaas.

"So then when we're finishing up the planting, it tells us the time: *dzhaas dzhaas dzhaas dzhaas.*"

Q: Ima-ta dzhaas dzhaas?
what-INT

"What is *dzhaas dzhaas*?"

70. Dzhuluy, kan-wan-ta riku-ra-nchi chi?
dzhuluy you-INST-INT look-PAST-1PL that

"The *dzhuluy* bird, was it with you we saw that one?"

71. Chi-ta-ta mana acerta-w-ra-ngi?
that-ACC-INT NEG ascertain-DUR-PAST-2

"Didn't you notice that then?"

Q: Um um; chasna kanta-n?
um hm like that sing-3

"Yes, is that how it sings?"

72. Ah ow chasna kanta-w-n; ura-ta ku-n ña las seis.
ah hah like that sing-DUR-3 hour-ACC give-3 now six o'clock

"Ah hah, that's how it sings, giving the time at six o'clock."

Q: A las seis chasna kanta-n?
at six o'clock like that sing-3

"At six that's how it sings?"

73. Nda a las seis-mi chasna chi dzhaas dzhaas dzhaas.
yes at six o'clock-EV like that that

"Yes, at six that's how it goes: *dzhaas dzhaas dzhaas.*"

74. Ña ura
now hour

"Then at that time,"

75. chay-ma tola-ta shita-sha (claps hands),
there-DAT stick-ACC throw-COR

"throwing the digging stick down over there,"

76. chay uras-mi kal^{y}pa-shka-l^{y}a wasi-ta rina a-n ña.
that hour-EV run-PERF-LIM house-ACC go be-3 now

"right then one has to go homeward, just running."

77. Ña wasi-ta wasi-ta ri-shun ni-sha ña ñukanchi shuk purun-bi
now home-ADV home-ADV go-1IMP want-COR now we one weedy patch-LOC
ayta-wan pariul kuti-l^{y}ata dzhaas dzhaas dzhaas.
step-INST equal again-ADV

"Then thinking let's go home, home, and right when we step into that weedy patch, again it goes *dzhaas dzhaas dzhaas*."

78. ña p$^{in^{g}}$ tutaya-w-nga.
now night-DUR-3FUT

"Then *p$^{in^{g}}$* it will be nightening."

79. Kal^{y}pa-shka-l^{y}a kal^{y}pa-shka-l^{y}a.
run-PERF-LIM run-PERF-LIM

"Just running just running."

80. Ña—
then

"Then—"

81. ñambi-ma l^{y}ukshi-gri-nchi, hatun ñambi-ma, ña wasi-ma paktana-wan
path-DAT emerge-TRNSL-1PL big path-DAT then home-DAT arrive-INST

"we go and emerge onto the path, the big path, and when we arrive home"

82. chi kuti-l^{y}ata dzhaas dzhaas dzhaas.
that again-ADV

"that one again says *dzhaas dzhaas dzhaas*."

83. p$^{in^{g}}$ tutaya-w-nga.
night-DUR-3FUT

"And *p$^{in^{g}}$* it will be nightening."

84. Chi kal^{y}pa-shka-l^{y}a rina a-k a-n, chasna-guna tuku-shpa.
that run-PERF-LIM go be-AG be-3 like that-PL become-COR

"And that's how, just running one has to go, when things like that are happening."

The sound-symbolic descriptions of the bird's cry and the darkening sky contribute to the narrator's sense of panic. Each time she uses these sound-symbolic utterances, she immediately follows with a description of her frantic running race with darkness. Overall, the narrative has a nightmare-like feel. It suggests a nightmare about something very important that one has forgotten to do. She's forgotten about the passage of time, because the rain clouds have hidden the sun.

Sherzer (1990: 91) noted that sound imagery contributed to the humorous narratives related by the Kuna. Moreover, he emphasized the dynamic interplay between the humorous and the poetic, stating that many of the devices used for humorous and playful effect, such as quoted dialogues, sound imagery, and exaggerated descriptions, overlap with artful, poetic techniques. Sound imagery is also used by the Pastaza Quechua for humorous effect. The following order was given to me in a playful way, by using the sound-symbolic adverb *mutsi*, which describes the sound and also the chewing movement of a *tsawata* "tortoise" as it eats papaya. Tortoises are often discovered in one's agricultural field at the base of a papaya tree busily chomping away at ripe papayas that have fallen. The woman who said the following to me had just given me a plate full of ripe papayas. She and the others present laughed good naturedly at her comparison between myself and the tortoise.

85. Mutsi mutsi miku-ngi Janet tsawata shina.
mutsi mutsi eat-2 Janet tortoise like
"Eat these *mutsi mutsi,* Janet, like a tortoise."

Another example of sound symbolism's playful function is evident in the following examples, where my friends teased me for falling by imitating the sound made by that falling. The conditions for falling couldn't have been more congenial: it was dark, and the ground was uneven and full of ruts. Nevertheless, I was reminded of this incident, complete with its sound-symbolic effects, more often than I would have liked during the course of my fieldwork. The adolescent girl who first noticed it described it as follows with sound-symbolic *p^{h}uxxx* describing my resultant collision with the ground.

86. Sarun agosto hista-y bulsa ruku-ndi p^{h}uxxx urma-sha may-ta-shi kal^{y}pa-k
other august festival-LOC bag big-INCL fall-COR where-ADV-EV runAG
ma-ra.
be-PAST
"During last August's festival, after falling *p^{h}uxxx* with her big bag and all, where did she then run off to?"

Another reference to this event was made by a woman who asked me upon my arrival at her house if I had fallen on the way. This description of that event used *pit^{h}ixxx,* which gestured my falling into an initial falling motion, *pi-* and a resultant collision with the ground, *-t^{h}ixxx.*

87. Mana sarun shina pit^{h}ixxx urma-ra-ngi?
NEG other like fall-PAST-2
"You didn't like last time fall *pit^{h}ixxx*?"

My friends' constant and unwelcome reminders of this incident can be explained as their attempts to enculturate me by teaching me the importance of strength, control, and fitness. Over the course of my fieldwork I was reminded time and time again of the importance of being in control of one's physical self, of not losing one's composure, and of being strong and capable. All of these positive qualities are represented in the verb *shayana* "to stand." The following short excerpt from a lowland Quechua song reveals this ideal.

> Whatever anybody wants,
> my desire is to keep on standing up
> in every type of work. (recorded by Harrison 1989: 139)

In teasing me over and over again for falling, my friends were softening what was intended as a reprimand for appearing weak, incapable, and clumsy. The softening of this reprimand was achieved with the use of sound symbolism, which gave their scolding a less harsh, teasing, and playful mood.

Identification

Sound symbolism is a particularly important device for communicating about Quechua peoples' daily experiences of birds. Feld (1982) has written extensively on the significance of birds' songs and sounds for the Kaluli of Papua New Guinea. The Kaluli, he states, "categorize and think about routine experiences of birds most often and most thoroughly in terms of the sounds they hear in the forest and at the village edges" (71). For the Pastaza Quechua as well, birds' sounds are of primary importance for their routine encounters with them. As is true for the Kaluli, the Quechua are far more likely to first identify a bird by its sound, while its physical features will be much less discussed. In the following example, a friend questions my knowledge of the *munditi*, a type of hawk, by asking me if I know its sound.

88. Munditi kanta-y uras hm$^{hm^{hm}}$ kanta-k-ta uya-ra-ngi-chu?
munditi sing-NOM time sing-AG-ACC hear-PAST-2-INT
"Have you heard, when the *munditi* sings, how it goes *hm*$^{hm^{hm}}$?"

The importance of birds' sounds is also evident by their nomenclature. Many birds' names are lexicalizations of the sounds they are said to make. The following are just a few of the statements made about birds whose names are based on their cries. The *shangwali* hawk:

89. Shang shang shang kapari-u-n.
shout-DUR-3
"*Shang shang shang* it shouts."

The *chukchukia*, a perching bird:

90. Chukchukiyaaaa kanta-k ma-n.
sing-AG be-3
"It sings *chukchukiyaaaa*."

The *dundu*, a perching bird:

91. Dun dun dun kanta-k ma-n; l^{y}akil^{y}a kanta-k ma-n.
    sing-AG be-3 sadly sing-AG be-3
    "*Dun dun dun* it sings; sadly it sings."

The *wishil^{y}a,* a perching bird:

92. Wishil^{y}a wishil^{y}a kanta-k, rigra-ta kushpari-sha, kushi-ya-n pay.
    sing-AG wing-ACC shake-COR happy-INCH-3 he
    "*Wishil^{y}a wishil^{y}a* it sings, flapping its wings, becoming happy, that one."

The *shishili,* a perching bird:

93. Shilishili tamya-shka-y uyari-k ma-n.
    rain-PERF-NOM sound-AG be-3
    "It is heard going *shilishili* when it rains."

The *titi*, a perching bird:

94. Ti ti ti ti kanta-k ma-n.
    sing-AG be-3
    "It sings *ti ti ti ti*."

In addition to their identificational function, lexicalized sounds made by birds also communicate limited kinds of messages. The *chikwan,* for example, is a small, brown perching bird. I first became aware of it one day while walking with a friend in her agricultural field. My friend interrupted what I was saying to call my attention to this bird's chirping. She told me, teasingly, that since the bird was saying "*chi chi chi chi chi*," she could believe what I was telling her. If instead the bird had said "*chikwan chikwan*" while I was speaking, then my words couldn't be trusted.

The significance of birds' songs and sounds for the Pastaza Quechua is complex. Their importance can be understood by considering the role of sound in Pastaza Quechua cosmology. In general, sound in the form of song is integral to many kinds of magical practices. Shamans must learn to *takina* "to sing for magical purposes" as part of their apprenticeship; for it is through songs that they bring about whatever changes are sought. The songs are structured as invocations to spirits who are told what to do for a patient. One curing session, for example, was conducted for the purpose of uniting an estranged husband and wife. The shaman's song directly addressed a number of spirits of the forest, including a vine woman, a sap woman, and a smoke woman. Each of these deities, through its own natural powers, was expected to bring the husband and wife back together again: the vine woman by wrapping herself around them; the sap woman by causing them to stick together; and the smoke woman by wafting herself in and out of their nostrils, causing them to be contagiously attracted to each other.

Sound, then, is a mediating force between the world of humans and that of spirits. Through their sounds, birds frequently act as mediating agents between these worlds.[1] One myth relates how a deceased man's spirit took the form of a *witi rusa* bird who visited his widow, crying sadly to her while she worked. The connection between birds and spirits is also evident by the occasional confusion on the part of Quechua speakers, between sounds made by birds and sounds made by forest spirits or *supays*. The following is a representation of a conversation that took place between a father and daughter who were spending the night in the forest. It illustrates the daughter's confusion about an unfamiliar sound, which she assumed to be a type of hummingbird. Realizing that it wasn't a hummingbird, however, the father immediately began blowing smoke from his cigarette in the direction of the sound, a gesture that indicated his fear of a malevolent forest spirit.

95. Siri-sha uya-kpi hiiiiiiiiiiiiiiiiiiiiiiiiiiiiiiiiiiiiiiiiiiiiiiiiiiiiiiiiiiiiii-mi silba-shka shina.
lie-COR hear-SWRF -EV whistle-PERF like
"Lying there I heard *hiiiiiiiiiiiiiiiiiiiiiiiiiiiiiiiiiiiiiiiiiiiiiiiiiiiiiiiiiiiii,* as if someone whistled.

96. Yaya uya-y! L^yawsa kindi-ta ni-ni-mi ñuka!
father listen-IMP saliva hummingbird-ACC say-1-EV I
"'Father listen! It's the Saliva hummingbird,' I said."

97. Mana mama-ku! Ima chari?
NEG mother-DIM what perhaps
"No little daughter; what could it be?"

98. Mana samay-bas pitirik-chu silba-n uya-ngi-chu? ni-wa-ra.
NEG breath-INCL cut-NEG whistle-3 hear-2-NEG say-ACC-PAST
"Not running out of breath it whistles, do you hear?' he said to me."[2] . . .

99. Mandzhari-ra yaya, tobako-wan puka puka ra-sha shaya-w-ra.
be afraid-PAST father tobacco-INST blow blow do-COR stand-DUR-PAST
"Father stood there, afraid, blowing blowing with his tobacco."

Epistemic

For the Pastaza Quechua, the use of sound symbolism for identification links up with greater cosmological matters involving the cultural and natural world, and a theory of causation which links these domains. Sound-symbolic utterances articulate Quechua cultural constructions of the natural world and thereby mediate between perception, bodily experience, and nature. Sound-symbolic language provides them with one way of achieving a sense of management of the natural world. Their use of sound symbolism is an attempt to use bodily movements to imitate their own ideals of what is natural and what is not. The movements of the mouth, the shaping of the vocal tract, and the fluctuating pitch of the voice are all uses of the body to imitate movements and processes of perceptual experience. By imitating these movements and processes, they achieve a sense of control over them. In this way, sound-symbolic language becomes a physiological force integrated with the natural and cosmological world, rather than an abstract, detached code of signification. The preceding example concerning the confusion between a bird's cry and a spirit's sound illustrates how important one's physiological capacities are for understanding nature. The assessment of this sound uses the body as a model for what is unusual. The sound is too continuous, according to the narrator's father, to be any kind of natural life form. Everything that sounds has to run out of breath. Further examples that support these claims about the interconnections between sound symbolism, nature, and one's bodily capacities and perceptual experiences come from narratives of personal experience. In many of these narratives, sound-symbolically described impressions are considered to index a life-changing event, often involving something tragic, such as death or illness, or something inexplicable. In such narratives, the quality of a sound or other sensory impression rendered with sound becomes part of peoples' constructions of what went wrong. These stories are important because they reveal a Quechua sense of what is unnatural or unusual, which is based on their own bodily capacities and perceptual experiences.

Some narratives were catalyzed when questions about sound symbolism triggered an account of a personal experience for the purpose of exemplifying a sound-symbolic word. For example, I once asked, "How does one come, going *talang talang*?" A friend was immediately reminded of the sound of a blowgun and dart quiver knocking against each other as a hunter comes home empty-handed, without any meat to feed his family. And this association triggered a specific, rather extended narrative about the breakup of an uncle and aunt's marriage. The marriage ended, as it happened, because her uncle was giving away all of the meat he had caught to another woman before returning home empty-handed to his wife and children. It was the hollow sound of his blowgun and dart quiver knocking *talang talang* against each other which indicated to his wife even before she saw him that there was no meat draped over his shoulders. The perception that this sound was somehow not right, then, provided the man's wife with an excuse for following her husband and discovering him with his lover. And it was this sound that remained vivid in her memory because it had aroused her initial suspicions of her husband's infidelity.

In the following narrative exerpt, sound-symbolically rendered impressions form part of an explanatory framework that accounts for a vengeance raid conducted by a small band of Achuar. This vengeance raid resulted in the assassination of a Quechua shaman whose descendants I knew well. The Achuar, who are linguistically unrelated to the Quechua, believe that most of their deaths are homicides caused by physical violence, sorcery, or avenging souls of the dead. When a death is attributed to sorcery, Quechua shamans are typically blamed, and physical retaliation in the form of a vengeance raid against that shaman is often undertaken. For the purposes of my argument, the following account is interesting because a bird's chirping, along with other sound-symbolically described occurrences, are said to signal the vengeance raid. Tragically, the shaman refuses to acknowledge the conjunction of signs. The bird whose warning was ignored is the *chikwan,* which was briefly discussed in the previous section on sound-symbolic identification. I discovered from this narrative that its chirping not only indicates the truth value of someone's utterance but also portends something ominous. In this context there's a quality about the *chikwan*'s chirping that doesn't accord with peoples' typical perceptual construct of birds, and for this reason it becomes ominous in this context. What is unnatural is its incessancy. It's described with a much longer and intonationally elaborate set of repetitions than other birds' cries. This bird's cry, and other natural and atmospheric signals as well, are said to act in concert, so that the death of the man is seen as a sort of cosmological conspiracy. The narrative begins with the shaman's wife's recreation of her first suspicions triggered by the *chikwan*'s chirping.

100. Chi-ga ña yapa-shi chikwan rima-n ni-ra mik^{y}a Lola: chi chi chi chi chi chi
so-TOP now a lot-EV chikwan speak-3 say-3PAST aunt Lola
chikwan! Ruya hawa-manda ni-u-sha-mi ni-sha-shi ni-n; lomo rama-y
chikwan tree high-from say-DUR-COR-EV say-COR-EV say-3 manioc branch-LOC
tiyari-k shamu-n ni-ra chi chi chi chi chi chi
sit-AG come-3 say-3-PAST

"Well, now, the *chikwan* bird is speaking a lot,' said aunt Lola: '*chi chi chi chi chi chi* *chikwan*. Speaking from the top of a tree, it is saying this,' she says; 'then on a manioc branch it comes to sit saying *chi chi chi chi chi chi*.'"

101. Ña rima-nga-shi ra-w-ra runa, ima a-sha pobre chikwan-ga.
now tell-3FUT-EV do-DUR-3PAST person what be-COR poor chikwan-TOP

"Now it was going to tell about a person, a poor soul, the *chikwan* bird was."

102. Chi-shi ni-ra ima pi-ta runa-chu wañu-chiun shamu-nga ra-u-n? Ima
that-EV say-PAST what who-QN person-QN kill-SUB come-FUTINF do-DUR-3
nasha-ta kasna chikwan rima-n? ni-ra-shi.
why-INT like that chikwan speak-3 say-PAST-EV

"So she wondered 'what or who is it? Will someone come to kill somebody? Why does the *chikwan* speak like that?' she wondered."

In the next example, the shaman's wife decides that the bird is warning them and says as much to her husband by repeating the bird's chirping.

103. Kan-da-cha chi chi chi chi chi chi chi chi chi -shi ni-n ni-ra.
you-ACC-EV -EV say-3 say-PAST

"'It's to you, maybe, that it says *chi chi chi chi chi chi chi chi chi*, she said."

What makes this chirping incessant is its deviation from descriptions of typical bird cries, which are only repeated twice. The chikwan, by contrast, is always described with at least five repetitions, and sometimes as many as twelve. The longer duration of this bird's chirping is unnatural because only humans speak utterances with extended duration. The longer duration of this bird's chirping therefore suggests an urgent message.

In the next example, the narrator describes what her mother and father, who had been visiting, had observed right before leaving the scene of the assassination. They report seeing a human-like shadow that seemed to cause ripe fruit to fall from a tree and they relate the sound of the fruit's falling. This very unusual falling of the fruit from a tree, and the human-like shadow were yet more evidence that something ominous was looming.

104. Ñuka mama, ñuka yaya ri-naw-ra.
my mother my father go-3PL-PAST
"My mother and father left."

105. Riku-l^{y}ayta-shi puku-shka ruya-ga runa shina-shi yana-n shayari-n ni-naw.
look-ADV-EV ripen-PERF tree-TOP person like-EV black-ADV stand-3 say-3PL-PAST
"While they looked right over there something like a person's black shadow was standing by a ripened tree."

106. Yana-n shayari-sha putu putu putu putu-shi puku-shka-ta urmachi-n ni-ra.
black-ADV stand-COR -EV ripen-PERF-ACC make fall-3 say-PAST
"'The black shadow standing there made the ripened fruit fall *putu putu putu putu*,' said aunt Lola."

Then in the next example even more configurations of signs using sound-symbolic impressions are described.

107. Rupa-y tamya s^{h}ayyyyyyyyyy tutututu s^{h}ayyyyyyyyyy paho-ta ra-ra riku-ngi-ma.
burn rain danger-ACC make-PAST look-2-CNDL
"And you would have seen how a burning rain *s^{h}ayyyyyyyyyy tutututu s^{h}ayyyyyyyyyy* made danger."

A "burning rain" is a brief downpour that takes place while the sun is shining. The sound-symbolic *s^{h}ayyyyyyyyyy* describes the sheeting-like quality of the rainfall, and the repetitions of *tutututu* describe the droplet-like quality of its falling. In general, any rain that falls on a sunny day and the rainbows that accompany it are believed to index a state of danger.

The bird's chirping, the falling of the ripe fruit from the tree, and the "burning rain" are all considered experientially unusual from a Quechua point of view. Together, these signals conspire to seal the shaman's fate with the inexorability of a scientific law. His death is described not as a tragic accident that could have been avoided, but as an inevitable outcome of what was clearly indexed by sound-symbolic impressions. Even the shaman's refusal to listen to the warning signs is attributed to sounds. This refusal was explained by suggesting that the Achuar were able to bewitch their intended victim, making him powerless to escape, by singing to him from a distance.

One final example from a narrative of personal experience reveals the role of sound-symbolic impressions in evaluating the meaning of one's perceptions. This narrative describes how months of work on a dugout canoe were rendered useless when the just finished canoe began to split apart. To appreciate the significance of this dramatic event, it is necessary to understand the connections between canoes and analogical tropes of death. Whitten (1976: 39) found that death is often figured as a journey to an underwater underworld.[3] This underworld is considered accessible through a river's whirlpools, which then lead to underworld rivers. Because canoes transport one to these underworld rivers, they are part of burial practice symbolism. A corpse is buried in a container which is symbolically conceived as a canoe (138). Under ordinary circumstances, of course, canoes are an essential part of daily life for those who live along the river. However, when a canoe "behaves" in such an unnatural way, its death symbolism becomes foregrounded in peoples' minds. The man who had been carving this canoe interpreted its splitting as an ominous index of his own death, which in fact took place about three months after this event. The narrative begins with a description of the uncle's final day of work on the canoe. The narrator's recollections of that day begin with the sounds of her uncle's tool as it repeatedly hits the canoe's surface.

108. Ñuka hachi-mi kanoa-w-ra haaatun kanoa-ta.
I uncle-EV make canoe-DUR-PAST biiig canoe-ACC
"My uncle he was making a canoe, a biiiiig one!"

109. Kanoa-w-ra pay kimsa kil^{y}ata-ta taraba-ra.
make canoe-DUR-PAST he three month-ACC work-PAST
"He made that canoe, working on it for three months."

110. Chi-mi ñuka-ga—
that-EV I-TOP
"So then I, um—"

111. Pay taw taw taw taw taw taw taw taw asiol^{y}a-n al^{y}a-w-kpi.
he planer-INST dig-DUR-SWRF
"He was digging with the planer *taw taw taw taw taw taw taw taw*."

She then describes how she prepared *aswa* to bring to her uncle who was too busy to come and drink it.

112. 'Aswa-ta upi-k shamu-y' ni-kpi
aswa-ACC drink-AG come-IMP say-SWRF
"And when I said 'Come and drink *aswa*,'"

113. 'kayl^{y}a-ta tukuchi-u-ni' ushushi ni-wa-n.
this-LIM-ACC finish-DUR-1 daughter say-1ACC-3

"he said to me, "I'm just finishing up this little bit, daughter.'"

114. Chi-ga upichi-gri-sha-l^{y}a ni-sha shungu yuyari-sha ñuka—
that-TOP give drink-TRNSL-1FUT-LIM say-COR heart think-COR I

"And so thinking to myself 'I'll just go and give him to drink'—"

115. aswa-ta al^{y}i al^{y}i ra-sha
aswa-ACC good good do-COR

"preparing preparing the *aswa* well,"

116. yaku-ta apa-sha, yaku, chi-ta apa-sha—
water-ACC take-COR water that-ACC take-COR

"bringing water, bringing that water—"

117. mangay l^{y}api l^{y}api ra-sha—
pot-LOC squeeze squeeze do-COR

"squeezing squeezing the *aswa* in the pot—"

118. hachi-ta upichi-gri-ni yaku pirtu-y ri-sha.
uncle-ACC give drink-TRNSL-1 water shore-LOC go-COR

"heading for the water's shore, I go and give my uncle something to drink."

When she arrives at her uncle's side, he alerts her to the beginning of the splitting, which he says he can hear. The narrator describes the visible crack at the rear of the canoe resulting from the splitting, with the sound-symbolic *shaka*, which describes a sound and an image of a lengthwise tearing.

119. Chi-mi upichi-u-shka-y—
that-EV give drink-DUR-PERF-NOM

"So then, having given him something to drink—"

120. 'Mama-ku, yanga chari ra-w-ni ña, yanga chari, kasna tarabos-ta
mother-DIM uselessly perhaps do-DUR-1 now uselessly perhaps like this laborious-ADV
pasa-w-ni' ni-wa-ra.
pass-DUR-1 say-1ACC-PAST

"'Uselessly, perhaps, I'm doing this, little daughter; uselessly perhaps I'm laboring away' he said to me."

121. 'Chiga?' ni-ra-ni.
that-EV say-PAST-1

"'What do you mean?' I said."

122. 'Uya-y! Uyari-kta-n partiri-u-n' ni-wa-ra.
listen-IMP hear-ADV-INST split-DUR-3 say-1ACC-PAST

"'Listen! It's splitting enough to be heard,' he told me."

123. 'May?'
where
"Where?"

124. Uya-kpi, kasna siki-ga kasna shak^{aa} wawa ma-ra riki.
listen-SWRF like this rear-TOP like this baby was-PAST look-IMP
"Upon listening, um, the rear was a little *shak*^{aa}, you see."

125. Kay-l^{y}a wawa-shi siki-ybi.
here-LIM baby-EV rear-LOC
"Just a little bit of a split there at the rear."

126. Ña pay siki mana-chu siki parti riku-ra-ngi-chu kanoa siki-ta?
now it rear no-NEG rear part see-PAST-2-NEG canoe rear-ACC
"Now it was at the rear, you've seen, haven't you, the canoe's rear?"

127. Chi.
that
"That's where it was."

128. Ña chi-manda chi intiru-ta.
now there-from that entire-ACC
"Then from there the entire thing."

She tries to persuade her uncle to repair the split. He doesn't heed her advice, and the splitting progresses. Her description includes the sound image of its splitting, *t^{h}as*, and the resultant visual image, *shaka*. With the progression of the splitting her uncle expresses his apprehensions about its significance. These apprehensions are affirmed by the narrator's own metanarrative comments.

129. 'Mana hachi!' ni-ni. 'Chi kuskay kilaba-y!' ni-ni.
No uncle say-1 that straight nail-IMP say-1
"'No, uncle!' I say. 'Nail it back together,' I tell him."

130. 'Shuk shuk shuk kaspi-wan, tawla, pala-wan' ni-ra-ni.
a a a stick-INST pole board-INST say-PAST-1
"'With a—a—a—stick, a pole, or with a board,' I said."

131. Mana uya-wa-ra-chu.
NEG listen-1ACC-PAST-NEG
"He didn't listen to me."

132. Chi-ga ña t^{h}asssss uyari-shka-n-ga sha^{ka} chi intiru-ta ri-u-n.
that-TOP then sound-PERF-INCL-TOP that entire-ACC go-DUR-3
"So then having sounded *t^{h}asssss,* it goes *sha*^{ka} an entire section."

133. Kuti t^{h}asssss uyari-shka-n-ga ña chi sha^{ka}.
again sound-PERF-INCL-TOP then that
"Again sounding *t^{h}asssss,* then another section *sha*^{ka}."

134. Ña chasna uyari-u-sha.
now like that sound-DUR-COR
"Now like that it sounds."

135. Chi-ga 'yanu-shka-ta miku-k shamu-y.'
that-TOP cook-PERF-ACC eat-AG come-IMP
"And so then I said, 'Come and eat the cooked food.'"

136. Kay-ma riku-wa-ychi ñuka kanoa tapia-n ni-ra
here-DAT look-1ACC-PLIMP I canoe portend-3 say-PAST
"And he said, 'Look here, all of you; my canoe portends.'"

137. Tapia-sha-shi chasna tuku a-k a-shka ñuka hachi wañuna a-kpi.
portend-COR-EV like that become be-AG be-PERF I uncle die be-SWRF
"Portending it had become like that, as my uncle was to die."

138. Wañuna-y kanoa a-w-ra rik-i!
die-NOM canoe be-DUR-PAST look-IMP
"It was a death canoe, you see."

The canoe's splitting took place over the course of an afternoon. Condensing her description of its splitting by means of sound-symbolic adverbs, the narrator presents the splitting as a speeded-up, continuous, time-lapsed event by performatively simulating its component images. The adverb *shaka* is given its most performatively lengthened articulation in the next example, to describe how the splitting traveled the entire length of the canoe.

139. Ña punda-ma shaka$^{a^{aa}}$."
now point-DAT
"Then from that point it went splitting *shaka*$^{a^{aa}}$."

In the next line, sound-symbolic *awing* communicates the image of the gaping openness resulting from the completed lengthwise split. Then the compound consisting of sound-symbolic *tas* and *kal^{y}a* focuses on the depth dimension of the fissure. By contrast with *awing,* which communicates an idea of a lengthwise splitting, *kal^{y}a* focuses on a fissure that penetrates along a vertical axis. The narrator is in effect saying that the splitting apart of the canoe was not only along its entire length, but it was along its vertical dimension, and therefore deep as well.

140. Awing ña tas ka^{lya}.
now
"Then gaping open *awing,* it completely fissured *ka*^{lya}."

With the horizontal and vertical sundering of the canoe, its two component parts simply fell to the ground, as is described below.

141. Ña chay-ma chay-ma kanoa urma-ra rik-i!
then there-DAT there-DAT canoe fall-PAST look-IMP
"And there and there the canoe halves fell, look!"

142. Paktachi-shka kanoa!
finish-PERF canoe
"A finished canoe!"

143. Ñuka mik^{y}a waka-ra.
I aunt cry-PAST
"My aunt just cried."

144. Tarabos-ta chusku mingay-ta ra-sha aysachi-ra-ni' ni-ra.
laborious-ADV four minga-ACC do-COR make pull-PAST-1 say-PAST
"'Laboriously, over four *minga*s, I had it dragged,' he said."

145. Chusku minga-ybi-mi aysana-w-ra puhal-manda chi kanoa-ta.
four minga-LOC-EV pull-DUR-PAST trunk-from that canoe
"They pulled that canoe while still a tree trunk, over four *minga*s."

This narrative is a particularly eloquent testament to the significance of sound-symbolically rendered experience. It opens with the sound of the uncle's repetitive pounding as he finished carving his canoe. The canoe's initial splitting is said to have been auditorily evident. The splitting itself, which happened slowly, over the course of an afternoon, is condensed into a vivid, time-lapsed, sound-symbolic series of images. Finally, the narrator's perception of the event as a whole is causally linked with her uncle's own death three months later.

For Puka yakuans, sound-symbolic style is a modality for representing what is significant about experience. Sound-symbolic utterances are integral to their articulations of the order of things. They are crucially important for organizing their memories, for articulating their understanding of natural and unnatural processes, for identifying their perceptions, and for communicating about their experiences. The formal linguistic conception of language as an abstract code disconnected from the material world and from the body of the speaker is inadequate for the lowland Quechua. Sound-symbolically rendered impressions are felt, sensed, and embodied. When they formally amplify a sound-symbolic impression with performative foregrounding, Quechua speakers use the body to intensify their participation in the perceptual processes they simulate. The body becomes a resonance chamber for the sounds, rhythms, and processes of the natural world.

Nonlinguistic evidence attesting to the interrelatedness of sound, the body, and nature is evident in figure 6-1, a poster that was conceived and painted by two men from a village near Puka yaku. This poster announces an annual meeting of the Organización de Pueblos Indigenas de Pastaza, also known as OPIP. The central concern of this organization is the conservation and protection of indigenous lands from multinational business interests, particularly oil companies. Its poster proclaims indigenous rights to the land by means of verbal slogans and a dramatic visual representation. One of the artists explained this image to me by drawing out the connections between the man

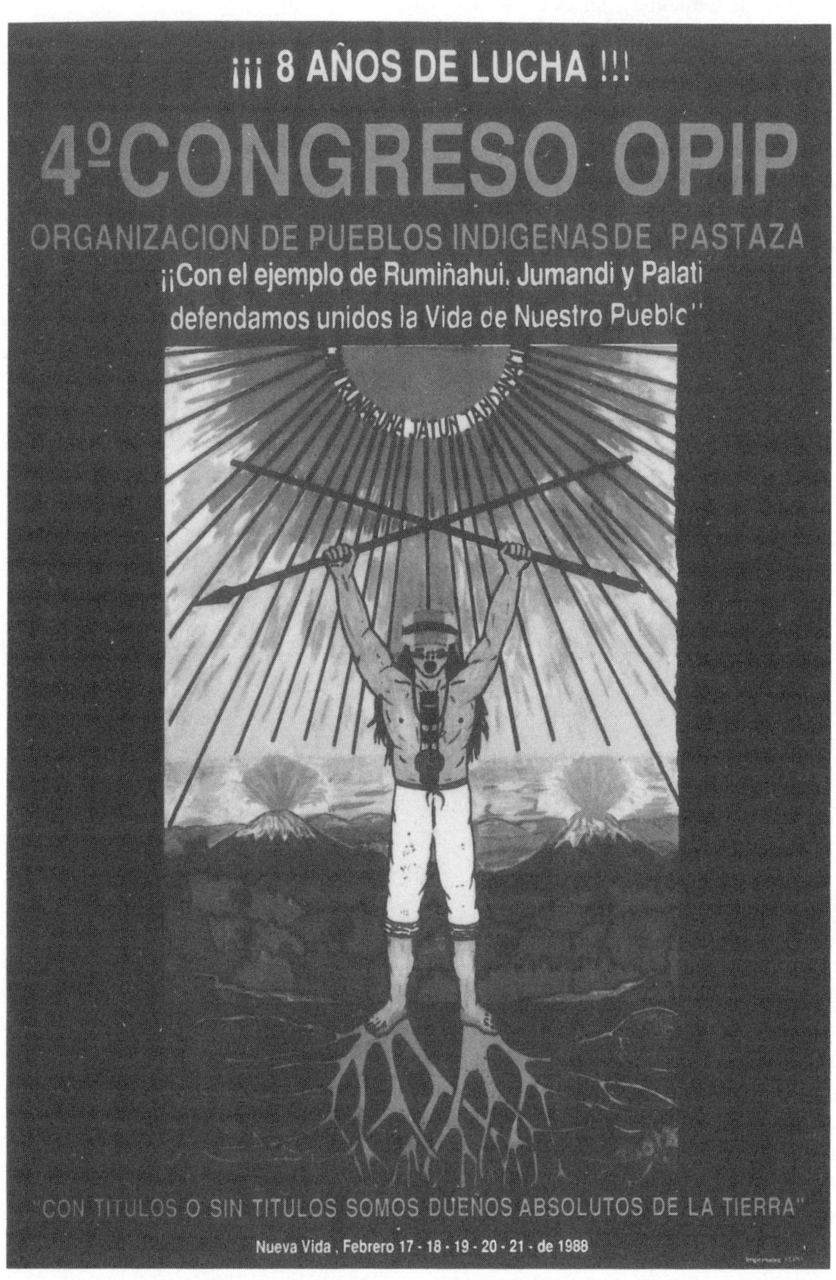

Figure 6-1 Poster proclaiming indigenous rights to the land and announcing a meeting of the Organización de Pueblos Indígenas de Pastaza.

and the earth. The openness of the man's posture, especially his outstretched arms, bespeaks an alignment of unity with the natural world. His legs are also slightly open and his body is metaphorically tree-like, his feet rooted into the ground, anchored into the earth. The man and the earth are further united by their shared anger. The earth's anger is indicated by the volcanoes erupting in the background and also by the blazing red sun. The man's anger is evident in his defiant, war-like demeanor. His arms are raised up, ready for battle with spear and blowgun. The man's open mouth allows an angry cry to reverberate through his body and out into the world, thereby providing a definitive link between sound, the body, and the natural world.

Summary: Comparative Observations

This chapter has analyzed the multiple uses of sound-symbolic style, not to emphasize the distinctiveness of each of its functions. The poetic, referential, modal, instructional, inferential, metalingual, identificational, and epistemic functions of sound symbolism crosscut, overlap, and mutually ramify with each other. Other functions have not been discussed. One which is not yet well understood is the use of sound symbolism in reported speech. Do such usages directly quote another person's discourse, do they communicate the "gist" of what was said, or do they re-present another's voice in the speaker's own way? The unrestrictedness of its use and the performative energy invested in its articulation suggest that sound symbolism is a modality for representing what is significant about Pastaza Quechua experience. Language use is modeled on sounds, patterns, movements, and rhythms of the natural world and of one's bodily experiences in it. Linguistic sound symbolism represents the material qualities of the natural sensible world, and thereby articulates Quechua peoples' cultural constructions of it. Preliminary comparative observations suggest that the stylistic markedness of sound symbolism is sensitive to subtle shifts in cultural values during formative moments of transformation. Literacy in conjunction with social, political, and economic change is affecting sound-symbolic style in eastern Amazonian Ecuador.

Because sound symbolism is most effectively used in face-to-face communication, it has been associated with oral traditions and styles of expression (Diffloth 1972). Literacy, which removes language from the body of the speaker, is at odds with the essentially discursive design of sound-symbolic language and presents other problems as well for the conceptual orientations of sound-symbolic language users. With literacy comes the disembodied word, detached and transcendent truths, concepts of doctrine, codification, and systematization (Goody 1977, Gellner 1988). Preliminary comparison between Puka yaku and another village, Sara yaku, reveals that literacy is connected with the transformation and reinterpretation of sound-symbolic style. Literacy, along with social, political, and economic change, is transforming the nature of Sara yakuans' everyday life and creating experiential frameworks that are cognitively dissonant with sound-symbolic discourse.

The two villages, Sara yaku and Puka yaku, present striking contrasts and similarities. Both are situated along the Bobonaza River, in eastern Amazonian Ecuador, about a day's journey from each other by dugout canoe. Both are relatively isolated and unreachable by roads. And in both villages people practice subsistence-based slash-and-burn horticulture in addition to hunting and fishing. In many other respects, however, they are strikingly different. Sara yakuans are relatively more involved with literate forms of communication than Puka yakuans. Although Sara yaku, like Puka yaku, is geographically isolated, it is the home village for many leaders and officials of a national level indigenous organization. All of these leaders and officials have received formal education, many in universities in Quito, and all speak Spanish besides their native Quechua. Because Sara yaku is home for many of these leaders, it is also an unofficial hub for the organization's activities. As such, it has a small airstrip to accommodate the organization's fleet of single-engine Cessnas which are in constant use by officials traveling to meetings. Organization officials are extremely active in articulating the village's attitudinal alignment with forces of modernization. Their main concern is to affirm and conserve their own traditional values and at the same time select what they want from what modern life has to offer. They have solicited funds for development projects, resulting in the building of several schools in Sara yaku. They have successfully repelled unwanted forms of modernization in the form of international exploration by petroleum companies. The organization's officials have also attempted to implement linguistic change in the form of a *Quichua Unificada* Unified Quechua," which combines lexical and grammatical features from a variety of dialects. Although Quichua Unificada has not been widely accepted in Sara yaku, the attempt to promote its use bespeaks an interest in codification, standardization, and other kinds of literacy-influenced practices.

Consider by contrast, the village of Puka yaku. Eighteen months of fieldwork revealed that the majority of adults do not read or write, nor are they able to converse in Spanish. The children of Puka yaku attend the village's only school sporadically. The villagers are not involved in the organization that is so prominent a presence in Sara yaku. Nor are they overly concerned when forces of modernization threaten to disrupt their land and its resources. When I left Puka yaku in 1988, an oil company was beginning to do exploratory work there. In both villages, then, forces of modernization are effecting change. In Puka yaku people are largely unreflective about these changes. In Sara yaku, however, people are attempting to control the rate and type of changes that occur, even initiating some of their own designs for change, as for example, with their language. In Puka yaku sound symbolism is an important form of expression but will diminish in use as traditional ways of living and thinking are discarded by a community that will become increasingly literate and increasingly connected with the market economy and with modern technological culture. How, then, is sound symbolism used in Sara yaku, where literacy is already relatively established, and yet traditional ways of living and thinking are at the same time affirmed? How do Sara yakuans retain, adapt, or reinterpret the functions of sound-symbolic discourse to accommodate new experiential frameworks?

Preliminary observations suggest that in Sara yaku sound symbolism is becoming functionally restricted and undergoing much less formal amplification. Its functional restriction is evident in two interrelated usages. It has become associated with a complex of features that mark women's speech from men's. And it has become an emblem of authenticity, of something distinctively "Quechua," which has no equivalent in the literate, Spanish-speaking world. As an emblem of authenticity, it is associated with features that distinguish between cultural "insiders" and "outsiders." These observations are based on my sporadic contact with Sara yakuans over the course of my eighteen months of work in Puka yaku. I was acquainted with many Sara yakuans and came to know particularly well one family whom I visited on a regular basis. They are also based on a year's intense work with a man from Sara yaku whom I brought to the United States. In general, Sara yakuans' style of speaking differs from Puka yakuans in its heavy use of Spanish verbs that have been "Quechuafied" with the infinitive suffix. For example: Spanish *saludar* "to greet" becomes Quechua *saludana*; Spanish *conquistar* "to conquer" becomes Quechua *conquistana*, etc. This is particularly true of university-educated Sara yakuans, such as the man I worked with in the United States. Another important difference is that the Sara yakuans I knew used much less sound symbolism than Puka yakuans. Furthermore, when they did use it, it was much less formally amplified by performative foregrounding than Puka yakuans'. At times this difference seemed to indicate a gender contrast. For example, the man I worked with in the United States admitted that the sound-symbolic forms I had analyzed and written about were an important feature of the language. Yet when I used them myself he often laughed, and when I attempted to elicit them from him he often became embarrassed, saying that it was a *warmi tono* or "woman's tone" of speaking.

My friend's dismissal of sound symbolism as a woman's form of speech does not, however, explain all of the complexities of its use by Sara yakuans. A couple of Sara yaku women whom I visited regularly in Ecuador also seemed reluctant to use sound-symbolic forms with me. They were not university educated; however, they had been living in a fairly large town for a couple of years. These woman spoke a much more hispanicized, nonsound-symbolic form of Quechua with me than with members of their community. For them, I suspect, the use of sound symbolism indicated an "insider" status which I did not have. Its use as an emblem of authenticity, as something distinctively Quechua, which has no equivalent in the Spanish-speaking world, is also evident in data from a newsletter that was published by Sara yakuans. This newsletter, entitled *Amanecer Indio* "Indian Dawning," used to appear monthly with reports of indigenous activities, meetings, and conferences. The orientation of this newsletter was ostensibly political. It advocated the rights of indigenous peoples throughout Ecuador to control their own lands without interference from the national government. It also contained political cartoons and features of cultural interest to the indigenous community. For example, the issue published in December 1986 contains a *taki* or shaman's song addressed to the fertility goddess *Nunguli* who is considered the "mother of manioc." This short *taki* has been translated into Spanish with the exception of a couple of sound-symbolic forms which appear with footnotes of explanation. The sound-symbolic *tst tsi*, for example, is explained as *Expresión para indicar el tirar de algo con fuerza* "an expression to indicate the pulling of something with force" (*Amenecer Indio*, December 1986: 16). Another sound-symbolic expression, *sac sac sac sac sac sac sac,* also appears with a footnote explaining *Expresión para indicar el dispersar de algo que cae a tierra* "an expression to indicate the dispersal of something that falls to the ground" (ibid.).

My preliminary hypothesis, then, is that among Sara yakuans, sound symbolism is becoming a functionally restricted style of speaking. Sara yakuans' greater interconnectedness with complex societies creates experiential frameworks that require increasingly literate forms of expression. Literacy, which removes language from the body of the speaker, is at odds with the discursive design of sound-symbolic language. Literacy also affects peoples' ways of thinking about language. There is a marked decrease in sound symbolism among Sara yakuans who have been university educated or transplanted from their village. Typically, men rather than women become university educated. It is also more usual for men than women to leave the village for extended periods of time. This particular confluence of gender, educational, and demographic factors has contributed to the reinterpretation of sound-symbolic speaking style. In general, its use connotes "insider status" and a cluster of other values as well, such as authenticity, intimacy, and affectivity. Because women are most often in the position of being cultural insiders, it has also become associated with a woman's style of speaking.

II

THE SOUND-SYMBOLIC CONSTRUCTION OF SPATIOTEMPORAL EXPERIENCE

7

Sound-Symbolic Iconicity and Grammar

> We believe that it is dangerous to establish, in advance, a distinction between grammatical elements on the one hand, and certain others that are called agrammatical, on the other; between an intellectual language and an affective language. The elements referred to as agrammatical or affective can, in effect, obey grammatical rules that one has not yet succeeded in extricating. (translation mine)
>
> L. Hjelmslev, *Principes de grammaire generale,* 1928, p. 240

Part I laid the conceptual foundations for understanding the interconnections between sound symbolism, aspect, and performance. Sound-symbolic utterances exploit the embodied properties and constraints of language. The linguistic sign vehicle is intrinsically durative because it consists of a spoken chain of significant differences. It is also intrinsically completive because of the limitations of the human breath which must spend itself at regular intervals of articulation. These given features of linguistic communication are then enhanced through performative movements of the mouth, shapings of the vocal tract, and fluctuations in voice pitch, all of which imitate movements and processes of perceptual experience. Sound-symbolic performances create a heightened sense of an action's unfolding, providing subtle, nuanced specifications of tempo, rhythm, process, and movement. Such specifications have a definite place, or ecological niche, within the grammatical architecture of Pastaza Quechua. Sound-symbolic utterances allow speakers to tread their way through chained series of coreference structures without compromising grammatical clarity and expressive force.[1] Sound-symbolic usage also ramifies with deeper cultural concerns. For the Pastaza Quechua sound is a modality for understanding and communicating about experience. The most significant events of peoples' lives are interpreted against a backdrop of sound-symbolically rendered impressions which represent ideas about the naturalness or unnaturalness of perceptual experience. Furthermore, the character of sound-symbolic style and functional markedness is variable and is probably sensitive to shifts in social, political, educational, and economic parameters.

Part II presents a detailed discussion of forty-three sound-symbolic adverbs that are of central importance in Pastaza Quechua discourse. The adverbs are grouped into chapters defined by such cognitively basic experiences as falling, opening and closing, making contact with surfaces or penetrating through barriers, making deformative movements and gestures, experiencing sudden realizations and other highly salient perceptions. Each sound-symbolic adverb will be defined verbally, and if possible, with an imageic diagram. I make no claims about the validity of these diagrams for Quechua-speaking people. I offer them as alternative schematizations which clarify the links between aspect and spatiotemporal experience. The contexts of each adverb's use, and their affective significance are discussed briefly. The articulatory and acoustical properties which lend themselves to iconic communication are identified. Each of the verbs that cooccur with a sound-symbolic adverb is listed in order of its frequency of use. The verbs most commonly used with a sound-symbolic adverb will be listed first. The unique configurations of semantic properties synthesized by sound-symbolic adverb/verb combinations are described. Finally, the discourse contexts of sound symbolic usage is analyzed, giving particular attention to their functions and the ways in which these functions are enhanced through performance.

All of the foregoing claims made about sound symbolism, including its grammatical role, its stylistic significance, and its cognitive salience, are limited to the Pastaza Quechua dialect. Sound-symbolic use in other Quechua dialects may share some of the features and functions outlined here; however, the data are not available. León ([1950?] n.d.) who wrote a grammar of the Canelos variety of Pastaza Quechua, mentions no sound-symbolic words in his word list. Cole (1985: 216–17) lists ideophones for the Imbabura dialect of northern Ecuador; however, he provides no information about their syntactic, morphosyntactic, or discourse characteristics. Ross (1979: 158) reports onomatopoeia for highland dialects of Ecuador, stating that sound-symbolic adverbs are used with a finite form of the verb *nina* "to say." Some Quechua dialects outside of Ecuador do report sound-symbolic words used to form verb stems fully inflected for tense, person, and number. Parker (1969: 75–76) lists over forty sound-symbolic stems for Ayacucho Quechua, a dialect spoken in south-central Peru, all of them based on a disyllabic root that is then repeated once or twice. Mannheim (personal communication) states that speakers of Cuzco Quechua, a closely related dialect, are also able to form verbs from sound-symbolic adverbs. Weber (1989: 37) reports that onomatopoeic sounds are an open class of substantives in Huallaga Quechua, and they can function as verbs by suffixation with an inchoative morpheme.

In none of these Quechua dialects, then, do sound-symbolic words have the unique constellation of grammatical and discourse features found in Pastaza Quechua. Many can be derived with proper suffixation into verb forms, and there is no indication from their description that they are in any way semantically or syntactically special. Nevertheless, there are reports from nonrelated languages of ideophones that share many crucial features of Pastaza Quechua's sound-symbolic adverbs. Koehn and Koehn state that in Apalai, a Carib language spoken in northern Brazil, the ideophone is "a noninflected onomatopoeic word that denotes an action that is normally expressed by a finite verb form" (1986: 124). They also mention Apalai ideophones' ability to substitute for a verb or an entire sentence, the slight variations they exhibit from normal Apalai phonology, and the frequency of their use in everyday conversation and storytelling

(124–125.) The use of ideophones as verb substitutes has also been reported for another Amazonian language, Canela Krahô, a Ge language spoken in central Brazil (Popjes and Popjes 1986: 198). All of this suggests that sound symbolism in Pastaza Quechua is an areal rather than a genetic feature of the language. More research is necessary, however, particularly on nonrelated dialects that are in closer geographical proximity with Pastaza Quechua, before definitive conclusions can be reached.

Pastaza Quechua sound-symbolic adverbs are distinctive as a class by their morphological, syntactic, and semantic properties. Although monosyllabic words ending in stops and fricatives are quite rare in the lexicon, there are nine of them among the forty-three adverbs analyzed here. Sound-symbolic adverbs are also distinctive by their word-initial affricates: eight adverbs among the forty-three adverbs to be analyzed have word-initial affricates. The affricate *dz*-, which occurs word initially in sound-symbolic *dzas*, *dzing*, *dzir,* and *dzawn,* only occurs in the lexicon in word-medial position, as an allophonic variant of the phoneme /z/. The palatalized *ch*^{y}-, which occurs word initially in *ch*^{y}*u,* does not occur elsewhere in the lexicon. The few examples of verbs from the lexicon with the word-initial affricate *ts* probably originated from sound-symbolic adverbs. The question of the origin of sound-symbolic adverbs as a distinctive class cannot be treated here, yet there must be assimilative processes between this class and the rest of the lexicon. For example, the verb *tsuntsuyana* "to become ragged, tattered" is derived from *tsuntsu* "ragged, tattered" and can be inflected as any other verb in the lexicon. By contrast, sound-symbolic adverbs never take a verb's inflectional endings, although they can be used as substitutes for a verb omitted by a speaker. The ability of sound-symbolic adverbs to substitute for verbs, predications, and even entire propositions without confusing or disorienting Quechua speakers suggests something of their unique semantic properties, yet it would be misleading to suggest that sound-symbolic adverbs simply "substitute" for other kinds of structures. Diffloth has noted that "In trying to paraphrase an ideophone with ordinary words of the same language, we find that several sentences are often needed, and, even then, the paraphrase is not wholly satisfactory" (1972: 441).

To fully appreciate the sound symbolism of Pastaza Quechua adverbs and the cognitive implications of their iconicity, it is necessary to justify the use of the term *image schema* by clarifying the ways in which their structure deviates from the traditional building block principles of morphology discussed earlier. In stating that they are schematic, it is claimed that sound-symbolic adverbs make use of gestalt-like structures that are directly meaningful. Lakoff (1987: 279) explains that both image schemas and basic-level categories function in our preconceptual experience. Image schemas deviate from the conceptual structures of objectivist semantics in that they are directly meaningful, though not necessarily primitive. Furthermore, although they are structured, their structure is not the result of applying fully productive rules of semantic composition. The structure of sound-symbolic adverbs cannot be calculated, predicted, or understood as a sum of abstract, phonemic, or morphemic elements. They communicate through their physiological embodied qualities. The articulatory movements of the vocal tract and the acoustical impressions that resonate from them simulate experientially basic images of movement, process, cessation, completion, and suddenness, which are directly meaningful. The embodied nature of sound symbolism was recognized long ago by Sapir (1929) and Newman (1933), both of whom conducted a series of experimental studies that found correlations between ideas of largeness and smallness and the kinesthetic experience of shaping the vocal articulatory tract into a relatively larger or smaller resonance chamber with the pronunciation of vowel sounds. More recently Diffloth has suggested that "the sensations produced in the vocal tract by the articulation of sound" may be more important than acoustic qualities in sound symbolic communication (1976: 262).

Syllable structure is one way in which Pastaza Quechua sound-symbolic adverbs communicate through their embodied properties. Monosyllabic adverbs typically represent an action or event as realized, while disyllabic adverbs break an action or process into component movements and gestures. Such a distinction is directly meaningful because it is communicated through one's basic understanding of the difference between a simple realized-ness, as experienced by the pronunciation of a monosyllable, and the more complex realized-ness of a disyllable. The distinction between a simply realized action and a complex one is then further enhanced through performative features of voice pitch, loudness, and rhythm, which emphasize the uninterruptedness of a simple, realized action, or the contrast between an initial gesture and a final concluding gesture. In addition to syllabic length, the closure or openness of a syllable—that is, whether it ends in a consonant or not—embodies a range of sensations and experiences. A closed final syllable can imitate a gesture of closure, the completion of an action, the cessation of a movement or of the possibility for movement, the bounding or circumscription of an image, or the abrupt contact of one surface with another. Some of these phenomena can also be iconically described by a constriction of the articulators, as is created by lip rounding. The openness of a syllable, by contrast, is iconic of a sound unfolding in time, an expansiveness, a continuous movement, a lack of obstruction, or an absence of clear definition or boundedness.

In word-internal positions, a contrast between the high vowels and low vowels, as between an initial-syllable high *i* and a final-syllable low *a*, or between the front vowel *i* and the back vowel *u*, can intensify the contrast between component movements described by a disyllabic adverb. A contrast between a rounded, articulatorily constricted vowel, such as *o*, and an unrounded, open vowel such as *a*, can be iconically expressive of a gesture involving a closing and an opening. Other iconically expressive features within an adverb are the presence or absence of obstruction in the vocal tract and the production or nonproduction of a turbulent airstream during an adverb's pronunciation. A lack of obstruction in the vocal tract can be iconic of an unimpeded movement through space. An obstruction in the vocal tract is iconically expressive of contact with a surface, a gesture of closure, the completion of an action, and the cessation of a movement or of the possibility for movement. A lack of turbulence within the oral tract, which characterizes the pronunciation of the lateral liquid *-l-* can be iconic of a visual smoothness, such as that of an uninterrupted surface, an effortless movement through space, or a movement that is light and lacking in force. The fricatives and affricates *s*, *sh*, *ts*, and *dz*—all of which are pronounced with a turbulent airstream—can be iconic of a movement, a frictional movement, the uninterruptedness of a movement, the uninterruptedness of a surface, the uninterruptedness of a sound unfolding in time, or the spatial trajectory of a movement.

In general, the word-initial consonant or vowel of a sound-symbolic adverb will carry the least iconic significance (cf. Diffloth 1976: 260). This accounts in part for the instability of word-initial affricates. Word-initial *dz-* sometimes becomes *z-*, and word-initial *ts-* sometimes becomes *t-* and sometimes *s-*. Moreover, the voicing of word-initial affricates is also unstable. There is free variation between word-initial *dz-* and *ts*, particularly in the variant forms of the sound-symbolic adverb *dzir*. The tendency for the initial part of a word to be less iconically significant than the final part is also evident by the overwhelming tendency for disyllabic adverbs to have more complex performative elaborations on their second syllables than on their first syllables. Most of a speaker's performative energy is focused on the second syllables of sound-symbolic adverbs. Furthermore, the second syllables of sound-symbolic adverbs are overwhelmingly more complex in their morphology than initial syllables. The following disyllabic sound symbolic adverbs all exhibit this tendency: *po-lang*, *a-ki*, *wa-l^yang*, *wi-kang*, *a-wing*, *pa-lay; pa-tang*, *wa-ling*, and *tsu-ping*. In any case, whether an adverb is disyllabic or monosyllabic, it will usually receive more performative foregrounding on its final sounds than on its initial sounds.

Verb/Adverb Relationships

Sound-symbolic adverbs have a variety of structural and semantic relationships with their verbs. First, a sound-symbolic adverb can simply restate the meaning of its verb. This is exemplified by the adverb *t^yapi* and the verb *l^yutarina* "to stick to." In such adverb/verb combinations, the verb is the sound-symbolic adverb's primary verb insofar as it comes closest to characterizing its semantics. However, the adverb is not just a restatement of the primary verb; it is analogous to an image of the action described by that verb. The synonymity between a sound-symbolic adverb and its primary verb, then, is rather general. They actually involve different modalities of communication: the verb refers to an action, and the sound-symbolic adverb is a vocalic gesture of an action.

Second, the sound-symbolic adverb is so semantically general that is have no primary verb. *Tas* is an example of a semantically general adverb. Its generality is evident by its ability to cooccur with a large number of verbs. *Tas* is somewhat comparable to the English particle "up" in such constructions as "eat up," "finish up," and "straighten up." What unites these various instances of "up" is that they affect the lexical aspect of their verbs with a completive value, yet it would be difficult to relate the aspectual completiveness of these constructions to the specific semantics of "up." The meaning of the construction as a whole cannot be atomized into its parts. The adverb and verb are semantically unified and interdependent. If *tas* undergoes multiple repetition, it continues to be semantically dependent on its verb, becoming an image of the action referred to by that verb.

Third, the adverb/verb combination is the reverse of the preceding situation (in which the verb's meaning was more central than that of the adverb): in this construction, the sound-symbolic adverb assumes more semantic importance than the verb it modifies. For example, in combination with *toa* "a complete turning over," the verb *rana* "to do, make" means "to turn something over." With *sa* "scattered movement away from a center," *rana* "to do, make" means "to throw something, scattering it." Other verbs that often participate in this kind of construction include *rina* "to go";

shamuna "to come"; *tiyana* "to be" *rikurina* "to appear." In such constructions the verb can be compared to a frame within which the more pictorial or gestural image of the action described by an adverb is presented.

Fourth, sound-symbolic adverbs can be rephrased as prepositional phrase constructions. For example *ang* is translatable as "with mouth wide open" in combination with the verb *chapana* "to wait." An adverb such as *tus* can also be translated with a prepositional phrase when it is used to refer to an idea of a crisp sound. For example, in combination with the verb *kanina* "to bite," it can be translated "to bite with the sound *tus*." Included in this category also are the metaphorical uses of sound-symbolic adverbs. *Ping*, for example, describes a complete change from light to darkness. In conjunction with the verb *tutayana* "to become night," it can be translated "as if with a *ping* it became night."

Fifth, sound-symbolic adverbs may encode a covert predicate. In the following translation the covert predicate encoded by *ping* appears in parentheses: "So, (having closed his eyes with a) *ping*, he was lying there." As this example also illustrates, the aspect encoded by the covert predicate may be different from the aspect of its finite verb. The aspect of the covert predicate is completive while that of the finite verb is durative. In another example, *toa* "to turn something over" can occur with the verb *pambana* "to bury." The translation of such a construction would be "(to turn something over) *toa* and bury it."

These five types of adverb/verb constructions cannot be correlated in a consistent way with specific verbs or adverbs. Any given sound-symbolic adverb can participate in all of the constructions described. Its structural status changes with the semantics of its verb. Moreover, the particular sense of a verb's semantic characterization is frequently subject to the influence of the sound-symbolic adverb with which it occurs. Despite the futility of attempting to assign each adverb to a consistent semantic and syntactic structural type, it is clear that sound-symbolic adverbs affect the lexical or predicate level aspect of the verbs with which they occur. A sound-symbolic adverb is relevant to the encoding of predicate level aspect when it concerns the action of the finite verb in relation to its participatory or circumstantial roles. By "participatory role" is meant such entitites as agent and patient. A "circumstantial role," as described by Andrews (1985: 69–71), is an entity that forms the background to an event, rather than actively participate in it.

The Aspect Values of Sound-Symbolic Adverbs

Sound-symbolic image schemas intersect with aspect grammar by representing ideas of basic experiences which are salient, in part, because their performative articulation in language enacts the closure, completiveness, or instantaneousness of the action, event, or process itself. Most of the sound-symbolic adverbs analyzed here specify that an action is closed within its frame and are therefore perfective. The following adverbs signal closure within their frames by their momentaneous, punctual meanings: *dzas* "a quick action," *dzir* "a quick sliding action," *palay*"a quick stealthy action," *dzing* "a sudden awareness," *tupu* "the moment of falling into water," *polang* "the moment of emerging from underwater," *patang* "the moment of hitting a ground surface with force," *pak* "the moment of falling with a splat," *tak* "the moment of making contact with a surface," *t'ʸapi* "the moment of making contact with a surface and sticking to it," *tsak* "the moment of making a shallow puncture," *tus* "the moment of bursting or puncturing something fleshy," and *tsuk* "the moment of removing a piece of something cleanly away from its whole."

The next group of adverbs signal closure by their completive or resultative meanings. These include *ang* "a wide open mouth," *ing* "a splitting open or a slit," *t'ʸam* "a complete turn," *toa* "a complete turning over," *ton* "a complete filling up," *awing* "a complete opening up," *taw*"a complete closing off," *ling* "a complete enclosure or crossing of boundaries," *polo* "a complete penetration through a barrier," *ping* "a complete change from light to darkness," *wikang* "a verticality completely detached from a surrounding space," *ch'ʸu* "a complete cutting off," *kal'ʸa* "a complete fissure," *shaka* "a complete tear," *shaw* "a completely continuous two-dimensional entity," *saw* "a completely continuous fluid movement," *tay* "a complete lack of movement," *tsung* "a complete drenching," and *tsuping* "a complete bareness." Another type of closure is signaled by the aorist adverbs that describe a total configuration of low animacy entities. These include *waling* "a pattern of positive/negative space," *ki* "a configuration of similar objects that have fallen," *sa* "a random movement or arrangement away from a center," *dzawn* "a movement or arrangement toward a center," *cham* "a distribution of objects throughout a space," and *chinda* "a jutting outward from a base by a group of vertical shapes."

Most sound-symbolic adverbs have mixed aspects. *Ping*, for example, was defined here as a completive adverb describing a complete change from light to darkness. However, it could as well have been defined as a sudden change from light to darkness and been included with the punctual adverbs. The adverb *tak* also has a completive meaning in addition to its punctual one. The mixing of aspect values within one adverb also involves crossing over into subcategories that are imperfective. For example, *palay* describes both a quick stealthy movement, which is punctual, as well as a series of rapidly falling objects or entities, which is iterative. And the family of adverbs called *dzir* describe quick sliding movements, which are punctual, as well as sustained gliding movements across surfaces, which are imperfective, and sustained sliding movements in a downward or upward direction, also imperfective. And *ling* describes both a complete enclosure and an iterative, rapid, back-and-forth movement. A few adverbs are almost always repeated at least twice. *Aki* "a swaying back and forth," *huy* "a dangling back and forth," and *wal'ʸang* "a movement of light and shadow" are typically iterative; however, all three can be used in aspectually perfective ways. *L'ʸu* "a shine, glint or sparkle" is used with equal frequency either in a single occurrence to describe a completely shiny surface or in multiple repetitions to describe an iterative glinting or sparkling.

Although these adverbs represent a significant component of the aspectual system they cannot be neatly arranged into categories such as completive or resultative. A typical adverb has more than one aspect value. Moreover, a good number of them exhibit synesthesia, which is to say that they encode descriptions of sensations from different sensorial domains. The adverb *tsak*, for example, describes the moment when a shallow puncture is made, as well as an idea of the sound of striking a match. *Ton* describes both a complete filling up and an idea of the sound of an explosion.

The complexities of sound-symbolic semantics and their obvious relevance to aspect make clear the inadequacy of a point/line conception of grammatical aspect. The point/line schema is only the most abstract way of thinking about aspect. Aspect is linked to the sensible world of spatiotemporal experience. If a grammatical description of aspect is to be ethnographically sensitive, then it must consider the ways in which native speakers articulate and foreground their experiences of the sensible world they inhabit. For the Pastaza Quechua, sound symbolism renders actions, processes, and events into distinctive temporal contours of shapes and forms as outlined in the following chapters.

8

Sound-Symbolic Contrasts of Sensible Experience

Although sound-symbolic adverbs form a distinctive word class, they share certain semantic characteristics with the rest of the lexicon. One such characteristic is their ability to pattern in oppositional relationships. This chapter describes twelve sound-symbolic adverbs that are semantically related by their contrast. These twelve adverbs pair into six sets of contrasts. *Sa* and *dzawn* describe an opposition between an internally complex action or event which is centrifugally oriented (moving away from a center) versus one that is centripetally oriented (moving toward a center.) *Tʸam* and *toa* describe an opposition between a complete, 360-degree angle turn around, and a 180-degree turn, which is typically upside down as well. *Polang* and *tupu* can be described as a contrast between the moment of emerging from underwater to the surface and the moment of dropping down into water from above. *Huy* and *aki* describe an opposition between an uncontrolled hanging and a controlled swaying. *Lʸuw* and *walʸang* describe an opposition between a shininess and a shadowy, indistinct movement. *Wikang* and *chinda* describe an opposition between an unattached, vertically positioned object in space and a vertical jutting out into space from a base.

Sa

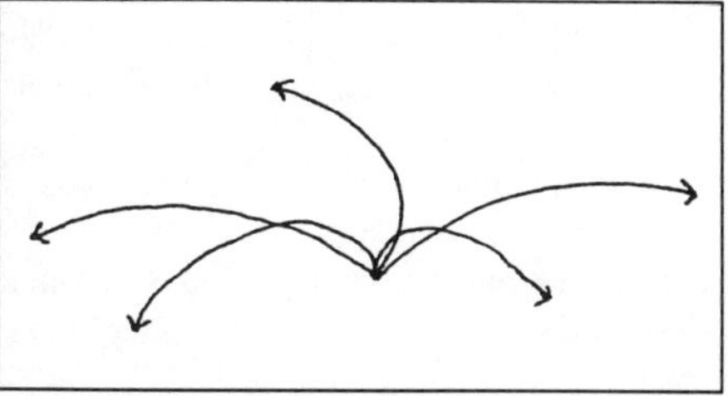

DEFINITION Describes expanded or random movement from or within a locus, by one or more entities or agents. Aspectually aorist, durative.

COMMENT *Sa* describes not a neat radial pattern, marked by symmetry and balance, but, rather, the disorderly order that results when various objects or entities that were concentrated in one space have spread out from it. *Sa* can describe an aesthetic apperception, such as the pattern defined by turtle hatchlings leaving their nest in the sand and going off in every direction. Its use evokes a range of affective values. A parent once remarked with sadness about the inevitability of children scattering from their families when they grow up, to go off and live in other places. Someone else mentioned the threat posed by members of an enemy tribe hidden and scattered *sa* at various places throughout the forest.

ICONIC PROPERTIES The iconicity of *sa* is related to its initial fricative, *s*-; to its vowel, *a*-; and to the openness of its syllable. The initial fricative, *s*-, which is articulated with a continuous airstream, is iconic of the continuousness of the movement outward from center. Because its articulation involves enough constriction to create a turbulent airstream, the fricative *s*- also contrasts with the openness of the oral tract while pronouncing the following vowel, *a*-. The contrast between the initially constricted and subsequently more open position of the articulators is imitative of the initial clustering and subsequent expansion outward of a movement described by *sa*.

Sa occurs with the following verbs.

1. sa shitana
   throw
   — to scatter anything, e.g., salt on food, empty fruit pods on the ground, a wide net over water
2. sa tuksina
   throw
   — to throw, scattering
3. sa rana
   do
   — to do anything with a scattering or dispersing motion
4. sa icharina
   spill
   — to spill, scatter, or sprinkle anything
5. sa tukuna
   become
   — to become scattered, e.g., children when they mature and go off to live in various places
6. sa sirina
   lie
   — to lie scattered throughout a given space, e.g., clothes all over a house, members of an enemy tribe throughout the forest
7. sa ishpana
   urinate
   — to sprinkle urine, e.g., rats running along beams of a house at night
8. sa ismana
   defecate
   — to defecate, scattering, e.g., a sloth hanging from a tree
9. sa paskarina
   open
   — to open up, spreading randomly, e.g., logs of a floating balsa raft when their moorings are untied
10. sa l^{y}ukshina
    emerge
    — to emerge randomly from a place, e.g., newly hatched turtles from a nest in the sand
11. sa urmana
    fall
    — to fall randomly, e.g., clothes to the ground when the line on which they hang falls
12. sa harkana
    obstruct
    — to impede or obstruct by placing obstacles every which way
13. sa mitikuna
    hide
    — to hide all over a given area, e.g., members of an enemy tribe
14. sa sakirina
    remain
    — to be left in a scattered or disrupted condition, e.g., the way sand looks when something underneath it emerges

In the following example, multiple repetitions of *sa* gesture the act of seasoning turtle meat by sprinkling a garlic-flavored fungus all over it. The speaker is instructing me in this context, by means of sound-symbolic *sa*.

15. sa sa sa sa sa sa sa sa shita-ni, sumak, kachi-ta shina.
throw-1 nicely salt-ACC like

"I throw (it) *sa sa sa sa sa sa sa sa*, nicely, like salt."

Sa is performatively foregrounded here by multiple repetitions, each of which can be understood as a vocal gesture of the action it describes. *Sa*'s function here is instructional: the speaker is explaining a process in the preparation of turtle meat. The fact that these repetitions of *sa* are circumscribed by an increase and subsequent decrease in pitch makes clear that it is the configuration of the action as a whole which is also of interest to the speaker.

The next example, taken from a myth, describes the way a basket of peanuts carried on someone's back was inadvertently scattered until emptied by the person carrying it.

16. Ña apari-sha, waska-ndi ña sa sa sa ichari-shka
then carry-COR rope-both now sprinkle-PERF

"Then, carrying (the basket) with the rope, she sprinkled it *sa sa sa*."

Each repetition of *sa* describes an instance of scattering, and the telic pitch progression considers each of these instances as progressive realizations of the complete emptying of the basket. Here *sa* functions poetically, to highlight the intrinsic qualities of the scattering motion that takes place while the woman is walking in the sky, visiting star people.

In the next example, taken from a narrative of personal experience, *sa* describes the way a clump of earth was hurled through the air in an attempt to chase away a malevolent forest spirit.

17. Puku-shka washa, intiru alpa-ta-s s^haaaaaaa-mi shita-ra.
blow-PERF after entire earth-ACC-INCL -EV throw-PAST

"After blowing (on it) he threw the entire (clump of) earth *s^haaaaaaa*!"

Sa is performatively foregrounded here by its lengthening and by the strong puff of aspiration that devoices its vowel. The lengthening communicates both aspectual durativity, and also an image of an extended expansion in space. The aspiration communicates the force of the throwing action. *Sa*'s function here is emphatic: it communicates an idea of a deliberate and forceful action.

In the following, *sa* describes the pattern created by the spreading out of a balsa raft's logs after their moorings were untied.

18. Ña chʸu chʸu piti-nchi ango-ta ni-ra, s$^{a^{a}}$ kacha-n, pulʸu pulʸu-shi ri-nawn ni-ra.
then cut-1PL vine-ACC say-PAST send-3 stump stump-EV go-3PL say-PAST

"'Then we cut the vines *chʸu chʸu*, he said, and *s$^{a^{a}}$* (he sends them), and they go stump stump,' he said."

Sa is performatively foregrounded here by an upglide in pitch, which considers the complete extent of the balsa logs' spreading out. Here *sa*'s function can be understood by analogy with a director's use of a wide-angle shot. Wide-angle shots present the essential features of a pattern that are best observed from a distance. It is a relatively distant view of the spreading out of the logs which the speaker intends to communicate, by considering the complete expanse of the logs' spreading out. In this sentence *sa* also functions to lend imageability and therefore credibility to a statement from someone else's narrative of personal experience.

Dzawn

DEFINITION An action, process, or event that involves a clustering together of individual agents, such as people, birds, bats, or insects. Aspectually aorist.

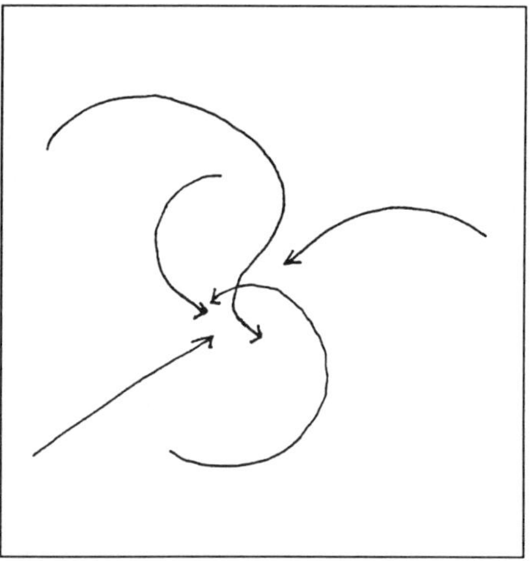

COMMENT Just as *sa* is descriptive of a disorderly, outward-moving movement or pattern, *dzawn* is descriptive of a disorderly, inward movement or pattern. *Dzawn* can be applied to a friendly group of people gathered for a *minga* "work party." I have also heard it used to describe angry, volatile mobs that erupted into violence. Any insects that swarm or teem are also described with *dzawn*.

ICONIC PROPERTIES The iconicity of *dzawn* is related to its initial affricate *dz-*, to its vowel and approximant *-aw-*, and to the closure of its syllable. The initial affricate *dz-*, which is articulated with a continuous airstream, is iconic of the motion of whatever moves toward a center. The lip rounding accompanying the vowel and approximant *-aw-* creates articulatory constriction, which is iconic of the circumscribed, clustering together described by *dzawn*. The final *-n*, which is sometimes dropped, closes the syllable, imitating an idea of boundedness.

Dzawn occurs with the following verbs.

1. dzawn tandarina — to gather together
   gather
2. dzawn maka-naku-na — to fight as a group
   fight-RCP-INF

3. dzawn shamuna — to come as a group
   come
4. dzawn hatarina — to rise in a swarm
   get up
5. dzawn sirina — to lie as a group
   recline
6. dzawn mana — to be gathered together
   be

In the following example, taken from a myth, *dzawn* describes the way a swarm of predatory bats come to a house full of sleeping people. The sentence was not finished off with a finite verb because the narrator interrupted herself to inject metacommentary about the eventual outcome of the story.

7. Punu-shka-y-ga ña dzaw shamu-sha.
   sleep-PERF-NOM-TOP then come-COR
   "When they've all fallen asleep, (the bats) having come *dzaw* in a swarm."

Dzawn does not undergo formal amplification. It functions grammatically, by affecting the coreference verb *shamusha* "coming" with an aorist aspect value, because it describes a complex configuration as a whole.

In the next example, taken from a myth about the origins of animals' markings and colors, *dzawn* describes the way all animals had once been gathered in one woman's house. In this part of the story, the old woman who had painted all of the animals discovers that they've left her.

8. Pay-wan runa shina kasna dzaw siri-k-guna-ga il^{y}a-n!
   her-INST people like like this lie-AG-PL-TOP be lacking-3
   "The ones who, as if (they were her own) people, had *dzaw* lay near her, crowded like that, were gone!"

Dzawn does not undergo formal amplification in this example. It functions grammatically, to indicate the aorist aspect of the phrase *sirikgunaga* "the ones who are lay-ers."

In the next example, *dzawn* describes the way flies that had gathered on a molting snake rose up in a swarm when a person approached.

9. Putan dz^{h}awww hatari-ra!
   fly rise-PAST
   "The flies rose up *dz^{h}awww*!"

Dzawn is formally amplified by lengthening, by its aspiration, and by the low-pitched breathy voice over its vowels. Its formal amplification simulates the rising movement of the swarming insects. By drawing out its pronunciation, the speaker focuses on the dramatic contrast between the durativity of this rising movement and the immediately preceding state of the flies' stillness.

In the next example, dzawn describes the way flies were swarming over a freshly killed animal.

10. Kuru mama putan dz^{h}awww tandari-shka ma-ra.
worm mother fly gather-PERF be-PAST
"The worm mother flies were gathered *dz^{h}awww.*"

Dzawn is performatively foregrounded here by its lengthening which simulates an idea of the ongoingness of the flies' swarming movement, and also considers the clustering configuration as a whole.

In the following example, *dzawn* describes a fighting mob of people.

11. Dz^{h}aaawwnnn maka-naku-shka-wna!
fight-RCP-PAST-3PL
"They were fighting with each other *dz^{h}aaawwnnn!*"

Its performative lengthening functions to focus attention on an image of ongoing fighting. At the same time that it focuses on the image described by *dzawn,* the performative lengthening also enhances the aspectual durativity which is implied by the reciprocally suffixed verb *makanakushkawna* "they were fighting with each other."

T^{y}am

DEFINITION To revolve, roll, or turn, in a complete revolution; to make something turn, roll, or revolve. Aspectually completive, resultative.

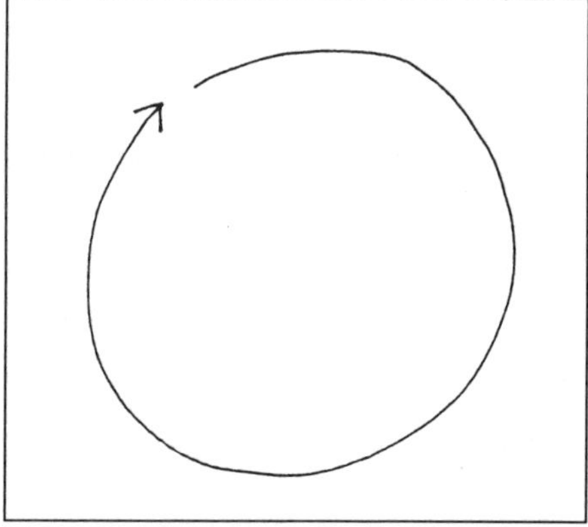

COMMENT One of the most frequent imperative statements uttered by Quechua speakers is *T^{y}am upingi!* "Drink, making your bowl turn over *t^{y}am!*" The drink is always *aswa*, a mildly fermented beverage made from cooked and masticated manioc. The ideal *aswa* drinker is someone who can gulp it so fast that the bowl can be turned upside down almost as soon as the drinking has begun. It's this complete turning over of the bowl which is the essential image of *t^{y}am.* This turning over image described by *t^{y}am* is also used metaphorically as a conceptual image for a change of heart. Someone who experiences a dramatic change in their feelings is said to have turned over *t^{y}am.*

ICONIC PROPERTIES The iconicity of *t^{y}am* is related to its palatalized *t^{y}*- and to the closure of its syllable. The palatalization of the initial consonant *t^{y}* creates, by its high front tongue position, less closure than that required for an unpalatalized consonant. This lesser degree of closure, then, creates an articulatory contrast with the word-final closure of the lips for *-m*. This opening and closing of the articulatory positions presents a complete range of contrast and thereby gestures the contrast implied by a complete revolution.

T^{y}am occurs with the following verbs.

1. t^{y}am voltiarina
   turn
   to turn completely around, e.g., a soldier ordered to do so, or to look at what is behind one; to roll over, e.g., a dying snake, a dugout canoe; to roll back, e.g., the eyes of a corpse
2. t^{y}am voltia-chi-na
   turn-CAUS
   to turn something around, e.g., a stone to examine it, a blowgun to use the opposite end, a ladder to make who's climbing it fall off (myth)
3. t^{y}am upina
   drink
   to drink up by drinking everything from a clay bowl or hollowed out gourd, thus turning it over
4. t^{y}am rana
   do
   to turn over or to turn something over
5. t^{y}am kushparina
   shake
   to shake by rolling or turning over and over, e.g., an animal on the ground, a fish out of water
6. t^{y}am tigrana
   turn
   to turn over, e.g., a canoe
7. t^{y}am pasa-chi-na
   pass-CAUS
   to slice through a piece of meat along a horizontal axis, while turning the top half over
8. t^{y}am mana
   be
   to be turned over, e.g., the edge of a clay jar
9. t^{y}am rikuna
   look
   to turn one's eyes away from someone because of shame, e.g., a child being rebuked by parents; to eye someone by sweeping the gaze all over them
10. t^{y}am pil^{y}urina
    wrap
    to wrap around something, e.g., to wrap long hair all the way around one's wrists to prevent that person from going away (myth)

In the following example *t^{y}am* describes the way someone walking in the forest turned completely around to see what was making noise behind her.

11. T^{y}am voltiari-sha riku-ra-ni; il^{y}a-n!
    turn around-COR see-PAST-1 be lacking-3
    "Turning around *t^{y}am* I looked; there was nothing there!"

T^{y}am is not formally amplified in this context. It functions grammatically, to indicate the aspectual closure of the coreference verb *voltiarisha*. It is the speaker's use of *t^{y}am* with the coreference verb *voltiarisha* "turning" which makes it clear that the act of turning is in this context aspectually resultative.

In the next sentence *t^{y}am* describes the way an unsuspecting traveler might be turned around in his or her sentiments by a powerful type of love magic, rendering that person helpless to return home.

12. Shina a-sha-ga t^{y}a^{m} (pause); nukanchi l^{y}akta-ta mana tigra-shun!
like that be-COR-TOP our place-ACC NEG return-1PLFUT

"And just like that *t^{y}a^{m}* (pause); we won't return to our place."

T^{y}am is performatively foregrounded here by an upglide, by an immediately following pause, and by its syntactic isolation. All of these foregrounding techniques heighten the modal/emotive function that *t^{y}am* is serving in this context. The elaborated image of a complete turnaround heightens the impact of the statement's warning: this magic is so powerful that it causes a complete turnaround in one's sentiments.

In the next example *t^{y}am* describes the way each member of a group of men became drunk by drinking up their individual bowls of breadfruit beer.

13. Turi-guna t^{y}am, shuk-bas t^{y}am, shuk-bas t^{y}am, wañu-k Loberto ña, riku-l^{y}ayta-shi
brother-PL one-INCL one-INCL die-AG Loberto then watch-ADV-EV
macha-ra.
become drunk-PAST

"The brothers (drank up) *t^{y}am*, one (bowl) *t^{y}am*, then another *t^{y}am*, and the late Loberto, instead of just watching, also became drunk."

T^{y}am is foregrounded here by its repetition and by its syntactic isolation which condense a series of activities into a succinct image. The action of drinking up all of the breadfruit beer is presented with an image of a completely turned over bowl. *T^{y}am*'s function here is both aesthetic and grammatical; it presents a clear, compressed image of a relatively complex activity in order to highlight its completiveness.

In the next example, taken from a myth, *t^{y}am* describes the way a man wrapped his wife's hair around his hand in tighter and tighter coils to prevent her from running away while he slept.

14. Chi-ga ña rina-manda-ga akcha-y-ga t^{y}am t^{y}am t^{y}am t^{y}am -shi pil^{y}uri-sha-shi
so-TOP then go-from-TOP hair-LOC-TOP -EV wrap-COR-EV
puñu-ra.
sleep-PAST

"So then, (to prevent her) from going, (having) wrapped her hair (around him), *t^{y}am t^{y}am t^{y}am t^{y}am* he slept."

T^{y}am is performatively foregrounded here by its repetition and by the telic pitch progression over the repetitions. Its function is both aesthetic and grammatical in this context. Each repetition of *t^{y}am*, by its progressively higher pitch, represents an incremental subevent toward the completion of the larger action considered as a whole. This performative foregrounding is comparable to a cinematographer's use of juxtaposed shots to represent the various stages of an activity leading to its completion. Through performative foregrounding, the narrator simulates the passage of a complete interval of time.

Toa

DEFINITION To turn or be turned from an upright position to an upside-down position. Aspectually completive, resultative.

COMMENT While the essential image of *tʸam* is the completion of a revolution along any axis, the meaning of *toa* almost always implies that something has turned only far enough to be in a face-down position with respect to some surface, although not necessarily touching that surface. Objects described as turning *toa* typically have both a spherical and a flat dimension. These include clay bowls for drinking *aswa*; dugout canoes; and round *pilʸchi* gourds that have been split in half, hollowed out, and used for drinking *aswa*. All of these objects are rounded insofar as they are containers, but also flat because their open side can be turned upside down to rest evenly on a flat surface. Some actions described with *toa*, such as a dying man collapsing face down or a man lying face down in a canoe to protect himself from an assault, have to be considered extensions of the essential image of *toa*. In these extended usages, it is the face-down aspect of *toa*'s meaning, rather than the spherical-object-coming-flatly-to-a-rest aspect of its meaning, that becomes centrally important.

ICONIC PROPERTIES The vowel sequence *-oa* is present only in this sound-symbolic adverb and is totally absent from the rest of the Quechua lexicon. Its use by Quechua speakers in *toa* may have been influenced by the existence of the sequence *-oa* in the Spanish word *canoa*. Furthermore, since the image of a canoe turned upside down is often described with *toa*, this may be a case of a lexical item, or at least, a vowel sequence from a lexical item, assuming a particular iconic value that is related to an image of the lexical item itself. The iconicity of *toa* could be related to the contrast between the initial constriction caused by the lip rounding of the vowel *-o-*, which is then opened up with the vowel *-a*. This articulatory constriction, followed by opening is analogous to the containment and subsequent spilling which are often consequences of actions described with *toa*.

Toa is used with the following verbs.

1.	toa churana put	to put something upside down, e.g., a drinking bowl after washing it
2.	toa rana do	to put anything upside down
3.	toa upina drink	to drink until the drinking bowl or gourd can be turned completely over, i.e., to drink up[1]
4.	toa talina spill	to spill everything in a container by turning it upside down
5.	toa arma-chi-na bathe-CAUS	to drench something or someone by turning a container full of any liquid upside down
6.	toa shitana throw	to throw any liquid by turning its container upside down

7. toa pambana — to bury something, turning it upside down
   bury
8. toa rina — to go upside down
   go
9. toa voltiarina — to roll over and turn upside down, e.g., a canoe
   overturn
10. toa sirina — to lie face down
    lie
11. toa siri-chi-na — to make someone lie face down
    lie-CAUS
12. toa hapirina — to hold oneself face down over a surface, e.g., for protection from an assault
    catch
13. toa wañuna — to die lying face down
    die
14. toa urmana — to fall or collapse face down
    fall

In the following example, taken from a myth, *toa* describes the way a large clay jar was turned over to hide someone.

15. Hatun manga-wan toa ra-sha, toa ra-shka-y, pay yaya ruku shamu-kpi ña
    large pot-ADV do-COR do-PERF-NOM their father big come-SWRF then
    kara-naw-ra.
    feed-3PL-PAST

    "Turning the large pot *toa* upside down, having turned it *toa* upside down, they fed their big old father when he arrived."

Toa does not undergo formal amplification here. It functions grammatically, by affecting the aspectual reading of the coreference verb *rasha* "doing" with completiveness.

In the next example, taken from a narrative of personal experience, *toa* describes the way a man whose body had just been riddled with bullets collapsed face down.

16. Ni-ka, $\text{to}^{\text{a}^{\text{-ma}}}$ (pause) urma-shka-ra.
    say-TOP -DAT fall-PERF-PAST

    "(After) saying that, $\textit{to}^{\textit{a-}^{\textit{ma}}}$ (pause), he'd collapsed (face down)."

Toa is performatively foregrounded here by its upwardly gliding pitch and its immediately following pause, both of which invite the listener to pause for a moment and consider the implications of this action's result. Rather than stating the obvious fact that the man has just died, the narrator simulates an image of his collapse, which is powerfully evocative of a mood of finality.[2]

In the next example *toa* is used along with the sound-symbolic adverb *t*^{y}*am* to describe the way a canoe traveling in a rain-swollen river was turned upside down when it collided with a tree branch hidden underwater.

17. Takari-ga, kanoa t^{y}am, $t^{o^{a}}$ (pause) voltiari-shka!
knock-TOP canoe turn over-PERF

"Having bumped (into it), the canoe (going) *t^{y}am* $t^{o^{a}}$ (pause) turned over and upside down."

Toa is formally amplified here by an upglide in pitch and an immediately following pause, both of which function to create a catastrophic mood. Instead of stating that the canoe turned completely upside down, an event that has disastrous implications for its passengers, the narrator uses imagery suggesting these implications.

In the next sentence, taken from a myth, *toa* describes the way a gourd filled with black vegetable dye was turned completely over so that it spilled all over a bird, making its feathers completely black.

18. Kay pawshi-ta, ña kay-ma al^{y}i shinki l^{y}api-shka-an-ga, $t^{o^{a}}$ (pause).
this bird-ACC now here-DAT good black squeeze-PERF-INST-TOP
"Having squeezed (the seeds) until (the water) was very black, (she turned it over) $t^{o^{a}}$ (pause) on the *pawshi* bird."

Toa is formally amplified with an upglide, an immediately following pause, and its syntactic isolation. All these techniques enhance its overwhelmingly aesthetic function, which is to communicate an image of the *pawshi* bird becoming completely black.

Polang

DEFINITION (1) Describes the moment of emergence from underwater to the surface. Aspectually punctual, completive, and resultative. (2) Describes a floating or gliding across water. Aspectually durative. Both *polang*$_1$ and *polang*$_2$ describe movements in water that take place with relative ease, a minimum of effort, and an absence of thrashing sounds.

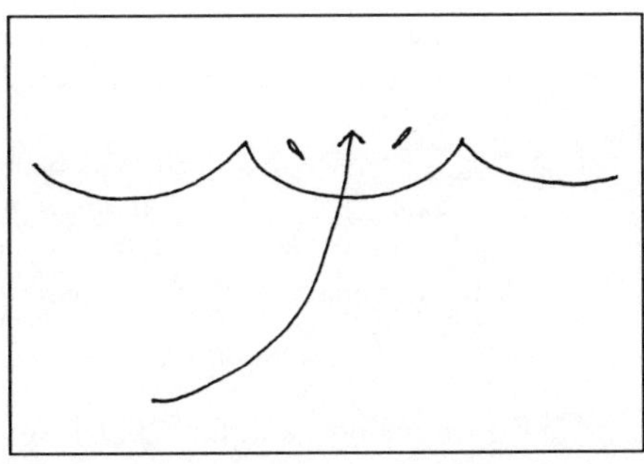

COMMENT The description of floating movement in water almost always involves the use of *polang*. *Polang*$_1$ can describe very dramatic images, such as that of an anaconda surging to the surface, or matter-of-fact images, such as that of a canoe standing afloat near the shore or weeds appearing to float on the surface. *Polang*$_2$ is typically used by speakers to evoke a feeling for the ease of gliding and the lightness of buoyancy.

ICONIC PROPERTIES The iconicity of *polang* can be related to its disyllable structure, its liquid *-l-*, and its final velarized nasal *-ng*. Its disyllabic structure provides a framework within which a speaker can performatively gesture either a contrast between down underwater and above water, or a continuous, smooth, gliding movement over water. The liquid *-l-* enhances an idea of movement in water that is relatively effortless because it is articulated without producing a turbulent airstream. The articulation of the word-final nasal stop, *-ng,* creates, by the lowering of the velum, an obstruction in the airstream, which is iconic of the cessation of movement that occurs when something has emerged to the water's surface and has no medium left in which to move. However, when a speaker wants to communicate an idea of a gliding floating movement across water, which is unobstructed, then the second syllable of *polang* is performatively lengthened, thereby overriding the lack of movement implied by the word final velarized nasal *-ng*.

Polang occurs with the following verbs.

1.	polang wamburina float, fly	to emerge from underwater to the surface, e.g., an anaconda's head; to float or glide across the water's surface e.g., a canoe, fish, etc.
2.	polang wambu-china float-CAUS	to raise something from underwater to the surface, e.g., an animal its head
3.	polang shamuna come	to come or arrive by canoe; to glide effortlessly, without having to row or maneuver, e.g., when traveling downriver
4.	polang rina go	to move on the surface of water, e.g., a canoe or balsa raft; an oar dropped into the water; an anaconda; the hair of a person who dives underwater
5.	polang shayana stand	to remain in place on the water's surface, e.g., a canoe that is tied to something
6.	polang rikuna look	to emerge from underwater in order to see something, e.g., any animal in pursuit of its prey
7.	polang rikurina appear	to appear to be floating on top of water, e.g., weeds growing from underneath, or a cluster of dead logs
8.	polang wañuna die	to float across water as a lifeless entity, e.g., any dead animal
9.	polang waytana swim	to swim bobbing up above the water's surface, e.g., a turtle, or to swim by simply floating across the water's surface, allowing the current to carry one downstream
10.	polang l^{y}ukshina emerge	to emerge by gliding up from underwater, e.g., a submarine

In the following example, taken from a narrative of personal experience, *polang* is used to describe the way a canoe that was passed underneath a fallen tree reemerged by springing back up to the water's surface.

11.	Yaku uray-ma	pasa-chi-ra-nchi,	yaku uku-ta,	kanoa-ga po^{lang}
	water downriver-DAT	pass-CAUS-PAST-1PL	water under-ACC	canoe-TOP

"We passed it (in the direction of) downriver, under the water, and the canoe (emerged) *po^{lang}*!"

Polang is performatively foregrounded by the upjump over its second syllable and also by its syntactic isolation. By its high/low contrast, the upjump gestures the component movements of the canoe's springing up to the water's surface. *Polang*'s function in this context is instructional. The speaker is relating how to free a canoe that has been trapped by a fallen tree, without having to lift its impossibly heavy bulk up out of the water. The performative elaboration of *polang* presents, instead, an alternative strategy that exploits the lightness, buoyancy, and ease of its movement from underwater to the surface.

The next sentence contrasts with the preceding because it describes a gradual process of rising to the water's surface rather than a sudden springing up. Here *polang*$_1$ describes an anaconda's surging from underwater to the surface.

12. Poll^{h}ang wamburi-n, rik-i !
    float-3 look-2IMP
    "Look! He rises *poll^{h}ang*."

Polang is performatively foregrounded by a combination of lengthening on the first syllable and strong aspiration at the beginning of the second syllable. These foregrounding techniques exploit its disyllabic structure to gesture the anaconda's rise and resultant surge to the water's surface. The rise is represented by the lengthening of the initial syllable, while the surge is represented by the aspiration over the second syllable.

The next example repeats *polang*$_1$ to describe the repeated bobbing to the surface from underwater of a large catfish which had just been speared. The bobbing movement resulted from its resistance to being pulled in by the man who had speared it.

13. Pay-ga hawa-ma, hawa-ma polang polang polang, chawpi kay chakkk^{h} kanoa-ma !
    he-TOP above-DAT above-DAT middle this canoe-DAT
    "He (appeared) on top, and on top, *polang polang polang*, then, right in the middle (of his head, they hit him) *chakkk^{h}*, and into the canoe (they pulled him)."

Polang is formally amplified here by its multiple repetitions and by its syntactic isolation. By repeating the image of the catfish's resistant movements, the speaker uses *polang*'s image of light, buoyant movement to simulate a dramatic and difficult struggle.

Polang$_2$, which describes a floating or gliding across water, has an epistemic function in the following sentence taken from a description of an apparition. The narrator describes a vision of a water person, i.e., a being who is human-like, but is believed to live in an underwater world. For the narrator, this vision was significant because it indicated a possible calling for shamanistic abilities which she never made use of. In the following example, she uses *polang*$_2$ to describe the way the water person's hair floated across the surface of water when it dived underwater.

14. Akcha-ga pola^{aa}nnnnng yaku-ta ri-ra.
    hair-TOP water-ACC go-PAST
    "The hair *pol^{aa}nnnnng* on the water went."

Polang is performatively foregrounded here by its lengthening, by the variation in pitch over that lengthening, and by its syntactic displacement from the verb *rira* "went." The lengthening of the second-syllable vowel, together with its slight pitch fluctuation, can be understood as a vocal gesture of the appearance of movement of the hair across the water's surface. This pitch fluctuation gestures an idea of movement because it is itself a deviation from a baseline pitch. By moving away slightly from this baseline pitch, it performs an idea of the movement which it describes. This image functions to make more credible the description of the water person, by focusing on one of the more ordinary aspects of its physical appearance.

In the next example *polang*$_2$ is extended to describe the gliding across water of a canoe full of men whom the narrator used to encounter frequently.

15. Montalvo-y-ga chasna polaaa-xx-l^yaaaa, kay señor Anibal-guna shamu-k
Montalvo-LOC-TOP like that -ADV this mister Anibal-PL come-AG
a-naw-ra.
be-3PL-PAST
"Mister Anibal and others used to come to Montalvo, *polaaa-xxl^yaaaa*, like that (floating in canoes they arrived)."

The suffixation of *polang* with an epenthetic velar fricative, as well as an emphatic *-l^ya,* allows its speaker to prolong the duration of its pronunciation, thereby gesturing more precisely, an idea of movement across space, as well as the aspectual durativity of that movement. Here *polang*'s function is modal. It evokes a sentimental feeling for bygone days. The simulated movement of men arriving in canoes brings images from the past clearly into the listener's present awareness

Polang$_2$ also describes a spatial expanse with the same extended pronunciation that was just used; however, the following example describes an expanse of weeds that are not actually moving, although they are floating on the water's surface. The other sound-symbolic adverb *ba* portrays their spreading out, while *polang* simulates their buoyancy.

16. Kiwa hawa-y, baaa kucha-guna-y, polaaa-xx-l^yaaa-ng chasna rikuri-k ma-n.
weed top-LOC lake-PL-LOC -ADV-INST like that appear-AG be-3
"The weeds (spreading out) *baaa*, on top of the lakes appear *polaaaxxl^yaaang*, like that."

This particular use of *polang* above features an adverbializing morpheme *-ng* in addition to the epenthetic velar fricative and the emphatic *-l^ya* suffix. This example differs from the previous one, then, by what it describes, and also by one suffixal morpheme. It is tempting to consider examples 15 and 16 a minimal pair, differing only by the closure of the word-final syllable, and attribute their different meaning to the presence or absence of word-final closure. Example 15 describes a free unrestricted movement across space and ends in an open syllable. Example 16 describes a collective configuration, i.e., an area of weeds floating on the water's surface, which has a definite shape and closure. In any case, *polang*'s function here is aesthetic: it simulates a perception of a buoyant expanse of weeds on the water's surface.

Tsupu

DEFINITION (1) Describes an idea of the sound of the moment of falling into water. Aspectually punctual. (2) Describes the path of a movement under water after falling into it, or the shallow splashing sound made by such a movement when whoever or whatever splashes is only partially submerged. Aspectually durative.[3]

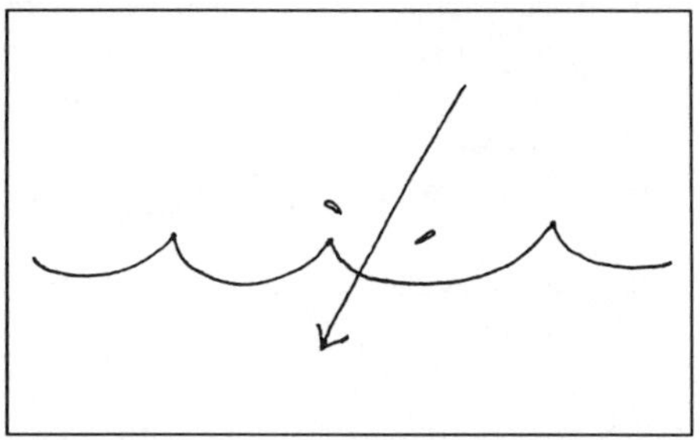

COMMENT There are several sound-symbolic adverbs in addition to *tsupu* which are descriptive of various sounds and images made by moving in water or by the movements of water. *Tsupu* is distinctive from these insofar as it implies a certain scenario. According to this scenario, something which was out of water, or at least partially above the water's surface has fallen into it, and in doing so, made enough of a noise to be heard. Insofar as it describes a path of movement underwater, *tsupu* calls attention to the fascination on the part of Quechua speakers for whatever lives beneath the water. Interestingly, there is a belief that there is another world beneath the water, which resembles the abovewater world, although it has distinctive forms of life, including human-like creatures.

ICONIC PROPERTIES The iconicity of *tsupu* is related to its disyllabic structure, its bilabial stop, *-p-*, and its final open syllable. Its disyllabic structure provides a framework within which a speaker can performatively gesture either an idea of the sound of falling into water or a falling and a subsequent path of movement underwater. The medial bilabial stop, *-p-*, the articulation of which involves a momentary cessation of air through the vocal tract, together with its immediately following vowel, which allows air to again pass freely through the vocal tract, are iconic of the brief contact and subsequent movement by an object through water. If a speaker wants to describe an extended path of movement underwater, then the second syllable, -pu, is performatively lengthened. The openness of the final syllable is iconic of unobstructed movement through water.

Tsupu occurs with the following verbs.

1. tsupu saltana (leap) — to leap and fall into water, e.g., catfish, freshwater dolphin
2. tsupu urmana (fall) — to fall into water, e.g., an animal, piece of fruit, etc.
3. tsupu zambulina (plunge) — to plunge or immerse oneself underwater
4. tsupu rina (go) — to go into water by leaping, falling, or plunging
5. tsupu shitana (throw) — to throw something into water, e.g., a piece of bait for fishing

6. tsupu ichana — to disperse by throwing into water
   disperse
7. tsupu ichuna — to get rid of by throwing out into water, e.g., accumulated rainwater from a canoe
   abandon
8. tsupu kachana — to send, drop something into water, e.g., a machete knife by a careless child
   send
9. tsupu kacharina — to release something into the water
   release
10. tsupu uyarina — to be heard falling into water
    sound

In the following example, *tsupu* describes how a large rodent called a *kapiwara* quickly dove into the river to avoid being detected by the speaker herself who was washing clothes nearby.

11. Kasna taksari-kbi chay l^{y}uka-kbi, ñukanchi tiya-shka pungu-y, tup^{h}uu; tupu
    like that wash-SWRF there crawl-SWRF our dwell-PERF door-LOC
    salta-k-ga, yaku-y chingari-n!
    leap-AG-TOP water-LOC be lost-3

    "(And so I was) washing clothes like that, and there it was crawling near the clearing where we live; *tup^{h}uu* (it went); leaping into the water *tupu*, it was gone!"

When she uses *tsupu* the first time, she foregrounds it with a strong puff of air over the second syllable. This explosive puff of aspiration can be understood as a performative gesture of the force of the animal's fall. Although the first *tsupu* is intended to simulate the quality of the sound made by the animal, it also functions aspectually because it describes the punctual moment when the speaker first became aware of the animal's presence. This first *tsupu* has an inferential function because it is used to describe the speaker's realization of the animal's presence. The second, less performative *tsupu* modifies the agentivized verb *saltak* "leap-er," which, without modification by *tsupu*, would be unspecified for aspectual punctuality.

In the next example *tsupu*$_1$ describes a water dog's chasing of a catfish. The other sound-symbolic adverb, *dzas*, describes any punctual action. Here *dzas* describes a catfish's punctual leaping out of the water; *tsupu* describes its punctual falling back in.

12. Bagri dzas tupu salta-sha urma-n, pay-was tsupu, timpu salta-chi-gri!
    catfish leap-COR fall-3 he-INCL time leap-CAUS-TRSLC

    "(Whenever) the catfish leaped *dzas* and fell *tupu*, he (the dog) also went *tsupu,* and in no time went and made it leap back out of the water."

There is very little performative foregrounding either of *dzas* or *tsupu* in this sentence. Neither sound-symbolic adverb is given intonational elaboration. The first occurrence of *dzas* and *tsupu* together is grammatically motivated: both adverbs modify the coreference verb *saltasha* "leaping," affecting it with aspectual punctuality. Only the second *tsupu* is slightly foregrounded by its syntactic displacement from the verb *saltachigri* "goes and makes leap." It is interrupted from modification of this verb by the adverb *timpu* "in no time." This second occurrence of *tsupu* also functions grammatically by enhancing the punctuality that is implied by the translocative suffix *-gri*.

In the next example *tsupu* and its variant *tupu* undergo multiple repetitions to describe the way several large rodents called *lomocha*-s[4] were heard jumping into the river and swimming. Their jumping into the river is described with *tsupu*$_1$; their swimming is described by *tsupu*$_2$.

13. Chi-ga, kucha sapi-manda uya-kbi tsup^{h}uuuuuu tsupu tsupu tsupu tsupu tsupu
that-TOP pond end-from listen-SWRF
tsupu tupu tupu tupu; tsup^{h}uu, tsup^{h}uu tsup^{h}u tup^{h}u uyari-mu-ra.
sound-CIS-PAST

"So then, from the end of the pond, what I heard was *tsup^{h}uuuuuu tsupu tsupu tsupu tsupu tsupu tsupu tupu tupu tupu, tsup^{h}uu tsup^{h}uu tsup^{h}u tup^{h}u* it sounded."

Tsupu$_1$ is represented by the four aspirated forms. Each of these is a sound-symbolic performance of the four animals falling into water. The force of the fall is represented by the explosive puff of air created by their aspiration. The other occurrences of *tsupu* are performatively foregrounded by their multiple repetition, which is rhythmically regular and very quickly executed to imitate the fast pace of their swimming. Each aspirated *tsupu* is aspectually punctual at the predicate level. The repetitions of *tsupu* considered as a series are aspectually iterative at the propositional level. The formal amplifications of *tsupu*$_1$ and *tsupu*$_2$ also function modally in this context to recreate the anxiety felt by the narrator upon hearing these sounds and not knowing what was making them. It was night, and she couldn't see the animals. Furthermore, her husband had just left her alone to go and get help hauling in a giant turtle which they had just speared. By performatively simulating the quality of these sounds, without first revealing what was making them, the narrator evokes the same apprehensions she felt during the experience itself.

In the next example, taken from a myth, *tsupu*$_2$ describes the way a person who has just had his eyes pecked out by a hawk goes and falls into a river and then travels some distance underwater before he turns into a freshwater dolphin. The other sound-symbolic adverbs, *b^{h}ux* and *kar*, describe, respectively, the dolphin's subsequent burst out of water and the trailing arc created by that movement.

14. Yaku-y tup^{h}uuuuuuuu urma-k-ga, chimbay -shi b^{h}uxxx karrrr-shi l^{y}ukshi-ra.
water-LOC fall-AG-TOP across-EV -EV emerge-PAST

"Falling into the water *tup^{h}uuuuuuuu* (it went until it reached) across, and there, *b^{h}uxxx karrrr* it emerged."

Tupu is performatively foregrounded here by lengthening of its final syllable, which describes the spatial extent of the dolphin's movement underwater. Its formal amplification functions aesthetically to simulate a feeling of the duration of movement and its extendedness in space.

In another example taken from a myth, *tsupu*$_2$ describes not only the spatial extent of an underwater movement but also its depth. The sentence describes an anaconda's journey to its underwater abode.

15. Yaku-y-ga tupu$_{u_{u_{uu}}}$ urma-ra yaku-y.
water-LOC-TOP fall-PAST water-LOC

"In the water he fell (and went) *tupu$_{u_{u_{uu}}}$* (down into) the water."

*Tsupu*2 is performatively foregrounded by the extension of its final syllable. It is additionally foregrounded by a successive lowering of the speaker's voice over the extension of *tsupu*'s final syllable. This successive lowering of the speaker's voice is a performative gesture of the increasingly lower depth traveled by the anaconda. *Tsupu* functions aesthetically to simulate a feeling of the duration of a movement, and the extent of its depth as well.

Huy

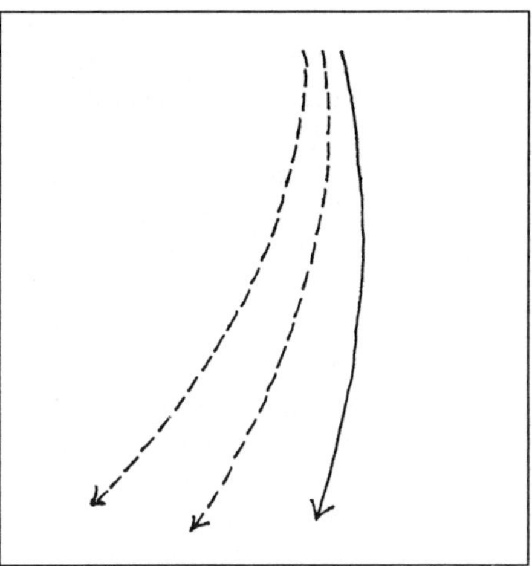

DEFINITION To be hanging, dangling, or suspended, or to move while hanging, dangling, or being suspended. Aspectually durative, completive, resultative.

COMMENT The essential image of *huy* is of an object or entity at rest, or at its most natural in a hanging, suspended state. Sloths hanging from trees, fruit pods hanging from branches, babies hanging in a sheet tied between posts, and a man hanging in a hammock are all images described by *huy*. This essential image of *huy*-ness can lend drama to an image of something that should not be hanging or suspended, but is. For example, a military plane that crashed because it had been overloaded with cargo was observed by people who had watched its take-off to be hanging *huy* at its tail end. Another dramatic image described with *huy* is that of a partridge killed by a snake that had torn its skin and left it hanging *huy* away from its flesh.

ICONIC PROPERTIES The iconicity of *huy* is related to its lack of stop consonants. Its word-initial velar fricative *h-* produces a turbulent airstream that allows for the movement of air through the vocal tract. This free movement, which is also continued during articulation of its following vowel and approximant *-uy*, imitates the free movement of whatever is suspended, dangling, or hanging.

Huy occurs with the following verbs.

1.	huy warkuna hang	to be hanging or dangling, e.g., meat from rafters
2.	huy warku-chi-na hang-CAUS	to hang or dangle something, e.g., a toy in front of a baby
3.	huy warkurina hang	to hang oneself on something, e.g., the way a sloth hangs from a tree
4.	huy puñuna sleep	to sleep hanging, e.g., a baby in a sheet tied between posts
5.	huy sirina lie	to recline hanging, e.g., in a hammock
6.	huy pugl^{y}ana play	to play with any long cord, rope, or vine, by shooting or casting it about
7.	huy apana take, carry	to take or carry anything that hangs
8.	huy aparina bear, carry	to bear fruits or pods which hang prominently
9.	huy rina go	to go, hanging in space, e.g., the tail of an airplane that has just taken off
10.	huy tukuna become	to deviate from any fixed point or path of movement by drooping or hanging, e.g. an airplane's tail
11.	huy hapina catch	to catch something, thereby hanging it, e.g., a fish suspended by hook and line
12.	huy hapirina catch	to catch oneself onto something, e.g. a sloth on a vine
13.	huy likirina tear	to tear something, leaving it hanging, e.g., the way a large snake kills a partridge, by biting and then tearing its skin, leaving it hanging away from the flesh

The following two examples use *huy* to describe the same object in motion—an airplane—in two different ways. In the first example, *huy* is used to communicate an image of smooth, continuous, unbroken movement; it describes how the tail of a plane, as seen by bystanders, seemed to be hanging too low right after take-off.

14. Ña kasna ri-ra chupa-ga huy$_{yyyyyyyyy}$.
then like this go-PAST tail-TOP
"Then this is how the tail went *huy*$_{yyyyyyyyy}$."

The lengthening of its pronunciation is a performative gesture of the uninterrupted duration of the plane's movement across space. There is also a slight descending pitch across the pronunciation of *huy*, which suggests a feeling of lowness about this movement. These qualities of *huy*'s pronunciation were possibly meant by the speaker to foreshadow the plane's crash, that was in fact imminent.

In the next example *huy* describes rough, choppy, repeated movements. This sentence concerns a different incident. It describes how it felt to be inside a small plane that was being bounced around in stormy weather. The other sound-symbolic adverb, *aki*, describes the deviation from and then return to the plane's position of equilibrium. *Huy* describes the feeling of suspension all by itself.

15. Kasna ma-ra ak^{h}iiii ak^{h}iiii h^{h}uyyyyy h^{h}uyyyyyyy!
like this be-PAST
"Like this it was, *ak^{h}iiii ak^{h}iiii h^{h}uyyyyy h^{h}uyyyyyyy*!"

Huy is performatively foregrounded here by repetition, strong aspiration, some lengthening, and its syntactic isolation. The speaker's strong aspiration of *huy* is a vocal gesture of a feeling of unobstructed movement. The lengthening expresses both the spatial extent of that movement and its duration. This gesture adds drama to the description because the feeling of unobstructed movement suggests a lack of stability which, in this context, is terrifying.

The next example is taken from a legend about a giant hawk that would swoop down and pluck people out of their canoes and carry them off. At this moment in the story the hawk has just picked up a man. *Huy* describes how his legs looked dangling in mid-air.

16. Chaki-l^{y}a huy huy huy huy huy urku punda-ta apa-n.
foot-just mountain top-ACC take-3
"Only his feet (are seen) *huy huy huy huy huy* (as) it carries him to the mountain top."

Huy is performatively foregrounded here by its multiple repetition and its syntactic isolation. It is repeated quickly and rapidly to simulate the struggling movement of the poor victim's legs as they dangled in midair. Its function is modal. It evokes terror in the mind of the listener, as well as pity for the unfortunate victim.

The next sentence, taken from a fable, consists of a turtle's instructing a jaguar to cross a river by sliding himself across a vine that the turtle has hung from a tree on the other side. The other sound-symbolic adverb, *dzir*, describes the way the jaguar is supposed to slide along the vine.

17. Kunan kay-ta wawki, ni-n-shi huy huy huy hapiri-sha warkuri-sha;
now this-ACC brother say-3-EV grab on-COR hang on-COR

dzir dzir dzir dzir dzir dzir chimba-gri-ngi.
cross-TNSL-2

"Now here, brother, holding and hanging on, *huy huy huy*, go and cross over,

dzir dzir dzir dzir dzir dzir."

Huy is formally amplified by its multiple repetitions and also by the progressively higher pitch of these repetitions. Each repetition of *huy* indicates an incremental subevent toward the completion of the jaguar's movement across the river. This performative foregrounding is comparable to a cinematographer's use of juxtaposed shots to represent the various stages of an activity leading to its completion. By instructing the jaguar in this way, and suggesting that the crossing is something that is as good as accomplished, the turtle is able to trick him into crossing the river, which leads to his own demise.

In the next example *huy* is part of a description of the way a large snake peeled the skin of a partridge completely back, so that it was hanging away from its flesh. This description is part of an account of a pit viper's attack on a partridge, including the way it crushed the animal, plucked its feathers, and finally tore its skin away from the animal's flesh.

18. Yutu kara-ta, ña wil^{y}ma-ndi h$^{u^y}$ (pause); chay-ma-mi liki-shka-ra.
partridge skin-ACC now feather-INCL that-DAT-EV tear-PERF-PAST

"The partridge's skin, and even its feathers *h*$^{u^y}$ (pause), to there had been torn."

Huy is performatively foregrounded here with an upglide, an immediately following pause, and displacement from its verb *likishkara* "had torn." The upglide, pause, and displacement focus one's attention on the image described by *huy* in the same way that a cinematographer's close-up shot causes one to look at something with a more narrowly circumscribed point of view. In this instance, the close-up image emphasizes the completeness and thoroughness of the snake's deformation of the partridge. This final image is meant to describe the last, horrible act of this whole process.

The final example is taken from a discussion of the appearance of different kinds of fruit bearing trees. *Huy* describes the appearance of long, pod-shaped fruits that hang all over a tree.

20. Puka kambi randi, pay-ba rama-ta karan rama-ta apari-n huyyyyyy-xx-l^{y}a.
red guava instead it-POSS branch-ACC each branch-ACC bear-3 -ADV
"The red guava, rather, on each of its branches it bears (fruit) *huyyyyyy-xx-l^{y}a*."

Huy is performatively foregrounded here by its lengthening. This lengthening simulates an idea of a spatial expanse. In simulating this expanse, the speaker instructs me on the appearance of the tree and also communicates the salient aesthetic qualities of its appearance.

Aki

DEFINITION To move by deviating from and returning to a central axis, usually because of lack of control. Aspectually durative and punctual. Possibly originates from Spanish *aqui* "here." Could be the source of another sound-symbolic adverb *ki*.

COMMENT While *huy* describes a suspension or hanging which is at rest, *aki* describes a suspended swaying which is by definition not at rest because it is attempting to restabilize itself. One of the scariest experiences described with *aki* is that of being inside a small plane that sways from side to side because of bad weather. However, *aki* can also describe an aesthetically pleasing image. Some of the nicer images described with *aki* include the movement of large hawks that sway from side to side as they fly. There is also a dance done by women, described with *aki*, involving a sharp dipping of the upper torso and tossing of the hair from side to side.

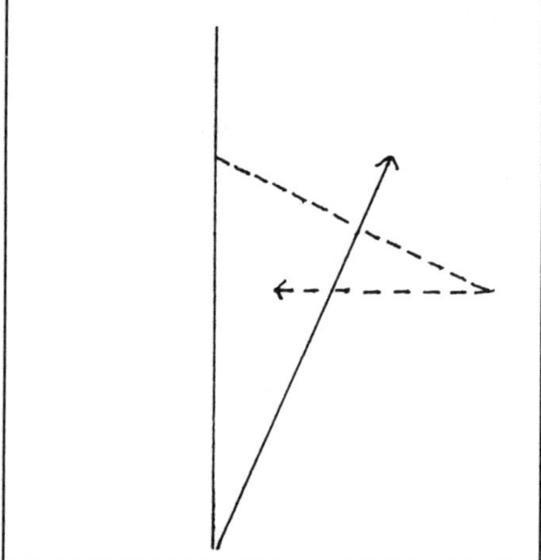

ICONIC PROPERTIES The iconicity of *aki* is related to its disyllabic structure and to its medial velar stop, *-k-*. The disyllabic structure of *aki* allows a speaker to performatively distinguish between the initial unstable part of a movement and its subsequent return to stability. The medial velar stop, *-k-*, by its brief cessation of the airstream movement, is iconic of the center of stability upon which any pivotal movement depends.

Aki occurs with the following verbs.

1.	aki kushparina move back and forth	to tip or roll from side to side, e.g., small plane in bad weather, a dugout canoe in water
2.	aki chimbana cross	to cross a space, swaying unsteadily, e.g., to cross a stream by stepping on any available rocks or fallen trees
3.	aki baylana dance	to dance by dipping the upper torso and tossing the hair from side to side
4.	aki shamuna come, approach	to come or arrive tottering because of drunkenness
5.	aki kal^{y}pana run	to run by tipping from side to side, as when running in deep sand
6.	aki pawana fly	to tip from side to side while flying, e.g., hawks playing with the wind

In the following example *aki* describes the way condors look when they dip from side to side while flying.

7. Kondor-guna aki aki aki aki pawa-nawn, wayra-ta pugl^{y}a-chi-sha.
   condor-PL fly-3PL wind-ACC play-CAUS-COR
   "Condors fly *aki aki aki aki*, playing with the wind."

Aki is performatively foregrounded here by its multiple repetitions. It functions aesthetically, by recreating a feeling of the iterative swaying movement of the bird.

In the next example *aki* describes an uncomfortable, subjective experience of swaying. This sentence describes the way a plane tipped from side to side in a bad storm. The other sound-symbolic adverb, *huy*, describes the suspended-like feeling resulting from the plane's sudden dropping upon hitting an air pocket.

8. Ña avion h^{h}uyyy al^{y}pa-l^{y}ata-ta ri-u-n, h^{h}uuyyyy, al^{y}pa-l^{y}ata-ta ri-u-n, a^{h}aaki a^{h}aaki
   now plane ground-just-to go-DUR-3 ground-just-to go-DUR-3
   a^{h}aaki a^{h}aaki !

   "Now the plane is going *h^{h}uyyy* toward the ground, *h^{h}uuyyyy*, toward the ground; (it's going) *a^{h}aaki a^{h}aaki a^{h}aaki a^{h}aaki*!

Aki is performatively foregrounded by its multiple repetition, by the lengthening of the first syllable of each repetition, and by its syntactic isolation. The speaker's drawing out of the first syllable of *aki* gestures the precarious tipping movement of the airplane. By prolonging the first syllable, the speaker heightens the feeling of scariness by emphasizing what seemed like a long time to be in a state of unsteadiness.

The next sentence describes the way one sways when crossing a stream by stepping on whatever logs are there.

9. Kaspi-ta chura-shka-ta, aki aki aki aki chimba-ra-ni.
   stick-ACC put-PERF-ACC cross-PAST-1

   "(Stepping) on the logs that had been put there, *aki aki aki aki* I crossed over."

Aki is performatively foregrounded above by its multiple repetition and also by its word-final stress. The word-final stress breaks the cadence of the multiple repetitions and in doing so emphasizes the stabilizing portion of the movement when contact is made with the logs.

L^{y}u

DEFINITION (1) Describes a shine, glint, or sparkle of any chromatic value. Aspectually resultative, completive, and iterative. (2) Describes a meandering, curved, or swirling movement. Aspectually iterative. A variant form, not often used, is *lu*.

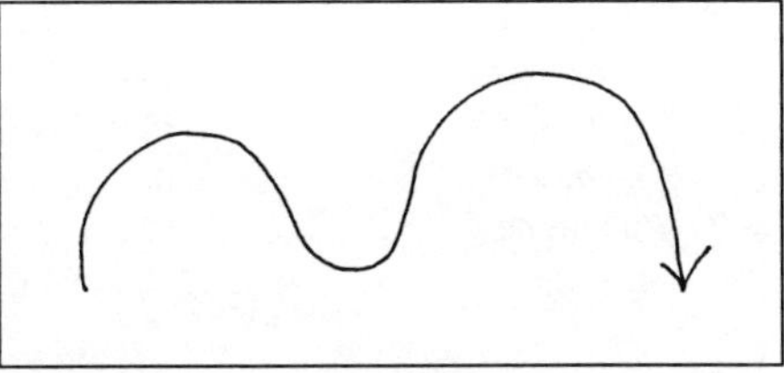

COMMENT $L^{y}u_{1}$ describes all of the kinds of images that are typically considered with the English words "bright" and "shiny," such as glass objects, golden or silvery metallic objects, and flashes of lightening at night. It also describes other chromaticities of brightness, in addition to those that are clear, white, or golden. For example, there is a large fly with a bright blue-green abdomen that is described with $l^{y}u_{1}$. The flesh of an animal that is exposed by the flaying of its skin is described with $l^{y}u_{1}$. Teeth dyed black with a vegetable juice are also described with $l^{y}u_{1}$. The connection between $l^{y}u_{1}$ and $l^{y}u_{2}$ is unclear. $L^{y}u_{2}$ describes both an actual curving movement, such as that of a snake, and a feeling of movement suggested by an inanimate shape, such as the curved line defined by a river's path. The images described by $l^{y}u_{1}$ and $l^{y}u_{2}$ are almost always considered aesthetically pleasing.

ICONIC PROPERTIES The iconicity of l^yu_1 is related to its palatalized liquid l^y- and the openness of its syllable. The palatalized liquid l^y- can be considered a "smooth, even" sound, insofar as there is no audible friction from the airstream produced during its articulation. This sound lends itself to imitation of a shiny surface, because a visual pattern that is shiny has the appearance of an uninterrupted, even surface. The openness of its final syllable lends itself to imitation of a smooth, uninterrupted surface because it implies a lack of boundedness. The iconicity of l^yu_2 is also related to its palatalized liquid, l^y-; its high back vowel, *-u-*; and the openness of its final syllable. The palatalization of the liquid creates a high front tongue position, which provides a sharp articulatory contrast with the immediately following high back vowel, *-u-*. This contrast between front and back vowels lends itself to imitation of a swirling, curved movement because such a movement is defined by a contrast—that is, a deviation in opposite directions—while it moves progressively toward a fixed point. By its lack of boundedness, the openness of its final syllable is iconic of the idea of motion implied by a curved movement.

$L^y u$ occurs with the following verbs.

1.	l^yu rikurina appear	to shine or glitter, e.g., glass beads in the sun, lightening at night, skin of a catfish, wet hair, polyester clothing, teeth blackened with a leaf juice; abdomen of a fly, fur of a black jaguar
2.	l^yu rana do, make	to make shiny, e.g., a clay pot with varnish
3.	l^yu l^yuchuna peel	to peel an animal's hide, exposing its shiny flesh
4.	l^yu rikuna look	to roll one's eyes
5.	l^yu maskana search	to search by circling all over rather than following a direct route
6.	l^yu muyuna circle	to move by curving or circling about, e.g., a snake; to meander, e.g., a river
7.	l^yu barana insert	to swish or swirl around with an inserted object or instrument, e.g., to apply medicine to the inside of a baby's mouth

In the following sentence *$l^y u$* describes the shininess of the fur of a *sacha $al^y ku$* "forest dog."

8. Pay-ba wil^{y}ma chasna-ga $l^y u^{u^{u}}$ (pause) rikuri-k ma-n, bagri kara shina.
   he-POSS fur like that-TOP appear-AG be-3 catfish skin like

   "Its fur appears *$l^y u^{u^{u}}$* (pause) like the skin of a catfish."

$L^y u$ is performatively foregrounded by its upglide, its lengthening, and its immediately following pause. By gliding the pitch of *$l^y u$* upward, the speaker is vocally gesturing the complete extent of the evenness of the shine on this animal's fur. This performative description also calls attention to these qualities because they are aesthetically pleasing.

The next example describes the appearance of an animal's flesh after its skin has been completely peeled away.

9. Chi-ta-ga $l^yu^{u^{u^u}}$ l^yuchu-nchi kara-ta chakichi-ngawa.
   that-ACC-TOP peel-1PL skin-ACC dry-FINF

   "We peel that (until it is) *$l^yu^{u^{u^u}}$* in order to dry the skin."

L^yu is performatively foregrounded by its upglide and lengthening. This technique vocally gestures the complete shininess of the animal's flesh. The aesthetically pleasing quality of this image is grounded in the speaker's conception of a task—the preparation of a monkey's meat for drying—which has been carefully, skillfully, and completely executed. By formally elaborating this image, she invites a listener to ponder the aesthetically pleasing feeling of pride over the completion of one step in the preparation of the animal's meat.

L^yu_1 can also describe a glinting or sparkling surface. In the next sentence, taken from a fable, it describes the appearance of a trunk full of gold.

10. L^yu l^yu l^yu l^yu l^yu l^yu l^yu rikuri-k kuri mashti-ta-shi apamu-shka.
    appear-AG gold thing-ACC-EV bring-PERF

    "He brought a thing (trunk) of *l^yu l^yu l^yu l^yu l^yu l^yu l^yu* appearing gold."

L^yu is performatively foregrounded here by its multiple repetition and by its circumscribing rise and fall in pitch. The repetitions are comparable to an enumerative gesture of the sparkles. The incremental pitch variations, by their distribution throughout a range of levels, suggest that the sparkling was distributed all over a certain visual field. This description simulates the image of sparkling gold for aesthetic effect.

Repetitions of *l^yu_1* can also be used to describe flashes of lightning.

11. Rayu-guna l^yu l^yu l^yu rikuri-n tuta-y.
    lightning-PL appear-3 night-LOC
    "(Flashes of) lightning appear *l^yu l^yu l^yu* at night."

This sentence is performatively foregrounded by its multiple repetitions that simulate the aesthetically pleasing qualities of the lightning's intermittent flashing against the blackness of the night sky.

L^yu_2, which describes a meandering or curved movement, is always repeated. The man who said the following sentence embellished his repetitions by making repeated curved gestures with his index finger to describe the meandering curves of a river. This sentence occurred while we were dicussing the things one can see when traveling in an airplane.

12. Bobonaza yaku l^yu l^yu l^yu l^yu puri-k ma-n.
    Bobonaza river travel-AG be-3
    "The Bobonaza River travels *l^yu l^yu l^yu l^yu*."

L^yu is performatively foregrounded by its multiple repetitions and also by the hand gesture that accompanied it. These repetitions and the accompanying gesture imitate a feeling of movement and the aesthetic pleasure of apprehending it from a distant vantage point.

Wal^yang

DEFINITION Describes a movement of shadowy forms, or an alternating pattern of light and darkness. Aspectually iterative, resultative.

COMMENT While *l^yuw_1* describes shininess and brightness, the essential image described by *wal^yang* is a shadowy and indistinct movement. Typically, such movements are described as taking place at night. However, the intermittant light and darkness of rainclouds seen from inside an airplane can also be described with *wal^yang*. The images described with *wal^yang* usually make people feel afraid.

ICONIC PROPERTIES The iconicity of *wal^yang* is related to its disyllabic structure, its word-medial palatalized liquid *-l^y-*, and the closure of its final syllable. Its disyllabic structure allows a speaker to gesture vocally, a movement of form, or an alternating pattern of light and darkness. The first syllable, *wa-*, can correspond to what is seen before a movement, and the second syllable, *-l^yang*, to the visible difference in a pattern as a result of movement. Alternatively, the first syllable can be analogous to a movement, while the second syllable is analogous to a movement coming to a rest. As there is no audible friction from the airstream produced during its articulation, its medial liquid *-l^y-* is iconic of the movements it describes, which are lacking in forcefulness. The final closed syllable completes the image by its articulation, which obstructs the airstream and effectively concludes the image.

Wal^yang occurs with the following verbs.

1. wal^yang rina (go) — to create shadows or to be visible as shadows while moving or going
2. wal^yang shamuna (come) — to arrive at night, appearing as a shadowy figure
3. wal^yang kuyurina (shake) — to shake, or flutter, creating shadows
4. wal^yang rikuna (see) — to see only a shadow of a form
5. wal^yang rikurina (appear) — to appear as a shadowy movement

In the following sentence *wal^yang* describes a glimpse of a shadowy form seen at night with only the illumination of a burning fire.

6. Amsa a-shka, nina pundzha-l^{y}a wal^{y}ang -mi riku-ra-ni.
   darkness be-PERF fire day-LIM -EV see-PAST-1
   "As it was dark, (with) only the firelight, I saw *wal^{y}ang* (dimly)."

Wal^{y}ang is not performatively foregrounded here. It affects its verb *rikurani* "I saw" with an aspectually aorist value because it describes a contrastive movement of light and shadow seen as a single complete vision.

In the next example *wal^{y}ang* is part of a description of an accidental encounter with a jaguar, hidden from view by a tree's foliage. *Wal^{y}ang* describes a moment of the leaves' movement which makes evident the jaguar's presence. This particular use of *wal^{y}ang* was actually elicited indirectly by myself because it was used to paraphrase another sound-symbolic adverb, *sang*, which I didn't at the time understand. The narrator's description, as well as my own question which caused her to paraphrase the image with *wal^{y}ang*, follow.

7. Ruya-ga kasna urma-shka-ra hawa-ta urma-shka-ra; rama rama rama
   tree-TOP like this fall-PERF-PAST above-ACC fall-PERF-PAST branch branch branch
   rama rama!
   branch branch
   "The tree had fallen like this (catching itself on another tree), above, it had fallen; (there were) branches, branches, branches, branches, branches."

8. Kil tik^{h}aaaaaa ruya, chi-mi, imina chari s^{h}aaaang ra-shka shina rikuri-ra!
   Kil cluster tree there-EV how perhaps do-PERF like appear-PAST
   And the *kil* flowers were clustered all over the tree; and there it appeared to go *s^{h}aaaang*.

   Q: Ima shina sang a-ra?
   how like be-PAST
   "How was it *sang*?"

9. Kuti wa$^{l^y ang}$ kasna kuyuri-ra.
   well like this shake-PAST
   "Well *wa$^{l^y ang}$* like that it shook!

Wal^{y}ang is performatively foregrounded here by the upjump of pitch and by its syntactic displacement from its verb *kuyurira* "it shook." Its upjump provides a pitch contrast that iconifies a conceptual contrast, which enhances the description of a resultant state. The first syllable, *wa-*, corresponds to the pattern that was seen before the leaves fluttered; the second syllable, *-l^{y}ang*, corresponds to the visible difference in that pattern as a result of the leaves' shaking, which was caused by the jaguar. In this example *wal^{y}ang* is used in a combination of inferential, instructional, and modal functions. The image described by *wal^{y}ang* is represented by the speaker as important in her own realization of the jaguar's presence. Further, her use of this image is part of her explanation of how she came to this realization. Finally, the image itself is intended to evoke a startled, alert, and fearful feeling upon seeing this slight fluttering movement without knowing its source.

In the next example, *wal^{y}ang* describes a pattern of shadowy movement created by people walking at night.

10. Runa-guna amsa-y wal^{y}ang wal^{y}ang rikuri-sha puri-nawn, mandzhana-ya-kta.
    people-PL darkness-LOC appear-COR walk-3PL be afraid-ICH-until
    "People go around in the darkness, appearing frighteningly *wal^{y}ang wal^{y}ang*."

Wal^{y}ang is minimally foregrounded by its reduplication, which is a shorthand for aspectual iterativity. It functions grammatically and referentially to refer to a shadowy movement which caused the speaker to be fearful.

In the final example, *wal^{y}ang* describes the contrasting pattern of light and shadow created by rainclouds seen from inside a small airplane.

11. Chi-mi puyu kasna wal^{y}ang wal^{y}ang wal^{y}ang wal^{y}ang wal^{y}ang ri-shka-y, kay-bi
    then-EV cloud like this go-PERF-NOM here-LOC
    ri-shka-y, kay-bi urku a-w-kpi . . .
    go-PERF-NOM here-LOC hill be-DUR-SWRF
    "Then the clouds having gone like this *wal^{y}ang wal^{y}ang wal^{y}ang wal^{y}ang wal^{y}ang,* here is this hill . . ."

Wal^{y}ang is performatively foregrounded by its multiple repetition, which simulates the repeating pattern of lightness and darkness. Its function is modal. It evokes a feeling of fear felt by the speaker who described how this lack of visibility nearly resulted in the plane's crash into a hillside. It describes the repetition of a contrasting pattern of light and darkness, and therefore affects this sentence with aspectual iterativity.

Wikang

DEFINITION To stand or be positioned vertically in space, unattached and independent of the surrounding environment. Aspectually resultative, completive, durative.

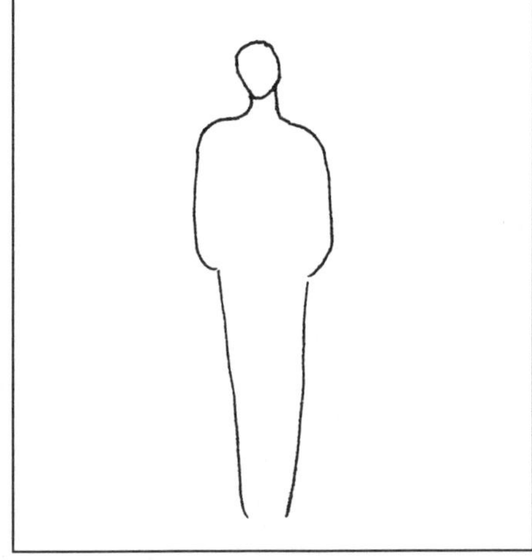

COMMENT *Wikang* is a sound-symbolic image modeled on the bodily and emotional experiences of standing and of feeling singular and apart from everything else. For the Quechua the physical posture of standing connotes strength, resolve, endurance, and vulnerability. People who fall, for whatever reason, are looked down on or teased. Nevertheless, the strength of one's standing posture can also make one vulnerable in certain contexts. Someone once used *wikang* to describe what it felt like to stop in the middle of the forest upon hearing an unidentifiable sound, and stand there all alone, frightened.

ICONIC PROPERTIES The iconicity of *wikang* is related to its disyllabic structure; its medial velar stop, *-k-*; the contrast between the high vowel *-i-* in its initial syllable and the low vowel *-a-* in its final syllable; and its final velarized nasal, *-ng*. Its disyllabic structure is iconic of the distinction between foreground and background. The initial syllable, *wi-*, is iconic of the background, and the final syllable, *-kang*, is iconic of the foregrounded vertical image. The distinction between foreground and background is further enhanced by the contrast between the high vowel *-i-* and the low vowel *-a-*. Because its articulation involves a complete obstruction of the airstream and a subsequent burst of sound, the medial velar stop, *-k-*, provides a definitive focus for the shift from background to foreground. The final velarized nasal, *-ng*, completes the framing of the image of verticality by its articulatory obstruction of the airstream, which effectively concludes the image.

Wikang occurs with the following verbs.

1. wikang shayana — to stand straight up
   stand
2. wikang mana — to be positioned vertically in space
   be
3. wikang rikurina — to appear vertically positioned in space
   appear
4. wikang l^{y}ukshina — to emerge upward, in a vertical shape, e.g., something from underwater
   emerge
5. wikang rina — to go along in a way which makes one's vertical dimensions most prominent., e.g., a worm carrying a leaf stem in its mouth (myth)
   go
6. wikang al^{y}sana — to lift up so that one's vertical dimension is most prominent, e.g., a sting ray's tail
   lift
7. wikang tiya-chi-na — to position something vertically in space
   be-CAUS

The following sentence is taken from a personal experience narrative about a bizarre discovery. While walking deep in the forest, a woman discovered a man who, although dead, had only been partially buried. *Wikang* is used to describe the way the dead man's foot was sticking straight out of the ground.

8. Ña shuk chaki hawa-y wi^{kang} chaki rikuri-ra.
   now one foot above-LOC foot appear-PAST
   "And one foot (was pointing) upward, *wi*^{kang} (that) foot appeared."

Wikang is performatively foregrounded by the upjump over its second syllable and by displacement from its verb *rikurira* "appeared." The upjump provides a pitch contrast that is iconic of the conceptual contrast between foreground and background. In this instance, the initial syllable, *wi-*, is comparable to the neutral background, while the second upjumped syllable, *-kang*, is comparable to the dramatic foregrounded image of the foot sticking straight out of the ground. In this context, the straight up-ness of the image described with *wikang* evokes feelings of shock and irony experienced by such a startling discovery. The image of strength connoted by *wikang* is extremely ironic in this context, because the being in question is deceased.

In the next example *wikang* describes the way the long inner section of a blowgun stood straight up after being poked into a jaguar's flesh. The jaguar in question had attacked and killed the narrator's father's dog. In this sentence the narrator is repeating what her father had told her about how he'd done away with the jaguar using only his blowgun as a weapon.

9. Ña kay-bi sha-ya-w-n, ni-ra-mi, pukuna tulʸu-ga wi^{kang}!
now here-LOC stand-DUR-3 say-PAST-EV blowgun bone-TOP
"'Now here, he said, is (how) the bone of the blowgun is standing up, *wi*$^{\textit{kang}}$.'"

Wikang is performatively foregrounded here by its upjump and syntactic displacement. The upjump provides a pitch contrast that enhances the description of a resultant state, which, in this case, is the state of the blowgun's end sticking straight out of the jaguar. The narrator's father uses this image to emphasize the strong effect he had on the jaguar, which he did eventually kill.

In the next example *wikang* describes an image of someone standing alone in the forest. The speaker is describing how she felt upon hearing unidentifiable sounds.

10. Kan-chu mana mandzha-ngi-ma? Kan-ga pi-wan-da kwinta-naku-ngi-ma
you-NEG NEG be afraid-2-CNDL you-TOP who-INST-ACC talk-RCP-2-CNDL
sapa-lʸa wi^{kang} sacha-y? Alʸku-lʸa-ng!
alone-LIM forest-LOC dog-LIM-INST
"Wouldn't you be afraid? You, who would you talk with, (standing) alone, *wi*$^{\textit{kang}}$ in the forest with only a dog!"

Wikang is performatively foregrounded by its upjump and also by its syntactic isolation. The upjump provides a pitch contrast that enhances the description of a resultant state, in this case, the state of standing still, all alone in the forest. *Wikang* in this sentence evokes a feeling of vulnerability. The strength connoted by the image of standing up straight makes one more visible and therefore open to attack from unknown forces in the forest.

The next example was offered as a description of the way a type of forest spirit walks by turning a somersault, and then standing straight up. The sound-symbolic adverb *tʸam* describes its somersault and *wikang* describes its standing straight up again.

11. Shalama supay tʸam wi^{kang} tʸam wi^{kang} tʸam wi^{kang} puri-k ma-n.
Shalama spirit walk-AG be-3
"The shalama spirit walks (by going) *tʸam wi*$^{\textit{kang}}$ *tʸam wi*$^{\textit{kang}}$ *tʸam wi*$^{\textit{kang}}$."

Wikang is performatively foregrounded by its multiple repetition and by the upjump over each repetition. Each upjump in pitch can be understood as a gesture of the spirit's standing straight up. Each instance of this standing up, as represented by *wikang*, can be considered aspectually resultative. The combination of images of rolling and then standing straight up again evoke a whimsical feeling.

The following example is taken from a Quechua version of the biblical tale of Noah's ark. According to this version, God had flooded the world so deeply that it was impossible to steer one's way around in the water with a pole because there was no ground to be reached with the pole. The speaker's use of *wikang* describes a miraculous moment when a steering pole was raised straight upward from underwater by a rising of the ground.

12. Riku-kpi tawna-ga wika$^{a\,a\,a\,a}$aaannggg l^{y}ukshi-shka.
    look-SWRF pole-TOP leave-PERF

    "What he saw was that the pole emerged *wika*$^{a\,a\,a\,a}$*aaannggg*."

Wikang is performatively foregrounded by lengthening and a circumscribing pitch rise and fall. These techniques present a vocal gesture of an uninterrupted, continuous image. The lengthening describes the way more and more of the pole gradually emerged from under the water as the ground under the water rose. The rise and fall in pitch over the lengthened syllable circumscribes the image of the pole's rising and also breaks the monotony of the lengthening. This image functions both aesthetically and epistemically. From a listener's perspective, it lends credibility and concreteness to a miraculous moment. At the same time, within the story itself, the image serves as an index of something beyond the ordinary. It allows the biblical protagonists to know that *yaya d^{y}os* "god the father" is on their side.

Chinda

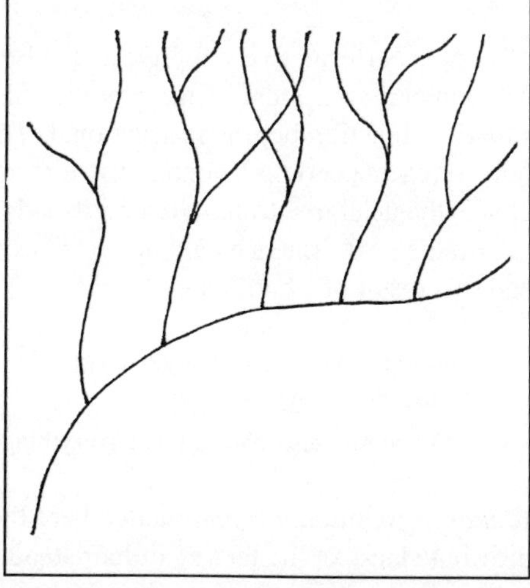

DEFINITION (1) Describes a group of long vertical shapes that jut out or upward from a base. Aspectually aorist. (2) Describes the movement of anything with a prominent vertical extension. Aspectually durative.

COMMENT While the essential image described by *wikang* is of a singular, unattached vertical prominence, *chinda* describes a plurality of long shapes jutting out from a base. The English word "spikiness" comes close to describing *chinda*, although it also implies sharpness, which *chinda* does not. The way hair seems to stand up on skin when one shivers is described with *chinda*. The image of a canoe filled with long bunches of manioc branches that are stood upright is another common image described with *chinda.*

ICONIC PROPERTIES The iconicity of *chinda* is related to its disyllabic structure; the contrast between its initial syllable high vowel *-i-* and its final syllable low vowel *-a*; its closed initial syllable, *chin-*, and the openness of its final syllable, *-da*. Its disyllabic structure is iconic of the distinction between foreground and background.

Chinda occurs with the following verbs.

1. chinda rina go	to jut up and outward from a base, e.g., the long spindly branches of a type of coral, hair on a body that shivers
2. chinda wiñana grow	to grow straight up, e.g., hair which is plucked out or which has fallen out during pregnancy
3. chinda l^{y}ukshina leave	to emerge sticking straight out, e.g., the antennae of a fresh water shrimp coming out of a hole
4. chinda apana take, carry	to carry something that juts out or upward, e.g., a canoe carrying long bunches of manioc branches that are stood upright
5. chinda ana be	to be jutting out, e.g., limbs of a dead tree trunk lying on its side
6. chinda muyurina circle	to make circling movements that have a vertical prominence, e.g., a freshwater dolphin swimming underwater with only its dorsal fin showing above the water

In the following example *chinda* describes the branches that stick out of a tree trunk lying on its side.

7. Chi playa punda-y-mi kay intiru kaspi siri-u-ra ni-ni chinda chinda chinda
   that beach edge-LOC-EV this entire trunk lie-DUR-PAST say-1
   kaspi a-ra.
   trunk be-PAST

   "I mean that there, at the edge of the beach, this entire trunk was lying there; *chinda chinda chinda*, it was."

Chinda is performatively foregrounded by multiple repetition. These repetitions are an enumerative gesture of the plurality of branches jutting out from the tree trunk. *Chinda*'s function here is instructional. The narrator is clarifying an explanation of how to reach a certain lagoon in the forest. One of the landmarks in the surrounding area is the dead tree trunk lying on its side, with bare branches jutting out around it.

In the next sentence *chinda* describes the feeling of one's body hair standing on end as a result of a bad scare.

8. Intiru aycha ña wil^{y}ma-guna-s chinda chinda ri-wa-n.
   entire flesh now hair-PL-INCL go-1ACC-3

   "All of my flesh, the hair and everything, *chinda chinda* it went on me."

Chinda is minimally foregrounded here by its reduplication. It refers to the all over distributedness of the feeling of hair standing up on one's body.

In the next sentence *chinda* describes an image of a canoe filled with bundles of manioc branches that have been stood upright. The other sound-symbolic adverb, *ton*, describes the completedness of the filling of the canoe.

9.

Lomo kaspi-ta-ga	wangu	wangu	wangu	chunga	wangu-ta	wangu-sha	hatun
manioc branch-ACC-TOP	bundle	bundle	bundle	ten	bundle-ACC	bundle-COR	big

kano-y-ga	$t^{o^{n}}$	chind^{h}aaaa-xxl^{y}a	apamuna	a-n.
canoe-LOC-TOP		-ADV	bring	be-3

"Making bundles and bundles and bundles with the manioc branches, making ten bundles, and (then filling) a big canoe with them $t^{o^{n}}$, they bring them *chind*^{h}*aaaa-xxl*^{y}*a*."

Chinda is performatively foregrounded by lengthening, aspiration, and its suffixation with an epenthetic velar fricative and the emphatic suffix -*l*^{y}*a*. The suffixation of *chinda* with an epenthetic velar fricative, as well as an emphatic -*l*^{y}*a*, allows its pronunciation to be prolonged. In this context, the duration of *chinda*'s lengthening gestures not just an idea of the manioc branches' movement across space as the canoe carries them; it also gestures the spatial distribution of the vertical prominences defined by these bundles. The image described by *chinda* is aesthetically pleasing in this context. The bunches of branches filling the canoe represent the completion of one stage of a long, difficult task. One of the preliminary stages of this task is the cutting and gathering together of cuttings from mature bushes for propagation in a new field. The description presents an image of this particular task's completion.

The final example of *chinda* describes the vertical prominence of a freshwater dolphin's dorsal fin as it circles just beneath the water's surface.

10.

Kal^{y}ari-ga	kay	l^{y}akta-gama	shamu-k	ma-ra,	chinda-nnnnng	muyu-ria-k
beginning-TOP	this	place-as far as	come-AG	be-PAST	-INST	circle-DUR-AG

a-naw-ra.
be-3-PAST

"A long time ago they would come even as far as this place, (appearing) *chinda-nnnnng* they would circle about."

Chinda is performatively foregrounded by lengthening. Its lengthening is a vocal gesture of an an ongoing uninterrupted movement through space. *Chinda*'s function here is aesthetic: it describes an image of movement that is particularly enjoyed by the Quechua because it is only rarely seen. The freshwater dolphin has become almost extinct in this area due to overhunting.

9

Sound Symbols of Contact and Penetration

This chapter consists of six sound-symbolic adverbs describing various kinds and gradations of contact and penetration. *Tak* describes the moment of contact between two surfaces.[1] *T'api* elaborates the notion of contact by describing instances in which contact results in adhesion. *Dzir* describes situations in which contact between surfaces is maintained even though one or possibly both surfaces are moving. The first real adverb of penetration is *tsak*. It describes the shallowest degree of penetration, such as that experienced by an insect's sting. *Ling* describes a deeper degree of insertion usually involving empty or enclosed spaces. The final adverb *polo* describes the greatest degree of penetration because it describes a complete passing through or breaking through a barrier.

Tak

DEFINITION (1A) The moment of contact between two surfaces, one of which, typically, is manipulated by a force higher in agency than the other. The positioning of an object within a definite point in space. (1B) An idea of the sound resulting from a deliberate and swift contact between two relatively firm surfaces. Aspectually punctual.[2] (2A) An expanse of contact between two entities, such that the surface of one is coextensive with the surface of another, although they remain separable. (2B) Any feature or quality considered as extended in space; any attribute, state, or action considered in, or performed to, its utmost limit. Aspectually completive, resultative, aorist.[3] When used in its punctual sense, its final velar stop is sometimes voiced. When *tak* describes the expanse, limit, or extent of an action or attribute, the final velar stop is often lengthened and fricativized.

COMMENT *Tak*$_1$ can be understood by analogy with a cinematographer or videographer's use of a close-up shot: it is the *moment* when contact is made between two sur-

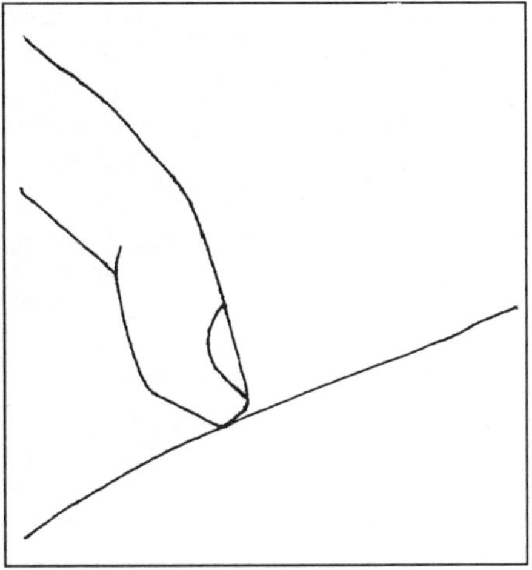

faces that is focused on with tak_{1A}. There is often a sense of urgency about an action so described. One grabs onto small children *tak* to remove them from danger. A weapon is grabbed *tak* to prepare for defense or assault. The central meaning of tak_{1A}, which is to describe the moment when contact is made between surfaces can be extended to describe a definite positioning of something in space. For example, a snake positions its tail *tak* in the air when it is about to strike. Tak_{1B} can describe any number of sounds resulting from contact between two relatively hard surfaces. An aluminum pot filled with water is placed *tak* on a cooking fire of logs. Bullets hit tree bark *tak*. Tak_2 can be considered a three-dimensional version of tak_1. While tak_1 describes a point-like contact between surfaces, tak_2 describes an extended expanse of contact between surfaces, such as that between a container and what fills it. A bottle filled with a liquid or a river after a heavy rain are described with tak_2. Similarly, the idea of filling can be used metaphorically. A swelling throughout any body part is described with tak_2.

ICONIC PROPERTIES The iconicity of tak_1 is related to its monosyllabicity and to its final velar stop, *-k*. Its monosyllabicity means that tak_1 cannot be diagrammatically analyzed, as can disyllabic sound-symbolic adverbs, into component vocal gestures corresponding to component parts of a movement. Its monosyllabicity, then, is iconic of the punctual nature of the moment when two surfaces make contact. Because it involves a complete closure of the articulators, blocking the free movement of the airstream through the mouth, its final velar stop, *-k*, is iconic of the cessation of movement resulting when two surfaces make contact. The iconicity of tak_2 is also related to its monosyllabicity and to the closure of its syllable. Its monosyllabicity is iconic of the noncomplexity of something considered as a complete expanse. The closure of its syllable is iconic of the boundedness of whatever is considered to fill up a space or expand throughout it.

Tak occurs with the following verbs. Its punctual sense is far more commonly employed than its completive. However, sometimes the same verb is used on one occasion punctually and on another completively. Further, there is occasional overlap between aspectual punctuality and completion, within one definition of usage.

1. tak hapina
   catch
   to grab onto a person, animal, or object, e.g., to remove a child from danger, to catch prey, or to prepare for defense or assault; to make the sound of hitting against a surface, e.g., by bullets hitting tree bark
2. tak hapirina
   catch
   to press oneself against an object, person, or surface; to be indelibly "caught" all over a surface, e.g., plant dye to a face

3. tak hapi-chi-na
   catch-CAUS
   to cause contact between two entities by placing them together, e.g., to place a drowning person's hand at the edge of a canoe or a nipple to a baby's mouth
4. tak churana
   put
   to purposely place some object in a position, e.g., a snake placing its tail in striking position; to put something over an expanse of a space, e.g., a long vine over the width of a river or the mouth over the hole of a blowgun; to put something into a container, filling it completely, e.g., liquid inside a bottle; to put out everything possible, e.g., food for a feast
5. tak churarina
   get dressed
   to be dressed to the hilt
6. tak chura-chi-na
   put-CAUS
   to allow, encourage someone to get dressed by placing everything out for them
7. tak hundana
   fill
   to fill completely, e.g. a river after a heavy rain
8. tak hunda-chi-na
   fill-CAUS
   to load something up, e.g., a canoe with provisions, a bag with oranges, a trunk with clothes
9. tak montonana
   pile up
   to pile up anything, e.g. plaintains
10. tak montonarina
    pile up
    to be piled up
11. tak mana
    be
    to be attributed with some quality or condition to the fullest possible extent, e.g., a girl completely matured, soldiers armed to the hilt, a face covered with pimples
12. tak tukuna
    become
    to undergo a complete change, e.g., to turn from a boy to a giant-headed anaconda (myth); to turn from a normal forest into one overgrown with thorns, (myth)
13. tak l^{y}utarina
    stick
    to touch something and cling to it, e.g., a magnet to metal, a chigger to skin, a small carniverous sardine to flesh
14. tak l^{y}uta-chi-na
    stick-CAUS
    to place two surfaces together, causing them to stick, e.g., a decapitated head onto its neck (myth)
15. tak nanana
    hurt
    to feel a painful pressure all over a body part, e.g., a leg
16. tak pungina
    swell
    to be completely swollen from infection, e.g., a body part or the genitalia of some female mammals during estrus and immediately preceding parturition
17. tak amulina
    place in mouth
    to put something into one's mouth, e.g., an anaconda its prey
18. tak amuli-chi-na
    put in mouth-CAUS
    to cause to put in the mouth, e.g., to place a stick into an alligator's mouth
19. tak mikuna
    eat
    to peck at food, e.g., birds at worms
20. tak pil^{y}una
    wrap
    to wrap something completely, e.g., boa strangling a tapir
21. tak pil^{y}urina
    wrap
    to cover the wrists by wrapping strands of beads around them
22. tak watana
    tie
    to bind a captive's hands firmly together; to tie a handkerchief around a head, completely covering the eyes

23. tak watarina — to tie something around one's head
 tie
24. tak l^yawturina — to decorate the head by surrounding it with a feathered band
 feather band
25. tak kuruna — to crown one's head with a headdress
 crown
26. tak tiyarina — to sit down in a definite place, e.g., a bird alighting on a tree branch; to swell to prominence, as if "sitting up," e.g., lymph nodes within the groin
 sit
27. tak tiya-chi-na — to set something, making it "sit," e.g., a rock
 be-CAUS
28. tak shayarina — to stand out prominently, e.g., breasts filling with milk during pregnancy
 stand up
29. tak shaya-chi-na — to stand something in a definite place, e.g., a pot over burning logs
 stand-CAUS
30. tak hatarina — to press all over, rising upward, e.g., a baby in the womb during pregnancy
 get up
31. tak kipirina — to hug a person affectionately; to hug a tree to pull oneself from water; to hug a lance in preparation for a battle
 hug
32. tak tapana — to plug or cover something up, e.g., a hole in a tree with a termites' nest (myth), ears with cotton, a head with a hat
 cover
33. tak harkarina — to be completely stuck, e.g., a tree which, when cut, falls against another, or a jaguar trying to go through a hole too small for it (myth)
 be obstructed
34. tak harkachina — to impede completely by blocking off, e.g., an animal's escape
 obstruct
35. tak rikuna — to look someone directly in the eyes, e.g., to facilitate amorous magic
 look
36. tak rikurina — to appear as a vast expanse, as does the sky when a river is so wide that its opposite shore disappears from view
 appear
37. tak riku-chi-na — to place something directly within someone's view, e.g., a bowl of *aswa*, to make them drink
 look-CAUS
38. tak l^yukana — to crawl completely flat against the ground, e.g., to hide
 crawl
39. tak kilabana — to nail something completely shut
 nail
40. tak pal^{y}ana — to harvest everything possible from a given source, e.g., all the fruit from a tree
 harvest
41. tak karana — to serve guests all of the food a host has
 give to eat
42. tak kuna — to give everything of anything
 give
43. tak chimbana — to cross a given space, such as a ravine, by bridging over it with a log, touching the other side
 cross
44. tak l^yukshi-chi-na — to position something outside of a given area, e.g., to place someone's face above water to help them avoid drowning
 leave-CAUS
45. tak awirina — to paint one's body up with vegetable dyes
 paint
46. tak nitina — to be completely pressed or crushed, e.g., by a landslide
 press

47.	tak shamuna come	to come from every direction
48.	tak chikichina tickle	to surprise someone with a light touch or graze
49.	tak kargana load	to fully load a gun
50.	tak kacharina let go	to let something completely go, e.g., the release on a gun
51.	tak rana do	to do anything in a complete way, e.g., to cover one's face with dye; to place something in position, e.g., the way a soldier places his hand in position for a salute or the way a boa positions its head after arranging its body into coils
52.	tak kimirina lean	to lean on something, touching it with only a tip or end, e.g., the way a rifle is leaned by its muzzle against a wall
53.	tak markana carry	to hold onto a baby securely
54.	tak pungarana become pitch	to stick onto something simply by touching it
55.	tak sakirina remain	to remain in contact with a surface
56.	tak kamana try	to test the ripeness of a gourd by tapping it, making the sound *tak*
57.	tak rupa-chi-na hot-CAUS	to touch something hot to someone or something, burning them
58.	tak tarpuna plant	to plant an entire field
59.	tak apana take	to pick something up and take it away, e.g., a piece of kindling from a fire or a bird downed by a poison dart
60.	tak apa-mu-na take-CIS	to bring a large quantity of something
61.	tak pitina cut	to cut something, e.g., a plaintain stalk, making the sound *tak*
62.	tak piti-ri-na cut-RFL	to cut oneself by biting down *tak* into one's own flesh, e.g., a mythic bat
63.	tak angl^{y}ana choose	to pick everything
64.	tak takana touch	to touch something
65.	tak takarina touch	to bump into something, e.g., a canoe that collides with an underwater tree branch

Tak$_1$

In the following example *tak*$_{1A}$ describes the quick grabbing of a rifle.

66. 'Il^{y}apa-ta tak hapi-sha, chawpi il^{y}apa-ra-ni' ni-ra pay.
rifle-ACC grab-COR middle shoot-PAST-1 say-PAST he

"'I *tak* grabbed the rifle and shot right through (i.e., in the middle) the air,' he said."

Tak is not performatively foregrounded here. It accompanies the coreferenced verb root *hapisha* "grabbing" to specify the punctual contact between a hand and the rifle it grabbed. In this sentence its aspectual function is most important because it effectively delineates the action of the coreferenced verb from that of the finite verb by making clear that its achievement was punctually completed.

The next example uses *tak* to describe the moment of contact between a magnet and a piece of metal, resulting in their clinging together.

67. Tak taka-kpi hawa-manda l^y^utari-n.
touch-SWRF above-from stick-3
"Once (he) touches (it) *tak*, it clings from above."

Tak is not performatively foregrounded here. It functions primarily to specify the aspectual punctuality of the switch reference verb *takakpi* "he touches," which would otherwise be unspecified for aspect.

The next example describes the way a large snake plucks the feathers from a partridge it will eat. *Tak* describes the moment of contact made by the snake's mouth with the partridge. *Purus* is a sound image of the actual plucking.

68. Riku-kpi, yanga tak amuli-n, purus! tak amuli-n, purus!
look-SWRF just put in mouth-3 put in mouth-3
"Upon looking, (we saw) it just *tak* put it in its mouth and *purus* (pluck it out), *tak* put it in its mouth, and *purus* (pluck it out)!"

Tak is not performatively foregrounded in this example. It functions to specify the aspectual punctuality of the verb *amulin* "it puts in its mouth."

The meaning of tak_{1A}, which is to the describe a moment of contact between surfaces, can be extended to describe the way any object or entity is positioned at a definite point in space. In this extended use there is no actual physical contact between surfaces. Rather, there is an idea of contact because the object or entity is being positioned in a definite point in space. The following example uses tak_{1A} in this extended sense to describe the way a large snake placed its tail in mid-air, ready to strike, after arranging its body into successive coilings. The coilings are described with the sound-symbolic adverb *dziri*. *Tak* describes the final punctual placement of its tail in position ready to strike.

71. Ña kay-bi-ga dziriri dziriri dziriri dziriri dziri ri ri tak chupa-ta hawa-y.
then here-LOC-TOP tail-ACC above-LOC
"Then here (it coiled itself) *dziriri dziriri dziriri dziriri dziri ri ri tak* (and placed its) tail above ."

Tak is performatively foregrounded by its high-pitched pronunciation and its syntactic isolation. It functions to simulate an image of the punctual moment in time and placement in space of the snake's tail, making the narrative description vivid and also terrifying. *Tak* is also grammatically important for its role in encoding aspectual punctuality. This is a particularly important function because both *tak* and *dziri* are syntactically isolated. They bear full aspectual responsibility as there are no finite verbs in this sentence.

Tak$_{1B}$

Tak is also used as a sound image of an aspectually punctual action. In the following example it presents an idea of the punctual sound of setting a pot on top of a cooking fire.

69. Ñuka yanda-ta apamu-ni, nina-ta hapichi-ni, shayachi pasa-ni ishka-ndi
    I wood-ACC bring-1 fire-ACC light-1 set finish-1 two-INCL
    irmanga-ta ^{tak}.
    pot-ACC
    "I bring the wood, light the fire, and finish setting (them) in place, both of the pots (set in place) ^{tak}."

Tak is performatively foregrounded by its higher pitched pronunciation and also by its syntactic displacement from the verb phrase *shayachi pasani* "I finish setting in place." By displacing *tak* from its verb phrase and making it the last element of its utterance, the speaker foregrounds more effectively what *tak* is meant to express. In this context *tak* expresses the final punctual moment when a series of actions concerning food preparation have been completed. By its appearance in sentence final position it imitates this idea of "last-ness."

Tak$_{2A}$

Tak$_2$ is semantically distinguished from *tak*$_1$ because it concerns a three-dimensional image. Images described with *tak*$_2$ concern contact, either physical or conceptual, over an expanded domain. In the following example, *tak* describes the completeness of the filling up of a jar with vegetable peelings in order to propagate grubs.

72. Chunda kara-ta tak hundachi-u-ga, chasna chura-nawn.
    chonta peel-ACC fill-DUR-TOP like that put-3PL
    "Filling up the chonta peelings *tak*, that's how they put (them)."

Tak is not performatively foregrounded in this sentence. Its main role is to specify the predicate level completiveness of its verb. Without *tak* its verb *hundachiuga* would have to be translated as "filling." The speaker's use of *tak*, however, requires that its verb be translated as "filling up." With respect to its position in temporal space, that is, its propositional status, this sentence is aspectually durative. Since its verb is modified by *tak*, however, the sentence is aspectually completive at the predicate level.

In the next sentence the three-dimensional contact implied by *tak*$_2$ describes the cresting of a river which had risen quite high. It is the way the river was filled up that is focused on with *tak*.

73. Yaku-ga, t$^{a^{k}}$ ña al^{y}pa-ga kay-bi al^{y}pa a-w-kbi, ña kasna-mi
water-TOP now ground-TOP here-LOC ground be-DUR-SWRF then like this
kata-w-ra.
cover-DUR-PAST

"And the water, $t^{a^{k}}$ now the ground here; if the ground is here, now this is (how far) the water was covering (it)."

Tak is performatively foregrounded by its upglide and also by syntactic displacement from its verb *katawra* "was covering." The upglide over *tak*, which spans the extent of the speaker's voice, can be understood as a gesture of the extent of the river's filling. *Tak*'s function here is explanatory and also grammatical. It is used to clarify the extent to which the river was filled and to grammatically specify the completeness of the river's filling.

In the next sentence *tak*$_{2}$ describes a complete swelling of lymph nodes in the groin after walking an extremely long distance.

74. Ishka-ndi changa-ma papa muyu t$^{a^{k}}$ tiyari-wa-shka-ra, pungi-wa-shka-ra.
two-INCL leg-DAT father seed sit-1ACC-PERF-PAST swell-1ACC-PERF-PAST

"Into both of my legs, thc big nodes (in my groin) $t^{a^{k}}$ had pressed up in me, had swelled up in me."

Tak is performatively foregrounded by its upglide in pitch and by the very tensed voice[4] of its pronunciation. Its upglide can be understood as a gestural enactment of the completeness of the lymph nodes' swelling. *Tak*'s function here is both grammatical and emotive. At the conclusion of the upglide, the listener can consider the process of swelling as accomplished. At the same time, the completeness of this process evokes an idea of a forceful, painful pressure.

Tak$_{2B}$

Tak$_{2B}$ describes a feature or quality that is extended in space, without necessarily making contact with any other entity or surface. The following sentence, taken from a myth, uses *tak*$_{2B}$ to describe an expanse of peanut fields spread out across the sky. It describes how they look to an ordinary man who sees them while visiting the sky for the first time.

75. Kasna indzhik chagra ña t$^{a^{a^{xxxx}}}$!
like this peanut field now

"Like this the peanut field, now $t^{a^{a^{xxxx}}}$ (was spread out)!"

Tak is performatively foregrounded by its lengthening, by its upglide, by the fricativization of its final velar consonant, and by its syntactic isolation. All of these foregrounding techniques contribute to a performative enactment of a spatial expanse, which is grammatically and expressively significant. The completeness of the expanse is grammatically relevant because the sentence has no finite verb. *Tak* therefore bears full aspectual responsibility. The vastness of this expanse, communicated by performative lengthening, impresses the listener's aesthetic sensibility.

In the next sentence *tak*$_{2B}$ is repeated to describe how, when one reaches an extremely wide part of a river, the opposite shore is so far away that it seems to blend into the sky, making the sky appear as if it extends wherever one looks.

76. Sacha-ga il^{y}a-k il^{y}a-k il^{y}a-k, cielo tak tak tak cielo-l^{y}a-shi rikuri-k a-n
    forest-TOP lack-AG lack-AG lack-AG sky sky-just-EV appear-AG be-3
    chay-bi.
    there-LOC
    "The forest is gone, gone, gone; (and) the sky *tak tak tak*; only the sky appears there!"

Tak is performatively foregrounded here by its multiple repetition, by the telic pitch progression imposed on the repetitions, and by displacement from its verb *rikurik* "appears." The multiple repetitions of *tak* and their telic pitch progression are functionally analagous to a filmmaker's use of a zoom out, which presents an image with an increasingly wider angle shot for aesthetic effect. Each repetition of *tak* is intended to present a more complete extent of the sky's expanse. At the same time, these repetitions are grammatically significant because they affect their verb *rikurik* "appears," which is otherwise unmarked for aspectuality, with perfectivity.

Tak$_{2B}$ can also be used to describe an attribute or action considered in, or performed to, its utmost limit. In the next sentence *tak* describes how a girl filled out when she matured.

77. Chi wawa pukuri-shka washa, shina tak raku ma-ra.
    that child mature-PERF after like fat be-PAST
    "That child after she matured, she was *tak*, like fat all over."

Tak is not performatively foregrounded here; it functions in this sentence to specify an aspectually resultative state, that of being completely matured.

T^{y}api

DEFINITION (1) Describes the moment of contact between two surfaces, which usually results in their clinging together. Aspectually punctual. (2) Describes the resultant clinging together of two entitities which have made contact. Aspectually completive, resultative. Also used adjectivally to describe a nose or buttocks that are relatively flattened out or otherwise nonprominent.

COMMENT This sound-symbolic adverb seems to have more nonordinary contexts of use than any other. There are several ghost stories involving severed limbs, decapitated heads, and so on, which can cling *t^{y}api* to all kinds of surfaces. There is also an account of a magic stone which, like a magnet, attracted objects and also people to itself, *t^{y}api*, for some unspecified malevolent purpose. There is a feminine forest spirit, called the *wiki warmi* "sticky woman," who is associated with various sticky substances and saps obtained from trees and is sometimes invoked in love magic for her ability to make people cling *t^{y}api* to each other. Insofar as it describes contact between two entities that can remain separable, *t^{y}api* overlaps with *tak*$_{1A}$; however, the meaning of *tak* is communicated, in part, by its iconic suggestion of the sound of contact. *T^{y}api*, by contrast, is not iconic of sound.

ICONIC PROPERTIES The iconicity of *t^{y}api* is related to its disyllabic structure, to the contrast between its initial syllable, low vowel *-a-*, and its final syllable, high vowel *-i*, and to the openness of its initial and final syllables. The disyllabic structure of *t^{y}api* allows a speaker to performatively gesture either the moment when something makes contact with something else or the resultant clinging of the two surfaces that have made contact. The distinction between these two subevents is iconically enhanced by the contrast between the initial syllable, low vowel *-a-*, and the final syllable, high vowel *-i*. The initial syllable, *t^{y}a-*, can be iconic of the moment when contact is made or of the movement by something toward another surface. The final syllable, *-pi*, can be iconic of the moment of contact or of the clinging considered as a resultant state. The openness of the initial and final syllables is iconic of the lack of a clearly circumscribed boundary between surfaces that stick together.

T^{y}api occurs with the following verbs.

1.	t^{y}api l^{y}utana cling	to touch two surfaces to each other, making them stick, e.g., a compress on skin; to bring two surfaces together so that one of them loses its separateness, e.g., the way a fire conforms around whatever it encounters
2.	t^{y}api l^{y}uta-chi-na cling-CAUS	same as above
3.	t^{y}api l^{y}utarina cling	to attach oneself, or a part of oneself to a surface
4.	t^{y}api hapirina catch	to catch oneself, or a part of oneself onto a surface
5.	t^{y}api hapi-chi-na catch-CAUS	to cause something to be caught with another surface
6.	t^{y}api ana be	to be stuck to something
7.	t^{y}api tukuna become	to become stuck to something; to become attached to another person, e.g., by falling in love
8.	t^{y}api munana want	to want someone so much, that one is helplessly drawn to that person
9.	t^{y}api aparina bear	to carry something or bear something, e.g., the way some fruit-bearing trees look, with long-stemmed fruit attached by their tips to the tree's branches

10. t^{y}api churana (put) — to put something into contact with a surface so that it clings to it

11. t^{y}api awana (make) — to create something by pressing its parts together, e.g., a clay pot out of coils pinched together

11. t^{y}api awana (make) — to create something by pressing its parts together, e.g., a clay pot out of coils pinched together

12. t^{y}api ugl^{y}arina (hug) — to hug someone securely

13. t^{y}api mitikuna (hide) — to hide by pressing oneself against something, e.g., a large tree trunk

The following sentence, taken from a fable about a tortoise and a jaguar, uses *t^{y}api* to describe the moment of contact made by a lit match with the jaguar's hide, resulting in his conflagration. The other adverb, *tsak*, describes an idea of the sound of striking the match stick.

14. Chi-ga fusfuru-wan-ga tsak hapichi-k, t^{y}aapi l^{y}uta-ga, ña sindi kal^{y}ari-shka.
that-TOP match-ADV-TOP light-AG stick-TOP then burn begin-PERF

"(After) lighting that match *tsak*, and making it stick (to the jaguar) *t^{y}aapi*, then the burning began."

T^{y}api is performatively foregrounded by a slight lengthening of its initial syllable vowel. This brief lengthening can be understood as a gesture of the punctual moment of contact between the lit match and the jaguar's hide. *T^{y}api*'s function here is grammatical, referential, and aesthetic. It refers to the punctual moment when contact is made between the lit match and the jaguar's hide. It also allows the listener to enjoy the perceptually salient image of that moment when the tortoise has his ultimate revenge on the jaguar.

The next sentence is taken from a myth about a star that takes the form of a woman and goes for a time to live on the earth. This sentence describes her return to the sky, despite all attempts by her human husband to keep her on the earth. Sound-symbolic *ts^{y}un* describes the sound she made while whizzing upward. The adverbial form of the word *pundzha* "day" describes the streak of light she created while moving. Finally, *t^{y}api* describes how she appeared to stick back into place in the sky.

15. Ts^{y}unnnnnn-shi ri-ra pundzha-nnng; riku-l^{y}ayta-shi, chasna-y-ga t^{y}a^{pi}-shi l^{y}utari-gri-ra.
-EV go-PAST day-INST watch-CIR-EV like that-LOC-TOP -EV stick-TRSLC-PAST

"She went *ts^{y}unnnnnn*, brightlyyyy; and as he watched, she went and stuck to the sky *t^{y}a^{pi}*."

T^{y}api is performatively foregrounded by the upjump over its second syllable. The upjump can be understood as an intonational gesture of the action described. The initial, lower pitched syllable is analogous to the initial movement, and the higher pitched second syllable is analogous to the final punctual moment when the star sticks back into place in the sky. Besides functioning grammatically to indicate the punctual moment when the star resumes its place in the sky, t^y*api* also functions modally to express a feeling of finality. Once she resumes her place in the sky, her human husband realizes that despite all of his attempts to keep her with him, she will never again return to the earth.

The next sentence uses t^y*api* metaphorically to describe the effect on a person of a love charm.

16. Pay-ba simayuka-l^ya-wan kan-ga t^ya^{pi} (pause), pay-ma tuku-nga ra-w-ngi
    he-POSS love charm-just-INST you-TOP he-DAT become-FINF do-DUR-2
    pay-ta riku-sha.
    he-ACC see-COR
    "With just his love charm you, t^ya^{pi} (pause) toward him you will become (drawn, upon) seeing him."

T^y*api* is performatively foregrounded by its upjump, by its immediately following pause, and by its displacement from its verb. The upjump and its pause cause one to focus attention on the grammatically resultant state of being drawn to someone. The upjump communicates this resultant state by providing a pitch contrast for the conceptual contrast between the way one is before being drawn to someone and the way one is after being drawn to someone. The image described by t^y*api* also functions modally to convey an emphatic sense of warning. The spell of a type of love magic is so powerful that it causes people to be drawn to each other as if stuck together.

In the next example t^y*api* describes the spatial distribution of ripe fruit all over the tips of a tree's branches, as if stuck onto them.

18. Karan rama-ta, pacha-ga, yanga t^yapi-xx-l^yaaaa, kulpa-xxl^yaaa apari-shka-ta
    each branch-ACC wow-TOP just -ADV cluster-ADV bear-PERF-ACC
    riku-ngi ma!
    see-2 CNDL
    "On each branch, wow! You would see what it bore, just t^y*api-xx-*l^y*aaaa*, and clustered (all over)!"

T^y*api* is performatively foregrounded by its lengthening, which takes place over an epenthetic velar fricative, as well as over an emphatic suffix, -l^y*a*. The lengthening communicates an image of spatial distribution which is aesthetically pleasing because it suggests bounteousness.

Dzir

DEFINITION (1) To pull or slide an object across a surface. Aspectually punctual, durative. To move by sliding, scraping, slithering, or slipping across, over, or down a surface; to grow by seeming to slide across a surface. Aspectually durative. (2) An idea of the sound made by such movements. Aspectually durative.

COMMENT The essence of *dzir*'s meaning is friction. It is applied to obviously frictional movements involving rubbing or scraping. The way a forest pig wipes itself clean of mud by scraping itself along a tree trunk and the way a person slides down a muddy slope are both described with *dzir*. *Dzir* also describes subtler frictional movements, such as the dribbling of saliva down a cheek. *Dzir* can be used metaphorically to describe the way something seems to create friction as it moves; for example, the way a vine grows by seeming to slide along a surface is described with *dzir*.

ICONIC PROPERTIES The iconicity of *dzir* is related to its affricate, *dz-*, which is articulated by bringing the articulators so close together that a turbulent air flow results. The turbulence of this sound is imitative of sliding movements that create friction. The iconic properties of *dzir* can also be described for the variant forms it assumes. *Dzir* undergoes a couple of different processes, including apocope of its final *-r* and partial reduplication with simultaneous lengthening. Although most sound-symbolic adverbs do not exhibit free variation between voiced and voiceless consonants, *dzir* does. Forms belonging to the family of *dzir* include the following variants: *dzi* and *tsi*; *dziri*, *tsiri*, and *diri*, and $dz^{y}u$. There is an iconic sense in the use of these variant sets. The shorter forms *dzi* and *tsi* are used interchangeably to describe quick, punctual sliding actions. The partially reduplicated forms *dziri*, *tsiri*, and *diri* are all used to focus on the frictional dimension of sliding movements. The partial reduplication of the *-ir* is pronounced as a vowel and a flap, the articulation of which involves a very quick contact between the tongue and the roof of the mouth. This contact, then, is iconic of the repeated friction of one surface sliding over another. Finally, $dz^{y}u$ is used to focus on the smoothness of sliding movements. The absence of a flapped final *-r* is iconic of the absence of friction implied by this variant.

Dzir occurs with the following verbs.

1.	dzir aysana pull	to pull something out quickly, e.g., a weapon such as a knife or pistol, a dart from an animal; to drag something or someone, along the ground: variants include *dzi* and *zidi*.
2.	dzir sikana climb	to climb by sliding up along a surface, e.g., a type of bird which digs its beak into a tree trunk and slides itself up in increments, or a snake slithering up a tree
3.	dzir raykuna descend	to slide down, e.g., a tree; to lower something down by sliding it, e.g., a baby from its carrying sling by sliding it down one's back
4.	dzir urmana fall	to descend by sliding downward, e.g., saliva dribbling down a cheek
5.	dzir urma-chi-na fall-CAUS	to lower something by sliding it down, e.g., a snake lowering its tail down a tree (myth)
6.	dzir l^{y}uchuna peel	to peel by scraping, e.g., a papaya
7.	dzir rina go	to slide, e.g., a person or stick down a slope, an elevator along a shaft, a snake along the ground
8.	dzir kakuna rub	to rub something over a surface, e.g., a type of leaf believed to ensure results over a fish hook before baiting it

9.	dzir tangana push	to push something, e.g. a large wooden vat, making it slide along a floor
10.	dzir apana take	to take or grab an animal by pulling it, e.g., out of a hole or along a surface
11.	dzir rana do, make	to slide, e.g., a squirrel shot with a poisoned dart down a tree trunk
12.	dzir shamuna come	to come by sliding, e.g., the way a man unable to use his legs sat on a small wooden bench and slid himself along the ground; to come by slithering, e.g., a snake moving along the ground
13.	dzir al^{y}mana weed	to remove small weeds from the ground by grazing the blade of a machete sideways across the ground, cutting them away
14.	dzir paskarina open	to open by sliding, e.g., to loosen the knot of a sheet or blanket (tied for carrying a baby) by pulling it apart; to slide open, e.g., a snake out of a coiled position
15.	dzir uyarina sound	to make the sound of sliding, e.g., a snake sliding open from a coiled position
16.	dzir picharina sweep	to sweep oneself by rubbing, e.g., the way a pig wipes itself clean of mud by rubbing against the base of a tree
17.	dzir l^{y}awkana lick	to slide the tongue across a surface, e.g., the way a sucker mouth catfish eats what grows at the bottom of a river bed
18.	dzir kawchuna twist, roll	to roll over a surface, e.g., a piece of clay to form a coil
19.	dzir kushparina shake, roll	to roll over a surface, e.g., a dog rubbing its back on the ground to dry off its fur
20.	dzir pitina cut	to cut by sawing, e.g., the way an anaconda with an iron-toothed back sawed in half any boats that passed over it (legend)
21.	dzir dizmayana faint	to faint, sliding downward, e.g., a drowning person along the edge of a canoe
22.	dzir tukuna become	to yield to sliding, e.g., to fall asleep and slide into a slumped position
23.	dzir chimbana cross	to be dragged downstream by a rapidly flowing river while attempting to cross straight over to the opposite bank
24.	dzir waytana swim	to swim by gliding, e.g., a snake
25.	dzir wiñana grow	describes the way the earth raised itself during a great flood, enabling people to steer themselves with poles (myth)
26.	dzir wiñarina sprout	to grow by continous increments, e.g., the vine of a potato.
27.	dzir mirana increase	to grow uninterruptedly, along a continuous trajectory, e.g., a frog's penis (myth)
28.	dzir kuyuna shake	to slide by rocking and shaking, e.g., the earth during a quake

Dzir$_1$ is often shortened to *tsi* or *dzi* to describe the quick pulling out of a knife, pistol, or other object. In the following sentence it describes the quick pulling out of a knife to kill an animal.

29. Kuchil^{y}u-ta pay kay-ma watari-shka-ta tsi aysa-sha shayari-shka.
knife-ACC she here-DAT tie-PERF-ACC pull-COR stand-PERF
"Pulling out, *tsi*, the knife she had tied right here, she stood (ready to fight)."

Dzir is performatively foregrounded by its shortening to *tsi*, which is modally expressive. By shortening *dzir* to *tsi*, the speaker more emphatically gestures the quick action of pulling out the knife, which in this context also connotes forcefulness. *Tsi* also functions grammatically. Without *tsi*, the verb *aysasha* "pulling" would be aspectually durative since it is suffixed with the coreference marker. However, *tsi* makes clear the punctuality of the action of pulling out the knife.

Dzir$_1$ can also describe a repeated series of quick sliding actions. In the next example it is repeated by a mother who is instructing her child to go and scrape weeds with the tip of a machete blade.

30. Chinda-ta dzir dzir alma-gr-i!
outside-ACC weed-TNSL-IMP
"Go outside and weed *dzir dzir*!" (i.e., go with your machete and scrape the ground *dzir dzir*, removing the weeds)

Dzir is minimally foregrounded by its reduplication. The reduplication communicates the fact that the movements described by *dzir* are aspectually iterative. *Dzir* also has a conative function since it is part of an imperative statement oriented primarily toward the addressee.

The next two examples also describe iterated actions with *dzir*$_1$. In the following sentence, *dzir* describes the way a type of leaf is rubbed repeatedly over a fishing hook before casting it out in the water. It's believed that by doing this, one is sure to catch something.

31. Anzelo panga-ta anzelo kiru-wan dzir dzir dzir dzir kaku-ngi; chi-manda hapi-ngi.
hook leaf-ACC hook tooth-INST rub-2 that-from catch-2
"You rub the fish hook leaf over the tooth of the hook (going) *dzir dzir dzir dzir* then you catch (fish)."

Dzir is performatively foregrounded by its multiple repetition. The relatively fast pace of these repetitions is also performative because it gestures the quickness of the action described. *Dzir* functions both grammatically to indicate the iterativity of the action and also explanatorily as part of an instruction.

The next sentence describes how a man who was unable to use his legs could only slide himself forward little by little on a small bench.

32. Chi banko-wan dzir (pause) dzir (pause) dzir (pause), ñuka yaya shamu-n.
that bench-INST my father come-3
"With (the help of) that bench, *dzir* (pause) *dzir* (pause) *dzir* (pause) my father comes along."

Dzir is performatively foregrounded by its multiple repetitions, by the pause after each repetition, and by syntactic displacement from its verb *shamun* "he comes." The pause after each repetition gestures the interruptedness of the man's movement and the awkwardness and pathetic quality of his incapacitation.

Dzir$_1$ also describes a smooth unbroken sliding movement. The next example, taken from a myth, describes the way a person who had been enchanted into a deep sleep had to be dragged *ziri* along the ground by his sister.

33. Turi-ta chaki-manda ziririririri -shi aysa-sha ri-ra.
brother-ACC foot-from -EV pull-COR go-PAST
"Dragging her brother *ziririririri* by his foot, she went."

Ziri is performatively foregrounded here by its partial reduplication and lengthening, both of which gesture the dragging action described. *Ziri* has both a grammatical and aesthetic function in this context. It reinforces the aspectual durativity already implied by the coreference verb *aysasha* "pulling" which it modifies. At the same time, the dragging image simulated by *ziri* is aesthetically salient because the action it describes is made perceptually salient by its formal amplification.

The smooth unbroken sliding movement just described is used in the next example with an intonational shape that is somewhat unusual for sound symbolic adverbs. Here *dziri* describes how a drowning woman's grip on the edge of a canoe slipped down along its side as she fainted.

34. Kanoa shimi-y dziri ri ri ri riri ña dizmaya-shka kumari Manila.
canoe mouth-LOC now faint-PERF comadre Manila
"From the edge of the canoe, *dziri ri ri ri riri* (she slipped); now she'd fainted, comadre Manila had."

Dzir is performatively foregrounded by its partial reduplication, its lengthening, the lowering of pitch over its pronunciation, and its syntactic isolation. These techniques, especially the lengthening and pitch lowering, gesture the downward movement of the woman's descent into the water. The simulation of this descent into the water is emotively terrifying because it seems to indicate that she will drown.

In the next sentence the variant *dz*^{y}*u* describes a sliding movement that is seen as primarily smooth rather than frictional. The sentence, taken from a myth, describes a boa's ascent up a tree.

35. Kasna uchu putu intiru ruku-shi sikamu-ra dz^{y}uuuuuuuuu-shi shamu-n.
like that pepper palm entire big-EV climb-PAST -EV come-3
"In this way the big (old boa) climbed the entire pepper palm; *dz*^{y}*uuuuuuuuu* he came up."

Dz^y*u* is performatively foregrounded by its lengthening and by the speaker's use of creakiness over the final portion of the lengthening. The lengthening gestures the unbrokenness of the boa's sliding up along the tree, which is both aesthetically salient and grammatically durative.

Dzir$_2$ describes an idea of a sound made by a frictional movement. The final example sentence uses *dzir* to describe the way a boa constrictor uncoiled itself when someone stepped on a fallen tree trunk near where it was lying.

36. Chi ruya hawa-y aytari-wan pariul^{y}a dz^{h}iririririririri uyari-ra.
 that tree top-LOC step-INST equal sound-PAST
 "At the moment I stepped on that tree, *dz^{h}iririririririri* it sounded."

Dzir is performatively foregrounded here by its partial reduplication, lengthening, and initial forceful aspiration. The aspiration greatly reduces the voicing on the subsequent vowels. All of these techniques gesture the continuous sliding open motion of the snake from coiled position. In this context, the aspectual durativity of *dziri* is put in the service of a terrifyingly clear perception—that of a snake uncoiling itself near the speaker.

Tsak

DEFINITION (1) To make a shallow puncture. Aspectually punctual. (2) An idea of the sound of such a puncture or of the sound of striking a match. Aspectually punctual.

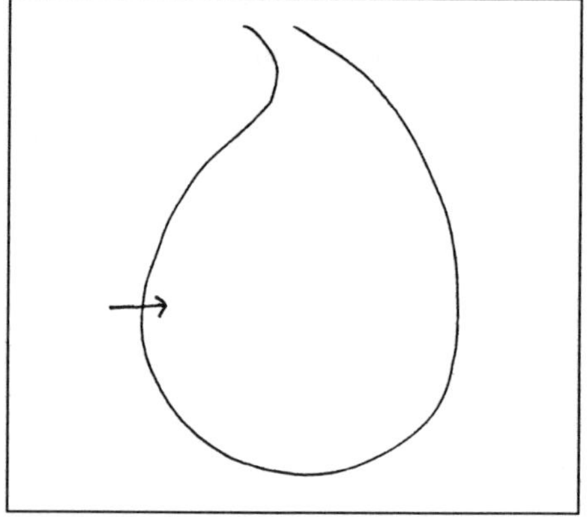

COMMENT What is essential to the meaning of *tsak*$_1$ is that whatever is pricked or pierced is not thereby significantly deformed. *Tsak*$_1$ is used to describe a piercing or puncturing into a medium that is firm, integral, and resistent. Insects pierce *tsak*, as does a dart from a blowgun. *Tsak*$_2$ exemplifies the principle of synaesthesia, whereby more than one sensation, in this case the sound of striking a match and the sound of piercing something, are represented by one form.

ICONIC PROPERTIES The iconicity of *tsak* is related to its monosyllabic shape; its affricate, *ts-*; and its final velar stop, *-k*. Its monosyllabicity is iconic of the punctual action described by *tsak*. By its articulation with a continuous airstream, its affricate, *ts-*; is iconic of the piercing part of the movement it describes. Its final velar stop, *-k*, the pronunciation of which involves a complete closure of the articulators, is iconic of the cessation of movement resulting when something has shallowly penetrated something else.

Tsak occurs with the following verbs.

1.	tsak tuksina pierce	to prick, pierce, or puncture with a sharp implement, e.g., the spearing of a fish or the sting of an insect
2.	tsak yaykuna enter	to enter by puncturing, e.g., a needle
3.	tsak shitana throw	to throw something, e.g., a dart from a blowgun, which pierces its target
4.	tsak kindzhana enclose	to enclose a space by sticking poles into the ground
5.	tsak shayarina stand	to dock oneself on the bank of a river by sticking a pole into the ground
6.	tsak al^{y}ana dig	to dig shallowly, e.g., with the point of a knife blade, in order to remove new growths of weeds from the ground
7.	tsak mana be	to be capable of pricking, piercing, or puncturing
8.	tsak rana do	to pierce something; to light a match
9.	tsak hapichina light	to light a fire, making the sound *tsak*, with a match stick
10.	tsak sindichina ignite	to ignite, making the sound *tsak*, with a match stick

Tsak$_1$ is used in the following sentence to describe the moment when a canoe was brought to a standstill by stabbing the riverbank with a steering pole.

11. Chi-ga ña tsak shayari-k shamu-sha, 'maykan-da angichi kay-bi guardia-ga'
that-TOP then stand-AG come-COR which be-2PL here-LOC guard-TOP
ni-ra-mi.
say-PAST-EV

"So then, coming *tsak* to a standstill, (one of them) said, 'Which of you is the guard here?'"

Tsak is not performatively foregrounded in this sentence; its function here is primarily grammatical. By modifying the coreference verb phrase *shayarik shamusha* "coming to a standstill" *tsak* affects the aspectual reading of the sentence with punctuality.

The next sentence, taken from a legend, describes how a giant hawk swooped down over a canoe and plucked one of its passengers right out and carried him off. *Tsak* describes the hawk's puncturing of the person's head with its beak. The other sound-symbolic adverb, *tak*, describes the moment when the hawk grabbed onto the rest of the man's body with its feet.

12. Chawpi korona-y-shi tuksi-k a-shkara ^{tsak} kiru-wan, runa-ta kay-manda tak
middle crown-LOC-EV pierce-AG be-PERF-PAST beak-INST man-ACC here-from
chaki-wan.
foot-INST

"He would pierce ^{tsak} with his beak, right in the middle of a man's crown, (and then) from here (he'd grabbed onto him) *tak* with his feet."

Tsak is performatively foregrounded by its leveled pitch rise and by its syntactic displacement from the verb phrase *tuksik ashkara* "had pierced." By raising its pitch above the utterance's baseline, the speaker gestures the punctual moment when the hawk pierced the crown of the man's head. *Tsak* affects the predicate-level aspect of its verb with punctuality. At the same time, it makes the extraordinary occurrence it describes more accessible to the listener's imagination because it describes in grisly detail the mechanics of the giant hawk's attack on humans.

The next example of *tsak* is taken from a myth. It describes how lots of leaf-wrapped bundles of *aswa* pulp were tainted by a forest spirit who pierced each of them with a poison-tipped lance.

13. Chi shamu-sha-ga, shuk-ta tsak shuk-ta tsak shuk-ta tsak shuk-ta tsak tuksi-shka.
    that come-COR-TOP one-ACC one-ACC one-ACC one-ACC pierce-PERF
    "So, coming, he pierced one *tsak* and another *tsak* and another *tsak* and another *tsak*."

Tsak is performatively foregrounded by its multiple repetition. Each repetition of *tsak* is a gesture of piercing, which functions here to make the action as perceptually sharp and as clearly focused as a close-up shot in a film.

Tsak$_2$ is used next to describe the sound of lighting a match.

14. 'Tabako-ta fosforira-n tsak hapichi-sha, chupa-shaaa, ama puñu-sha ni-sha'
    tobacco-ACC match-INST light-COR suck-COR NEG sleep-COR want-COR
    tiya-ra-ni ni-ra.
    be located-PAST-1 say-PAST
    "'Lighting the tobacco *tsak* with a match, dragginnng (away on it), not wanting to sleep, I sat there,' he said."

Tsak is not performatively foregrounded in this sentence. It functions to specify the aspectual punctuality of the coreference verb *hapichisha* "lighting."

Ling

DEFINITION (1) To insert into an enclosed space. Aspectually completive, resultative. To enter a physically bounded space or to cross an obvious boundary, as between a forest and agricultural field. Aspectually completive, resultative. (2) To move quickly with back-and-forth or in and out motions. Aspectually iterative.

COMMENT The essential image described by *ling* is one of containment. *Ling*$_1$ describes the action of putting something into an enclosed space or a malleable medium such as earth, wood, water, or fire. One puts a stick *ling* into a hole to probe its depth, a manioc cutting *ling* into the ground to propagate a new plant, or a plaintain *ling* into a fire to roast it. *Ling*$_1$ also has an intransitive version. Rather than putting some entity or object into a container, an agent or entity contains itself by entering an enclosed space. Some of the images described by intransitive *ling*$_1$ include the way a person goes into a house, the way an armadillo goes into a hole, and the way a tortoise goes into a mat of decaying leaves. *Ling*$_2$ is a metaphorical extension of the core containment image described by *ling*$_1$. It is the movement from one point to another, which is implied by the act of containment, that becomes central for *ling*$_2$, with the added semantic features of repetition and quickness. Images described with *ling*$_2$ include the body of a trembling person, the quickly flicking tongue of a snake, or the earth during a quake.

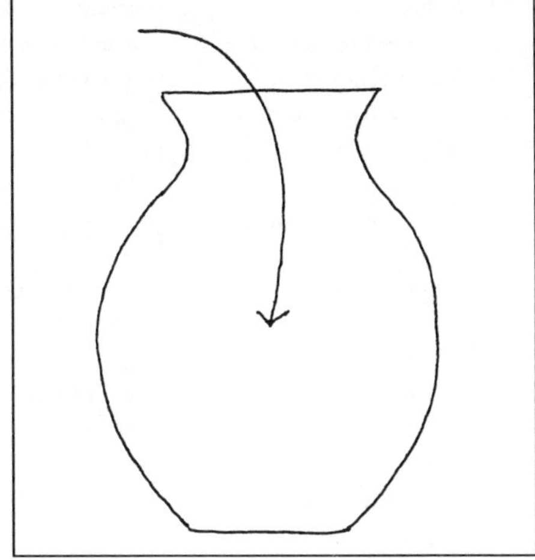

ICONIC PROPERTIES The iconicity of *ling* is related to its final closed syllable and its monosyllabicity. Its monosyllabicity is iconic of the relative noncomplexity of actions or events described with *ling*. Insertion and enclosure are relatively simple because they only require the crossing of boundaries. The final closed syllable, which is articulated with a word-final nasal *-ng*, creates, by the lowering of the velum, an obstruction in the airstream, which is iconic of the cessation of movement when enclosure or insertion has happened.

Ling occurs with the following verbs.

1. ling satina
insert — to insert into an enclosed or bounded space, e.g., a stick in a hole, clothes in a bucket of water, anything into a fire to roast it
2. ling satirina
insert — to insert oneself into a bounded space
3. ling churana
put, place — to put into an enclosed or bounded space
4. ling churarina
get dressed — to slip an article of clothing over the body, e.g., a dress over the head
5. ling barana
poke — to poke a hand, finger, or object into a hole or orifice; to poke something out from an enclosed space
6. ling kilabana
nail — to nail or pound something, e.g., a steering pole into a river bank
7. ling tarpuna
plant — to plant by sticking a cutting into the ground
8. ling chuntina
stoke — to stoke a fire by pushing the ends of burning logs closer to its center
9. ling tiya-chi-na
be located-CAUS — to put someone inside of something, e.g., to hide them
10. ling pasa-chi-na
pass-CAUS — to pass through by insertion, e.g., bait through a hook, a canoe past a fallen tree by ducking it through, underwater
11. ling kani-chi-na
bite-CAUS — to insert the point of a knife into a surface, such as wood, and leave it stand there

12. ling nil^{y}puna — to swallow something whole, gulp something down, e.g., the way a snake consumes its prey
    swallow
13. ling nil^{y}pu-chi-na — to give or make someone swallow something whole, e.g., a pill
    swallow-CAUS
14. ling kachana — to send into a contained or defined space, e.g., to sweep trash through a hole in the floor
    send
15. ling hunda-chi-na — to put things into a contained space, filling it up
    fill-CAUS
16. ling kawina — to row by carefully placing the oar into the water with as little noisy splashing as possible
    row
17. ling yaykuna — to enter any bounded space, e.g., a person into a house, an armadillo into a hole, a snake into water, a tortoise under a covering of decaying leaves
    enter
18. ling paktana — to arrive at a house unexpectedly and walk right in; to emerge from the forest upon an agricultural field
    arrive
19. ling shamuna — to arrive unexpectedly; to penetrate, e.g., mythic worm into a human female; to move progressively through a space, e.g., a carniverous sardine through flesh
    come
20. ling ñawpa-chi-na — to lead someone into a bounded space
    lead-CAUS
21. ling mikuna — to eat through, e.g., a small carniverous sardine through the flesh of its victims
    eat
22. ling shayarina — to stand up into a bounded space, e.g., the way an anaconda raised itself up into a rack of drying meat, in order to steal from it (myth)
    stand
23. ling sikarina — to climb up into a bounded space, e.g., the way a catfish raises its head above water and inserts it between a palisade of floating logs, in order to sleep
    climb
24. ling rana — to poke out, e.g., a snake its tongue; to copulate, e.g., a mythic worm into human female
    do, make, copulate
25. ling mandzharina — to be frightened into shaking
    be afraid
26. ling chukchurina — to shake or tremble, usually from fright, but also from extreme physical trauma, such as multiple gunshot wounds
    shake, tremble
27. ling kuyuna — to rock or shake, e.g., an earthquake
    rock, shake

In the following example, *ling* is used along with an insertion gesture made with a finger, to describe the act of planting a manioc cutting into the ground.

28. Kasna ling tarpu-nchi.
    like this plant-1PL
    "We plant *ling* like this."

Ling is not performatively foregrounded. It functions to specify the aspectual completiveness of the verb *tarpunchi* "we plant" by making clear the spatial and temporal boundedness of the action of planting the manioc cuttings.

In the next sentence, taken from a hunting narrative, *ling* describes the use of a stick to probe the depth of a hole, to search for a bird.

29. Chi-ga chi kaspi-ga linnnnng, chi-y sakiri-ra.
that-TOP that stick-TOP that-LOC remain-PAST
"Then that stick (went) *linnnnng*, and there it stopped."

Ling is performatively foregrounded by its lengthening and by its syntactic isolation. The lengthening is a gesture of the spatial extendedness of the hole. The termination of the lengthening, evident by the phrase *chiy sakirira* "there it stopped," indicates the point at which the stick reaches the end of the cavity. *Ling*'s function here is explanatory. It describes how the narrator was able to catch a *kilpundu* bird by probing a hole.

In the next example repetitions of *ling* describe planting a field with manioc cuttings.

30. Lomo kaspi-ta asta-nchi; asta-shka washa paki-nchi; paki-shka washa
manioc stick-ACC pile up-1PL pile up-PERF after break-1PL break-PERF after
tola-shka-y-ga ling ling ling ling ling; lomo kaspi puchu-kpi, kuti
make hole-PERF-LOC-TOP manioc stick remain-SWRF again
tola-sha, tukuy ña tukuchi-nchi.
make hole-COR all then finish-1PL
"(First) we pile up the manioc sticks; after piling them up we break them; after breaking them (we plant them) in the holes that we've made *ling ling ling ling ling*; if there are any manioc branches left, again making holes, we finish (planting) all of them."

Ling is performativeley foregrounded by its multiple repetition, by the telic pitch progression over the repetitions, and by its syntactic isolation. The multiple repetitions of *ling* gesture the action of planting manioc sticks in the ground. The telic pitch progression makes clear that it is a complete cycle of planting that is being described. Each of the holes that has been made in advance is going to be filled with a cutting. *Ling*'s function, then, is explanatory. It simulates, with a telic pitch progression, an image of a complete cycle of planting.

The next sentence, taken from a myth, uses *ling* to describe the protaganist's entrance into a hole in the ground in order to hide from a forest spirt.

31. Shina ra-sha pay-ga kunan chi uktu-y ling yayku-sha, kumishin-wa tas tapari-shka.
like that do-COR she-TOP now that hole-LOC enter-COR termite-INST
close-PERF
"Doing it like that, then entering that hole *ling*, she closed it *tas* with a termites' mound."

Ling is not performatively foregrounded. It modifies the coreference verb *yaykusha* "entering," specifying the completiveness of the protagonist's entrance into the hole.

In the next example *ling* describes the way wild forest pigs tend to go into holes.

32. Pundzhana, ima-s uktu-y $l^{i^{ng}}$ (pause) al^{y}pa uktu-y a-sha, ruya pul^{y}u uktu-y
pig what-INCL hole-LOC ground hole-LOC be-COR tree stump hole-LOC
a-sha, yayku-k ma-n.
be-COR enter-AG be-3

"A pundzhana, or whatever, into a hole (it goes) $l^{i^{ng}}$ (pause); if there's a hole in the ground, or in the stump of a tree, it enters."

Ling is performatively foregrounded by its upglide, by its syntactic isolation, and by its immediately following pause. The upglide can be understood as a performative gesture of the animal's entrance into the hole. At its termination, the animal is in the hole, and the resultant state of its being there is foregrounded by the immediately following pause. *Ling* therefore functions grammatically because it supplies the only aspectual information, given the absence of a verb in this sentence. It also functions to make the explanation more emphatic.

The next example of *ling* describes the surging of an anaconda from underwater to the surface as observed by a man who was defecating in the water, near the spot where the anaconda emerged.

33. Lll^{h}iing-shi shamu-shka.
-EV come-PERF

"It came (up to him) *lll^{h}iing*!"

Ling is performatively foregrounded by its lengthening and by aspiration. The lengthening gestures the initial part of the animal's surging movement. This image is modal in its function. By simulating the anaconda's surging forward, the speaker evokes a threatening and dangerous mood. The emphasis on the surge suggests the man's vulnerability to attack.

Ling$_2$, which describes a quick back and forth, in and out, or trembling movement is always repeated. In the following example *ling* describes the repeated spasms of the body of a man dying from a self-inflicted gunshot wound. The other sound-symbolic adverb, *ti*, which is repeated much more rapidly, describes the pulsing of blood out of his body.

37. Ña amo ling ling ling ling tititititititititi ling ling ling charak kawsa-w-ra-mi.
then man yet live-DUR-PAST-EV

"Then the man (shook) *ling ling ling ling tititititititititi ling ling ling*; he was still alive."

Ling is performatively foregrounded here by its multiple repetition and by its syntactic isolation. Each repetition of *ling* can be understood as a gesture of the man's shaking movement. *Ling* affects the aspect reading of this sentence with iterative durativity, and it also evokes the pathos of the image of a dying man's last moments.

In the final example, *ling*$_2$ describes a person's direct face-to-face encounter with a snake, focusing on the in-and-out flicking motion of the snake's tongue.

38. Uma-ta alsa-sha riku-wa-shka-ra ling ling ling ling ling ling ling ling ling ling ling ling.
head-ACC raise-COR look-1ACC-PERF-PAST

"Raising its head, it had looked at me (going) *ling ling ling ling ling ling ling ling ling ling ling ling.*"

Ling is performatively foregrounded by its syntactic isolation, by its multiple repetition, by the pitch contour over the repetitions, and by the extreme speed with which the repetitions are executed. The rapid repetitions gesture the fast flicking movement of the snake's tongue. The rising and falling pitch contour circumscribes these repetitions by setting them off from the rest of the utterance. *Ling* affects the aspect reading of this sentence with iterative durativity, and it also functions modally, to strike fear into a listener, by simulating the terrifying face-to-face image experienced by the speaker.

Polo

DEFINITION To pass completely through an object, body, or substance. Aspectually completive, resultative.

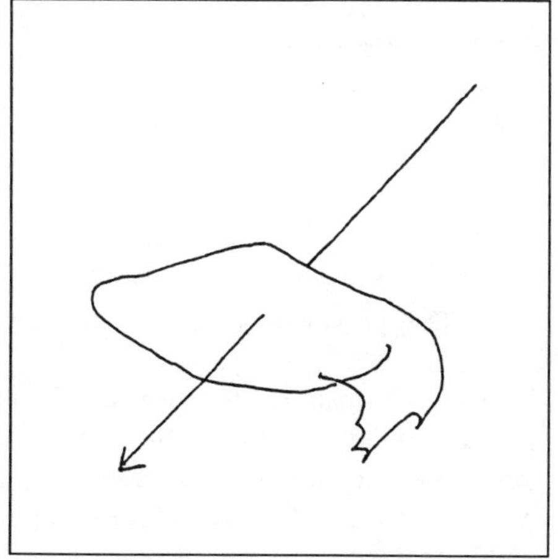

COMMENT The essential image described by *polo* is one of breaking through a barrier, whether it is perceived to require great effort or almost none at all. Animals are often described as emerging *polo* from a confined space, such as that defined by a decaying tree trunk. Bullets pass *polo* through wooden canoes. A needle goes *polo* through an ear lobe that has been pierced.

ICONIC PROPERTIES The iconicity of *polo* is related to its disyllabic structure; its lateral liquid, *-l-*; and its open final syllable. Its disyllabicity allows a speaker to performatively distinguish between the initial part of the movement, before a barrier has been penetrated, and the final part of the movement, after the barrier has been penetrated. The medial lateral *-l-* is iconic of the ease of penetration because it is articulated without producing a turbulent airstream. The final open syllable is iconic of the lack of obstruction once the barrier has been penetrated.

Polo occurs with the following verbs.

1. polo pasana — to pass through
   pass
2. polo pasa-chi-na — to pass something through
   pass-CAUS
3. polo l^{y}ukshina — to emerge through a barrier
   leave
4. polo il^{y}apana — to shoot (with a rifle) through a surface
   shoot
5. polo uktuna — to pierce or puncture through
   pierce
6. polo barana — to poke through
   poke
7. polo mana — to be burrowed or tunneled
   be

The following example, taken from a myth, describes the murder of a wicked old woman by shoving a stick through her head.

8. Kaspi-wan polo bara-shka-wna.
   stick-INST insert-PERF-3PL
   "With a stick they poked all the way through *polo*.

Polo is not performatively foregrounded. It affects the aspect reading of its sentence with completiveness.

In the next example, taken from a personal experience narrative, *polo* describes the way a leaf was funneled into a cup for catching rainwater, and then secured by poking a stick through it, thereby enabling a group of men lost in the forest to survive.

9. Kay-ta kaspi-ta po^{lo} pasa-chi-nawn.
   here-ACC stick-ACC pass-CAUS-3PL
   "They pass the stick right through here *po*^{lo}."

Polo is performatively foregrounded by its upjump. The upjump can be understood as a performative gesture of the action it describes. The first, lower pitched syllable can be understood as the movement which precedes the passing through; the second syllable describes the moment of the passing through. *Polo* affects the aspect reading of this sentence with completiveness and it also has an explanatory function. The speaker uses it to explain one of the survival techniques used by the lost men.

In the next sentence, taken from a myth, *polo* describes a rabbit's emergence through a barrier.

10. Ña po^{lo} (pause); shuk parti-manda-shi l^{y}ukshi-shka.
    then one part-from-EV leave-PERF
    "Then *po*^{lo} (pause); he emerged from another side."

Polo is performatively foregrounded by its upjump, by its immediately following pause, and by displacement from its verb *l^{y}ukshishka* "emerged." The upjump over *polo* gestures the difference between the initial part of the action and the final breaking through the barrier. The image of its breakthrough functions aesthetically. By displacing *polo* from its verb, so that it actually occurs before the verb itself is uttered, the speaker highlights the speed of the animal's movement, as well as its cleverness. The animal's action is executed with such speed and cleverness that it happens before the listener is completely made aware of it by means of the verb *l^{y}ukshishka* "emerged."

In the next example *polo* describes how bullets fired by hostile Peruvian soldiers went right through a wooden canoe, barely missing the Ecuadorean men for whom they were intended.

11. Kanoa-ta polo polo polo (pause); runa-ta mana hapi tuku-nchi-chu ni-ra-mi.
    canoe-ACC people-ACC NEG catch become-3PL-NEG say-PAST-EV

    "'(Although they went right through) the canoe *polo polo polo* they missed us,' (lit.: we people didn't get caught), he said."

Polo is performatively foregrounded by its syntactic isolation, by its multiple repetition, by the telic pitch progression over the repeated series, and by the pause immediately following its repetitions. The telic pitch progression is a way of presenting the subevents leading to the completion of an activity or process. Each progression takes us closer to its termination. After the final, highest pitched repetition of *polo*, the listener knows that everything is over because the speaker states that no one was hit by any of the bullets. *Polo*'s function is modal. It evokes sentiments of suspense, anticipation, and anxiety over the possibility that one of the members of the party could have been hit by the bullets.

In the final example, repetitions of *polo* describe a series of probes through a decaying tree stump in search of a wild pig hidden inside. The pig was caught by probing through the inside of the trunk with a stick after first plugging up all other openings. The other sound-symbolic adverb, *ch^{y}u*, describes the act of cutting away at the stump.

12. Chi-ta karan-manda tapa-sha-ga piti-ni ch^{y}u ch^{y}u, polo polo polo polo; ña
    that-ACC each-from plug-COR-TOP cut-1 then
    pakta-ra-ni!
    reach-PAST-1

    "Plugging each of its (holes), I cut ch^{y}u ch^{y}u (and probe), *polo polo polo polo*; then I reached (it)."

Polo is performatively foregrounded have by its syntactic isolation, by its multiple repetitions, and by the telic pitch progression over the repetitions. Each of its repetitions is a gesture of an individually completed probe through a section of the stump. The telic pitch progression indicates the increasing proximity to the animal with each successive probe. That the final, highest pitched probe is in fact the last one is indicated by *ña paktarani* "then I reached (it)." *Polo*'s function here is explanatory, aesthetic, and modal. It explains by simulating a clear image of a series of actions, each of which is charged with a mood of expectation that it might be the final one.

10

Sound Symbols of Opening and Closing

This chapter analyzes six sound-symbolic adverbs of opening and closing, most of which are based on bodily orifices. *Ang* describes a gaping, wide open mouth. *Ing* describes a slit-like opening, such as a smile, or a split on the surface of the skin. *Awing* describes the act of opening or exposing a hollow or enclosed space, which is typically noncorporeal. *Tus* describes the bursting open of something crisp or fleshy. *Taw* describes the closing up of a hollow space, or a hollow sound which can be corporeal or noncorporeal. *Ping* describes the act of closing the eyes and is metaphorically extended to describe an atmospheric change from light to darkness.

Ang

DEFINITION To open a mouth widely, completely. Aspectually completive, resultative.

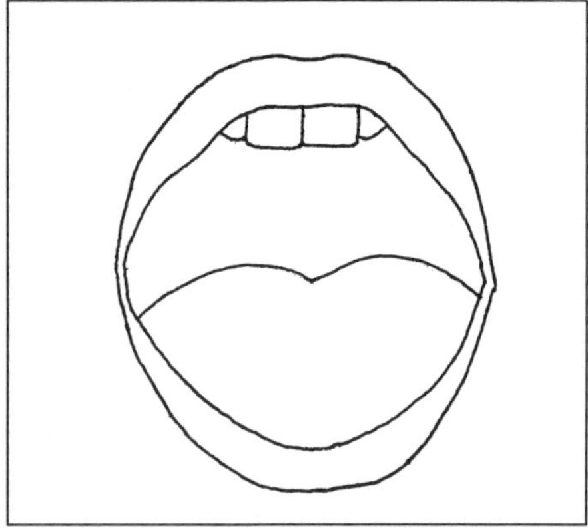

COMMENT The images described with *ang* have a range of affective values. They are as frightening as the wide open mouth of a predatory animal, such as an alligator poised for attack; as unusual as the wide open mouth of a catfish asleep; as mundane as the wide open mouth of someone yawning; or as winsome as the gaping beaks of baby birds waiting to be fed. Sometimes *ang* is used for hyperbole or satire, as when it is used to tease someone whose mouth hangs slightly open, panting because of tiredness.

ICONIC PROPERTIES The iconicity of *ang* is related to its initial open vowel, *-a*, which causes the mouth to be open rather than restricted during its articulation. For an expressively explicit effect, speakers sometimes open the mouth much wider than is necessary during its pronunciation.

Ang occurs with the following verbs.

1. ang paskana open	to open the mouth as far as possible, e.g., to yawn, or to nurse (of a baby); to open the mouth of an animal, e.g., a young bird, to feed it
2. ang rana do	same as above
3. ang chapana wait	to wait with mouth open, e.g., baby birds waiting to be fed
4. ang sirina lie	to lie with mouth open, e.g., an anaconda trying to disgorge what it has swallowed or a person trying to drink an entire pond (myth).
5. ang puñuna sleep	to sleep with mouth open, e.g., several types of fish
6. ang rikuna look	to stare with mouth open, e.g., an alligator assuming a threatening look
7. ang sambayana become tired	to become so tired that one's mouth hangs open, panting

In the following example *ang* describes how a bird was fed by opening its mouth up completely.

8. Bul^{y}us-l^{y}a ra-sha ang paska-sha, uku-y uku-y sati-k a-ra-ni.
   ball-LIM make-COR open-COR inside-LOC inside-LOC insert-AG be-PAST-1
   "Making little balls, opening its mouth up *ang*, I would insert them inside, inside."

Ang is not performatively foregrounded. It specifies the aspectual completiveness of the coreference verb *paskasha* "opening."

In the next example *ang* is part of a dramatic description of the way a deadly poisonous snake made one last effort to bite the person who had just sliced off its head. The complete slicing off of its head is described by the sound-symbolic adverb *ch^{y}u*. *Ang* describes the complete opening of its mouth. *Taw* describes the complete closing of its mouth right before it died.

9. Shura-y ch^{y}u piti-shka, ña $^{\text{ang taw}}$ kani-shpa chay-mi wañu-ra palo.
   one-LOC cut-PERF then bite-COR that-EV die-PAST snake
   "In one (fell swoop) (his head) *ch^{y}u* was cut off, then (opening its mouth up) ^{ang}, and ^{taw} biting down, there the snake died."

Ang is performatively foregrounded by its syntactic isolation and by the slightly raised pitch of its pronunciation. Its function here is aesthetic and modal. By evoking a clear image of the snake's wide open mouth, the narrator suggests the terrifying possibility of being bitten by it.

In the next example *ang* describes how a catfish appeared with its mouth wide open, resting on dead tree branches that accumulated in a bend near the river's shore.

10. Ñuka kusa ni-ra, puñu-u-u-shka-shi ni-ra, annng (pause) hawa-y
my husband say-PAST sleep-DUR-DUR-PERF-EV say-PAST above-LOC
palisara hawa-y.
palisade above-LOC
"'It was sleeping,' my husband said, (with its mouth opened) *annng* (pause) above, on top of the palisade (of branches)."

Ang is performatively foregrounded here by its lengthening, its pronounciation with a slightly higher and louder pitch, and its immediately following pause, all of which function to highlight the aesthetic qualities of this extremely unusual sight.

In the next example *ang* describes the way a baby might repeatedly open its mouth when afflicted with a fungal infection which makes it impossible to nurse.

11. Chi wañu upus-manda ang ang ra-sha mana chuchu-nga.
that die thrush-from do-COR NEG nurse-3FUT
"Because of that deadly thrush, (even though) a baby goes *ang ang* he will not nurse."

Ang is performatively foregrounded here by its repetition, which simulates the repeated efforts of the baby to feed. Even though *ang* is only minimally foregrounded, in this context its repetition evokes a mood of extreme pathos at the image of a hungry child who cannot be satisfied.

Ing

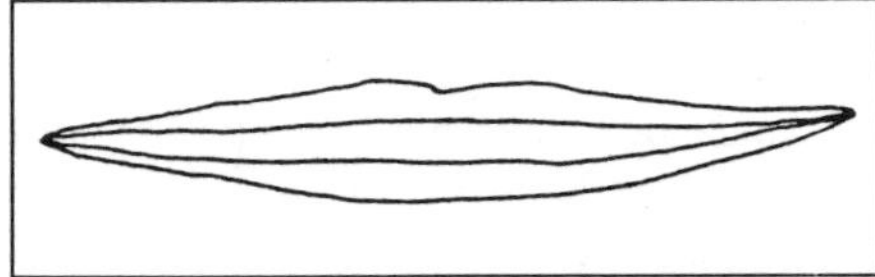

DEFINITION To open in the shape of a slit or to split open. Aspectually completive, resultative, aorist.

COMMENT The essential image of *ing* is of a slit-like opening which is not a permanent deformation. The image of a smile or of an animal's baring of its teeth is temporary and gestural rather than rigid and permanent. When *ing* describes a splitting or cracking of a surface, such as skin it is almost always a shallow split, which is relatively temporary, rather than a deeply, and permanently deformative fissure.

ICONIC PROPERTIES The iconicity of *ing* is related to the articulatory position of the mouth, which is spread open during its pronunciation. The opening of the mouth while pronouncing *ing* requires a slight spreading of the lips, which emphasizes its slit-like shape, thereby enhancing the iconicity of *ing*'s meaning.

Ing occurs with the following verbs.

1. ing partina part	to divide lengthwise, e.g., to score the surface of wet clay with a line
2. ing rana do	to make a slit, e.g., by baring teeth or by scoring something, e.g., cooked meat or a fired clay jar
3. ing rina go	to split open, e.g., infected skin
4. ing chakirina dry up	to dry up to the point of splitting, e.g., skin overexposed to the sun
5. ing tostarina toast	same as above
6. ing asina laugh	to laugh with mouth open in the shape of slit, e.g., the way humans and some other primates do
7. ing shamuna come	to come at something or someone with teeth bared, e.g., a jaguar

In the following example *ing* is used in a discussion of techniques for repairing pottery, to refer to the splitting open of a recently fired clay jar. The other sound-symbolic adverb, *taw,* refers to the sound of the clay jar's bursting apart.

8. Kay, ima, t^haw tuvya-sha, mana-chu ing ra-n?
this what burst-COR NEG-NEG do-3

"You know, don't you, how bursting apart *t^haw* it splits open *ing*?"

Ing is not performatively foregrounded here. It functions grammatically, affecting its verb *ran* "it makes, does" with resultativity. Its function is also referential. It refers to the complete splitting open of a jar in order to clarify a fine point in a discussion of techniques for repairing pottery. Moreover, since the finite verb it modifies is virtually empty of semantic content, *ing* bears full semantic responsibility in this adverb/verb construction.

The next example, taken from a myth, uses *ing* to describe the smile on a little baby's face when it is discovered hidden away in a heap of refuse. The baby is the result of a union between a human man and a star woman who has many habits that are directly opposed to human ways of doing things.

9. Innnnng asi-sha-shi ishkay-l^ya kiru-yuk-shi a-shka.
laugh-COR-EV two-LIM teeth-POSS-EV be-PERF

"As he was laughing *innnnng*, (it was apparent that) he only had two teeth."

Ing is performatively foregrounded above by its lengthening which focuses a listener's attention on the image of the baby's smile. The function of this image is to communicate an aesthetically appealing picture of a happy baby, which introduces some semblance of normality into a bizarre domestic arrangement. Despite the fact that the star woman has baffled her human affines with her many strange habits, such as keeping the baby hidden away in a heap of refuse, she has at least given them a happy, smiling baby.

In the next sentence *ing* is featured in a description of a procedure which is said to prevent jaguars from returning to one's agricultural field. The procedure involves digging up the jaguar's footprint from the ground, splitting it with a knife, and then burning it up, along with hot peppers. *Ing* describes the splitting of the foot's imprint.

10. Pay-ba chaki shungu-ta parti-ra-ni ing ing ing al^{y}pa-ta.
    he-POSS foot heart-ACC part-PAST-1 ground-ACC
    "I split the ground open *ing ing ing* (which bore) the heart of his footprint."

Ing is performatively foregrounded by its multiple repetition, which functions both grammatically insofar as it makes explicit the iterative aspect of its predicate, and also explanatorily, because it demonstrates the action of the splitting.

In the following example *ing* describes a visual pattern of cracks all over a foot caused by an infection.

11. Chaki yanga ing ing ing ing ing ing ri-kbi, pay tuksiri-ngaw shamu-ra.
    foot just go-SWRF he pierce-FINF come-PAST
    "As his foot had gone *ing ing ing ing ing* (all over), he came to get himself injected."

Ing is performatively foregrounded here by its multiple repetition and by the rise and fall of pitch over the repeated series. The pitch rise and fall imitate an idea of spatial distribution by their enumeration of a range of voice pitches. *Ing*'s function here is modal. By emphasizing the image of the cracks' distribution all over the skin, the speaker evokes pity for the afflicted person.

Awing

DEFINITION To open, uncover, or otherwise expose a space; to be opened, uncovered, or otherwise exposed. Aspectually completive, resultative.

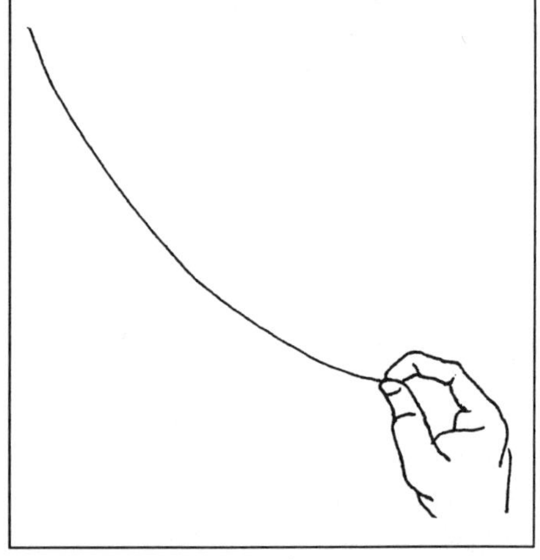

COMMENT The essential image of *awing* is of an enclosure of any kind, whether elaborately constructed or found in nature, that has been uncovered, exposed, or otherwise opened up.

ICONIC PROPERTIES The iconicity of *awing* is related to its disyllabic structure and to its initial open syllable, *a*-, and final closed syllable, *-wing*. Its disyllabic structure allows a speaker to gesture vocally, the component subactions making up an action described with *awing*. The initial open syllable, *a*-, is iconic of the opening gesture, while the final closed syllable, *-wing*, which is articulated with an obstruction in the airstream during pronunciation of *-ng*, is iconic of the cessation or completion of the opening up of a space.

Awing occurs with the following verbs.

1.	awing paskana open	to open or uncover a space, e.g., an animal's hiding place, a mosquito net, a door to a room, mouth of an animal, etc
2.	awing rana do, make	same as above
3.	awing partirina split	to split open, e.g., a wooden canoe or clay jar
4.	awing tangana shove	to open by shoving a barrier aside
5.	awing ana be	to be open

In the following example, taken from an account of a dream, *awing* describes the uncovering of a hole.

6. Awing ra-sha riku-kpi, runa akcha lulus ukuy siri-u-shka-ra.
   do-COR look-SWRF person hair matted inside lie-DUR-PERF-PAST

   "Opening it up *awing* and looking, (what I saw was that) a person's matted hair was lying inside."

Awing is not performatively foregrounded here. Its function is primarily grammatical insofar as it specifies the aspectual completiveness of the coreference verb *rasha* "doing."

In the next example an aspectually completive *awing* describes the opening up of a mosquito net.

7. Toldo-ta awing paska-sha riku-ra.
   mosquitonet-ACC open-COR look-PAST

   "Opening the mosquito net up *awing*, he looked."

Awing is not performatively foregrounded here. Its function is primarily grammatical insofar as it specifies the aspectual completiveness of the coreference verb *paskasha* "opening."

In the next sentence *awing* describes a person's awareness of an animal's escape by the openness it created when it pushed through a barrier.

8. Riku-kbi a^{wing} (pause) ña chay-ma tanga-shka-ra.
   look-SWRF then there-DAT shove-PERF-PAST

   "(What I) saw, then (was that) it *a*^{wing} (pause) had been pushed right through there."

Awing is performatively foregrounded here by an upjump, a following pause, and by its syntactic displacement from its verb *tangashkara* "had pushed." The image described by *awing* has an inferential function in this context, serving to alert the speaker to the unknown animal's escape.

In the following example *awing* is part of a description of the successive cutting away and opening up of the entrance to the hiding place of an armadillo.

9. Chi-ga chasna ra-sha awing awing awing paska-sha riku-ni.
   that-TOP like that do-COR open-COR look-1
   "So, opening (it) like that, *awing awing awing*, I look."

Awing is performatively foregrounded by its repetition, which describes the gestures of opening away in the attempt to get to the armadillo. The repetitions create a mood of expectation that at any moment the armadillo will be discovered.

Tus

DEFINITION (1) To burst open or to be burst open by pressure, sudden impact, or a sharp puncture. Aspectually punctual, completive, resultative. (2) An idea of the sound of a burst, puncture, break, or crack, for example of a bone, or of something crisply fleshy, such as a raw vegetable root, breaking. Aspectually punctual.

COMMENT The image underlying tus_1 is of a three dimensional object or entity, whose outer skin or covering is punctured or burst open. Tus_2 extends this meaning because it applies to objects that may be inside a three-dimensional entity, such as a bone inside a body, or attached to it, such as the root of a tuberous vegetable. Tus_2, then, describes the breaking of something relatively firm or crisp that has an outer skin or covering, whether or not that outer skin or covering was itself burst open. Many images described by *tus* are overwhelmingly graphic and harrowing. They include the sound of a person's neck burst open by the constrictive pressure of a wire tied around it, the sound of a demon's eye bursting in a fire (myth), or the sound of a bat puncturing human flesh as it drinks its blood (myth).

ICONIC PROPERTIES The iconicity of *tus* is related to its monosyllabicity and to its word-final fricative *-s*, which is a continuous, unobstructed sound. Its monosyllabicity is iconic of the aspectually punctual action it describes. Its word-final *-s*, by its articulation without an obstruction in the airstream, is iconic of the yielding of an object or entity to being burst or punctured open.

Tus occurs with the following verbs.

1.	tus tuvyana burst	to burst open, e.g., a hen's egg
2.	tus tuvya-chi-na burst-CAUS	to burst something open, e.g., a blister
3.	tus kanina bite	to bite something, making it burst, e.g., the egg of a louse, eye of a roasted bird, *naranjilla* fruit, or hot pepper
4.	tus upina drink	to puncture and then drink juice from something, e.g., a piece of fruit
5.	tus pitirina cut	to cut by bursting open with a constrictive pressure, e.g., a neck strangled by wire; to cut something off, sounding *tus*, e.g., the root of a tuberous vegetable
6.	tus partirina divide	to divide by splitting open *tus*, e.g., the long pod of the *pakay* fruit when twisted
7.	tus pakirina break	to break, bursting open, e.g., a light bulb when it falls
8.	tus pakina break	the sound of breaking something hard, such as a bone
9.	tus pilana pluck	to pluck a piece of something off, making the sound *tus*, e.g., a tuberous vegetable from the ground, by snapping it off at the root
10.	tus chayana become cooked	to become cooked to such an extent that a piece of meat's outer skin can be broken off *tus*
11.	tus rupana burn	to burn something to a crisp

In the following example, taken from a hunting narrative, *tus* describes the puncturing of a dog's neck by a jaguar. The other sound-symbolic adverb, *pata*, describes the subsequent shaking of the dog's tail while it died.

12. Tus kay-ta; imina-ta kawsa-nga? ña chay chupa-lʸa patatatatatatatatatatatata;
 here-ADV how-ADV live-3FUT now that tail-LIM
 ña wanu-y pasa-n.
 now die-NOM pass-3
 "(When he's been bitten) *tus* here, (on the neck), how will he live? Only that tail (shook) *patatatatatatatatatatatata*; then he died."

Tus is performatively foregrounded here by its syntactic isolation, by its slightly raised voice pitch, and by the rhetorical stance of its utterance. Its syntactic isolation and raised voice pitch present a graphically descriptive rendering of the exact moment when the dog's life began to end. By framing the foregrounding of *tus* within a rhetorical question—"When he's been bitten *tus*, how will he live?"—the speaker asks the listener to imagine what is hoped for, but impossible, thereby effectively communicating his own affection for the dog and grief over its death.

In the next example, taken from a myth, *tus* describes the killing of a woman by a group of jaguars which, after flinging her to the ground, bit into her neck.

13. Al^{y}pa-ma urma-chi-k-guna ña kay-bi ^{tus}.
ground-DAT fall-CAUS-AG-PL then here-LOC
"The ones who had made (her) fall to the ground then (bit into her) ^{tus}, right here."

Tus is performatively foregrounded here by its syntactic isolation and by the higher pitch of its pronunciation. These techniques focus the listener's attention on the image of the woman's neck being punctured by the jaguar's bite, allowing the listener to imagine the viciousness of the animals.

In the next example *tus* describes the way a partridge's bones had been broken and crushed by a pit viper.

14. Kani-shka-s mana tiya-ra-chu, ^{tus} paki-shka-l^{y}a ma-shka-ra.
bite-PERF-INCL NEG be-PAST-NEG break-PERF-LIM be-PERF-PAST
"There wasn't even a bite, it had only been broken up ^{tus}."

Tus is performatively foregrounded here by the higher pitch of its pronunciation. This foregrounding contributes to a general mood of amazement and also horror at the methodicalness of the pit viper, which has been described in great detail by the man who witnessed its attack of the partridge, including its plucking of all of its feathers before attempting to swallow it.

In the next example, taken from a ghost story, *tus* describes the sound of a demon's eye bursting in a fire.

15. Nina-y-ga t^{h}ussssssssssss-shi tuvya-n.
fire-LOC-TOP -EV burst-3
"It burst *t^{h}ussssssssssss* in the fire."

Tus is performatively foregrounded here by its lengthening, which simulates the continuous quality of the sound of the bursting, and also by the aspiration of its initial *t*-, which devoices its following vowel, thereby affecting the sound with a kind of sizzly quality. Its foregrounding prolongs the drama of the demon's demise by allowing listeners to savor the duration of its eye's bursting.

The following example, taken from another ghost story, concerns a man who has died and returns as a rotting, worm-infested corpse. Upon returning to his family, he asks that someone remove the lice in his hair; however, there are only the worms feeding on his flesh. He therefore asks that the worms be handed to him and he bites *tus* into each one of them, savoring their flavor.

16. Tak hapi-k, tus ummmmmm! tus ummmmmm! tus ummmmmm! kani-u-n pay.
grab-AG bite-DUR-3 he
"Grabbing (them) *tak*, he bites *tus* ummmmmm! *tus* ummmmmm! *tus* ummmmmm!"

Tus is performatively foregrounded here by its repetition. By presenting an image of the man's biting into the worms as an ongoing activity, the narrator horrifies her listeners who are appalled not only by the gruesomeness of the action but also by its repeatedness, which suggests normalcy and ordinariness.

Taw

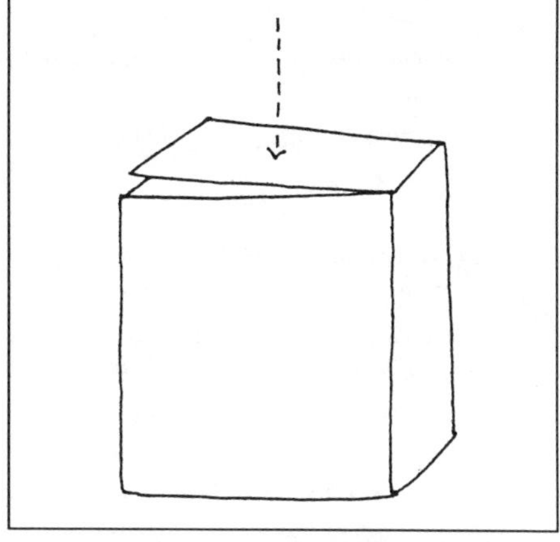

DEFINITION (1) An idea of the sound of closing or enclosing. To close up a hollow or three-dimensional space; to enclose an object within a three-dimensional space (cf. *pak_3*). Aspectually punctual or completive. (2) An idea of the sound of something hollow breaking open or of a hollow sound made by contact between something hard and something relatively soft. Aspectually punctual or completive.[1]

COMMENT The closing described by *taw* can apply to naturally hollow spaces, including those in the body, and to constructed spaces, such as houses, rooms, or cages.

ICONIC PROPERTIES The iconicity of *taw_1* is related to its monosyllabic structure and to its final central approximant, *-w*. Because it is relatively noncomplex, its monosyllabic structure is iconic of an idea of a punctual action. The lip rounding accompanying the central approximant, *w*, creates articulatory constriction, which is iconic of the idea of constricting a space by closing it off. Its final approximant, by its lack of cessation of the airstream in the oral tract, creates a reverberative-like resonance appropriate for the sound of a hollow space. The iconicity of *taw_2* is secondary, as it depends on an idea of a hollow sound which is then extended to describe a hollow-shaped object breaking open or a hollow-like sound of something soft that is struck against something hard.

Taw occurs with the following verbs.

1.	taw tapana close	to close off or enclose completely, e.g., a mouth, a room, or an animal within a cage
2.	taw rana do	same as above
3.	taw amulina put in mouth	to put something in the mouth and close it
4.	taw kanina bite	to bite down on something and close the mouth
5.	taw hapina grab	to grab something and close with it, e.g., the skirt of a dress over legs spread apart
6.	taw nitina press	to press shut, e.g., to press legs together
7.	taw $al^{y}ana$ dig	to dig, sounding *taw*, e.g., a steel blade into wood to carve out a canoe
8.	taw taksarina wash clothes	to wash clothes by slapping them *taw* against something, e.g., rocks

9. taw pikana — to chop something, e.g., meat, with a knife, making the sound *taw*
   chop
10. taw pitina — to cut, sounding *taw*, e.g., a balsa tree with an ax
   cut
11. taw waktana — to hit something *taw*, e.g., a tree trunk with a stick
   hit
12. taw tuvyana — to burst, break apart, sounding *taw*, e.g., a large clay jar or an egg
   explode

The following example is taken from a bizarre myth about worms that invade a woman by entering her and then reproducing inside. In this episode she attempts to prevent the worms' entering by pressing her legs together *taw* and then turning over the skirt of her dress to cover herself. The other sound-symbolic adverb, *pak*, describes the turning over and covering up with the skirt.

13. Changa kal^{y}a-w-ta taw niti-sha, l^{y}achapa-n ^{pak} (pause); imata-ta yayku-nga?
    leg split-DUR-ACC press-COR clothes-INST how-ADV enter-3FUT

    "Pressing the spread-apart legs together *taw*, with her clothes she (covered herself) *pak*; how could anything enter?"

Taw is not performatively foregrounded in this sentence. It modifies the coreference verb *nitisha* "pressing," specifying its aspectual perfectivity.

In the next sentence *taw* is part of a complex description. It describes the way a poisonous snake made one last effort to bite the person who had just sliced off its head. *Ch^{y}u* describes the complete slicing off of its head. *Ang* describes the complete opening of its mouth. *Taw* describes the complete closing of its mouth right before it died.

14. Shura-y ch^{y}u piti-shka, ña ^{ang} ^{taw} kani-shpa chay-mi wañu-ra palo!
    one-LOC cut-PERF then bite-COR that-EV die-PAST snake

    "In one (fell swoop) (his head) *ch^{y}u* was cut off, then (opening its mouth up) *ang* *taw*, and biting down, there the snake died."

Taw is performatively foregrounded here by its raised pitch and by the fact that, as the final sound-symbolic adverb of a complex description, it concerns the last, fearful act of the snake before it died.

In the next sentence *taw* describes the way a stone that was believed to possess special qualities was covered up with a drinking bowl after it was discovered in the forest.

15. Shuk mukaha-wan-ga ta$^{w^{w}}$ tapa-sha, ila sapi-bi sumak kindzha-sha saki-ra-ni.
    one bowl-INST-TOP close-COR ila base-LOC nice enclose-COR leave-PAST-1

    "Covering it up *ta*$^{w^{w}}$ with the bowl, nicely enclosing it, I left it at the base of the *ila* tree."

Taw is performatively foregrounded by the upglide of pitch, which imitates an idea of a completely realized action because it spans the complete extent of the speaker's voice range. Its function here is both grammatical, because it modifies the coreference verb *tapasha* "covering," and aesthetic because it focuses on the clear image of something completely covered up. In this context, the care and attention she gives to completely covering up this stone and marking off the place where she left it are related to its greater significance within her life history. Her encounter with this magical stone indicated to her that she had a "calling" to become a shaman. As her feelings about the possibility of fulfilling this calling were extremely mixed, she attempted to get rid of the stone by leaving it in the forest. By marking the place where she'd left it, she left open the possibility of retrieving it.

In the next example *taw*$_2$ is repeated to describe the carving movements made by a blade used to dig a canoe out of a tree trunk.

16. Chi-mi ñuka-ga pay taw taw taw taw taw taw taw taw asiol^{y}a-ng al^{y}a-w-kpi
that-EV I-TOP he planer-INST dig-DUR-SWRF
'aswa-ta upi-k shamu-y' ni-kpi, 'Kay-l^{y}a-ta tukuchi-u-ni ushushi'
aswa-ACC drink-AG come-2IMP say-SWRF here-LIM-ACC finish-DUR-1 daughter
ni-wa-n.
say-1ACC-3

"Then, while he's digging *taw taw taw taw taw taw taw taw* with the planer, I tell him, 'Come and drink *aswa,'* and he tells me, 'I'm finishing with only this little bit more, daughter.'"

Taw is performatively foregrounded here by its repetition, which makes aesthetically salient the durative aspect grammatically encoded in the coreference verb *al^{y}awkpi* "digging." The auditory impression of the man's carving of the canoe remained vivid in this speaker's memory because the man was her uncle and this would be the very last canoe he would ever carve. The sounds of his blade hitting the wood, therefore, have a peculiarly sad sound for her.

Ping

DEFINITION A complete change from light to darkness, usually as a result of shutting the eyes. Aspectually punctual, completive.

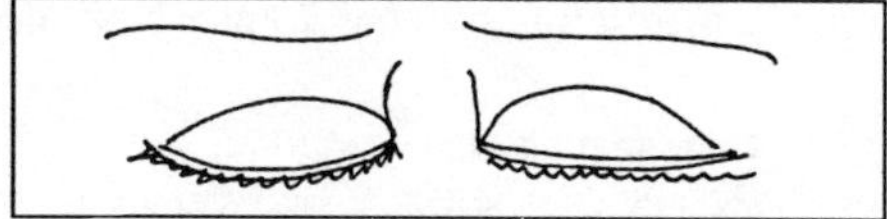

COMMENT Darkness, which occurs not only as a result of shutting the eyes but also atmospherically, is often described with *ping* when it seems to happen instantaneously.

ICONIC PROPERTIES The iconicity of *ping* is related to its monosyllabic structure, to its high vowel *-i-*, and to the fact that it ends in a closed syllable. Its monosyllabicity, by its relative noncomplexity, is iconic of a punctually completed action. Its high vowel, *-i-*, is iconic of the lightness and effortlessness (cf. Waugh 1990: 8) required to complete the action it describes. Its word-final closure is iconic of the act of closing one's eyes.

Ping occurs with the following verbs.

1. ping tapana — to shut the eyes
   close, shut
2. ping wañuna — to die out, e.g., light of a flashlight, candle, or gas flame
   die
3. ping tutayana — to turn rapidly and completely from dusk to night
   become night
4. ping chapana — to wait with eyes closed
   wait
5. ping sirina — to lie with eyes closed
   lie
6. ping tiyana — to stay or be in a place, with eyes closed
   be located
7. ping shayarina — to stand still with eyes closed
   come to a halt
8. ping puñuna — to shut the eyes and sleep
   sleep

The following example describes the sudden and complete darkness that results when a flashlight goes out.

9. Linterna ping wañu-ra.
   flashlight die-PAST
   "The flashlight died out *ping*."

Ping is performatively foregrounded here by the raised pitch of its pronunciation, which calls attention to the way the darkness, by its suddenness, stood out in someone's awareness. *Ping*'s function is both grammatical, because it affects its verb *wañura* "died" with punctual aspect, and aesthetic because it describes the clarity of this image for its own sake.

The next sentence features two *ping*s, one in a fragment of quoted speech, the other in a description. The sentence is taken from an episode in a myth that features a hawk instructing two children to shut their eyes.

10. Ñawi-ta ping tapa-ngi ni-kpi, turi wawa-ndi-shi tapa-naw-ra
    eye-ACC shut-2 say-SWRF brother baby-INCL-EV shut-3PL-PAST
    ñawi-ta ping (pause)-shi tapa-naw-ra.
    eye-ACC -EV close-3PL-PAST
    "When he said, 'Close your eyes *ping*,' the brother and his little sister closed their eyes; *ping* (pause) they closed them."

Ping is not performatively foregrounded in its first occurrence. It modifies the verb *tapangi* "you close" by specifying its punctuality with the most cognitively salient imitation of the action itself. In its second occurrence, where it describes the shutting of the brother and sister's eyes, it is performatively foregrounded by a raised pitch and by an immediately following pause, both of which assist its aesthetic function. The raised pitch and the pause call attention to the act of shutting the eyes and create a cognitive space whereby an image of complete blackness can be imagined by the listener.

In both of the preceding examples, *ping* was used as an adverb that added an aspectual punctuality to its verb and which also foregrounded the event or action described by that verb. In the next example, taken from a fable about a tortoise and a jaguar, *ping* is part of a description of the way the tortoise tricked the jaguar into lying at the bottom of the hill with his eyes closed, so that he was unable to see that the tortoise was preparing to crush him by sending an enormous boulder down the hill.

11. Chi-ga ping (pause)-shi siri-u-shka.
    then-TOP -EV lie-DUR-PAST
    "So then, (having closed his eyes) *ping*, he was lying there."

Ping is performatively foregrounded here by its raised pitch, the immediately following pause, and its syntactic isolation as the sole representative of an underlying predicate "he closed his eyes *ping*." All of these foregrounding techniques are aesthetic in function because they highlight the image of complete blackness described by *ping*, as well as its consequences, the jaguar's imminent demise. At the same time, due to its complete syntactic isolation, *ping* is the only indicator of its underlying predicate's aspectual punctuality.

In the next sentence, taken from a different episode of the same fable, *ping* describes the way a frog keeps letting its eyelids fall rather than keeping them open, which will enable the tortoise to throw sand in its eyes.

12. 'Kan yapa-mi ping tiya-ngi pani kuwa' ni-shka-shi.
    you a lot-EV be-2 sister frog say-PAST-EV
    "'You keep (letting your lids fall) *ping*, sister frog,' he said."

Ping is performatively foregrounded here by its raised pitch, which focuses one's attention on a single act of shutting the eyes. In combination with the quantificational adverb *yapa* "much, a lot," the aspectually punctual covert predicate encoded by *ping* becomes iterative at the level of the proposition, that is, the level that specifies a predicate in temporal and modal space. At the same time, the image of the frog's repeated blinking of its eyelids functions humorously because it suggests the frog's gullibility.

The next example features *ping* within the advice given by a mother to her child. She cautions the child about what to do if a stranger is encountered while walking in the forest. *Chun* describes a complete silence, *tay* describes a complete lack of activity, and *ping* describes the complete darkness resulting from a punctual shutting of the eyes.

13. Ima Awka, ima Peruano, ima-ta riku-sha-s, chun tay ping -shi shayarina!
    what Achuar what Peruvian what-ACC see-COR-INCL quiet -EV stand still
    "Whatever Achuar or Peruvian you might see, (you are) to stand *chun tay ping*."

Ping is performatively foregrounded here by its its raised pitch and by its final position in the sound-symbolic series. The progressive pitch rise over each adverb presents them in a hypothetical sequence of completion, even though the actions described are meant to happen simultaneously. *Ping*'s function is both grammatical, insofar as it affects its verb *shayarina* "to stand" with punctual aspect, and instructional because it is part of a mother's advice to her child. The urgency of this message is communicated by the foregrounded series of sound-symbolic images, which clearly describe what is necessary behavior for a particular situation of danger.

11

Sound Symbols of Falling

This chapter analyzes four sound-symbolic adverbs, all of which concern various types of falling. *Palay* describes the rapid falling of a group of objects or entities from a relatively high vantage point. *Pak* describes the contact made by a falling object or substance which is in some way reconfigured by that fall. *Patang* describes the contact made by someone or something that falls, but which does not suffer any evident loss of shape as a result of the fall; it also usually involves a fall from a relatively low vantage point. *Ki* describes a deliberate tossing, throwing, or sprinkling of a collection of objects or entities, as well as the configuration resulting from this tossing, throwing, or sprinkling.

Palay

DEFINITION (1) To fall rapidly and/or peltingly, as a collectivity of entities. Aspectually iterative. (2) To move quickly, stealthily; to skulk. Aspectually punctual, resultative.[1]

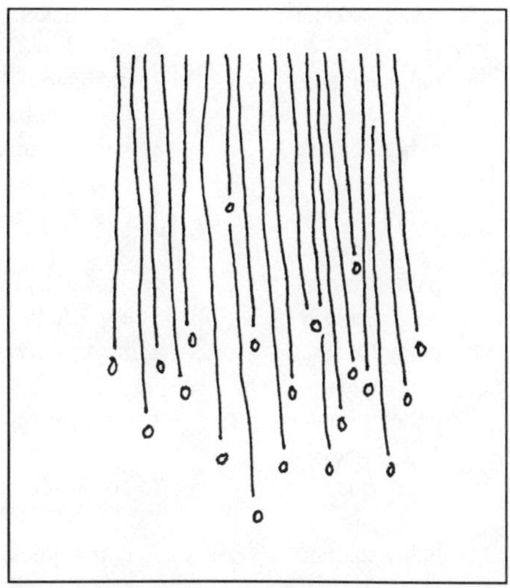

COMMENT *Palay*$_1$ imitates the sheer movement of falling rather than the eventual contact made by the falling objects with a ground surface. Furthermore, *palay*$_1$ is always used to describe the falling of objects or entities which from a human scale are small. It is applied to pelting rainfall, to the falling of many ripe fruits from a tree, and to what animals such as sloths defecate from up in a tree. It is also used to describe heavy bleeding from a deep wound, profuse crying, and vomiting. The relationship between *palay*$_1$ and *palay*$_2$ is unclear. The image of an action described with *palay*$_2$ involves movement from one point to another in a way that minimizes the mover's visibility. Besides humans, dogs are said to go around *palay*$_2$ because they often wander into other peoples' homes to steal food and then skulk out, their heads lowered, so as not to attract attention. One morning I heard a mother say to her daughter who was leaving for school, "Don't leave *palay* like a dog, without even saying goodbye."

ICONIC PROPERTIES The iconicity of *palay*$_1$ is related to its disyllabic structure, its lateral liquid *-l-*, and its open final syllable. Its disyllabic structure provides a frame for the vocal gesturing of a falling motion. Its initial syllable, *pa-*, and its final syllable, *-lay*, may be considered, respectively, the upward-to-downward movement of the falling object. Its lateral liquid *-l-*, which is articulated without producing a turbulent airstream, is iconic of the lack of turbulence created by small falling entities. The final open syllable is iconic of the lack of obstruction required for the action of falling. The iconicity of *palay*$_2$ is also related to its disyllabic structure and to its lateral approximant, *-l-*. Its disyllabic structure provides a framework for the gesturing of a surreptitious movement. The initial syllable, *pa-*, imitates the movement itself, while the final syllable, *-lay*, imitates the coming-to-rest position of the mover. The lateral liquid *-l-*, because of the lack of airstream turbulence during its articulation, imitates the quiet, undisruptive quality of a stealthy movement.

Palay occurs with the following verbs.

1. palay urmana (fall) — to fall peltingly, e.g., a heavy rain or ripe fruits from a tree
2. palay tamyana (rain) — to rain peltingly
3. palay wakana (cry) — to cry buckets, i.e., tears streaming down a face
4. palay ismana (defecate) — to defecate falling pellets, e.g., of sloths hanging in trees and the *mutu walo* and *shiringa* worms
5. palay k^{w}inana (vomit) — to vomit chunks of food
6. palay l^{y}ukshina (leave) — to emerge profusely, i.e., blood gushing out of a wound
7. palay ichuna (abandon) — to discard by throwing lots of objects down from a high place, e.g., shells of seeds eaten by an animal
8. palay tuksina (throw) — same as above
9. palay mirana (increase) — to multiply profusely, e.g., worms in rotting meat, and fall out
10. palay rina (go) — to go off secretly, quietly, quickly
11. palay shamuna (come) — to come quickly, stealthily, without calling attention to oneself

12. palay kal^{y}pana — to run somwhere by darting in and out of hiding places
    run
13. palay shayana — to go and stand somewhere in order to hide oneself
    stand

Palay$_1$ describes a heavy rainfall in the following sentence.

14. Palay palay palay tamya-ra.
    rain-PAST

    "It rained *palay palay palay*."

Palay is performatively foregrounded here by its rapid repetition, which communicates the peltingness of the rain's falling.

The next sentence is taken from a ghost story. It describes the return of a dead man, in the form of a rotting corpse, to the realm of the living and his attempt to eat the food his wife offered him. *Palay* describes the way the food he ate dropped out from a hole in his decaying throat.

15. Pay kasna miku-shka, kay-manda chi uktu wawa palay (pause) palay (pause) palay
    he like that eat-PERF here-from that hole little

    (pause) -shi urma-ra.
    -EV fall-PAST

    "Having eaten like that, (his food) fell from a little hole right here, *palay* (pause), *palay* (pause), *palay* (pause)."

Palay is performatively foregrounded here by its repetition, by the pause following each repetition, and by each repetition's slightly raised pitch. All of these techniques focus attention on the intermittent rhythm of the falling, thereby affecting the verb *urmara* "fell" with a durative aspect reading. The repetitions of *palay* also, by the regularity they imply, suggest a surreal and bizarre mood of normality and simultaneous abnormality.

In the next example *palay* describes the impression made on someone walking below by a sloth hanging from a vine and defecating.

16. Palay palay palay palay palay palay, munis^{y}on muyu-ta shina-mi isma-n!
    ammunition ball-ACC like-EV defecate-3

    "*Palay palay palay palay palay palay* he defecates (what are) like shots of ammunition."

Palay is performatively foregrounded here by its multiple repetitions, by their extremely fast-paced rhythm, and by the rise and fall in pitch that circumscribes them. The multiple repetitions imitate an idea of a multiplicity of falling objects. The fast pace of the repetitions is iconic of their speed. The circumscribing rise and fall in pitch over the repetitions relieves their monotony, at the same time that it foregrounds them from the utterance. The repetitions of *palay* function grammatically to indicate the iterative durativity of the falling and also modally, as part of a humorous slice-of-life narrative about a rarely encountered sight.

In the next example $palay_2$ is featured in a Quechua speaker's paraphrasing of a soldier's instructing one of his men to go on a reconnaissance mission.

17. Ima, ima tiya-kbi, may uya-sha pa^{lay} (pause) sindzhi shamu-ngi.
    what what be located-SWRF where hear-COR strong come-2
    "Whatever you hear about, wherever it is, *pa*^{lay} (pause) come back quickly (and report it)!

Palay is performatively foregrounded here by its syntactic displacement, by the upjump of pitch over its second syllable, and by the immediately following pause. It is syntactically displaced from its verb *shamungi* "you come." The upjump over its second syllable foregrounds that part of the stealthy movement that represents its coming to a rest. The pause gives the listener an opportunity to participate in the imagination of all of this. *Palay*'s function, then, is grammatical because it affects the aspect reading of its verb with punctuality, and also modal. It suggests a mood of secrecy and of the care necessary for the spy's action.

In the following example $palay_2$ occurs in the context of a gossip session where one person was reported to have used it to describe how a woman went around at night to various households for amorous activities.

18. 'Shuk kari-wan palay, shuk kari-wan palay ri-n,' ni-sha-shi ni-shka.
    one man-INST one man-INST go-3 say-COR-EV say-PERF
    "'With one man *palay*, and another man *palay*, she goes around,' they say she said."

Palay is performatively foregrounded here by its repetition, which functions grammatically, affecting its verb *rin* "goes" with durative aspect, and also modally, by strongly alleging a rich scenario of illicit activity.

Pak

DEFINITION (1) Describes the moment of contact or an idea of the sound of contact made by an object or substance that falls on a surface and is reconfigured or changed by the fall. Aspectually punctual/completive/resultative. (2) Describes the moment of contact made by a turning over (cf. *t'yam*) or covering over of a surface. Pak_2 is sometimes shortened to *pa*. Aspectually completive, resultative.[2]

COMMENT In contrast with $palay_1$, which describes a falling rather than the contact with a ground surface resulting from a fall, pak_1 describes the moment of contact made by what falls. What is described as falling with pak_1 is often a liquid-like substance, but it can also be anything limp that is easily deformed by a fall, such as rotting meat. The English sound-symbolic adverb "splat" is comparable to Quechua's pak_1. The difference between pak_1 and pak_2 is that pak_2 uses the sound iconicity of pak_1 to describe contact resulting from a turning over movement, but this contact is not always auditorily salient. Pak_1 and pak_2 have been etymologically related by one Quechua speaker to another sound symbolic adverb, *tsapak*, which describes the way waves of water slap the shore. I was told that *tsapak* describes both the sound of the water hitting the shore and the way it turns over when it hits.

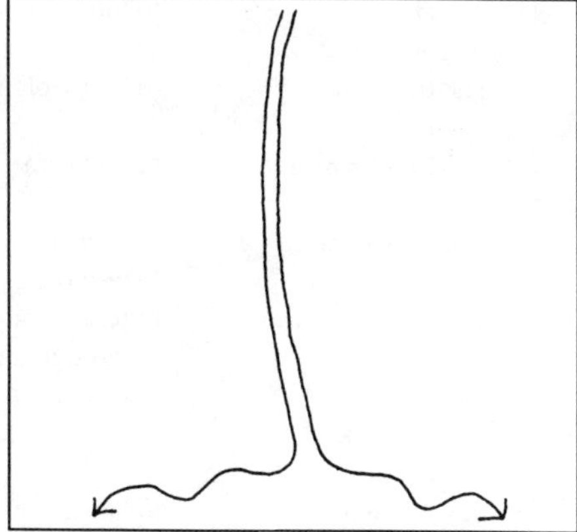

ICONIC PROPERTIES The iconicity of *pak* is related to its monosyllabicity and to its word-final velar stop, *-k*. Its monosyllabicity, which is relatively noncomplex, is iconic of the simple, punctual, and definitive contact made by a malleable substance with a firm, unyielding surface. The final velar stop, *-k*, which is articulated with an obstruction in the airstream, is iconic of the obstruction of whatever falls by the surface that stops its falling movement. The occasional shortening of pak_2 to *pa* indicates that the contact resulting from a turning over is not made with the same reconfiguring effect as takes place when something very malleable falls onto a firm surface. The absence of the final velar stop *-k*, then, is iconic of the absence of the obstruction by a firm surface of what falls onto it.

Pak occurs with the following verbs.

1. pak urmana
fall — to fall with a splat, e.g., tree sap onto the ground, roasting meat from a drying rack, clump of earth from an eroding riverbank
2. pak apamuna
bring — to bring something by turning over, e.g., the way a wave of water carries a shell with it and washes it onto shore
3. pak urma-chi-na
fall-CAUS — to make or let something fall with a splat, e.g., masticated food from the mouth
4. pak hunda-chi-na
full-CAUS — to fill a container by tossing portions into it, letting them fall sounding *pak*
5. pak apana
take — to take by turning over, e.g., to scrape sap oozing out of a tree, using a knife to turn it over and away from the tree's trunk
6. pak aparina
carry — to toss something over one's shoulder to carry it
7. pak rina
go — to turn over, e.g., skin peeled from flesh
8. pak warkuna
hang — to turn over and hang, e.g., skin torn from flesh
9. pak aysana
pull — to draw someone over to oneself by overcoming their resistance, e.g., through enchantment
10. pak l^{y}ukshina
leave — to leave quickly, as if pulled toward someone not present

11.	pak sirina lie	to turn over and lie on a surface (cf. *toa*)
12.	pak timbuna boil	to boil violently, sounding *pak*
13.	pak timbu-chi-na boil-CAUS	to boil something violently, making the sound *pak*
14.	pak paska-chi-na open-CAUS	to open up by turning over, e.g., by sliding a knife lengthwise through a piece of meat
15.	pak pasa-chi-na pass-CAUS	to pass through by turning over, e.g., by sliding a knife through a piece of meat, and turning the top layer of the meat over
16.	pak churana put	to place something over a surface
17.	pak ugl^{y}ana hatch	to hatch eggs by sitting over them, e.g., a hen
18.	pak watana tie	to tie over something, covering it
19.	pak hapina catch	to grab something, covering it up
20.	pak rana do	to knock over, e.g., the way an animal knocks down a barricade of sticks
21.	pak taparina close	to cover up, e.g., to close the eyes
22.	pak upina drink	to drink up, so that the drinking container can be turned over (cf *t^{y}am*, *toa*)

In the following example *pak* describes the way masticated food was made to fall on the ground.

23. Wawa pak urma-chi-ra muku-shka-ta.
baby fall-CAUS-PAST chew-PERF-ACC
"The baby let what he'd chewed fall *pak*."

Pak is not performatively foregrounded here. It functions to affect its verb's aspect reading with punctual completiveness, by imitating the cognitively salient sound made by the contact of food with a ground surface.

In the next example *pak* is repeated to describe the way pieces of stingray meat, which had not been properly dried, fell off of the drying rack on which they had been set. The sentence is one person's version of a conversation between herself and another woman about the proper way to dry meat. The other adverb, *pus*, is from the word *pusku* "foam" and refers to the way the meat was rotting away and frothing.

24. 'Kan mana al^{y}i chaki-chi-shka-ngi-chu,' raya, pay ismu-sha, ismu-sha,
you NEG well dry-CAUS-PERF-2-NEG stingray it rot-COR rot-COR
pay pak pak pak pus pus urma-w-ta, ni-ni.
it froth froth fall-DUR-ACC say-1
"Saying 'You haven't dried it well', I tell her that the stingray meat is rotting, rotting away, frothing frothing, and falling *pak pak pak*."

Pak is performatively foregrounded here by its syntactic displacement from its verb *urmawta* "falling" and by its multiple repetition. Its syntactic displacement focuses attention on the sound image of the meat's repeated falling, which functions modally to embarrass the incompetent woman responsible for wasting the meat.

In the next sentence, taken from a personal experience narrative, *pak*$_2$ describes the way a man turned over on his stomach to drink from a pond. The other sound-symbolic adverbs are *talaw*, which describes a collapsing motion, and *yun*, which describes the slurping of the water.

25. 'Talaw siri-ra-ni' ni-ra pak, yun yun yun yun yun yun.
lie-PAST-1 say-PAST
"'(Collapsing) *talaw*, I laid down,' he said, (and turned over) *pak*, (and drank) *yun yun yun yun yun yun*."

Pak is performatively foregrounded here by its syntactic isolation. By its isolation and also by its juxtaposition with other sound symbolic adverbs, it simulates the urgency of a series of actions that remained vivid in the memory of a man who had just encountered water for the first time in days, while he wandered lost in the forest.

Pak$_2$ sometimes occurs in a variant form, *pa*. In the following example, a resultative *pa* describes the way the skin of someone bitten by a snake falls back and over after being torn. The dropping of the final *-k* in this example is iconic of the absence of a hard, forceful contact. The other sound-symbolic adverb, *shaka*, describes the initial tearing of the victim's skin.

26. Chasna-shi runa-ta-s kani-k a-n, ña shaka pa!
like that-EV people-ACC-INCL bite-AG be-3 now
"That's how it bites people too, now, (tearing) *shaka* and (peeling it over) *pa*."

Pa is performatively foregrounded here by its syntactic isolation, which foregrounds an image of skin being turned over. The intended effect is to horrify.

In the next example *pak*$_2$ describes the way a piece of tapir meat is turned over as it is slit open lengthwise with a knife so that it can be salted. Again, the dropping of the final *-k* in this example is iconic of the absence of a hard, forceful contact. The other sound-symbolic adverb, *t^{y}am*, describes the successive rolling over of each section of the meat that falls *pa* as it is slit along a horizontal axis.

27. Chi-ta-s ña t^{y}am t^{y}am t^{y}am t^{y}am pa pa pa pa pa pa pa pa pa, chi-ta-was
that-ACC-INCL now that-ACC-INCL
pasa-chi-u-nchi aycha-ta.
pass-CAUS-DUR-1PL meat-ACC

"And that (foreleg) too, now *t^{y}am t^{y}am t^{y}am t^{y}am* (rolling it over) and *pa pa pa pa pa pa pa pa pa* (letting each section of that meat fall) also, we pass through it (with a knife.)"

Pak is performatively foregrounded here by its syntactic displacement, its multiple repetition, and the circumscribing rise and fall of pitch over its repetitions. Its syntactic displacement from its verb *pasachiunchi* "we pass" calls attention to the image of the meat falling over as it is sliced further and further. The images described by repetitions of *pak* and *tʸam* function as explanations to my inquiries about the preparation of meat for drying.

Patang

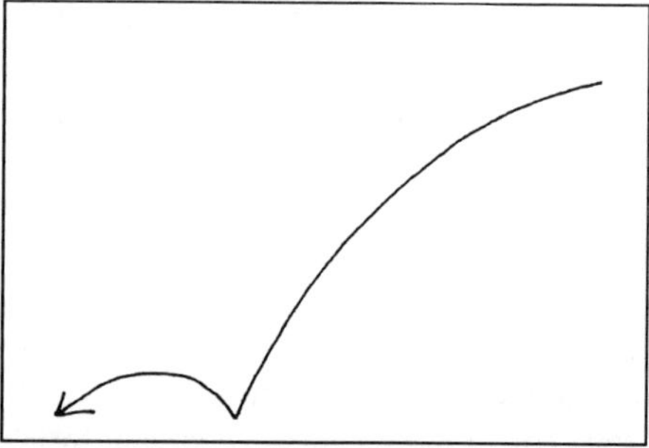

DEFINITION Describes the moment of contact, or an idea of the sound of contact made with a surface by falling upon or hitting against it, without any evident loss of wholeness or shape. Aspectually completive, resultative.

COMMENT Things that fall *patang* are usually somewhat heavy and substantial, which is why they don't suffer any obvious loss of shape. They include relatively inanimate objects such as tree trunks that fall over in a strong storm, as well as animate entities, such as the tail of a large snake, which is thrown down when it tries to grab an animal. Whoever or whatever deliberately hits *patang* deals a forceful blow which is intended to be disabling. English words describing a similar notion of falling or hitting are "thud" and "thump."

ICONIC PROPERTIES The iconicity of *patang* is related to its disyllabic structure; to its initial, medial, and final stop consonants, *p-*, *-t-*, and *-ng*; and to its final closed syllable. Its disyllabic structure provides speakers with a frame to performatively gesture the initial falling or hitting movement, *pa-*, and the final contact, *-tang*. Its initial, medial, and final stop consonants, *p-*, *-t-*, and *-ng*, create maximal obstruction in the vocal tract, which is imitative of the high degree of control maintained by the agent doing the hitting. Similarly, whatever falls or is hit *patang* can also be said to be relatively controlled because it suffers no evident loss of wholeness or shape. The final syllable, *-tang*, by its closure, imitates the definitive conclusion of a hitting or falling action.

Patang occurs with the following verbs.

1.	patang urmana fall	to fall down, e.g., tail of a snake, tree struck by lightening, bird shot with poisoned dart, and all kinds of fruit
2.	patang urma-chi-na fall-CAUS	to cause to fall down, e.g., an animal which is shot or a tree struck by lightning
3.	patang tuksina throw	to throw or fling something down, e.g., the way a large snake throws down its tail when attempting to grab an animal
4.	patang shitana throw	same as above

5. patang kushparina shake	to flail or thrash, hitting and thumping the ground, e.g., from a convulsive or traumatic fit
6. patang saltarina leap	to leap or jump up and down, e.g., while dancing
7. patang wañu-chi-na die-CAUS	to kill something, e.g., a snake, by hitting it against the ground with a stick, making the sound *patang*
8. patang waktana hit	to hit something, making the sound *patang*
9. patang mirana increase	to grow profusely and fall off sounding *patang*, e.g., ears of corn from their stalks (myth)

The following example features *patang* in a description of a woman's fall and subsequent convulsive fit.

10. Provincia de Loro-manda warmi-ga patang urma-sha atake-ta hapi-ra.
province of Loro-from woman-TOP fall-COR attack-ACC catch-PAST
"Falling *patang*, the woman from the province of Loro had an attack."

Patang is not performatively foregrounded here; it affects the aspect reading of the coreference verb *urmasha* "falling" with completiveness, and at the same time it communicates a dramatic image of that falling down.

In the next example a variant of *patang*, *potong*, describes the way lots of trees fell during a violent rainstorm. The other sound-symbolic adverb, *tay*, describes the sound of thunder.

11. Wayra-ga may-ta yanga potong potong potong potong potong potong,
wind-TOP where-ADV just
rayu-was t^{h}ayyy t^{h}aaayyy t^{h}aaayyy, rigri surduyana-ga!
thunder-INCL ear become deaf-TOP
"The wind (was making trees fall wherever) *potong potong potong potong potong potong*, and the thunder was deafening, *t^{h}ayyy t^{h}aaayyy t^{h}aaayyy* !"

Potong is performatively foregrounded here by its syntactic isolation and by its rapid repetition that imitates the rapid rhythm of the falling of the trees for dramatic effect and at the same time specifies their duration.

In the next sentence, taken from a myth, *patang* describes the way a group of spirits fell out of their hiding place, one after the other, having been smoked out by the burning of dried peppers. The series of repetitions is stopped by the narrator herself, who breaks them off to confirm with someone else the next event in the story.

12. Ña chawpi-ta hapichi-u-l^{y}a-shi urma-shk-awna shuk-bas patang shuk-bas patang
now middle-ACC light-DUR-LIM-EV fall-PERF-3PL one-INCL one-INCL
shuk-bas patang shuk-bas patang . . .
one-INCL one-INCL
"Then, just when the fire had caught half (of the tree stump), they (the spirits) fell out, one *patang* and another *patang* and another *patang* and another *patang* . . ."

Patang is performatively foregrounded here by its multiple repetitions, which imitate the forest spirits' successive falling out from the tree stump. Its function here is to suggest a kind of whimsical paradox. By attributing an idea of substantiality, of something solid that falls with a certain force, it gives the forest spirits a certain corporeal credibility.

In the next example *patang* describes the repeated hitting of a poisonous snake with a stick. The snake was a deadly variety of viper known in Quechua as *mutulu*, the bite of which kills almost instantly.

13. Kikin ruku pacha kal^{y}a kal^{y}a ra-sha, pa-t^{h}annng! (pause) Ruku pacha
real big EXCL do-COR big EXCL
pa-t^{h}annng (pause) kuti pa-t^{h}annng pa-t^{h}annng-mi wakta-n!
again -EV hit-3

"Standing with his legs apart, *kal^{y}a kal^{y}a* he hits this great big snake *pa-t^{h}annng*! (pause) This big thing, *pa-t^{h}annng*! (pause); and again *pa-t^{h}annng pa-t^{h}annng*!"

Patang is performatively foregrounded here by the slight break between its initial syllable, *pa-*, and its final syllable, *-tang*, which analyzes the component movements of the hitting action into an initial movement toward the animal, *pa-*, and the final violent contact with it, *-tang*. It is also foregrounded by the low-pitched, deeply resonant, and energetic burst of aspiration over its second syllable, *-tang*, which imitates the great force with which the snake was struck, making the eventual victory over it more impressive. *Patang* is further foregrounded by its multiple repetition, which gestures each act of striking, emphasizing how many it took to completely disable the animal.

In the following example *patang* describes how a large snake threw its tail to grab a dog, but missed and hit the ground. The speaker compares the force of the hit with that of a rotted log falling on the ground. The other sound-symbolic adverb, *dziri*, describes the sound of the snake's opening from coiled position.

34. Yanga dz^{h}iririri uyari-k-a, pa-t^{h}anng! (pause) ima ismu kaspi-ta shina tuksi-k
just sound-AG-TOP what rot log-ACC like throw-AG
a-shka chupa-ta!
be-PERF tail-ACC

"Just sounding *dz^{h}iririri* , (it went) *pa-t^{h}anng*! (pause), as if it were some rotted log it threw its tail down!"

Patang is performatively foregrounded here by its displacement from its verb *tuksik ashka* (lit.) "was a thrower," which presents the image before it is referred to. It is also foregrounded by the slight break between the first and second syllables which analyzes the action of throwing into an initial movement toward the dog, *pa-*, and a final contact with the ground, *-tang*. The aspiration over its second syllable, *-tang*, suggests the force with which the tail sailed through the air, and the pause after its pronunciation creates a brief suspenseful moment when the listener isn't yet certain that the dog has not been grabbed.

Ki

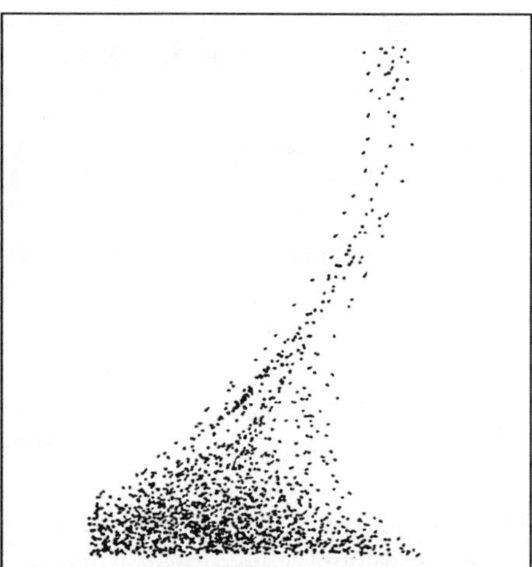

DEFINITION (1) To throw, spill, or sprinkle a collection of similar objects or entities. Aspectually completive. (2) To be heaped, piled, or randomly distributed within a space. Aspectually resultative, aorist.[3] Possibly originates from the sound-symbolic adverb *aki*.

COMMENT The images described with *ki* have associations of abundance, potential, and also wastefulness. One of the most common images described with *ki* is the spilling of the contents of a hexagonally woven basket, which occurs in myth and in narratives from everyday life. One woman described how frightened she became walking through the forest when she came so close to a poisonous snake that she nearly stepped on it. The unhappy result of this encounter was that she spilled the fish from her basket *ki*, which had taken an entire morning to catch, and ran away without even turning back.

ICONIC PROPERTIES The iconicity of *ki* is related to its monosyllabicity and to the openness of its syllable. Its monosyllabicity is iconic of the simplicity of a pattern perceived as a whole. The openness of its syllable is iconic of the scattered, noncontained quality of what is spilled. The iconicity of *ki* could also be due to its association with another sound-symbolic adverb rather than to its articulatory properties. If *ki* is related to the second syllable of the sound-symbolic adverb *aki*, which describes an unsteady swaying or rocking, then the falling, throwing, and spilling it describes could be a resultant image of the unsteady swaying described by *aki*.

Ki occurs with the following verbs.

1.	ki sirina lie	to lie in a pile or group, e.g., the way eggs look lying in a nest, the way lots of fish appear near the surface of a pond after the water is treated with venom
2.	ki talina spill	to spill or pour something nonliquid, e.g. rice, out of a container
3.	ki urmana fall	to fall, spilling all over, e.g. a basket of fish
4.	ki kuna give	to give a lot of, e.g., a "mountain" or pile of fruit
5.	ki ichuna abandon	to throw or spill something and leave it, e.g. a basket of fish
6.	ki shitana throw	to throw any particle-like medium such as dirt or sand

7. ki ichana — to sprinkle or scatter salt, ashes, or seeds
   sprinkle

In the following example, taken from a fable, *ki* describes a rabbit's flinging of a clump of dirt into the eyes of a frog.

8. Chi-ga al^{y}pa-wan-ga k^{h}iiii, ñawi-y shita-shka.
   then-TOP dirt-INST-TOP eye-LOC throw-PERF
   "Then with the dirt he threw *k^{h}iiii* into his eyes."

Ki is performatively foregrounded here by displacement from its verb *shitashka* "threw," its aspiration, and its lengthening. Its displacement from its verb foregrounds the image of the throwing, setting it off from the verb's reference to it. The aspiration imitates the force with which the throwing was accomplished. The lengthening imitates the path of movement of the dirt through the air. All of these techniques function aesthetically by their contribution to an image which is of key importance for the unfolding of the story's plot.

In the next example, taken from a fable with similarities to the Hansel and Gretel story, *ki* describes the sprinkling of corn and ashes by children to mark their route through the forest.

9. Ushpa wawa-ta ki, sara muyu chari, ushpa wawa chay ki ki ki ki ki icha-sha
   ash little-ACC corn seed perhaps ash little there sprinkle-COR
   ri-k a-naw-ra.
   go-AG be-3PL-PAST
   "A little bit of ash, *ki*, and some corn seed, perhaps, a bit of ash there, *ki ki ki ki ki* sprinkling they would go."

Ki is minimally foregrounded here by its multiple repetition, which imitates the action of throwing the seeds and ashes. In this context *ki* combines aesthetic and modal functions. By its performativity, the narrator simulates the particular qualities of an image of a series of actions, for the sake of the image itself. This image is significant for the story's plot since it is this series of actions that leads to the childrens' becoming lost. At the same time, by minimizing the actions' performativity, this image suggests a mood of effortlessness, lightness, and even an idea of flimsiness, which ramifies with the action's ultimate futility. As in the European version of this story, the birds of the forest ate all of the corn, and the wind swept all of the ashes away, making it impossible for the children to retrace their steps.

In the next example *ki* describes the way lots of fish lie in a configuration near the surface of a pond that has been treated with venom.

10. Kasna-y chuti, idzi sardina, kiiiiiii siri-shka.
    like this-LOC chuti idzi sardina lie-3past
    "Some *chuti* (type of fish), and *idzi sardina* (type of fish) laid there like this *kiiiiiii*."

Ki is performatively foregrounded here by lengthening, which is metaphorically imitative of the extension in space of the fish. This image is aesthetically motivated since it suggests the bounteousness and abundance of fish available for the catching.

In the next example *ki* is part of a complex composition of sound-symbolic adverbs describing the way a large clay jar will disintegrate after it has been fired if made from inferior clay. *Tan* describes an idea of how it sounds when the splitting begins. *Tas* describes the overall distribution of the splitting taking place in the entire jar. *Kal^{y}a* describes the fissured quality of the jar's cracks. *Awing* refers to the opening up of the jar as a result of its crackings and fissures. And *ki* describes the final outcome, which is the resulting pile of rubble consisting of the jar's broken fragments.

11. Uyari-nga-ta-ng partiri-nga tan tan tan tas tasss kal^{y}a awing kiii amo-ga
    sound-FUT-ADV-INST split-FUT owner-TOP
    waka-na ma-n.
    cry-INF be-3
    "It will split apart sounding *tan tan tan tas tasss*, (then) *kal^{y}a awing* (opening up) *kiii* (fissure), the one who made it has to cry."

Ki is performatively foregrounded here by its syntactic isolation, by its position as the last sound-symbolic adverb in a complex description, and by its lengthening. By contrast with the preceding example, where the lengthening of *ki* suggested a pleasant image of abundance, this lengthening suggests a depressing image of a useless collection of pottery rubble. In addition, the telic pitch progression over *kal^{y}a*, *awing*, and *ki* is iconically expressive of the progression in the jar's self-destruction.

In the final example *ki* describes the way women dance by tossing their hair while also bending their torsos from side to side. The image described with *ki* focuses on the tossing of the hair.

12. Akcha-yuk-guna kay-ma kiiiiii, chi-ma kiiiiii, gustu-ta rikuri-sha.
    hair-POSS-PL this-DAT that-DAT nice-ADV appear-COR
    "The ones with (long) hair (go) *kiiiiii* here, and *kiiiiii* there, looking really nice."

Ki is performatively foregrounded here by its lengthening and by its syntactic isolation. Its lengthening is aesthetically motivated: it imitates the path of movement of the hair through the air.

12

Sound Symbols of Deformation

This chapter analyzes six sound-symbolic adverbs that concern various types of deformative actions. All of these adverbs concern the description of actions or processes that cause the violation of an object or entity's integral structure. *Tsuk* describes the removal of something from its medium or structural mass. *Waling* describes an empty hollow left by a decaying, eating, or burning away. *Ch'ʸu* describes the deliberate cutting or breaking off of something, usually involving the use of a tool such as a knife. *Cham* describes what is typically an agentively low breaking or crumbling off of a piece or of pieces of something. *Kal'ʸa* describes the depth dimension of a fissure. *Shaka* describes the lengthwise dimension of a split or tear.

Tsuk

DEFINITION An idea of the sound of removing something from its medium or of taking a portion of something away from its mass. To remove something from its medium, or take a portion of something away from its structural mass. Aspectually punctual.

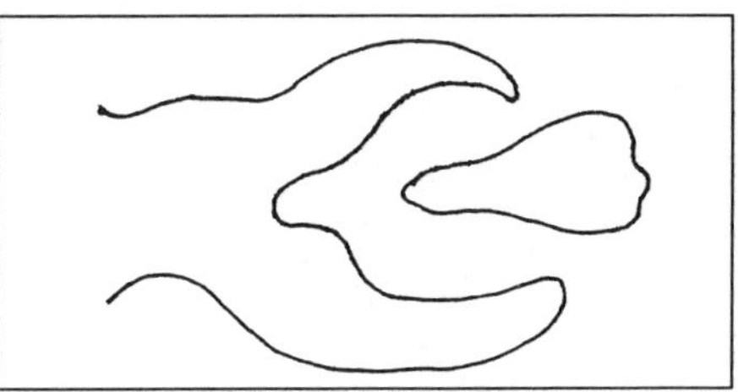

COMMENT What *tsuk* describes is the clean, surgical removal of something, typically from a living entity, whether plant or animal. The English word "pluck" comes close to describing *tsuk*. The removal of something *tsuk* from its medium or structural mass can disable or incapacitate in various degrees. When an animal, such as a rabbit, bites off a piece of a sweet potato *tsuk*, the plant is still viable as long as a lot of it is not consumed. But the heart of the *lisan* palm tree is plucked out *tsuk* and immediately consumed, only after most of the tree has already been chopped down. The most terrifying image described with *tsuk* involves a small carnivorous sardine, known in Spanish as the *coronera* and in Quechua as the *kaniru*, which is about an inch and a half long, whose attack can be fatal. It is said to be drawn to any orifice, and once it enters, it is prevented by sharp spiny prongs on its back from coming back out again. It therefore eats away at one's flesh, removing small pieces of it *tsuk*, working its way deeper and deeper into the body.

ICONIC PROPERTIES The iconicity of *tsuk* is related to its monosyllabicity and to its word-final velar stop, *-k*. Its monosyllabicity, by its noncomplexity, is iconic of the punctuality of actions described with *tsuk*. Its word-final velar stop, *-k*, by its complete cessation of the airstream mechanism, is iconic of the complete cessation of physical contiguity between what is removed and what it is removed from.

Tsuk occurs with the following verbs.

1. tsuk surkuna remove	to pluck out, e.g., a tuberous vegetable from the ground or a limb from its body
2. tsuk aysana pull	to pull out in one clean movement, e.g., the heart of the *lisan* palm tree
3. tsuk l^yukshi-chi-na leave-CAUS	to cause something to emerge from something else in one clean movement
4. tsuk chupana suck	to suck or bite off a piece of flesh, e.g., the way the *kaniru* sardine does when it attacks people
5. tsuk kanina bite	same as above
6. tsuk apana take	to take something away by quickly pulling it out of its medium or structural mass

In the following example, taken from a fable, *tsuk* describes the moment when a rabbit interrupts its hopping to steal a piece of sweet potato.

7. Chi-ga salta salta salta tsuk surkuri-sha-ga, conejo-ga kal^{y}pa-shka-shi.
   that-TOP leap leap leap remove-COR-TOP rabbit-TOP run-PERF-EV
   "So then leaping leaping leaping and then *tsuk* removing (a bite of sweet potato), the rabbit ran off."

Tsuk is not performatively foregrounded here. It affects its coreference verb *surkurishaga* "removing" with punctual aspect by simulating a cognitively salient image of the definitive removal of a piece of sweet potato.

In the next example *tsuk* describes the plucking out of the heart of a palm tree.

8. Tsuk aysa-sha pal^{y}a-nchi lisan yuyu-ta.
   pull-COR harvest-1PL lisan heart-ACC
   "We harvest the heart of the *lisan* palm, *tsuk* pulling it out."

Tsuk is not performatively foregrounded here. It affects its coreference verb *aysasha* "pulling" with punctual aspect by expressing the most cognitively salient image of the action of pulling out.

In the final example *tsuk* describes the way the small carnivorous *kaniru* sardine eats through flesh by biting off piece after piece, as it makes its way through a body.

9. Yari! Tsuk tsuk tsuk tsuk tsuk tsuk tsuk pay kani-sha ri-u-n na ima animal shina!
   think it bite-COR go-DUR-3 now what animal like!

   "(Just) imagine! *Tsuk tsuk tsuk tsuk tsuk tsuk tsuk* it's going, biting (it's way through) like what kind of an animal!"

Tsuk is performatively foregrounded have by its multiple repetition, by the rise and fall in pitch over the repetitions, and by its syntactic displacement from the coreference verb *kanisha* "biting." The multiple repetitions imitate the repeated action of biting. The rise and fall in pitch over the repetitions eases their monotony and at the same time suggests that the biting was distributed throughout a circumscribed space. The syntactic displacement of the series of repetitions from their verb foregrounds the image they describe as expressively distinct from the verb's mere reference to this action. All of these foregrounding techniques, particularly those suggesting the repeatedness and distributedness of the action, contribute to an overall gestalt of horror at the thought of one's body invaded by such a creature.

Waling

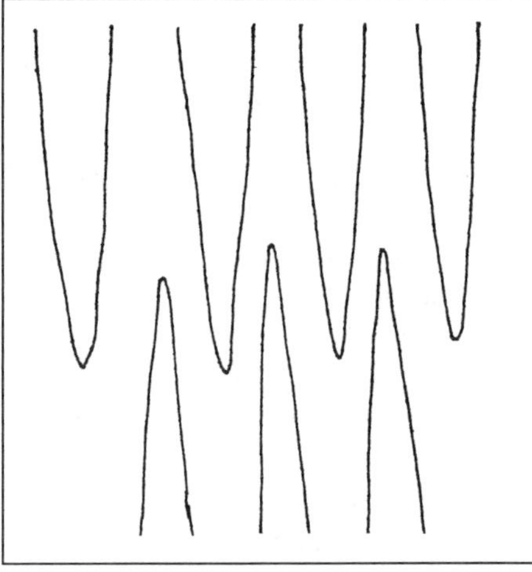

DEFINITION (1) To create empty space by eating away or burning up a portion of something; to be left partially eaten or burned away. Aspectually completive, resultative. (2) A pattern of positive/negative space. Aspectually aorist.

COMMENT *Waling* is a prominent death image for Quechua speakers, just as a bare human skeleton or a skull and crossbones are for us. However, the images described by *waling* are not as neat and clean as our skeletons and skulls. Many are so horrible they are fairly unimaginable. The image of flesh burned away almost down to the bone or of a body with most of the flesh consumed by a mythic bat are a couple of the more harrowing images described by *waling*. *Waling* is also a prominent image of decay, a force that is constantly at work in the rainforest ecosystem. One has to keep constant watch over produce harvested from the field. If left unguarded or uneaten, plaintains, potatoes, and manioc are quickly attacked by various kinds of insects which eat away at the flesh, leaving it *waling* full of cavities, rotting away.

ICONIC PROPERTIES The iconicity of *waling* is related to its disyllabic structure, the contrast between its initial-syllable low vowel *-a-* and its final-syllable high vowel *-i-*, and its final closed syllable all lend themselves to iconic interpretation. Its disyllabic structure provides a frame for the gesturing of the distinction between foreground and background. The initial syllable, *wa-*, is the background, or negative, empty space of the image, while the final syllable, *-ling*, is the foregrounded image of positive space. The contrast between the low and high vowels in the first and second syllables, respectively, further enhances the background/foreground distinction. The final closed syllable sets the image off from its surrounding utterance.

Waling occurs with the following verbs.

1. waling sakirina remain	to be left in a state of having been partially eaten away or burned away, e.g., ripe fruit or burned flesh
2. waling sirina lie	to lie in a state resulting from having been partially eaten away or burned away
3. waling rupana burn	to burn away flesh, leaving only bones
4. waling sakina leave	to leave emptied or hollowed out by eating away the flesh, leaving only bones
5. waling wañuna die	to die by losing an essential part of the characteristic appearance, e.g., the way trees lose their leaves, leaving bare branches exposed, or the way certain vines lose leaves while in a dormant phase
6. waling mikuna eat	to eat away the flesh of something, e.g., a piece of fruit by insects or small animals
7. wali mana be	to be characterized by a pattern of positive/negative space, e.g., the gap-toothed mouth of an alligator or the walls of an unfinished room stuck with support poles that are not yet covered up with cement
8. waling mikurina eat	to be eaten away, e.g., flesh of fruit marked with hollows; to eat the flesh of one's body, leaving only the bones, e.g., a mythic bat

The following example is taken from a myth about bats that consume people by eating their flesh, leaving only their bones. The first sound-symbolic adverb, *ch^{y}u*, describes its cutting into the flesh, and *waling* describes how it looks when the eating is finished.

9. Chi-ga shamu-sha-ga, yanga ch^{y}u ch^{y}u ch^{y}u ch^{y}u ch^{y}u ch^{y}u ch^{y}u tul^{y}u-l^{y}a-ta-shi
that-TOP come-COR-TOP just bone-LIM-ACC-EV
wa^{ling} saki-nawn.
leave-3PL

"So then, coming, and just (eating) *ch^{y}u ch^{y}u ch^{y}u ch^{y}u ch^{y}u ch^{y}u ch^{y}u* they left only the bones, *wa^{ling}*."

Waling is performatively foregrounded here by the upjump over its second syllable which, by its pitch contrast between the first and second syllables, imitates an idea of a distinction between foreground and background. Only the bones have been left, and it is this image of the remaining bones that is foregrounded by the intonational upjump over *waling*. This image is used by the narrator to create a mood of great anxiety and horror over the completeness of the victim's destruction by the bat.

The next example, taken from the same myth as the preceding one, describes the fate of a different victim.

10. Pay kusa-ta miku-shka, ña wa^{ling} (pause) tul^{y}u-l^{y}a siri-u-shka, sumak
her husband-ACC eat-PERF now bone-LIM lie-DUR-PERF nice
hihi shina l^{y}awka-shka.
grasshopper like lick-PERF
"(It) had eaten her husband, *wa*^{ling} (pause) so that only his bones lay there, as if licked nicely clean by grasshoppers."

Waling is performatively foregrounded here by its syntactic displacement from its verb *mikushka* "ate," by the upjump over its second syllable, and by the pause immediately following its pronunciation. Both its syntactic displacement and the pause immediately following *waling* allow a listener to actively imagine the image it describes apart from the verb's reference to it. The upjump over its second syllable by its pitch contrast between the first and second syllables imitates an idea of a distinction between foreground and background. The victim has been so completely consumed that only the bones remain, so bare that they look as if they've been licked clean.

The next example, taken from a different myth, features *waling* in a description of the way a forest was decimated by a spirit that ate all the leaves from the trees, leaving only the bare branches.

11. Ranchu panga-ga wa^{ling}! (pause) Puñuna panga-s wa^{ling}!
small house leaf-TOP sleep leaf-INCL
"The *ranchu* leaves *wa*^{ling} (were eaten); and the leaves for the sleeping house too, *wa*^{ling} (were eaten)."

Both uses of *waling* are performatively foregrounded here by their syntactic isolation and by the upjump over their second syllables. Their syntactic isolation places the entire descriptive and grammatical burden on these sound-symbolic adverbs. There are no verbs to specify aspect values nor to refer to the processes described. The upjump in pitch over its second syllable adds intonational foregrounding to the syntactic foregrounding, suggesting by its pitch contrast a before/after contrast between the way the forest looked normally and the way it appeared after all of its trees had been stripped bare. *Waling* functions grammatically, aesthetically, and modally. Given the sentence's absence of verbs, it encodes the only grammatical information about the aspectual completiveness of the process described. It also highlights the image of the bare forest for its shock effect, communicating to a listener the tremendous power of this spirit to wipe out an entire forest.

In the following example *waling* is used in its adjectival form, *wali*, to describe the positive/negative pattern of space defined by the gap-toothed mouth of an alligator.

12. Kay-l^ya kiru ruku-yuk-shi a-n wali wali kiru-yuk.
here-LIM tooth big-POSS-EV be-3 teeth-POSS
"It has big teeth like this; (it's a) *wali wali* possessor of teeth."

Wali is performatively foregrounded here by its reduplication, which gestures the multiplicity of the pattern's distribution at the same time that it specifies its aorist aspect.

Ch^y^u

DEFINITION To create a clean break by deliberately chopping, cutting, or cleaving an object or entity, usually by means of a sharp tool. Aspectually completive, resultative.

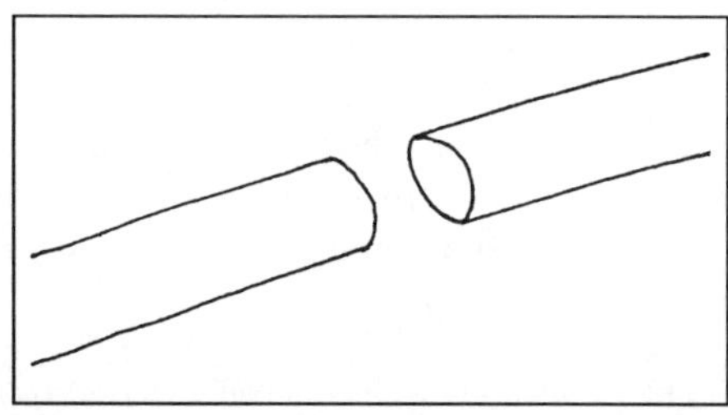

COMMENT *Ch^y^u* communicates an image of a clean break—of something definitively severed from something else. It is this dimension of separation which is most commonly used to describe the most ordinary activities, such as chopping pieces of meat to cook them or cutting a large leaf off its branch so that it can be used to wrap and roast fish. However, the image of a clean break is also extended metaphorically to describe, for example, the giving up of a habitual activity such as getting drunk or going on long treks through the forest because one is no longer able.

ICONIC PROPERTIES The iconicity of *ch^y^u* is related to its monosyllabic structure and to the openness of its syllable. Its monosyllabic structure is iconic of the noncomplexity of the image it describes. It is the clean break and not the more complicated chopping or cutting gesture that is described by *ch^y^u*. Because the openness of its syllable allows continuous movement of the airstream, it is iconic of the lack of a barrier between the disparate parts of what has been cut, chopped, or cleaved.

Ch^y^u occurs with the following verbs.

1. ch^y^u pitina (cut) — to cut off a portion of anything, e.g., a piece of wood, leaf, nylon cord, limb or portion of meat from an animal
2. ch^y^u pitirina (cut) — to cut off a part of oneself (mythic animal); to be cut cleanly, e.g., cord or rope by a resisting fish
3. ch^y^u kanina (bite) — to bite off a piece of something, e.g., food
4. ch^y^u pikana (chop) — to chop something into pieces; to mince
5. ch^y^u rutuna (cut hair) — to cut off hair
6. ch^y^u mikuna (eat) — to eat a piece of something; to eat something piece by piece
7. ch^y^u sakina (leave) — to completely abandon an activity, such as the pursuit of an animal, or a habitual action, such as getting drunk

8. ch^{y}u rupana — to burn off, e.g., a body part such as a hand, in a fire
   burn
9. ch^{y}u waktana — to hit something, causing it to break off, e.g., a papaya from a tree
   hit

The following example is taken from a narrative of personal experience about an encounter with a jaguar. *Ch^{y}u* is used to describe how the jaguar's tail was bitten off by a dog.

10. Chupa-ta ch^{y}u piti-ra, puma chupa-ta.
    tail-ACC cut-PAST jaguar tail-ACC.
    "The tail *ch^{y}u* he cut off, the jaguar's tail."

Ch^{y}u is not performatively foregrounded here. It specifies the completiveness of its verb *pitira* "he cut" by focusing on the most cognitively salient image of the cutting off.

In the next example *ch^{y}u* describes the harvesting of manioc by cutting off each tuber from its root.

11. Al^{y}a-sha ch^{y}u, chay-ma; al^{y}a-sha ch^{y}u, chay-ma.
    dig-COR that-DAT dig-COR that-DAT
    "Digging (them up, I cut them off) *ch^{y}u* (and throw them) over there; digging (them up, I cut them off) *ch^{y}u* (and throw them) over there."

Ch^{y}u is performatively foregrounded here by its syntactic isolation. It alone bears the burden of describing by means of a cognitively salient image the action of cutting the tubers off from their roots. In addition to its grammatical function, *ch^{y}u* has an instructional function in this context; it is intended to enlighten the anthropologist about the intricacies of manioc horticulture.

In the next example *ch^{y}u* describes the killing of an anaconda.

12. Ch^{y}u ch^{y}u pika-shka amarun-da.
    chop-PERF anaconda-ACC
    "He chopped up the anaconda *ch^{y}u ch^{y}u*."

Ch^{y}u is minimally foregrounded here by its reduplication, which is a shorthand for the multiple chops and cuts that actually took place. It functions grammatically, affecting its verb with iterative aspect, and also expressively. By minimizing the chopping with a simple reduplicated phrase, the speaker minimizes the effort required to kill the animal.

In the next example *ch^{y}u* describes the way an eel that had just been caught was cut up into portions and wrapped in leaves.

13. Angila ruku-ta ch^{y}u ch^{y}u ch^{y}u ch^{y}u ch^{y}u piti-sha sumak maytu-sha apa-ra.
    eel big-ACC cut-COR nicely leaf-wrap-COR take-PAST
    "Cutting up this big old eel *ch^{y}u ch^{y}u ch^{y}u ch^{y}u ch^{y}u*, wrapping it nicely, she took it with her."

Ch^{y}u is performatively foregrounded here by its multiple repetition and by the circumscribing rise and fall in pitch over the repetitions. The multiple repetitions gesture each of the repeated actions of cutting up the eel into portions. The circumscribing rise and fall in pitch over the repetitions sets them off as an image and also relieves their monotony. This image occurs in the context of a commentary about the undiscriminating palates of an upriver people. The speaker was a little surprised by the fact that people from upriver, in part because they have access to less protein, will eat a greater variety of water-dwelling creatures, including eels. Her performative elaborations of *ch^{y}u* with multiple repetitions and a circumscribing pitch rise and fall communicate an image of a process—the cutting up of fish for cooking—from beginning to end. By elaborating an image of this process in its entirety, the speaker lessens the unusualness of the image for herself, suggesting that what would be unheard of for her—the preparation of an eel for eating—is simply "business-as-usual" for someone upriver.

In the next example repetitons of *ch^{y}u* describe the successive cutting away at a tree stump to get at a wild pig hiding inside.

14. Tapa-shka washa piti-ni ch^{y}u ch^{y}u ch^{y}u ch^{y}u ch^{y}u piti-sha, ña aycha-y pakta-ra-ni.
cover-PERF after cut-1 cut-COR now meat-LOC arrive-PAST-1

"After plugging it up I cut *ch^{y}u ch^{y}u ch^{y}u ch^{y}u ch^{y}u* cutting away, then I get to the meat."

Ch^{y}u is performatively foregrounded here by its multiple repetition and by the telic pitch progression over its repetitions. The repetitions gesture each act of cutting away. By the time the last *ch^{y}u* of the series, which is also the highest pitched, is pronounced, the animal has been found. The repetitions and pitch progression create a mood of expectation which is heightened as the repeated series progresses. The expectation is rewarded with the phrase "then I get to the meat."

In the following example *ch^{y}u* describes how the owner of a canoe became aware that the rope he had used to tie it had been cut.

15. Kanoa waska ch$^{yu^{u}}$ (pause); kanoa il^{y}a-n!
canoe rope canoe be missing-3

"The canoe's rope (is cut off) *ch$^{yu^{u}}$* (pause); the canoe is gone!"

Ch^{y}u is performatively foregrounded here by its syntactic isolation, by the upwardly gliding pitch over its pronunciation, and by the immediately following pause. Its syntactic isolation places the full burden on *ch^{y}u* both for specifying the resultative aspect of its covert predicate and for expressing the most cognitively salient image of resultativity, the rope's clean break, which resulted in the canoe's drifting away. The upglide over *ch^{y}u* comes at a dramatic moment in this account concerning an anaconda's attack on a canoe which had been docked at the shore, its prow tied to a tree. The image of the rope's clean break and the canoe's disappearance fueled speculation that an anaconda had attacked the empty canoe in an attempt to attack its passengers.

Cham

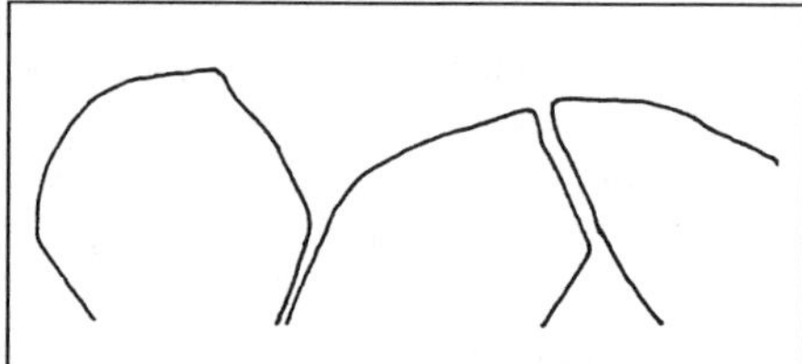

DEFINITION (1) To break, crumble off of an original whole. Aspectually completive, resultative. (2) To be distributed throughout a circumscribed space. Aspectually aorist.

COMMENT The break described by *cham* is not neat, as is the break described by *ch^{y}u*. Furthermore, in the vast majority of its uses, it is not a volitional break—that is, controlled by an agent. Things that crumble away in a number of pieces, rot off, or break off unevenly are described with *cham*. This image of the separation of segments then becomes the basis for the other sense of *cham*, describing the distribution of objects or entities throughout a circumscribed space. Such a distribution can apply to relatively inanimate objects, such as fruit hanging from a tree, or to more animate beings, such as worms emerging from a piece of rotting meat.

ICONIC PROPERTIES The iconicity of *cham* is related to its monosyllabicity and to its final bilabial stop. Its monosyllabicity is iconic of the noncomplexity of a breaking off. Its final bilabial stop which brings the lips together thereby sealing off the mouth's resonance chamber, is iconic of the separation of something from a greater whole.

Cham occurs with the following verbs.

1. cham pakirina (break) — to break off from a larger whole, e.g., a chip from a tooth or a branch from a tree
2. cham ismuna (rot) — to break off or crumble away because of rot, e.g., a vegetable not harvested in time
3. cham urmana (fall) — to break off and fall, e.g., a dart sticking out of an animal
4. cham waglina (spoil) — to spoil, breaking into pieces, e.g., rotting fish
5. cham aparina (bear) — to bear fruit all over a tree or vine, e.g., mango, guava, *genipa*, and grapes
6. cham mirana (increase) — to proliferate, e.g., the way worms multiply in anything that rots
7. cham l^{y}ukshina (emerge) — to emerge simultaneously from more than one place, e.g., the way worms emerge from a vegetable when its cooking water becomes hot, or from dried meat when placed in a fire
8. cham kanina (bite) — to bite something off messily or unevenly, e.g., a piece of an animal's tail by another animal while fighting

9. cham pakina — to break something unintentionally, e.g., an old ax while felling a tree; to break something off without using a cutting tool, e.g., a leaf or branch from a tree
   break

In the following example *cham* describes the breaking off of a branch, to be used to insert into a hole in order to probe its depth.

10. Shiwa panga-ta piti-sha, cham paki-sha, ninanda wata-sha, bara-ni.
    Shiwa leaf-ACC cut-COR break-COR securely tie-COR insert-1

    "Cutting the *shiwa* leaf, breaking it off *cham*, tying it securely, I insert (it into the hole)."

Cham is not performatively foregrounded here. It specifies the completiveness of its coreference verb *pakisha* "breaking" by describing the cognitively salient image of that breaking off.

In the next example, taken from a myth, *cham* describes the way a dart that had been shot into an animal broke off and fell when the protaganist attempted to pull it out. The other adverb *tsi*, a variant of *dzir*, refers to the attempt to pull it out.

11. Tsi aysari-sha ni-kpi ch$^{a^{m}}$ (pause); chay-ma-shi biruti urma-ra.
    pull-COR want-SWRF that-DAT-EV dart fall-PAST

    "Wanting to pull it out *tsi*, it (broke off) *ch*$^{a^{m}}$ and fell."

Cham is performatively foregrounded here by its upgliding pitch, by its immediately following pause, and by displacement from its verb *urmara* "it fell." The upgliding pitch focuses on an image of the resultant state of the dart's being broken off. The immediately following pause encourages a listener to imagine this image, as does the displacement of *cham* from its verb.

In the next example *cham* is repeated to describe the progressive disintegration of an ax.

12. Pay tay tay wakta-y-wan pariul, hacha-ga cham $^{\text{cham}^{\text{cham}}}$ -shi pakiri-ra.
    He hit-nom-INST equal ax-TOP -EV break-PAST

    "At the same time that he hit, (going) *tay tay*, the ax broke *cham* $^{cham^{cham}}$."

Cham is performatively foregrounded here by its multiple repetition and by the telic pitch progression over the repeated series. Its multiple repetitions gesture the individual subevents leading to the ax's disintegration. The pitch progression is iconic of the progressiveness of the action itself. By the time the last *cham* of the series, which is also the highest pitched, is pronounced, the ax has totally disintegrated. These repetitions can be compared to cinematic editing and juxtaposition techniques that compress the time spanned by a process or activity, presenting each subevent of the process or activity leading to its completion. The image of *cham*'s disintegration is deliberately speeded up for aesthetic effect, communicating an idea of a totally useless ax.

In the next example, taken from a myth, *cham* describes the worms inside a person's stomach.

13. Ña kasna-shi a-ra kuru-ga, wiksa ukwi-ga,
Now like this-EV be-PAST worm-TOP stomach inside-TOP

cham cham cham cham cham cham cham.

"Now the worms, they were inside the stomach like this:

cham cham cham cham cham cham cham."

Cham is performatively foregrounded here by its multiple repetition and by the slight rise and fall in pitch over the repeated series. The pitch rise and fall is iconic of the spatial boundaries of the worms' distribution. The slight rise and fall in the speaker's pronunciation of each adverb imitates an idea of the spatial distributedness of the worms inside the person's stomach. By beginning with a certain pitch, rising above it, and returning back to it on the last repetition, the speaker imitates an idea of starting somewhere, going everywhere else, and then returning to the initial starting point, suggesting the full exploration of a given space. This creates an icon for the bounds of the worms' spatial distribution. By suggesting the worms' distribution throughout the stomach, the narrator creates a tone of repulsiveness.

The following example, taken from a myth, describes the transformation of two sisters into trees, which suddenly bear fruit all over their branches. Unlike the preceding example, which uses multiple repetitions of *cham* to describe an image of spatial distribution, this example uses a single *cham* to describe the distribution of fruit throughout a tree.

14. Ña wituk, ura-y ch$^{a^{m}}$ (pause), manduru-was ch$^{a^{m}}$ (pause)-shi apari-ra.
now genipa short-LOC achiote-INCL -EV bear-PAST

"Then, in a flash, the *genipa* tree (was full of fruit) *ch*$^{a^{m}}$ (pause), and the achiote tree also, *ch*$^{a^{m}}$ (pause), it bore fruit."

Each *cham* is performatively foregrounded here by its upglide and immediately following pause. Here the speaker uses a single foregrounded *cham* to impress the listener with how quickly the tree, which has just been transformed from a woman, bore fruit. By uttering *cham* only once, the narrator impresses the listener with the instantaneousness and the completeness of the tree's transformation.

Kal^{y}a

DEFINITION Describes the deep, vertical dimension of a splitting or fissuring open, which can but usually does not result in complete separation (cf. *ing*). Aspectually completive, resultative, resultative/aorist.

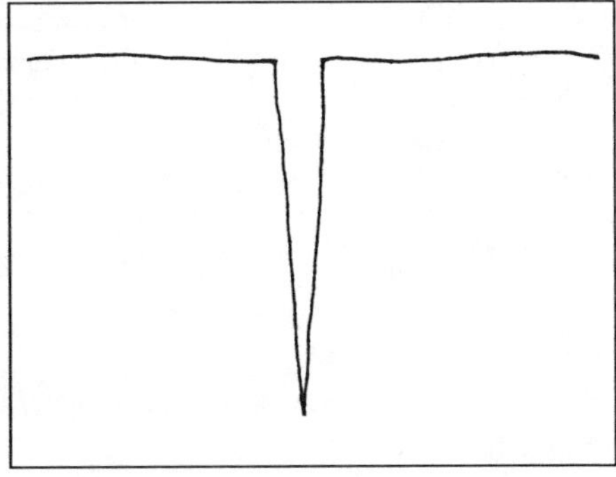

COMMENT The important difference between *ing* and *kal^{y}a* is that while *ing* can also describe a splitting open, it is always a relatively shallow splitting that doesn't disrupt the integrity of its entity. *Kal^{y}a*, however, describes an image of a deep fissure that significantly alters what it splits open. Cooked potatoes are split open *kal^{y}a* and served. Meat is split open *kal^{y}a* and salted before drying. The human body is also a model for this splitting. Evidence from the comments of several women indicates that they conceptualize their anatomical distinctiveness with *kal^{y}a*. A young girl told me a very short story about how men and women came to be physically different. According to her, a mythic man once became drunk and angry with his wife whom he then attacked with an ax, cleaving her and all future women *kal^{y}a*. The young girl's mother who was not far off, overheard her telling this story and reprimanded her daughter for speaking "uglily." But adult women also talk and think about their bodies with this image. A friend once described the experience of childbirth by comparing it to a feeling of being split open *kal^{y}a*. Moreover, there is a belief shared by all the women I knew that one should sleep on one's side and not on one's back. Sleeping on one's back exposes a female to the danger of being entered and impregnated by malevolent forest spirits. I suspect, however, that a less fantastic line of reasoning is also at work here: it is immodest to sleep on one's back even when fully clothed because of the danger of sprawling open *kal^{y}a*, a position suggesting extreme vulnerability.

ICONIC PROPERTIES The iconicity of *kal^{y}a* is related to its disyllabic structure; to its lateral liquid *-l^{y}-*; and to its final open syllable, *-l^{y}a*. Its disyllabic structure allows a speaker to gesture vocally the difference between the state of something before it is split open (the first syllable, *ka-*) and the image of something after it is split open (the second syllable, *-l^{y}a*). Its lateral liquid *-l^{y}-*, which is articulated with a slightly constricted high front tongue position, offers a distinctive contrast with the immediately following vowel, *-a*, which is articulated low and with an open mouth. This contrast enhances the iconic expressiveness of the final *-a* and thereby strengthens the total image of openness expressed by *kal^{y}a*.

Kal^{y}a occurs with the following verbs.

1. kal^{y}a partirina — to break open, fissure, e.g., roasted meat or wounded or infected flesh
   split
2. kal^{y}a partina — to split something open, e.g., meat to salt and dry it; to make a part in a head of hair in order to search for lice
   split
3. kal^{y}a paskana — to open by splitting, e.g. a sack of gold (fable)
   open
4. kal^{y}a waktana — to open by striking, e.g., wood with an ax
   hit
5. kal^{y}a chayana — to become well cooked to the point of splitting open, e.g., meat, fish, manioc, corn
   cook

6. kal^{y}a rana make, do	to be positioned with legs apart, e.g., in order to give birth or to anchor one's stance while killing an animal
7. kal^{y}a siririna lie	to lie with legs open, the way immodest or careless women do
8. kal^{y}a tiyarina sit	to sit open, e.g., a hen laying eggs
9. kal^{y}a kunguri-chi-na kneel-CAUS	to help someone kneel with legs apart to give birth

In the following example *kal^{y}a* describes one woman's version of the way it felt to give birth.

10. Chay sinti-ra-ni siki tul^{y}u; kal^{y}a ra-shka shina nana-wa-ra.
    there feel-PAST-1 ass bone do-PERF like pain-1ACC-PAST
    "I felt it there in my tail bone; it hurt me as if I was split apart *kal^{y}a.*"

Kal^{y}a is not performatively foregrounded here. It modifies the past participle *rashka*, literally "made, done," providing a cognitively salient image of a complete splitting open.

In the next example, taken from a fable, *kal^{y}a* describes the way a sack full of gold was split open and its contents spilled out.

11. Sira-shka-ta kal^{y}a paska-sha, yaku-y-shi tali-shka kuri-ta.
    sew-PERF-ACC open-COR water-LOC-EV spill-PERF gold-ACC
    "Splitting open *kal^{y}a* what had been sewn, he spilled the gold into the water."

Kal^{y}a is not performatively foregrounded here. It modifies the coreference verb *paskasha* "opening," specifying its aspectual completiveness with the cogitively salient image of a fissure.

In the next example *kal^{y}a* describes the splitting open of cooked potatoes to serve to hungry guests who had traveled a long way.

12. Hatun papa kosa-shka-ta kal^{y}a kal^{y}a kal^{y}a parti-sha hunda-kta chura-shka.
    big potato cook-PERF-ACC open-COR full-until put-PERF
    "Splitting open the big cooked potatoes, *kal^{y}a kal^{y}a kal^{y}a*, she put them (for us on plates) until they were full."

Kal^{y}a is performatively foregrounded here by its relatively rapid multiple repetition, which gestures the repeated action of splitting. By repeating this sound image quickly, the speaker presents a clear image of ideal hospitality. Not only should there be an abundance of food, but it should be speedily and willingly served.

The next example is taken from an episode in a myth concerning an invasion of worms into a woman who made the mistake of lying with her legs wide open. This sentence describes this position with *kal^{y}a.*

13. Ña dismaya-sha siri-k a-shka chi mama-ga, ña ka$^{l^yang}$.
then faint-COR lie-AG be-PERF that mother-TOP now -ADV
"Then fainting, she would lie there, that mother, *ka*$^{l^yang}$ (with legs wide open)."

Kal^{y}a is performatively foregrounded here by its syntactic displacement from its verb *sirik ashka* "would lie" and by the upjump over its second syllable. Its syntactic displacement allows a listener to imagine what *kal^{y}a* describes, apart from the verbal reference to it. The upjump over its second syllable performatively foregrounds the image of how the woman looked once her legs had sprawled open, effectively shocking and also amusing listeners.

The next example is taken from a narrative of personal experience about four men who wandered lost through the forest, starving for several months. Their desperation is evident by the fact that they actually consumed an anaconda, an animal whose meat is not ordinarily considered edible. In this sentence *kal^{y}a* describes the pattern of cracks and fissures all over an anaconda's skin after it has been cooked.

14. Kal^{y}a kal^{y}a kal^{y}a muna-y chaya-shka amarun aycha-ga ni-n.
desirable cook-PERF anaconda meat-TOP say-3
"'The anaconda meat cooked *kal^{y}a kal^{y}a kal^{y}a*, looking so delicious,' he said."

Kal^{y}a is performatively foregrounded here by its multiple repetition, which communicates the spatial distribution of the fissures all over the meat. The image of meat splitting apart after it's been cooked is a stereotypical one used to communicate a mood of delectability. The presence of fissures in any cooked meat usually indicates that it is high in fat and therefore tender.

The final example is taken from the final episode in a myth about a brain-thirsty spirit who steals brains from humans so that she can live. In this example *kal^{y}a* is first repeated to describe the successive parting of the victim's hair; is then used again to describe the spirit splitting open the victim's skull. The other sound-symbolic adverbs, *t^{y}ak* and *huwi*, describe, respectively, hitting of the skull and carrying off the victim's brain.

15. Kay-manda kal^{y}a kal^{y}a kal^{y}a kal^{y}a kal^{y}a kal^{y}a kal^{y}a kal^{y}a parti-shka, parti-shka
here-from open-PERF open-PERF
washa, al^{y}i riku-chi-n, t^{y}ak kal^{y}a ñuktu-ta huwi apa-ga ri-shka!
after well look-CAUS-3 brain-ACC take-TOP go-perf
"Starting from here, *kal^{y}a kal^{y}a kal^{y}a kal^{y}a kal^{y}a kal^{y}a kal^{y}a kal^{y}a* she parted (his hair); after parting it, aiming well, *t^{y}ak* (hits skull), *kal^{y}a* (splits skull open), carrying his brain *huwi* (hanging), she went off."

The first *kal^{y}a* is performatively foregrounded by its multiple repetitions and by the telic pitch progression over the series of its repetitions. The series of repetitions gestures the individual subevents leading to the victim's demise. It is iconic of the progressiveness of the action itself and is suggestive of cinematic editing that presents the time spanned by a process before presenting that process as accomplished. In this particular context, the progressive pitch has a grammatical and an aesthetic function: it communicates the completeness of the hair's parting, and it creates a sense of climax, which is appropriate, considering what's about to happen. After the last, highest pitched *kalʸa* of the series is pronounced, the forest spirit begins to attack the man and remove his brain.

When it describes the splitting of the victim's skull, *kalʸa* is performatively foregrounded by its syntactic isolation and by the upjump over its second syllable. Its syntactic isolation places the full expressive and grammatical burden on *kalʸa*, which describes a cognitively salient image of the splitting open of the victim's skull and also specifies the completiveness of that splitting. The upjump over *kalʸa*'s final syllable performatively gestures an idea of a contrast between the image of the skull before it had been split and after it had been split, evoking in graphic detail the horrific power of the *amasanga* spirit.

Shaka

DEFINITION A long splitting or tearing, or an idea of that sound, which can result in a complete separation; to divide a space visually by painting or scoring a long line over it. Aspectually completive, resultative.

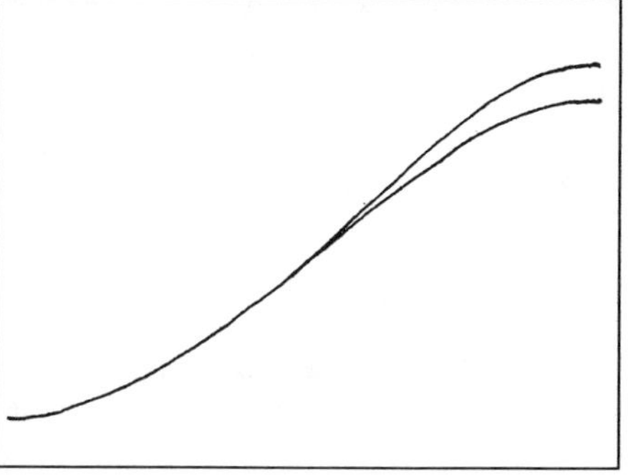

COMMENT A variety of substances and objects can be torn *shaka*. Many kinds of treebark are torn *shaka*, in long strips, from their trunk. Polyester clothing which quickly succumbs to mold and dampness is easily torn *shaka* and used for rags. Many objects have a natural grain that guides their splitting *shaka* into long parts. These include the pod of certain fruits, especially types of guava; certain cuts of meat; and the skin of many kinds of animals. There is a hawk called the *tejiras anga* "scissor-tailed hawk," whose tail feathers appear to have been split by tearing. According to a myth, this hawk, in the form of a man wearing a shirt, was grabbed by two women trying to prevent him from leaving them. When his shirt was torn, he immediately transformed back into a hawk, flying away with tail feathers torn *shaka*.

ICONIC PROPERTIES Although the initial consonants and vowels of sound-symbolic adverbs are not typically very strong in iconic properties, *shaka* is an exception. Its iconicity is related to its initial sibilant, *sh-*; its disyllabic structure; its velar stop, *-k-*; and its final open syllable, *-ka*. Its initial syllable, *sha-*, which is articulated with a continuous hissing airstream, is imitative of the continuous sound produced by the action of tearing something. Its velar stop, *-k-*, which is articulated by stopping the flow of the airstream, is iconic of the cessation of the action of tearing. Its final open syllable, *-ka*, is iconic of the openness of whatever is torn.

Shaka occurs with the following verbs.

1.	shaka likirina tear	to rip, tear apart, e.g., paper or clothing
2.	shaka partina divide	to divide something by tearing it lengthwise, e.g., meat of any animal or skin of a plaintain
3.	shaka partirina divide	to divide or split lengthwise, e.g., tree hit by lightning or wooden handle of an ax
4.	shaka rana make	to split or divide something lengthwise
5.	shaka rina go	to crack lengthwise, e.g., the very long pod of a type of guava fruit; to be divided visually, by painting with a line, e.g., the face for decoration; also said of a boa with long markings
6.	shaka awirina paint	to apply, paint, or appear to be applied or painted, any long line or mark, e.g., on a boa
7.	shaka pintarina paint	same as above
8.	shaka mana be	to be split
9.	shaka shil^{y}una scratch	to split or mark by scratching, e.g., a jaguar with its claws or a person with sharp fingernails
10.	shaka l^{y}ushtina peel	to peel or flay in strips, e.g., bark of a tree or hide of a jaguar
11.	shaka kanina bite	to bite, tearing the skin away, e.g., the way a viper attacks a partridge
12.	shaka mikuna eat	to eat, tearing apart into strips, e.g., tough dry meat
13.	shaka shalina cut	to cut or tear into strips, e.g., of tree bark
14.	shaka waktana hit	to split lengthwise by hitting, e.g., wood with an ax
15.	shaka ismuna rot	to become worn, tattered, and shredded, e.g., old clothing
16.	shaka tukuna become	to become split, e.g., the hull of a fruit when it grows to a certain thickness
17.	shaka apana take	to take something by holding on to a part of it and moving away from it, thereby tearing it into a strip, e.g., a man drawn apart by horses to which he is tied (fable)

In the following example from a personal experience narrative, *shaka* describes the way a snake bit a partridge and tore its skin.

18. Kay-ta shaka kani-shka-ra.
here-ACC bite-PERF-PAST
"Here it had *shaka* bitten (the partridge)."

Shaka is not performatively foregrounded here. It modifies the past perfect verb *kanishkara* "had bitten," specifying the cognitively salient image of a complete tearing.

In the next sentence, taken from a myth, *shaka* describes the tearing apart of an alligator which had bitten off the protagonist's leg.

19. Shaka parti-sha riku-kpi, chay-shi intiru changa tiya-w-shka-ra.
split-COR look-SWRF that-EV entire leg be-DUR-PERF-PAST

"Splitting (the alligator) apart *shaka*, and looking, (what he saw was that) the entire leg had been (in) there."

Shaka is not performatively foregrounded here. It modifies the coreference verb *partisha* "splitting," specifying its aspectual completiveness by describing the cognitively salient image of the alligator's complete splitting open.

In the next example *shaka* describes the image of a shirt ripping. The sentence, taken from the myth of the scissor tailed hawk, describes the moment when two women attempt to prevent the hawk from leaving them.

20. Kamisa-y hapi-kbi sh^{h}aka likiri-shka.
shirt-LOC grab-SWRF tear-PERF

"As (they) grabbed onto his shirt, it tore *sh^{h}aka.*"

Shaka is performatively foregrounded by the strongly aspirated initial *sh-*. This performative aspiration functions aesthetically by communicating the force of the tearing and gramatically by communicating the most cognitively salient image of the tearing's completeness.

In the next example *shaka* is repeated to describes the stripping of bark from the *shiwa* tree, which is then dried and used for illumination.

21. Shiwa rama-ta shak^a shak^a shak^a shak^a shak^a shali-nchi, nina-y chakichi-sha,
shiwa branch-ACC strip-1PL fire-LOC dry-COR
chi-wan-mi pundzh-ang ri-k a-nchi.
that-with-EV day-ADV go-AG be-1PL

"We strip a *shiwa* branch *shak^a shak^a shak^a shak^a shak^a*, then we dry it in the fire, and with that we go brightly."

Shaka is performatively foregrounded by its multiple repetition, by the upjump over each of its final syllables, and by the rise and fall in pitch over the repetitions as a whole. Its multiple repetition gestures the stripping of each piece of bark from the tree. The upjump over the final syllable of each repeated *shaka* imitates an idea of a before/after contrast between the tearing of the bark and its completion. The rise and fall in pitch over the series of repetitions is suggestive of a process distributed throughout a space, in this case, the area defined by the tree's trunk. These performative techniques assist the speaker's explanation of the processing of the *shiwa* tree's bark by making the explanation imageically clear.

In the final example *shaka* is part of a complex description of the way a dugout canoe, which had just been completely carved out of a tree trunk, suddenly began to split in half and continued until it was completely split open, each half falling away on the ground. This splitting was significant to the canoe's craftsman as a portent of his own death. The complete lengthwise splitting is described by *shaka.* Next, there is an image of opening, communicated by *awing*, which is to be understood as simultaneous with the splitting, since it is created by it. The next sound-symbolic adverb, *tas*, describes the completeness of the splitting at the same time that it acts as a conceptual pivot, switching the listener's attention from the lengthwise dimension of the splitting to its vertical dimension. The final sound-symbolic adverb, *kal*^{y}*a*, shifts the axis of the splitting to a vertical orientation to describe the final cleavage resulting in each half of the canoe falling away from itself.

22. Ña punda-ma, shak^{a} a^{wing} ña tas ka$^{l^{y}a}$ ña chay-ma chay-ma kanoa urma-ra!
then end-DAT then then that-DAT that-DAT canoe fall-PAST

"Then at the end, *shak*^{a} (lengthwise split),
a^{wing} (opening) *tas* (completeness) *ka*$^{l^{y}a}$ (vertical fissure),
and there and there the canoe fell."

Shaka is performatively foregrounded here by its syntactic isolation and by the upjump of pitch over its second syllable. Its syntactic isolation places the entire burden on *shaka*, both for expressing an image of the canoe's splitting and for specifying the completiveness of that action. The upjump over its final syllable foregrounds an idea of a before/after contrast between the splitting and its completion. The complex description of which *shaka* is part functions epistemically, as a way of understanding the link between a bizarre natural occurrence, i.e., the canoe's splitting in half, and the subsequent death of the canoe's craftsman. By describing this splitting as if it took place quickly and seemingly willfully, in a compressed time-lapsed image, the narrator suggests an analogical link between this split and the craftsman's own untimely death a few months later.

13

Sound Symbols of Suddenness and Completiveness

This chapter analyzes nine sound-symbolic adverbs that cannot easily be included with any of the previous chapters, but which are nonetheless important in the communication of schematic images that assist grammatical aspect. *Dzing* describes a sudden awareness or intuition. *Dzas* describes the punctual accomplishment of an action. *Tay* describes a nondynamic, permanent, or completely realized action or condition. *Tsuping* describes a complete bareness. *Tsung* describes the complete absorption of a liquid substance. *Saw* describes the unbroken movement of a fluid substance considered as a whole. *Shaw* describes the creation of a whole two-dimensional entity or a continuous two-dimensional gesture. *Ton* describes a complete filling or covering. *Tas* describes the completiveness, accomplishment, or extension in space of an action or condition.

Dzing

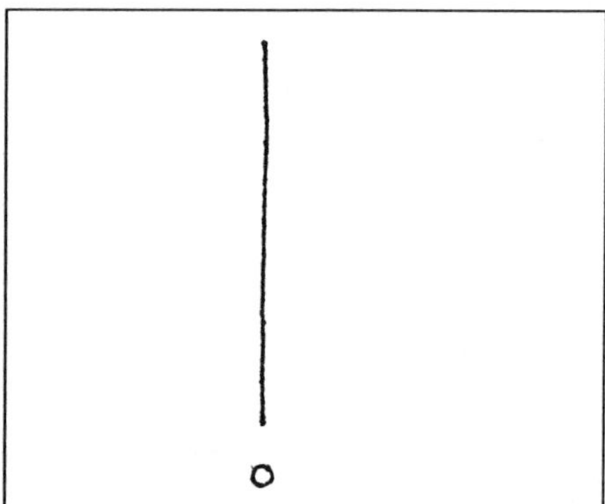

DEFINITION (1) A sudden awareness or intuition, especially one that causes fright. Aspectually punctual. (2) A sudden movement made as a result of a sudden awareness. Aspectually punctual.

COMMENT *Dzing* can be compared with a visual image from our own culture, that of the suddenly illuminated light bulb that is sometimes used in comics or cartoons to stand for a flash of insight. The important difference is that such flashes generally have a positive, illuminative value. For Quechua speakers, by contrast, what is realized by *dzing* often causes fright or panic. An awareness described with *dzing* was compared by one woman to an unpleasant jolt of electricity. Another explanation of *dzing* compared it to feeling as if the body has suddenly leaped, although it hasn't moved at all.

ICONIC PROPERTIES The iconicity of *dzing* is related to its monosyllabicity; to its initial affricate, *dz-*; to its high vowel *-i-*; and to its final closed syllable. Its monosyllabicity is iconic of the noncomplexity of a punctual realization. Its initial affricate *dz-*, which is articulated with a turbulent airstream movement, is iconic of a path of movement. A path of movement can be metaphorically descriptive of a realization because a realization takes one from a certain point, that of not knowing, to another point, that of having found out. Its high vowel, *-i-*, is iconic of the lightness and effortlessness (cf. Waugh 1990: 8) required for a sudden realization. Its final closed syllable is iconic of the lack of continuousness of a sudden, punctual realization.

Dzing occurs with the following verbs.

1. dzing tukuna (become) — to become sharply, acutely aware of something; to move quickly, suddenly, because of such an awareness, e.g., an animal that has been surprised
2. dzing mandzharina (be afraid) — to experience a sudden feeling of fright; to be given a start
3. dzing yuyarina (realize) — to suddenly realize or remember something important, e.g., the way a mother will have an intuition that her child is in trouble
4. dzing saltana (jump) — to move quickly, suddenly, because of fright or surprise
5. dzing mus^{y}ana (notice) — to suddenly notice or perceive something, e.g., an animal partially hidden by trees

In the following example *dzing* describes a mother's memory of a sudden intuition that her child was in trouble.

6. Ima shina ra-sha chari, dzing yuyari-ra-ni wawa-ta.
   what like do-COR perhaps realize-PAST-1 baby-ACC
   "What perhaps was I doing, when *dzing* I remembered the baby."

Dzing is not performatively foregrounded here. It specifies the punctuality of its verb *yuyarirani* "I remembered" by describing the cognitively salient sensation that reminded the speaker of her child.

In the next sentence *dzing* describes the startled way a snake moved when it became aware of a person walking near it.

7. Kasna riku-kbi dz^{hh}innng-mi tuku-ra pay, runa-ta mus^{y}a-sha.
   like this look-SWRF -EV become-PAST it person-ACC notice-COR
   "I looked and saw that it became *dz^{hh}innng*, upon seeing a person."

Dzing is performatively foregrounded here by its lengthening and by the momentarily forceful aspiration of its initial *dz^{hh}-*. The lengthening prolongs the speaker's focus on the image of the snake's movement. The moment of forceful aspiration, by the way it stands out, suggests the noticeability of the snake's split-second reflex resulting in its startled movement. The image of the snake's startled movement functions modally to create the same "jolted" feeling in a listener.

In the next sentence, taken from a myth, *dzing* describes the way a *wagra puma* "cow jaguar" became frightened upon seeing its own shadow.

8. Chasna-shi pay al^{y}ma-ta riku-n, dzi^{i}ing-shi mandzhari-n.
   like that-EV his shadow-ACC see-3 -EV become afraid-3
   "When he saw his shadow like that, he *dzi^{i}ing* became frightened."

Dzing is performatively foregrounded here by the sudden upjump over its medial vowel. The way the upjump stands out from the rest of the word imitates an idea of the way a startled feeling stands out from one's ordinary state of consciousness. At the same time, the momentariness of the upjump imitates an idea of the momentaneousness of a startled feeling. *Dzing*'s function here is ironic. The startled, frightened feeling it describes is in sharp contrast with the fierceness of the jaguar, particularly since its fear is of its own shadow.

In the last example *dzing* is part of a series of vivid impressions describing the sudden realization that what one is stepping on is a large boa constrictor. *Dzing* occurs with two expressively foregrounded lexical items, the words *kasha* "thorn" and *sarpa*, a shortened form of the Spanish *sarpullido*, a skin rash or eruption. It is used in Quechua, often in multiple repetitions, to describe any bumps on the skin, such as those resulting in raised welts, thickened scars, and so on.

9. K^{h}aaashaaa! S^{h}aaarpa! Dz^{hh}iiiing-l^{y}a tuku-ra-ni!
   thorny bumpy -LIM become-PAST-1
   "First, I felt something like thorns! Then bumps! And then *dz^{hh}iiiing* I became!"

Dzing is performatively foregrounded here by its lengthening, by the forceful aspiration over its *dz^{hh}-*, and by its suffixation with the emphatic *-l^{y}a*. Its lengthening allows the speaker to focus on the image of her fright. The forceful aspiration of the initial *dz-* imitates an idea of the forcefulness of the impact that this impression had on the speaker. While recounting this experience, she actually got up from her chair at one point, as if to walk away, saying that she couldn't even talk about it because it had been so traumatic for her.

Dzas

DEFINITION To do anything quickly or directly. Aspectually punctual.

COMMENT *Dzas* can be conceptualized with an arrow because it describes an action with a clearly defined trajectory. The trajectory described by *dzas* can be as short as an arm's length away or as far as another village away. Although *dzas* typically describes actions with fast and direct visible movements, such as getting up, leaping out

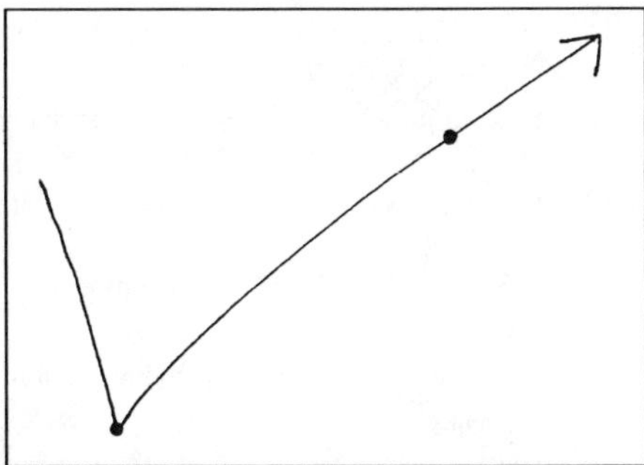

of water, or running off, it can be extended to describe instances of processes that seem to occur faster than usual, including dying, growing, falling asleep, learning, and becoming pregnant.

ICONIC PROPERTIES The iconicity of *dzas* is related to its monosyllabicity; to its initial affricate, *dz-*; and to its final fricative, *-s*. Its monosyllabicity is iconic of the noncomplexity of a quickly realized action. Its initial affricate, *dz-*, which is articulated with a turbulent airstream movement, is iconic of a path of movement. Its final fricative, *-s*, which is articulated with a continuous airstream, is iconic of the continuousness of a movement that is quick or direct. A movement that is quick or direct is continuous because it doesn't halt abruptly when it has reached its goal. It usually overshoots, extending somewhat beyond the goal.

Dzas occurs with the following verbs.

1. dzas hatarina — to rise, get up quickly, e.g., to greet or serve someone
   get up
2. dzas apana — to grab something quickly, furtively, e.g., to steal
   take
3. dzas saltana — to leap suddenly, e.g., the way a fish leaps out of water
   jump
4. dzas kal^{y}pana — to run off quickly
   run
5. dzas shamuna — to come or return from somewhere without stopping along the way or delaying
   come
6. dzas l^{y}ukshina — to get out of something, e.g., a canoe, quickly
   leave
7. dzas kuna — to quickly hand someone or something over to someone, e.g., a crying baby to its mother to be nursed
   give
8. dzas ichuna — to quickly get rid of something
   abandon
9. dzas pushana — to quickly go and fetch someone
   take
10. dzas rimana — to quickly go and tell some news or instruction
    tell
11. dzas churarina — to get dressed quickly
    get dressed
12. dzas tangana — to push something aside quickly, e.g., a bowl of *aswa*
    push
13. dzas aysana — to pull something out quickly, e.g., an identification card to show to the police
    pull
14. dzas wañuchina — to extinguish or put something out quickly, e.g., candle
    kill

15.	dzas wiñarina sprout	to sprout or grow up quickly, e.g., wild mushrooms
16.	dzas wañuna die	to die suddenly or unexpectedly
17.	dzas yachana know	to find out about something quickly, e.g., news or gossip
18.	dzas puñuna sleep	to fall asleep quickly
19.	dzas pitina cut	to cut something with a quick movement
20.	dzas surkuna remove	to take something or someone quickly out of something
21.	dzas wawayana become pregnant	to become pregnant in a short time
22.	dzas angl^{y}ana choose	to pick out quickly, e.g., stones from rice
23.	dzas mukuna chew	to chew something quickly, e.g., something with a crisp texture

The following example is taken from a brief account of a series of actions, beginning with the speaker's rising up *dzas* from a seated posture.

24. Dzas hatari-sha ri-ra-ni.
get up-COR go-PAST-1
"Getting up *dzas*, I left."

Dzas is not performatively foregrounded here. It specifies the punctuality of the coreference verb *hatarisha* "getting up" with the cognitively salient image of a trajectory, involving getting up and heading directly for another place.

In the next example *dzas* describes a catfish's quick leaping out of water in response to being chased by a dog.

25. Bagri ña dzas salta-kpi, pay-was l^{y}ukshi-n.
catfish now leap-SWRF he-INCL emerge-3
"The catfish then, having *dzas* leaped (out of the water), he (dog) also emerged."

Dzas is not performatively foregrounded here. It modifies the switch reference verb *saltakpi* "leaping," specifying its punctuality with the cognitively salient image of a trajectory, involving leaping out of the water and going back in at another place.

In the next example, taken from a myth, *dzas* describes each instance of piercing a fish. The lexical term for "white," *ruya*, stands for the flash of white seen when the fish is pulled out of the water.

26. Sardina-ta yapa tuksi-k a-shka dzas ruya-ng, dzas ruya-ng tuksi-k a-shka.
sardine-ACC lots pierce-AG be-PERF white-ADV white-ADV pierce-AG be-perf
"He speared lots of fish, *dzas*, a whiteness, *dzas*, a whiteness (one after the other.)"

Dzas is performatively foregrounded here by its repetition, which gestures each act of spearing a fish at the same time that it specifies the cognitively salient image of a trajectory, involving a direct movement toward the fish that will be speared. Here *dzas* functions hyperbolically to emphasize the prowess of the man catching the fish, by presenting an image of such rapidity, which contrasts strikingly with the typical difficulties encountered by nonmythic hunters.

In the next sentence *dzas* is used with a horizontal back-and-forth gesture of the hand to demonstrate how a sloppily written note may have been executed.

28. Rik-i pay kil^{y}ka-shka-ta dzas dzas dzas dzas!
look-2IMP his write-PERF-ACC
"Look at what he's written *dzas dzas dzas dzas*!"

Dzas is performatively foregrounded here by its multiple repetition, which gestures an idea of many sweeping movements across a piece of paper. Here *dzas* functions hyperbolically to imitate an idea of an overly hasty action. The girl who said this was critically examining the note, remarking on the sloppiness of the handwriting.

In the next example *dzas* describes the trajectory of movement defined by a freshwater dolphin quickly leaping out of water and through the air.

29. Shura-y dzasssssss polaya-y-mi sika-kta ri-ra!
short-LOC beach-LOC-EV climb-until go-PAST
"In a flash *dzasssssss* he went until he climbed as far as the beach!"

Dzas is performatively foregrounded here by its lengthening and by its syntactic displacement from its verb *rira* "went." Its syntactic displacement foregrounds the image presented by *dzas* apart from the verb's reference to that movement. The lengthening of *dzas*' final consonant is iconic of the duration of the dolphin's leap and also of the line of motion created by the trajectory of the leap. The function of *dzas* in this context is overwhelmingly aesthetic: it foregrounds an image that is appealing and beautiful to all, particularly as the animal it describes is now almost extinct in this region.

Tay

DEFINITION (1) Characterizes an action or condition as nondynamic, permanent, or realized as completely as is possible. Aspectually completive, resultative. (2) Describes an idea of the sound of rifle shots or thunder. Aspectually durative.

COMMENT *Tay*$_1$ might be derived from the adverb *tayl^{y}a* "tough, hard," which is related to *tay* by the notion of "unyieldingness," which in turn leads to notions of permanence, full realization, and nondynamicity. *Tay*$_1$ refers to a complete lack of physical movement, as of an animal watching and waiting to pounce on its prey or of a person walking through the forest who suddenly stands completely still in order to listen to an unfamiliar sound, or of someone who lies in a bed next to someone else, without moving or sprawling out, in order not to touch that other person. The idea of a complete lack of movement is then extended to describe an unyielding hold or grasp by something or someone of some object or being. A boa constrictor wraps itself *tay* around its prey. Two people fighting hold on to each other *tay*. A larval parasite, such as that left by the botfly, clings *tay* to its host. Tay_1 also describes the unyieldingness and impermeability of certain natural processes. When an unfired clay bowl that has been covered with slip dries up so that it is no longer burnishable, it is said to be dried up *tay* because it can no longer be worked with. Meat that is properly dried in the sun is said to have dried *tay* because it won't rot for a long long time. Finally, attitudes characterized by firm resolve or heroic endurance are described with *tay*. The use of tay_2 to describe both the sound of thunder and of gunfire may be explained by the etymological fact that the lexical item *il*^{y}*apa* was at one time used to describe both rifles and thunder.

ICONIC PROPERTIES The iconicity of tay_1 is related to its monosyllabicity and to the contrast between the low vowel, *-a-*, and the high palatal approximant, *-y*. Its monosyllabicity is iconic of the noncomplexity and nondynamicity of what is described by *tay*. The contrast between the low vowel, *-a-*, and the high palatal approximant, *-y*, is iconic of the completiveness or resultativity described by *tay* because the articulation of these contrasting sounds imitates a complete range of possibilities, in this instance, the possibilities for height within the vocal tract. The iconicity of tay_2 is related to its final open syllable. Its final open syllable, which is articulated without an obstruction in the vocal tract, is iconic of the continuousness of the sound of gunfire and also of the sound of thunder.

Tay occurs with the following verbs.

1. tay shayana stand	to stand still, e.g., in order to observe something or someone without being seen
2. tay shayarina stand up	to stop short in one's tracks while walking, e.g., upon hearing an unfamiliar sound
3. tay hapina take	to grab something tightly, e.g., the way an anaconda grabs a person, the way a person grabs a weapon or an opponent in a fight, or the way an elastic band grabs a bunch of hair
4. tay hapirina catch on	to attach tightly to something, e.g., severely burned skin to clothing when it is peeled away
5. tay chakirina dry up	to dry up, e.g., paint on unfired clay, meat in the sun, skin burned in the sun
6. tay chaki-chi-na dry-CAUS	to dry completely, e.g., meat so that it doesn't spoil
7. tay sakirina remain	to remain firmly in place, e.g., dye on skin
8. tay sirina lie	to lie very still without moving, e.g., someone playing dead or pretending to be asleep, or an animal waiting to attack its prey
9. tay tiyana be located	to be fixed in a certain place
10. tay tukuna become	to be realized in a condition or state as completely as is possible

11.	tay tiyarina sit	to sit without moving; to sit tight
12.	tay mitikuna hide	to hide, being very still
13.	tay watana tie	to tie something securely, e.g., an animal
14.	tay lazuna tie	same as above
15.	tay watarina tie	to tie oneself tightly, e.g., by wrapping hair around the head, so that it can't be grabbed while fighting
16.	tay puñuna sleep	to sleep so deeply, e.g., because of drugs or enchantment, that it is difficult to be roused; to sleep without moving or sprawling out, in order to avoid touching the person next to you
17.	tay wañuna die	to become stiff with rigor mortis
18.	tay taparina close	to close up as tightly as is possible, e.g., by twisting a cap or lid as far as it will go
19.	tay serana close	same as above
20.	tay churarina put-RFL	to place securely on one's body, e.g., a weapon
21.	tay katina follow	to pursue someone without letting up
22.	tay mandzharina be afraid	to be too frightened to move
23.	tay l^{y}utarina cling	to cling tightly, e.g., any larval parasite, such as that left by the botfly
24.	tay pil^{y}urina wrap	to wrap securely, e.g., a boa's tail around a tree or a person's long hair into a braid
25.	tay pil^{y}u-chi-na wrap-CAUS	to wrap something securely, e.g., an opponent's hair during a fight
26.	tay kipirina hug	to hug someone tightly
27.	tay kanina bite	to bite something and not let go, e.g., the way an animal inside a hole bites and holds onto a hand reaching for it
28.	tay awantana endure	to endure pain, suffering, or sadness without crying, complaining, or breaking down

In the following example *tay* is part of a recounting of a fight between two women, one of whom accused another of behaving flirtatiously with her husband. The woman who was accused used *tay* to describe the way she wrapped her opponent's hair so tightly that it immobilized her.

29. Tay akcha-ta pil^{y}u-chi-sha-ga, nina-y niti-k ma-ra-ni, mana kumari a-kpi.
hair-ACC wrap-CAUS-COR-TOP fire-LOC press-AG be-PAST-1 NEG comadre be-SWRF

"Wrapping her hair up *tay*, I might have pressed her into the fire, if she hadn't been my *comadre*.

Tay is not performatively foregrounded here. It modifies the coreference verb *pilʸuchishaga* "wrapping," specifying its completiveness by describing the most cognitively salient image of its action.

The next example features *tay* in a description of the way a stingray's lungs can be prepared and dried in such a way that they won't spoil.

30. Pusku shungu-was ña tay $w^{i^{n}}$ chaki-chi-shka, mana waglin-ga-chu.
    foam heart-INCL then all dry-CAUS-PERF NEG damage-3FUT-NEG

    "And the lungs also, (when) dried $a^{l^{l}}$ *tay*, will not spoil."

Tay is not performatively foregrounded here; instead, it occurs with another adverb *win* "all," which is foregrounded with an upglide. Both *tay* and *win* modify the participial *chakishka* "dried," making more emphatic its completiveness.

The next example is taken from a ghost story about a severed arm, which at times had a life of its own and at other times seemed quite dead. The sentence describes an unsuccessful attempt to join this arm to a body. *Tay* describes the arm's complete state of dessication.

31. Mana-shi lʸutari-ra-chu maki, ña tay chakiri-shka ruku.
    NEG-EV stick-PAST-NEG hand now dry-PERF old

    "The hand didn't stick back on; the old thing was dried up *tay*."

Tay is not performatively foregrounded here. It modifies the past participle *chakirishka* "dried," specifying its aspectual resultativity by describing the most cognitively salient image of that resultativity.

The next example, taken from a myth, describes how one of the protagonists had been enchanted into such a deep sleep that he couldn't be woken up. *Tay* describes this deep state of sleep.

32. Likcha-chi-ra-s, tanga-ra-s, $t^{a^{y}}$ (pause); ña mana-shi likchari-ra-chu!
    wake-CAUS-PAST-INCL shove-PAST-INCL now NEG-EV awaken-PAST-NEG

    "Although she tried to wake him, and even shoved him, (he slept) $t^{a^{y}}$ (pause); he didn't wake up."

Tay is performatively foregrounded here by its syntactic isolation, by the upglide of its pitch, and by its immediately following pause. Its syntactic isolation invites a listener to imagine the deep state of the man's sleep. By moving as far up in pitch as the speaker's voice will allow, the upglide foregrounds an idea of the completiveness of his deep state of sleep. The pause immediately following *tay*, by giving the listener a moment to imagine all of this, further foregrounds the image. In this context, *tay*'s function is grammatical since it alone bears the full responsibility for the absent verb, and it is aesthetic because it effectively communicates an image of a magical event—the enchantment of the protagonist—with an image borrowed from natural processes of everyday life.

In the following example *tay* occurs with two other sound-symbolic adverbs in a complex description. The sentence is taken from a fragment of advice given by a mother to her child. She cautions the child about what to do if a stranger is encountered while walking in the forest. Besides *tay*, the speaker also uses *chun*, which describes a complete silence, and *ping*, which describes the complete darkness resulting from shutting one's eyes.

33. Ima awka, ima Peruano, ima-ta riku-sha-s, chun tay ping -shi shayarina!
what Achuar what Peruvian what-ACC see-COR-INCL quiet -EV stand

"Whatever Achuar or Peruvian you might see, (you are) to stand *chun* (quiet) *tay* (not moving), *ping* (with eyes closed) !"

Tay is performatively foregrounded here by its its raised pitch and by its position in the sound-symbolic series. The progressive pitch rise over each adverb presents them in a hypothetical sequence of completion, even though the actions described are meant to happen simultaneously. *Tay*'s function is both grammatical, insofar as it affects its verb *shayarina* "to stand" with punctual aspect, and instructional because it is part of a mother's advice to her child. The urgency of this message is communicated by the foregrounded series of sound-symbolic images, which clearly describe what is necessary behavior for a particular situation of danger.

Tsuping

DEFINITION (1) To be completely bare of covering. (2) To be completely covered with dye (cf. *ton*$_{1B}$). Aspectually completive, resultative.

COMMENT The complete bareness described by *tsuping* can apply to a body stripped of clothes, an animal stripped of its skin in preparation for cooking, or land cleared in preparation for planting. That *tsuping* describes not only what is completely bared but also what is completely covered with dye may seem contradictory. However, a body that is completely covered with dye is comparable to bareness because it is visually uninterrupted. There are a number of dyes extracted from plants in the forest that have traditionally been used to cover oneself *tsuping* and continue to be used for aesthetic decoration. The dye most commonly sought for this purpose is extracted from a plant known as *wituk*, the fruit of which contains a clear juice that dries black on the body and remains that way for several weeks. The custom of covering one's entire body *tsuping* with black dye, which used to be considered quite beautiful, is only rarely practiced today, and chiefly by older women. Nowadays people are content to paint parts of their bodies with lines and decorative patterns.

ICONIC PROPERTIES The iconicity of *tsuping* is related to its disyllabic structure; to the contrast between its initial-syllable high back vowel, *-u-*, and its final-syllable high front vowel, *-i-*; and to its final closed syllable. Its disyllabic structure provides a frame for gesturing the difference between the gesture of stripping or covering with dye and the state of something after it is stripped or covered. The contrast between the initial-syllable back vowel, *-u-*, and the final-syllable front vowel, *-i-*, accentuates this difference. The closure of the final syllable establishes a conceptual closure or frame for the image of what is stripped bare or completely covered.

Tsuping occurs with the following verbs.

1. tsuping l^yatanana undress	to completely undress or to undress a part of the body, e.g., the upper torso
2. tsuping surkuna remove	to remove completely or flay, e.g., the skin of an animal before cutting it up into sections
3. tsuping waktana hit	to hit, chopping down everything; to clear an area, e.g., trees in a forest in preparation for planting
4. tsuping shitana throw	to throw a liquid dye all over someone or something
5. tsuping kakurina rub	to rub a dye or paint all over the body or all over one part of the body, e.g., the face

The following example, taken from a myth, uses *tsuping* to describe a man's undressing of his upper torso.

6. Pay kamisa-ta tsuping l^yatana-sha-ga, sumak kipi-sha, pay laro-y-shi chura-ra.
his shirt-ACC undress-COR-TOP nicely bundle-COR his side-LOC-EV put-PAST
"Removing his shirt *tsuping*, making a nice bundle of it, he put it by his side."

Tsuping is not performatively foregrounded here. It modifies the coreference verb *l^yatanasha* "undressing," specifying its completiveness with a cognitively salient image of a complete bareness.

In the next example, also taken from a myth, *tsuping* describes the complete covering of a woman with red dye.

7. Manduru-wan-ga tsuping shita-naw-ra.
achiote-INST-TOP throw-3PL-PAST
"He threw the achiote (liquid) *tsuping* (at the woman)."

Tsuping is not performatively foregrounded here. It modifies the verb *shitanawra* "threw," specifying its completiveness with the cognitively salient image of someone completely covered with dye.

In the next example *tsuping* describes the complete bareness of someone who has undressed.

8. Runa-guna-ga mana kalson-wan arma-k-chu a-nawn; tsu^{ping} l^yatana-sha
people-PL-TOP NEG shorts-INST bathe-AG-NEG be-3PL undress-COR
arma-nawn.
bathe-3PL
"People don't bathe with (under)shorts; undressing *tsu^{ping}* they bathe."

Tsuping is performatively forgrounded here by the upjump of pitch over its pronunciation. It modifies the coreference verb *l^yatanasha* "undressing," specifying its completiveness with the cognitively salient image of complete bareness. The upjump over its second syllable is instructionally expressive of a before/after contrast between a state of being dressed and a state of being completely undressed.

In the next example *tsuping* is part of an explanatory account of clearing land and planting it with manioc.

9. Kimi-shka washa, wakta-nga kal^yari-ra-ni, ñuka, win tsu^ping (pause) hatun-da
circumscribe-PERF after hit-FINF begin-PAST-1 I all big-ACC
chagrari-ra-ni.
make chagra-PAST-1

"After outlining (an area), I began to chop, all of it, *tsu^ping* (pause) I made a big *chagra.*"

Tsuping is performatively foregrounded here by the upjump of pitch over its second syllable, by the pause immediately following its pronunciation, and by its syntactic isolation. It functions grammatically since it alone bears the full semantic and grammatical responsibility for the absent verb, as well as instructionally by its use of an image to explain a series of procedures. The upjump over its second syllable imitates an idea of a before/after contrast between a field before it has been cleared and that same field after clearing.

In the following example *tsuping* describes the complete removal of a catfish's skin in preparation for drying.

10. Bagri-ta-ga ch^yu ch^yu ñawpa-ra, pichu kara-ta tsu^ping.
catfish-ACC-TOP lead-PAST breast skin-ACC

"First the catfish was (cut up) *ch^yu ch^yu*, then the breast skin (was removed) *tsu^ping*."

Tsuping is performatively foregrounded here by its syntactic isolation and by the upjump of pitch over its pronunciation. Its syntactic isolation means that it alone bears full grammatical and semantic responsibility for the absent verb. The upjump over its pronunciation simulates an idea of a before/after contrast between the fish before and after it has been skinned. Besides its grammatical significance, *tsuping* also functions aesthetically by simulating the pleasing image of a task well done.

Tsung

DEFINITION To absorb, cover, or drench with a liquid substance; to be drenched, covered by, or absorbed with a liquid substance. Aspectually completive, resultative.

COMMENT What *tsung* describes is not an image of wetness that is desireable and expected, such as the wetness of ground after a heavy rainfall. *Tsung* describes an image of wetness that is inappropriate, unwanted, unexpected—a wetness that deviates from what should be. A baby's diaper, clothing drenched in sweat after working hard or after being caught in a sudden downpour, and the thatched roof of a house that is so wet it begins to rot are all images described with *tsung*.

ICONIC PROPERTIES The iconicity of *tsung* is related to its monosyllabicity and to the closure of its syllable. Its monosyllabicity is iconic of the noncomplexity of being completely drenched. The closure of its syllable establishes a conceptual closure or frame for the image of what is completely drenched.

Tsung occurs with the following verbs.

1. tsung hukuna — to be soaked, e.g., with water, sweat, blood, or urine
   moisten
2. tsung huku-chi-na — to drench with water or sweat
   moisten-CAUS
3. tsung humbina — to be covered with sweat
   sweat
4. tsung upina — to drink all of a given liquid
   drink
5. tsung aysana — to draw all of the liquid from a container, e.g., by sucking it out
   pull

In the following example *tsung* is used in an account of a violent feud to describe the way a man soaked his shirt with blood by using it to absorb the blood emerging from a gunshot wound in his chest.

6. Raway l^{y}ukshi-kpi, kamisa-ta tsuping -shi Fausto l^{y}atana-sha, kaku kaku kaku kaku
   blood emerge-SWRF shirt-ACC -EV Fausto undress-COR rub rub rub rub

   kaku, raway-ta tsung pay-ba kamisa-n huku-chi-sha, w^{in} aycha-ta-shi armari-shka.
   rub blood-ACC he-POSS shirt-INST wet-CAUS-COR all flesh-ACC-EV bathe-PERF

   "As the blood was flowing out, Fausto undressed *tsuping*, and rubbed and rubbed and rubbed and rubbed and rubbed, soaking the blood up *tsung* with his shirt and bathing a^{ll} of his flesh in it."

Tsung is performatively foregrounded here by displacement from its coreference verb *hukuchisha* "soaking" for which it specifies aspectual completiveness. Its displacement invites the listener to imagine the shirt completely soaked with blood, apart from the verb's reference to it, and functions aesthetically, lending the description a "you-were-there" feeling.

The next example uses *tsung* to describe the wetness of a house's thatched roof.

7. Wasi kuruna ismu-kpi-shi ri-shka, kuruna tsung huku-sha-shi.
   house roof rot-SWRF-EV go-PERF roof wet-COR-EV

   "As the roof of the house had rotted, becoming completely soaked *tsung*, she went off."

Tsung is not performatively foregrounded here. It modifies the coreference verb *hukusha* "becoming wet," specifying its resultativity with the cognitively salient image of a completely soaked house roof.

In the following example *tsung* modifies the perfect participle *hukushka* "wet" to describe the way a man became completely soaked after being caught in a downpour.

8. Mana alilya-chu ñuka hachi shamu-ra, win tsung huku-shka.
   NEG well-NEG my uncle come-PAST moisten-PERF

   "My uncle didn't come back (looking) very well; he was all *tsung* drenched."

Tsung is performatively foregrounded here by the upglide over its pronunciation. By extending the speaker's voice pitch as far upward as it will go, the upglide expresses the total extent of the man's wetness. In this context, the image of the man's total wetness is expressively significant because it led to an illness which, in turn, led to his death a short time later.

Saw

DEFINITION A relatively brief, unbroken movement of a fluid substance or an idea of the sound made by such a movement. Aspectually completive, resultative, durative.

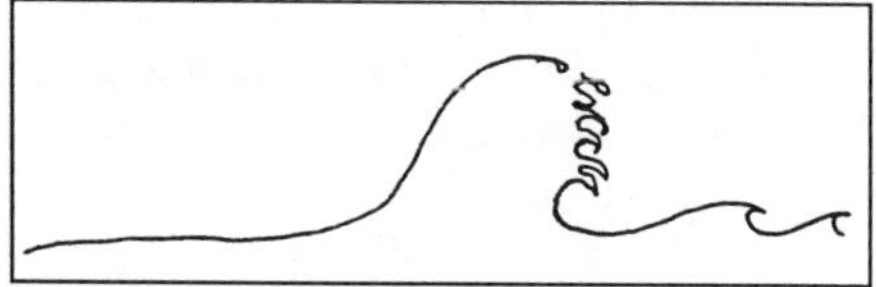

COMMENT The image described by *saw* of a brief, unbroken movement of fluid is often used to describe the movements of river water. After a heavy rain, the river crests, but if the rains let up for a sufficient time, then the water quickly goes down again. When it reverts back to a previous level, particularly if that previous level was relatively low, people say that it has dried up *saw*. What they mean to communicate is an image of a riverbed that has been left relatively drier after being filled by a brief, unbroken movement of river water. The changing levels of the river are important indices for the appropriateness of various activities. Traveling while the river is cresting is dangerous, because it often carries with it large bits of decayed trees, branches, and other objects, which would be dangerous in a collision. A cresting river is also dangerous because it often conceals obstacles to passage. A river that has dried up *saw*, however, is welcomed because the lower levels of water make fishing a much easier and more successful enterprise.

ICONIC PROPERTIES The iconicity of *saw* is related to its monosyllabicity; to its initial fricative, *s*-; and to its final central approximant, -*w*. Its monosyllabicity, by its noncomplexity is iconic of the simple sweep of whatever fluid moves. Its initial fricative, *s*-, the articulation of which is continuous, involving no obstruction of the airstream, imitates the continuousness, albeit brief, of the unbroken fluid movement. The lip rounding accompanying pronunciation of the central approximant, -*w*, creates a constriction of the mouth, although not a complete obstruction, which is iconic of the trailing off rather than of the abrupt cessation in the amount of water that flows as the source is depleted.

Saw occurs with the following verbs.

1. saw shamuna — to come in a sweeping movement, e.g., water onto a beach
   come
2. saw chakirina — to dry up quickly, suddenly, e.g., a river which had been very full
   dry up
3. saw talina — to pour a quantity of liquid, e.g., *aswa* into a bowl, or water over a body to bathe
   pour
4. saw churana — to put something in a place by pouring it there, e.g., *aswa* into a drinking bowl
   put
5. saw armana — to bathe by pouring water from a container over oneself
   bathe
6. saw k^winana — to pour forth with vomit (myth)
   vomit
7. saw uyarina — the sound of a continuous movement in water, e.g., of a large animal, such as a freshwater dolphin, catfish, or anaconda, or of wind rustling through trees
   sound

In the following example *saw* describes the way a mother, angry with her child over his misbehavior, doused him with water.

8. Piña-sha saw tali-ra yaku-ta.
   anger-COR pour-PAST water-ACC
   "(Because) she was angry, she dumped the water *saw*."

Saw is not performatively foregrounded here. It modifies the verb *talira* "poured," specifying its completiveness by calling one's attention to the cognitively salient image of water that has been completely dumped out of a container.

In the next example, taken from a myth, *saw* describes the unorthodox way of fermenting manioc used by a star transformed into a woman. Rather than masticating cooked manioc and then allowing it to ferment with her salival juices, she ate it raw and fermented it inside her stomach and then vomited it back into a jar.

9. Ña pay miku-shka-ta, il^{y}a-kta tinaha-y-ga saw saw saw hunda-kta-shi
   then her eat-PERF-ACC lack-until jar-LOC-TOP fill-until-EV
   pusku-xxl^{y}a-shi k^wina-k a-ra.
   foam-ADV-EV vomit-AG be-PAST
   "Then she would vomit into the jar *saw saw saw* until there was nothing left of what she had eaten, until the jar was foaming full."

Saw is performatively foregrounded here by its multiple repetition, by the telic pitch progression over the repeated series, and by displacement from its verb *k^winak ara* "would vomit." Each repetition of *saw* gestures a subevent of the larger activity of filling the jar by pouring into it. The displacement of these repetitions from their verb foregrounds the images of the pouring, apart from the verb's reference to this process. The telic pitch progression over the series of repetitions imitates an idea of the successive increase in the jar's volume and can be understood by analogy with a cinematographer's juxtaposition of a series of shots, each leading to the completion of a process or activity. The expressive significance of this telic pitch progression is that it lends normalcy and naturalness to a process which is anything but normal. By its progression, it suggests the unfolding and coming to conclusion of a natural process. Yet the star woman's method of making manioc is extremely offensive to her human affines, and the description of it as natural-like is ironically humorous.

In the next example *saw* describes the speed with which the level of water in a river lowers. In this sentence *saw* describes the river's lowering as if it happened in one complete movement. When asked for an explanation of *saw* in this context, the speaker paraphrased it with a mix of Quechua and Spanish, saying: *shuk rato* "in a flash," *win* "all," and *de golpe* "suddenly." The closest analogical image to the following would be that of a wave of water that washes away from a beach and back out to sea in a complete sweeping movement.

10. Chi tukuy t^haxx hunda-k-ga, saw chakiri-n.
that all fill-AG-TOP dry up
"(Although the water) fills all up *t^haxx*, it dries up *saw*."

Saw is not performatively foregrounded here. It modifies the verb *chakirin* "dries," specifying its resultativity at the same time that it describes that resultativity with the cognitively salient image of a brief, sweeping movement of water.

In the next example *saw* describes the sound made by a freshwater dolphin moving through water.

11. Kano-y-mi l^yapi-u-ra-ni; chi-mi kasna, ima-shi cha s^hawwwwwwww
canoe-LOC-EV squeeze-DUR-PAST-1; that-EV like that what-EV maybe
uyari-mu-kpi, kasna volteari-sha riku-ra-ni.
sound-CIS-SWRF like that turn-COR look-PAST-1
"I was squeezing (*aswa* pulp) in the canoe; then, what perhaps was a *s^hawwwwwwww*, sounded toward me, and turning around like that I looked."

Saw is performatively foregrounded here by its lengthening and also by the aspiration of its initial *s-*. The lengthened *saw* modifies the verb *uyarimukpi* "sounded toward," specifying its durativity and at the same time expressively gesturing that durativity by imitating the unfolding of that sound in time. *Saw*'s function in this context is inferential. It is represented by the speaker as part of her inference making about the presence of the dolphin underwater.

In the last example *saw* is extended to describe the way boiling water is poured through a series of holes leading to a long underground cavity, to kill snakes living inside.

12. Sawwwww, karan huktu-manda-mi yaku-ta tali-ra-nchi.
each hole-from-EV water-ACC pour-PAST-1PL

"*Sawwwww*, from each hole we poured water."

Saw is performatively foregrounded here by its lengthening and by syntactic displacement from its verb *taliranchi* "we poured." *Saw* specifies the durativity of its verb at the same time that it expressively gestures, by its lengthening, a cognitively salient sound image of moving water. Its displacement from its verb foregrounds the image of the pouring water apart from the verb's reference to it. *Saw*'s function is aesthetic and instructional. It informs a listener of a procedure for ridding one's agricultural field of venemous snakes by means of an expressive image of the procedure.

Shaw

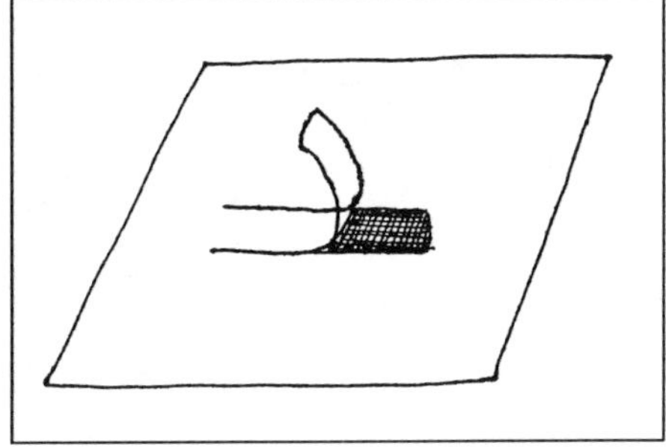

DEFINITION To create or define the borders of a continuous, two-dimensional entity by tearing, stripping, or pulling; to make a continuous two-dimensional gesture, such as a painted line. Aspectually completive.

COMMENT *Shaw* can be thought of as the positive version of *shaka*. While *shaka* describes the deformative effect of tearing and splitting, and therefore describes an empty space where there shouldn't be one, *shaw* describes what is newly defined or newly created by the action of tearing, stripping, or pulling. One of the entities most commonly defined by a *shaw* action is a strip of tree bark, which has a lot of different uses. Another product of the forest described with *shaw* is latex. Approximately thirty years ago, when it was still possible to make a profit by selling latex, people would tap it from trees, spread it out on an even surface, and when it had sufficiently dried, they would pull it up *shaw*, roll it up, and transport it in that form for sale.

ICONIC PROPERTIES The iconicity of *shaw* is related to its monosyllabicity; to its initial fricative, *sh-*; and to its final glide, *-w*. Its monosyllabicity by its noncomplexity is iconic of the simplicity of a tearing, stripping, or pulling movement. Its initial fricative, *sh-*, the articulation of which is continuous, involving no obstruction of the airstream, imitates the uninterruptedness of a surface that is stripped, pulled, or torn. The lip rounding accompanying pronunciation of the glide, *-w*, creates a constriction of the mouth, although not a complete obstruction, which is iconic of the tapering off rather than of the sharp-edged cutting off of a piece of something that is torn, stripped, or pulled away.

Shaw occurs with the following verbs.

1.	shaw aysana pull	to pull a continuous two dimensional portion of something, e.g., a piece of bark from a tree
2.	shaw anchuchina remove	to remove a continuous two-dimensional portion of something, e.g., a sheet of latex from a surface over which it has been spread
3.	shaw l^{y}uchuna peel	to peel a continuous two-dimensional portion of something, e.g., the skin of manioc, by removing it in one piece
4.	shaw partina part	To make a split which defines a continuous two-dimensional portion of something, e.g., in the skin of a plaintain
5.	shaw pichana sweep	to sweep with an unbroken movement, e.g., to shave hair from the body with a razor
6.	shaw l^{y}awkana lick	to lick something in a single continuous movement, e.g., a piece of cooked meat
7.	shaw awirina paint	to paint in an unbroken movement, e.g., the lips with lipstick

In the following example below *shaw* is repeated along with *shaka* to describe the stripping of bark from a tree. *Shaka* describes the split itself, while *shaw* describes the portion of bark created by that splitting motion.

8. Kasa kara-ta shaw shak^{a} shaw shak^{a} aysa-ra-ni, yanda-ta wangu-ngawa, waska
   Kasa skin-ACC pull-PAST-1 wood-ACC bundle-FINF rope
   il^{y}a-kpi.
   lack-SWRF
   "I pulled the *kasa* bark *shaw shak^{a} shaw shak^{a}* to bundle up the wood, as there wasn't any rope."

Shaw is performatively foregrounded here by its repetition, which gestures each act of pulling a complete strip of bark. *Shaw*'s function here is explanatory: it illustrates with a sound image the process of stripping bark from a tree for tying up bundles of wood.

In the next example *shaw* describes the way a large sheet of latex, which had been applied in liquid form all over a table and dried in the sun, was lifted off all at once, as one large piece.

9. Chi-ta ñuka yaya-ga shaw^{hhhhhhhh} aysa-sha l^{y}uch-k a-ra ña pacha tupu shina.
   that-ACC my father-TOP pull-COR peel-AG be-PAST now blanket size like
   "And that (latex) my father would peel, pulling it (with a) *shaw^{hhhhhhhh}* and it was like the size of a blanket."

Shaw is performatively foregrounded here by a strong, quickly released burst of air which filled out the speaker's cheeks. With this articulatory gesture the speaker imitates the release of the sheet of rubber from its surface and the concomitant release of air from underneath. *Shaw*'s function is evocative: the speaker is fondly recalling, by means of this sound image, the habits of her late father, who used to travel throughout the forest looking for latex trees to tap.

Ton

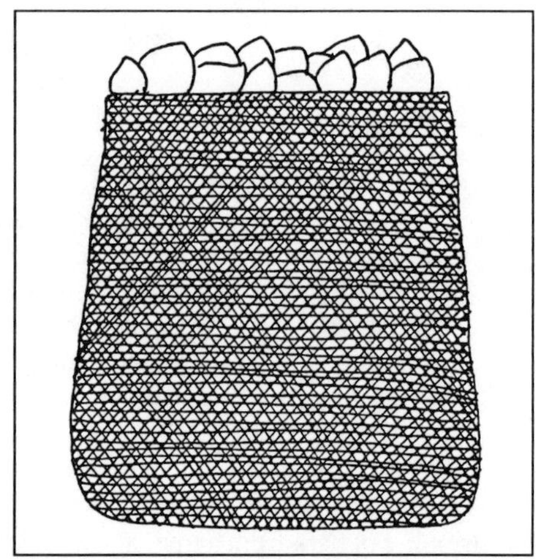

DEFINITION (1) To fill or be filled to utmost capacity; to cover or be covered, drenched with, or otherwise characterizeable by some attribute as completely as is possible (cf. *tak*$_2$). Aspectually completive, resultative. (2) An idea of the sound of an explosion, e.g., of dynamite; an idea of the sound, heard from a distance, of forceful contact between hard surfaces. Aspectually durative, punctual.

COMMENT Although *ton*$_1$ describes many different kinds of filling up, and by extension, covering up, it is most commonly used to describe an image of a filled-up canoe. To understand the significance of this image, it is necessary to appreciate how central river traveling is for many lowland Quechua. Everyone builds their houses, if not on the river, at least on a spot that ensures easy access to it because it is often necessary to travel by river to at least one of a family's agricultural fields. In addition to its importance for transportation, the river is important as an arena of display for lowland Quechua. Anyone traveling by canoe past a household is carefully scrutinized, interrogated about their destination, and, if appropriate, teased or at least gossiped about when they're no longer within earshot. Given the conspicuousness, then, of canoe travel, it isn't surprising that a canoe loaded with cargo would also attract attention and speculation. Canoes loaded *ton* with cargo are conspicuous visual displays of a day's work and wealth, whether harvested from the field, hunted in the forest, or caught in the river itself. They attract considerable attention and commentary from people who stop what they're doing to watch them go by, marveling at their contents and at the fortune or industriousness of their owners and often speculating about what, if anything, they themselves might be entitled to.

ICONIC PROPERTIES The iconicity of *ton*$_1$ is related to its monosyllabicity and to its final closure. Its monosyllabicity is iconic of the noncomplexity of what is completely filled, covered, or completely characterizable by an attribute. Its final closure is iconic of the finality of whatever is completely filled, covered, or completely characterizable by an attribute.

Ton occurs with the following verbs.

1. ton hundachina — to fill to the limit, e.g., a canoe with plaintains, fish, salt, or turtles
   fill
2. ton kargana — to load up to the limit
   load

3. ton hundarina — to fill up, e.g., a canoe with people or rainwater
   fill up
4. ton apana — to take a full load of something, usually by canoe
   take
5. ton apamuna — to bring a full load of something, usually by canoe
   bring
6. ton aparina — to bear fruit all over, even down to the base of the tree, e.g., the *chuku chuku* guava tree
   bear
7. ton awirina — to paint oneself black all over with the black vegetable dye *genipa* or with red *achiote* powder
   paint
8. ton armarina — to cover oneself with vegetable dye or powder; to be drenched with blood
   bathe
9. ton arma-chi-na — to cover someone all over with vegetable dye or powder
   bathe-CAUS
10. ton mana — to be filled, covered, or attributed with some salient quality or substance, e.g., a canoe with water, a priest with long vestments, or a woman with very long black hair
    be
11. ton pungina — to swell up all over, e.g., a body part
    swell
12. ton rawa-ya-na — to become drenched with blood from an open wound
    blood-ICH
13. ton nana-chi-na — to hurt all over
    pain-CAUS
14. ton rina — to go en masse, e.g., a canoe filled with soldiers or frightened animals running off
    go
15. ton shamuna — to come en masse
    come
16. ton tiyana — to be gathered en masse, e.g., canoes filled with people or provisions
    be located
17. ton ana — same as above
    be
18. ton tuvyana — to explode going *ton*, e.g., an airplane crashing or dynamite going off, etc
    explode
19. ton uyarina — to sound *ton*, e.g., an animal tapping on a hollow stump
    be heard
20. ton yandana — to chop wood making the sound *ton*
    cut wood
21. ton urmana — to fall going *ton*, e.g., a tree trunk
    fall

In the following example *ton*$_1$ describes a canoe filled with turtles.

22. Charapa-ta-ga kano-y-ga ton-mi apamu-nga ra-w-nchi.
    turtle-ACC-TOP canoe-LOC-TOP -EV bring-FINF do-DUR-1PL
    "We're going to bring a canoe *ton* (full) of turtles."

Ton is not performatively foregrounded here. It modifies the verb *apamunga rawnchi* "we're going to bring," specifying its completiveness by describing a cognitively salient image of a canoe full of turtles.

In the next example *ton* describes a canoe so completely filled with water that it had submerged under the water, with only its prow sticking out.

23. Pay singa-l^{y}a rikuri-sha, ña win ton yaku-wan ma-ra.
    it nose-LIM appear-COR now all water-INST be-PAST
    "It was all full with water, now, *ton*, with only its nose appearing."

Ton is not performatively foregrounded here. It modifies the verb *mara* "was," specifying its resultativity with the cognitively salient image of a canoe filled with water.

The next examples are taken from a conversation between myself and two other people about the journeys their fathers used to make to Peru to mine for salt. Both speakers use *ton* to describe the way canoes were filled as much as possible with the salt.

24. Speaker 1: Kanoa pakta-shka-ta hundachi-k a-naw-ray.
    canoe reach-PERF-ACC fill-AG be-3PL-PAST
    "They used to fill the canoes with as much as possible."

    Speaker 2: ‘$\text{T}^{\text{o}^{\text{o}^{\text{on}}}}$ hundachi-sha, ñuka yaya apamu-k a-ra-nchi,’ ni-k ma-ra—
    fill-COR my father bring-AG be-PAST-1PL say-AG be-PAST
    "‘Filling them $t^{o^{o^{on}}}$, we used to bring them,’ my father would say—"

    Speaker 1: $\text{t}^{\text{o}\,\text{o}\,\text{o}\,\text{o}\,\text{o}\,\text{o}}\text{onnn}$!

Speaker 2's use of *ton* is highly foregrounded by an upglide. By moving as far upward as her voice pitch will allow, the upglide imitates an idea of the extent of the canoes' filling. Since *ton* modifies the coreference verb *hundachisha* "filling," it also specifies its aspectual completiveness at the same time that it presents a listener with an intonational image of that completiveness. Speaker 1's rearticulation of *ton* with a more complex pitch contour indicates her cooperative involvement in speaker 2's presentation of the image. *Ton*'s function here is explanatory and evocative. By means of the image it simulates, it explains the extent to which people piled up their canoes with salt. At the same time, it evokes a complex set of feelings, including an idea of bounteousness and a longing for a time of great adventures and exotic experiences that has definitively passed and exists now only in peoples' memories or commemorated in a series of legends.

In the next sentence *ton* describes the way a man who had wandered in the forest for several months had become completely swollen from insect bites and exposure.

25. Ñuka kusa-ga $\text{to}^{\text{o}^{\text{o}^{\text{on}}}}$ -shi pungi-shka.
    my husband-TOP -EV swell-PERF
    "My husband was (completely) swollen $to^{o^{o^{on}}}$!"

Ton is performatively foregrounded here by its upglide, which imitates an idea of the extent of the man's swelling. At the same time that it simulates an image of this swelling, *ton* affects the perfect verb *pungishka* "swollen" with resultativity. *Ton*'s function is modal. It evokes pity for the poor man whose body was so ravaged by his wandering through the forest.

In the next example, from a narrative of personal experience, *ton*$_2$, describes the sound of an explosion which was believed to have originated from inside of a lake deep in the forest.

26. May-ta chari tuvya-ra, Janet, t^{h}ooooooooon tuvya-ra Santa Rosa kucha.
where-ADV perhaps explode-PAST Janet explode-PAST Santa Rosa lake
"Where perhaps, did it explode, Janet, *t^{h}ooooooooon*, Santa Rosa lake exploded!"

Ton is performatively foregrounded here by its lengthening, by the aspiration of its initial consonant, and by the low pitch of its pronunciation. Its lengthening performatively gestures the unfolding of the explosion in time while specifying its aspectual durativity. *Ton*'s function here is epistemic: the sound it describes was causally linked by the narrator to a long and difficult illness which she suffered shortly after hearing it. The explosion was compared to the sound of dynamite. Possibly, the shattering quality of the sound was metaphorically linked in the narrator's mind with the extreme disruption of her normal activities resulting from her illness.

Tas

DEFINITION Any action, condition, or state, considered as accomplished and complete or extended in space. Aspectually completive, resultative.

COMMENT There is overlap between *tas* and *tak*$_{2B}$, which describes any feature or quality considered as spatially extended or an action performed to its utmost limit. The decisive difference between *tak* and *tas* is that the central meaning of *tak* includes the idea of a particular moment of contact between entities, which is extended to describe an expanse of contact between entities, which is then further extended to describe any feature or quality as extended in space. *Tas*, by contrast, is more general. When it describes a spatially extended or completive action, state, or attribute, it is not grounded in a core sensory meaning as are the extended uses of *tak*. Further, it is its more general aspectual nondurativity that explains the presence of *tas* in compound sound-symbolic adverb constructions, the discussion of which follows. A verb modified by *tas* is comparable to a verb-particle construction in English such as "eat up," "cut off," or "fall down." The particles in these constructions are grammatically aspectual because all of them make clear the lexical level completiveness of their respective verbs' actions.

ICONIC PROPERTIES The iconicity of *tas* is related to its monosyllabicity and to its final closure. Its monosyllabicity is iconic of the noncomplexity of what is completely accomplished or extended in space. Its final closure is iconic of the finality of whatever is considered accomplished and complete or extended in space.

Tas occurs with the following verbs.

1.	tas pakina break	to break something open, e.g., an egg; to break something off, e.g., a piece of salt from a larger chunk
2.	tas pakirina break	to break off, e.g., part of a dart embedded in flesh
3.	tas kanina bite	to bite off, e.g., a portion of food
4.	tas ishkuna pluck	to pluck something off, e.g., a feather or piece of fruit
5.	tas mikuna eat	to eat a portion of something; to eat all of something
6.	tas pal^{y}ana harvest	to harvest all of the fruit from a tree; to take one piece
7.	tas pitina cut	to make a slit in something; to cut something off
8.	tas pitirina cut	to cut off from oneself, e.g., hair or fingernails
9.	tas riku-chi-na see-CAUS	to make something appear all at once, e.g., by shining a flashlight on it
10.	tas wañuchina kill	to put out a light
11.	tas watana tie	to tie something up, e.g., a dog; to tie something so that it is completely extended over or around something, e.g., a leaf over the rim of a glass to cover it
12.	tas watarina tie	to tie up some part of oneself, e.g., hair
13.	tas pasa-chi-na pass-CAUS	to pass something through, e.g., a strand of hair while braiding it
14.	tas apana take	to take everything, e.g., by fully loading a canoe
15.	tas pintana paint	to paint a mark or line, e.g., on the face
16.	tas upina drink	to drink up all of a given quantity
17.	tas upi-chi-na drink-CAUS	to make someone drink up, e.g., medicine
18.	tas hapina light	to light up a burner on a gas stove
19.	tas prohibina prohibit	to forbid absolutely, unconditionally, e.g., a rule made by the military
20.	tas nil^{y}puna swallow	to swallow down
21.	tas kindzhana enclose	to close off with a barrier, such as a fence
22.	tas paskana open	to open something up

23.	tas paskarina open	to open oneself up, e.g., the way a bird opens up the feathers on its head spreading them out, when it sings
24.	tas serana close	to be completely closed, e.g., a webbed foot
25.	tas tapana close	to close or shut something away
26.	tas taparina close	to shut oneself away, e.g., to hide
27.	tas chingarina be lost	to disappear completely, e.g., menstrual periods during pregnancy
28.	tas sakirina remain	to leave off or remain uniform throughout a given space, e.g., water left calm and unriled by waves
29.	tas sakina leave	to give up or abandon something, e.g., angry feelings or behavior toward another person
30.	tas tuta-ya-na night-ICH	to turn to the complete darkness of night
31.	tas amsa-ya-na dark-ICH	same as above
32.	tas harkana prevent	to obstruct in every possible way or from every possible direction
33.	tas aswana make aswa	to make a lot of *aswa*, e.g., for a celebration
34.	tas kichuna remove	to take away
35.	tas kacharina release	to let go of something
36.	tas rina go	to go off
37.	tas rana do	to do anything completely, e.g., to remove all weeds from an area
38.	tas l^{y}awturina crown	to completely surround one's head with a headdress
39.	tas tuvyana explode	to burst apart
40.	tas asina laugh	to be doubled up with laughter
41.	tas pukuna mature	to become completely ripened or fermented
42.	tas wiñana grow	to grow up everywhere, the way weeds do, covering an area
43.	tas il^{y}apana shoot	to shoot something down, e.g., any animal
44.	tas likcharina awaken	to wake up fully
45.	tas pichana sweep	to sweep up everything
46.	tas tamyana rain	to rain heavily
47.	tas mana be	to be fully characterizable by some attribute

In the following example, taken from a myth, *tas* describes the breaking open of an egg.

48. Lulun-da tas paki-sha, chawpi mar-bi tuksi-ra.
    egg-ACC break-COR middle sea-LOC throw-PAST
    "Breaking the egg open *tas*, he threw it out into the middle of the sea."

Tas is not performatively foregrounded here. It modifies the coreference verb *pakisha* "breaking," specifying its completiveness by describing the complete deformation in the egg's shape.

The next sentence, taken from a myth, uses *tas* to describe the way a dog's ears were plugged up with cotton.

49. Rinri-ta poto-wan tas tapa-ra.
    ear-ACC cotton-INST close-PAST
    "He plugged up the (dog's) ears *tas*."

Tas is not performatively foregrounded here. It modifies the verb *tapara* "plugged," specifying emphatically that the dog's ears were completely plugged up.

In the next sentence *tas* describes the complete peeling off of the hulls from each piece in a pile of breadfruit, which is then further processed to make a fermented beverage.

50. Chi kara-ta-s tas tas tas ri-shka-ta win l^{y}uchu-shka washa, indi-y
    that skin-ACC-INCL go-PERF-ACC all peel-PERF after sun-LOC
    shita-nawn.
    throw-3PL
    "And their hulls too, after peeling all of them (by having) popped them off *tas tas tas*, they throw them in the sun."

Tas is performatively foregrounded here by its relatively rapid multiple repetition, which gestures each popping off of a piece of breadfruit skin. By repeating *tas* relatively rapidly, the speaker imitates an idea of efficiency, making the process as a whole seem relatively effortless.

In the next example, taken from a myth, *tas* describes the way a bird plucked pieces of fruit from a tree to feed children who were being starved by their parents.

51. Chanda apiyu-ta-s, chasna-l^{y}a-ta tas tas tas ishku-sha, wawa-guna-ta
    then apiyu-ACC-INCL like this-LIM-ADV pluck-COR children-PL-ACC
    upi-chi-sha ashkata pal^{y}a-kpi tuta upi-k a-naw-ra.
    drink-CAUS-COR lots harvest-SWRF night drink-AG be-3PL-PAST
    "Then, plucking the *apiyu* fruits also, just like this, *tas tas tas*, harvesting a lot of them, they gave them to the children to drink at night."

Tas is performatively foregrounded here by its multiple repetition and by the telic pitch progression over the repetitions. Each repetition gestures an act of plucking a piece of fruit off the tree, specifying the completiveness of the coreference verb *ishkusha* "plucking." The telic pitch progression over the series of repetitions suggests a progressive increase in the quantity of fruits plucked, until the tree has been completely harvested. *Tas*'s function is aesthetic: by imitating an idea of the completeness of the tree's plucking, the narrator gratifies his listeners with the knowledge that children who were starved by their evil parents are now being properly fed and cared for.

In the next example *tas* is used by a young girl to describe the lines she plans to draw across her cheek with black *wituk* dye. She uses an index finger from each hand and starts at the ear. She then sweeps each index finger over each cheek while lengthening *tas*. Finally, the two lines meet at the tip of her nose, at which point she describes their moment of contact with *tak*.

52. Nuka tasssssss, chi-manda tasssssss tak pinta-nga ra-w-ni.
I there-from paint-FINF do-DUR-1
"I'm going to paint *tasssssss*, then (again) *tasssssss* (and) *tak*."

Tas is performatively foregrounded here by its lengthening which, together with the speaker's index finger movement across her face, gestures the action of drawing a line and at the same time specifies the complete extent of the line. *Tas*'s function here is explanatory and aesthetic: it explains the shape of the lines to be drawn be presenting a clear gestural image of those lines.

What distinguishes *tas* most interestingly from other sound-symbolic adverbs is its use by speakers in compound constructions of sound-symbolic adverbs. In such uses *tas* has an emphatic modifying function. It emphasizes the completiveness of whatever sound-symbolic adverb it modifies. In the last example, *tas* is part of a complex description of the *bogoniru* bird which spreads its head feathers straight out when it sings. The sound-symbolic adverb *chinda* refers to the spikiness of the feathers' spreading out, while *tas* emphasizes the completeness of their spreading out.

53. Bogoniru tas chinda-ng tas chinda-ng tas chinda-ng pay uma paskari-n,
Bogoniru -INST -INST -INST he head open-3
kanta-kpi.
sing-SWRF
"The Bogoniru bird's head (feathers) open up *tas chindang tas chindang tas chindang* when it sings."

Tas and *chinda* are performatively foregrounded here by their multiple repetition and by displacement from their verb *paskarin* "opens." Their multiple repetition gestures each action of the bird's opening up of its head feathers. Their displacement from their verb presents the listener with an image of the bird's head feathers opening up, apart from the verbal reference to that opening up. *Tas*'s function is to make more emphatic the image of the bird's feathers opening up. The image as a whole functions aesthetically and also to identify the bird. It simulates a series of movements which are distinctive and visually striking and which contribute to an observer's ability to distinguish this bird from others.

14
Conclusion

With their use of sound symbolism the Pastaza Quechua seek to integrate language with perceptual experience. From the perspective of Western science, this is an important task because of the difficulty, historically, of recognizing or representing the link between language as a cultural form and environmental phenomena, without reducing one or idealizing the other. The relationship between the two has always been deeply contested—hence the intractable debates on culture and nature and arbitrariness and motivation. But attempts to reconcile the two, and develop an integrated approach, have been few and far between. This book has focused directly on this problem and its possible solution by examing a phenomenon that has been troubling to all sides: sound-symbolic language. Linguistic sound symbolism is a performative technique for expressively communicating the salient sounds, rhythms, and psychophysical sensations that are drawn from perceptions of the environment and bodily experience. By examining the functions of these signs in discourse, we can recast the debate between the "natural" and the "conventional" aspects of language in terms less radically polarized than those commonly employed. The development of a theory that attempts to integrate grammar, cognition, semiotics, and aesthetically performative discourse is a first step in integrating several ancient and vexing dichotomies in the cultural and linguistic sciences.

Sound symbolism forges an important link between language and perception by its integration with the aspectual subsystem of Pastaza Quechua. The structure of the coreference clause "encourages" speakers to use sound-symbolic adverbs for maximum explicitness and conceptual clarity. At the same time, sound symbolism makes incalculable contributions to the expressive nuances of Pastaza Quechua discourse. So many subtleties of mood are linked to representations of the durativity or completiveness of an action, event, or process. Moods of catastrophe, futility, normalcy, beauty, lightness, and buoyancy are just a few of the more general ones. More specific moods include the forcefulness and even viciousness of a movement; the tediousness of a protracted effort; the remorseless working out of natural processes of decline, decay, and death; and the naturalness of the bizarre and the unexpectedness of what is most normal. Besides their affective significance, sound-symbolic adverbs have considerable performative potential for " filling out" relatively abstract grammatical concepts such as durativity and completiveness with semantically specific portraits of actions, events, and processes. The following are just a few of the semantically specific images of progression communicated through sound-symbolic performance: progressive proximity toward a long-awaited goal; progressive suspense with the unfolding of a dangerous process; a progressive increase of quantity in a contained space; and a progressive increase in one's perception of an unfathomably large expanse of space.

Although this work has concerned the "ecological fit" between sound-symbolic adverbs and Pastaza Quechua aspectual grammar, it would be a mistake to attribute too much uniqueness to Pastaza Quechua sound symbolism. There is suggestive evidence from Newman (1968: 110), for example, that sound-symbolic adverbs may function within the aspectual subsystem of the Hausa language as well. He cites the following data from Hausa, labeling the ideophones that occur with verbs as *intensifiers* or *descriptive adverbs*. However, the glosses he furnishes strongly suggest that the ideophones in question are not intensifying the actions of their respective verbs; rather, they appear to be affecting the lexical aspect of each verb with completive, resultative, and punctual aspect values. The examples as they appear in Newman (1968: 110) follow. The ideophones are italicized. My own assessments of their aspect values appear in parentheses.

(17) ya cika *pal*	he filled it to the brim (completive)
(18) ya kone *kurmus*	it burnt to the ground (resultative)
(19) ya tashi *farat*	he got up in a flash (punctual)
(20) ya fadi *sharap*	he fell headlong (inceptive/punctual)

The aspectual significance of ideophones, then, has not been adequately explored, even though much attention has been given to their phonological, morphological, syntactic, and semantic properties (cf. Antilla 1976; Courtenay 1976; Diffloth 1972, 1976, 1980; Emeneau 1969; Newman 1968; Nichols 1971; Samarin 1971). Furthermore, there have been no detailed studies, until now, of their performative, discourse characteristics.

Just as it would be wrong to attribute too much aspectual uniqueness to Pastaza Quechua sound symbolism, it would also be a mistake to overlook sound symbolism's most general functional affinities with other grammatical phenomena. Some of the work that gets done by the sound-symbolic adverbs here analyzed can be compared in a very general way with verb/particle constructions in English. Although the English language does not have coreference structures, it does make use of particles and prepositions to clarify the aspectual values of its verbs. These are evident in constructions such as *eat up*, *sit down*, *jump over*, *reach across*, *run out*, *walk in*, etc. In all of these constructions, the particle affects the verb's lexical aspect with perfectivity. An important difference, however, is that *up*, *down*, *over*, *across*, *out*, and *in* are never allowed to substitute for a finite verb, nor can they ever stand for an entire proposition. Their spatial meaning is often unrecognizable, as it is in the construction *eat up*, where the idea of finishing food cannot be linked in a very straightforward manner with an idea of up-ness, in the same way that seating oneself can be linked with a probable downward movement. Another significant way in which particles and prepositions are distinctive from sound-symbolic adverbs is that they are not the locus of performative elaboration. In addition to its use of such constructions for aspectual clarification, English also has a number of expressive adverbs such as "splat" and "thump" which are lexically encoded for perfective aspect values.

Nevertheless, these general similarities should not obscure the very important differences between Pastaza Quechua sound symbolism and the limited examples of onomatopoeia from English. What I hope has been made clear by the examples in this book is that Pastaza Quechua sound symbolism is quite distinctive in its discourse functions from the ways of speaking familiar to people living in a university or other kind of literacy-influenced culture. Most people would strongly defend their own language against charges that it lacked sound symbolism. All speakers feel intuitively that the sign is *not* arbitrary, yet most people living in a culture or subculture influenced by literacy would not engage in the elaborate sound symbolic performances with the frequency or for the variety of purposes that the Pastaza Quechua do. I have attempted to clarify Pastaza Quechua sound symbolism by an explication of the complex factors that contribute to its use. No one answer exists, and no one factor is necessarily primary. Performative elaborations of sound-symbolically rendered perceptions are one way of highlighting the sharedness of basic kinds of experiences. They help legitimize a Quechua cultural ideal of amiability and sociability. Further, sound symbolism represents an important link between one's personal experiences of nature, the significant events of one's life history, and the idiosyncracies of every individual's own aesthetic predilections. Finally, in Pastaza Quechua at least, the aspectual subsystem provides a convenient niche for sound-symbolic expression.

Lakoff's (1987) case studies from English provide compelling evidence for the schematic structuring of concepts, lexical items, and grammatical constructions. This work has shown that the schematic structuring of a class of lexical items is both grammatically and expressively salient in Pastaza Quechua. The point-line schema used for conceptualizing grammatical aspect is useful to a limited extent in describing Pastaza Quechua's aspect categories. However, a complete understanding of Pastaza Quechua's aspect expression necessitates consideration of the ways in which sound-symbolic schemas articulate perceptions of everyday experience. Basic, abstract aspect distinctions such as *punctual*, *durative*, and *perfective* do not adequately capture the cognitively salient images used to describe Quechua speakers' experience of aspectual time. Their sound-symbolic usage reveals a concern for the suddenness of a realization, the abruptness of a gesture, the definitive moment of contact with a surface, the sounds of sound unfolding in time, movements throughout an extended period of time or an expanse of space, and the full range of moods and affective values associated with these images. In Pastaza Quechua, grammatical aspect is not strictly speaking a separate grammatical subcomponent; it articulates with cognitive models of spatial and perceptual experience.

The cognitive structures expressed by sound-symbolic adverbs in Pastaza Quechua are probably universal. They are preconceptual structures that are grounded in peoples' bodily and perceptual experiences.; however, they are not necessarily linguistic in their expression. If we assume that the uses to which they are put in Pastaza Quechua are universal in some anthropological sense, then we might speculate on how other cultures achieve similar aims. All cultures, presumably, share ideas about sociability and strive at least in some contexts to emphasize the sharedness of basic kinds of experiences. I would suggest that many of the sound-symbolic schemas that are performatively communicated among the Pastaza Quechua for the enhancement of shared experiences are communicated in our own culture, nonlinguistically. The material conditions of Western scientific culture have made possible a vast array of technical resources and media for communication, and many of our embodied schemas are conveyed through visual technologies such as film and video. The functions of such modes of communication are extremely diverse, and some, such as the identificational, instructional, aesthetic, and modal, overlap with the uses of Pastaza Quechua sound-symbolic schemas. However, one common use of kinesthetic visual schemas is unique to capitalist consumer societies. Corporations, particularly food and restaurant companies, make abundant use of visual and also auditory kinesthetic schemas in television advertising to enhance good feelings among consumers for the purpose of enticing them to buy their products. A few of these images include liquid substances pouring out of containers, granular substances pouring out into a pile, images of the moment when something is definitively chopped in half or a piece of something is cut off, images of mouths wide open and also closing down over a piece of food, images of smiles and smiling faces, and so on.

Throughout this book I have deliberately compared sound-symbolic performative techniques with gestural and cinematic modes of communication. Terms such as "close-up shot," "wide angle shot," "juxtaposition," "montage," "fast motion shot," and "slow motion shot" made sense of much of the variability in sound-symbolic performance. All of this points to a view of semiotic systems which is not medium-specific. Gestures are not simply what we do with our body. They are also communicated through intonational patterns, as Bolinger (1985) first pointed out. Similarly, images are not only two-dimensional representations of visual perceptions; they are also three- and four-dimensional, as they unfold auditorily in temporal succession. And sound-symbolic discourse is not simply linguistic. It is comparable to gestural, imageic, and cinematic modalities of expression. Kristeva has suggested that other semiotic domains may illuminate the field of linguistic science:

> The importance of semiotic study consists of the fact that it reveals laws of the organization of signifying systems that were not observed in the study of verbal language. With these laws, language can probably be reconsidered one day to find there zones of "significance" that are being censored or repressed in the current state of linguistic science: zones appropriated by what has been called "art" in order for it to unfurl and explore them (1989: 318).

Further comparative study of sound symbolism in other languages promises to reveal much, not only about other linguistic cultures but also about the diverse kinds of processes involved in symbolization.

APPENDIX

CONJUGATION OF *RINA*

Present Indicative

ri-ni "I go"	ri-nchi "we go"
ri-ngi "you go"	ri-ngichi "you-all go"
ri-n "he/she/it goes"	ri-nawn, ri-n-guna "they go"

Past Tense

ri-ra-ni "I went"	ri-ra-nchi "we went"
ri-ra-ngi "you went"	ri-ra-ngichi "you-all went"
ri-ra "he/she/it went"	ri-naw-ra, ri-ra-guna "they went"

Narrative Past

——	——
——	——
ri-shka, ri-ra "he/she/it went"	ri-shk-awna, ri-naw-ra "they went"

Present Perfect

ri-shka-ni
"I've gone"

ri-shka-ngi
"you have gone"

ri-shka
"he/she/it, has gone"

ri-shka-nchi
"we've gone"

ri-shka-ngichi
"you-all have gone"

ri-shk-awna
"they have gone"

Past Perfect

ri-shka-ra-ni
"I had gone"

ri-shka-ra-ngi
"you had gone"

ri-shka-ra
"he/she/it had gone"

ri-shka-ra-nchi
"we had gone"

ri-shka-ra-ngichi
"you-all had gone"

ri-shka-naw-ra
"they had gone"

NOTES

Chapter 1 Introduction

1. In languages and language families where they have been attested, such as African (Childs 1989; Newman 1968; Samarin 1971), Indo-Aryan (Dimock 1957; Emeneau 1969), Japanese (Frei 1970), Mon-Khmer (Diffloth 1980), and Amerind (Durbin 1973), sound-symbolic words have been referred to as *ideophones* (Doke 1935; Samarin 1971), *expressives* (Diffloth 1972), *phonaesthetic words* (Henderson 1965), and *onomatopoeic words*.

2. Wescott noticed that sound-symbolic words from English also encode aspectual distinctions: "English examples . . . are . . . the word-pairs *smack~smash* and *crack ~ crash* in which the forms ending in stops seem to have an instantaneous sense, whereas those ending in fricatives seem to have—comparatively, at least—a durative or resultative force" (1976: 499). The existence of aspectually encoded sound-symbolic words in English does not weaken my stronger claim about their particular significance for Quechua linguistic culture, however, for two reasons: first, sound-symbolic words are functionally restricted in English speakers' discursive practice; second, they are not integrated with the grammatical system of aspect, as they are in Pastaza Quechua, where they modify a variety of coreference structures, specifying their aspectual values.

3. There is insufficient space here to discuss all of the interesting theoretical issues that are tied to sound-symbolic language use. Because it has been associated with nonliterate cultures, sound symbolism has been implicated in primitive mentality paradigms (Levy-Bruhl 1985: 147). Another ontogenetic view of sound symbolism was expressed by the developmental psychologist Heinz Werner, who was interested in the psychological implications of sound symbolism and of expressive language generally. Werner believed that sound-symbolic language use was based in a special perceptual mode, which he called *physiognomic*. Physiognomic perception contrasts with the *objective-technical* mode of perception that characterizes the modern outlook. People who perceive physiognomically are said to identify with what they perceive and endow their object of perception with dynamic and affective qualities. The problem with Werner's paradigm is that if it is interpreted in a strong form, as it has been, then sound-symbolic words would have to be considered presymbolic, or prelinguistic, utterances.

4. Friedrich's article outlines a theory of tropes designed, in part, to counteract the "metaphormania" that prevents an appreciation of the complexity of poetic language. One of Friedrich's main arguments is that, although metaphor is considered by many to be the most important literary device, its use in many cultures' poetic traditions is negligible. In Friedrich's classifica-

tion, all poetic language communicates by means of five general types and many subtypes of tropes or figures. These include image tropes, formal tropes, contiguity tropes, modal tropes, and analogical tropes. Metaphor is considered a subtype of analogical trope.

5. The term *Quichua* is sometimes employed to refer to the Ecuadorean dialects. I use *Quechua* however, because I believe Quichua only obscures the connection between the Ecuadorean dialects and the rest of the Quechua family.

6. The Pastaza and Napo dialects of Ecuador should not be confused with those of lowland Peru by the same name. See Wise (1985) for a description of the genetic classification and distribution of languages spoken in the adjacent lowlands of Peru.

Chapter 2 The Theoretical Dimensions of Aspect

1. An interesting conception of the interrelations between aspect, tense, and space is offered by Dombrovsky (1963), who discusses the specific roles of space and time notions in the development of the Indo-European tense-aspect system. Although I do not agree with most of the underlying assumptions of his argument, I acknowledge it here because of its essentially spatial conceptualization of aspect. Dombrovszky begins his essay with the assumption that tense and aspect evolved as separate systems in Indo-European, and he asks "Which came first?" He then argues that aspect must have preceded tense because aspect is a more primitive concept than tense. Aspect, he asserts, is a sort of intermediary category between a primitive present, which is predominantly spatial, and the later development of the more abstract notions of past and future time.

Dombrovszky's theory is that aspect and tense are closely linked to the evolutionary development of the social use of language. In the beginning, he speculates, it was only possible to use language to speak of actions that were spatially and temporally immediate. Only with the development of social life and culture did the narrative capacity of language, along with its expression of abstract notions of time such as past and future, evolve. He reasons further that aspect distinctions such as the aorist and the perfect represent the first attempt to abstract time from space. It is only an attempt, however, because the perfect is an intermediary form: it is still located primarily in the present, even if it is a present founded on past experience. While the Indo-European perfect is a projection of the past into the present, the imperfect, he believes, represents the full development of tense because it consists of the projection of a spatial present into the past. He attributes this development to the requirements of a new social skill, that of narration.

Although I do not agree with Dombrovszky's assumption that spatial awareness is a primitive perceptual ability and that the awareness of time reflects a more advanced abstractive conceptual ability, there is, I believe, some value in this scheme. Its value is that it allows aspect as a category to include both spatial and temporal dimensions.

2. I am indebted to Paul Friedrich who originally pointed this out.

3. Ejectives are sounds made by moving the glottis downward, thereby compressing the airstream, and then releasing it. Aspirates are made by prolonging the period of devoicing that ordinarily follows the pronunciation of a voiceless sound.

4. Mannheim includes *rawray* ~ *yawray* and *nina* which are unaspirated, but semantically associated with this set because they are incapable, for phonotactic reasons, of carrying the feature of aspiration. Aspiration requires the presence of an oral stop.

Chapter 3 The Grammatical Ecology of Aspect in Pastaza Quechua

1. There is no base form **awina*.

2. Orr and Wrisley (1981: 161) state that *-hu-* is a dialect variant used by Quechua speakers living along the Payamino and Napo Rivers, which is quite far north of the village where I worked.

3. There are two verbs in Quechua that can be glossed as "to be." The other verb, *ana*, is used to describe temporary conditions, locations, and character traits that are not considered intrinsic to a person's nature, or actions which are relatively low in agentivity. For example, in order to question someone about the whereabouts of someone else, speakers always use *ana* to ask the simple question "Was he there?"

A-w-ra-chu?
be-DUR-PAST-NEG

As another example, consider the next sentence, which uses *ana* to refer to the act of noticing something that someone else has misplaced.

Irma-wa sawli mana riku-k a-ra-ngi?
Irma-POSS machete NEG see-AG be-PAST-2

"You didn't see Irma's machete?" (lit.: You weren't a "see-er" of Irma's machete?)

To refer to an activity that is relatively agentive or a trait that is relatively intrinsic to an individual, however, *mana* is usually used.

Chapter 4 The Performative Expression of Durativity and Perfectivity

1. I exclude from consideration here examples of nouns or adjectives that are repeated for emphasis. In the following description, for example, *yana* "black" is repeated to describe the appearance of an anaconda.

Yana yana shinki ma-ra!
black black shiny be-PAST

"It was so black, pitch black!"

2. Furthermore, just as a series of multiple repetitions can vary considerably in pitch within the repeated series, so can the lengthened portion of a syllable. The most typical pattern is for the lengthened syllable to begin at a higher pitch than what preceded it, and to fall back down to the utterance's pitch as it ends. These pitch variations in the lengthened portions of syllables will not be represented in the examples.

3. The word *istileres* is a permutation of the Spanish *estrella*.

Chapter 5 Sound-Symbolic Involvement

1. In this respect it diverges from involved styles discussed in the literature, which are often interpreted as conflictive (Schiffrin 1984.)

2. Not all these authors have made explicit use of "involvement" and "detachment" as a conceptual scheme. Nevertheless, their work lends support to this framework. Labov (1972) provides evidence from interviews that black inner-city children are highly skilled at making arguments, reasoning, and creative expression; however, their linguistic culture, which emphasizes the importance of personal narrative experience, is quite different from the abstract, detached world of discourse offered by public schools. Similarly, Heath (1983) found that rural blacks who were able to read and write did not as a rule thrive intellectually in local schools. She traces their failure to a particular view of learning which values getting a feeling for the "shifting sands of reality" (1983: 84) rather than internalizing a fixed corpus of abstract, detached knowledge.

3. The translated narrative was bounded off as a text during the interview process itself. When it became obvious to me that my friend was embarking on a rather extended account, I asked her to backtrack and start from the beginning, so that I could record the entire narrative. It therefore has a well-marked beginning, indicated by the imperative "Look!" and a definitive conclusion, which is "And that's how I saw with these eyes what an anaconda caught." The entire narrative is internally organized according to the structural principles of line and verse.

4. This question of hers requires comment. Lowland Ecuadorean Quechua believe that anacondas are sometimes used by shamans as intermediaries. If an anaconda is seen, and especially if it behaves aggressively, people assume that it has been sent by a shaman, who will be referred to as its "owner."

5. In many of its uses, however, *tak* is the only indicator that an action has been punctually completed. Speakers do not always, as in line 14 make an action's completion explicit. When speakers are not completely explicit, for example, when they leave out the finite verb which *tak* is meant to modify, then the image-like quality of *tak* becomes grammatically important for its role in encoding aspectual punctuality.

6. Strictly speaking, *tsapak* should have been discussed in the first or second section of the exegesis, because it is a sound symbolic adverb of a sound and a movement. I discuss it here because its involvement function makes best sense when considered in relation to that of *pus*.

7. Admittedly, *kingu* "bend" is a lexical noun, not a sound-symbolic adverb. However, the lexicon is not without its own iconic properties. It would not be difficult to imagine how the sound qualities of *kingu* could lend themselves to iconic expression. The high front/high backness of the first and second syllable vowels, respectively, suggests a certain acoustical symmetry, which is congenial with the idea of a bend.

Chapter 6 Signs of Life in Sound

1. Whitten (1976: 44) reports that parakeets and other birds as well travel between many different natural and metaphysical domains and are believed capable of carrying women's songs to absentee men.

2. Immediately after saying this the narrator reported more instances of this sound. For brevity's sake, I've omitted these.

3. In my own fieldwork I also heard references to an underwater world. My impression is that this world is not exclusively a domain for those who have died, however, but is considered to be a realm inhabited by human-like creatures with extrahuman capacities, who occasionally visit the upper world to share their powers.

Chapter 7 Sound-Symbolic Iconicity and Grammar

1. In fact, coreference verbs are not the only type of structure that can be modified by sound-symbolic adverbs. Without modification by a perfective sound-symbolic adverb, a finite verb, an attributive verb, a coreference verb, and a switch-reference verb allow for the possibility that an action or event is ongoing within its event frame, but none of these constructions specifies ongoingness. This is the definition of the imperfective (Chung and Timberlake 1985: 236). When modified by a perfective sound-symbolic adverb, however, all of these constructions are thereby perfectively marked.

Chapter 8 Sound-Symbolic Contrasts of Sensible Experience

1. Far more common than the combination of *toa* with the verb *upina*, however, is *t*^{y}*am* with *upina*. When offered a clay bowl or a hollowed out gourd of *aswa*, one is almost always encouraged to drink it up with the imperative: *T*^{y}*am upingi*! "Drink it up *t*^{y}*am*!"

2. This sentence features a rare example of a sound-symbolic adverb suffixed with the dative case marker *-ma*.

3. A variant is *tupu*.

4. Probably the rodent native to South America which is called a "cavy," and which is a member of the family *Caviidae*.

Chapter 9 Sound Symbols of Contact and Penetration

1. *Tak* is probably derived from the Quechua verb *takana* "to touch," which could be related to Sp. *tocar*. However, among Quechua speakers *takana* itself is mostly used metaphorically to refer to sexual intercourse. Only rarely is it used to refer to ordinary touching.

2. This first set of examples will feature aspectually punctual functions of *tak*$_1$. The aspectual punctuality of *tak* is usually evident by its intonational shape, by the semantics of its utterance, and by certain distributional facts. One such fact is that punctual *tak* never modifies a verb suffixed with the continuous durative morpheme *-u-*. The intonational shape of punctual *tak* is either unelaborated or higher pitched than its utterance's baseline. Punctual *tak* never undergoes an upglide or lengthening. This is because upglides and lengthening imply a conceptual complexity that is incompatible with the idea of punctuality.

3. *Tak*$_2$ is distinguished from *tak*$_1$ in part by its aspectuality. *Tak*$_1$ cannot modify verbs that are suffixed with the continuous durative morpheme *-u-* because it encodes aspectual punctuality, and punctuality is conceptually incompatible with durativity. *Tak*$_2$, by contrast, may modify verbs that are formally durative. This is because *tak*$_2$ is aspectually completive, resultative, and aorist. And all of these aspect values can apply at the lexical or predicate level, while a seemingly conflicting aspectual durativity can be encoded at the propositional or narrative level.

4. The term "tense" is being used to designate a style of speaking in which the jaw is kept as closed as possible while speaking, and thus creates an impression of tenseness. This style of speaking is often employed throughout an entire sentence for dramatic emphasis.

Chapter 10 Sound Symbols of Opening and Closing

1. Whether *taw*$_1$ is interpreted as aspectually punctual or completive depends on whether it is interpreted as the action of closing up a space or as the sound produced by that action. The sound so produced is aspectually punctual because it implies that the act of closing off was done swiftly enough to produce a reverberative sound. The sound of closing off, is then extended to stand for the act of closing off, whether or not any sound resulted. The act of closing off therefore, can be either aspectually punctual or completive. In any case it is not always clear that these two senses of *taw*$_1$ are always separable, and it is therefore not always possible to decide between one aspect value and another, unless there are other manner adverbs such as *ukta* "quickly" that make it clear.

Chapter 11 Sound Symbols of Falling

1. *Palay*$_2$ is both aspectually punctual and resultative. When asked about its meaning, Quechua speakers often paraphrased it with adverbs such as *ukta* "fast" and *wayra shina* "like the wind." Its resultativity is related to the semantic feature of stealth. What is done secretly is often evident only as a result. Its punctual resultativity can therefore be related to a semantic configuration involving both speed and stealth.

2. *Pak*$_1$ may be punctual, completive, or resultative because the complete or resultant reconfiguration that takes place as a result of falling happens all at once. If used in a sentence that is transitive and in which the notional subject is high in agency and, or, animacy, then *pak*$_1$ will be considered punctual/completive. Otherwise it will be considered punctual/resultative.

3. *Ki* is either completive, resultative, or aorist because it describes a perfective action which is made evident by a total configuration of individual entities that are piled, heaped, randomly distributed, or otherwise grouped together.

BIBLIOGRAPHY

Anderson, Stephen R. (1982). "Where's Morphology?" *Linguistic Inquiry* 13 (fall): 571– 612.

——— (1985). *Phonology in the Twentieth Century*. Chicago: University of Chicago Press.

Andrews, Avery (1985). "The major functions of the noun phrase." In T. Shopen, ed., *Language Typology and Syntactic Description I*. Vol. 1: *Clause Structure*. Cambridge: Cambridge University Press. pp. 62–154.

Antilla, Raimo (1976). "Meaning and Structure of Finnish Descriptive Vocabulary." In Robert Harms and Frances Karttunen, eds., *Texas Linguistic Forum 5* (Papers from the Transatlantic Finnish Conference). Austin: University of Texas. pp. 1–12.

Arnheim, Rudof (1969). *Visual Thinking*. Berkeley: University of California.

——— (1957). *Film as Art*. Berkeley: University of California.

Aronson, Howard (1977). "Interrelationships between Aspect and Mood in Bulgarian." *Folia Slavica* 1(1): 9–32.

Basso, Ellen (1985). *A Musical View of the Universe*. Philadelphia: University of Pennsylvania Press.

Bauman, Richard (1977). *Verbal Art as Performance*. Prospect Heights: Waveland Press.

——— (1986). *Story, Performance and Event*. New York: Cambridge University Press.

Benveniste, Emile (1971). "The Nature of the Linguistic Sign." In *Problems in General Linguistics*. Coral Gables: University of Miami Press. pp. 43–48.

Binnick, Robert (1991). *Time and the Verb: A Guide to Tense and Aspect*. New York: Oxford University Press.

Bolinger, Dwight (1940). "Word Affinities." *American Speech* 15: 62–73.

——— (1950). "Rime, Assonance, and Morpheme Analysis." *Word* 6: 117–136.

——— (1985). "The Inherent Iconism of Intonation." In John Haiman, ed., *Iconicity in Syntax*. Amsterdam: John Benjamins. pp. 97–108.

——— (1986). *Intonation and Its Parts*. Stanford, Calif.: Stanford University Press.

Bright, William (1979). "A Karok Myth in Measured Verse: The Translation of a Performance." *Journal of California and Great Basin Anthropology* 1: 117–123.

Casson, Ronald (1983). "Schemata in Cogitive Anthropology." *Annual Review* of *Anthropology* 12: 429–462.

Cerrón-Palomino, Rodolfo (1987). *Lingüística Quechua*. Cuzco, Peru: Bartolomé de las casas.

Chafe, Wallace (1982). "Integration and Involvement in Speaking, Writing, and Oral Literature." In Deborah Tannen, ed., *Spoken and Written Language*. Norwood: Ablex. pp. 35–54.

Chatterjee, Ranjit (1988). *Aspect and Meaning in Slavic and Indic*. Amsterdam: John Benjamin.

Chung, Sandra and Timberlake, Alan (1985). "Tense, Aspect, and Mood." In Timothy Shopen, ed., *Language Typology and Syntactic Description*. Vol. 3: *Grammatical Categories and the Lexicon*. Cambridge: Cambridge University Press. pp. 202–258.

Cole, Peter (1985). *Imbabura Quechua*. The Hague: Mouton.

Comrie, Bernard (1976). *Aspect*. Cambridge: Cambridge University Press.

Courtenay, Karen R. (1976). "Ideophones Defined as a Phonological Class: The Case of Yoruba." *Studies in African Linguistics* (Supplement 6): 13–26.

DeReuse, Willem (1986). "The Lexicalization of Sound Symbolism in Santiago del Estero Quechua." *International Journal of American Linguistics* 52(1): 54–64.

Diffloth, Gerard (1972). "Notes on Expressive Meaning." *Chicago Linguistic Society* 8: 440–447.

——— (1976). "Expressives in Semai." Austroasiatic Studies 1. *Oceanic Linguistics*. Honolulu: University of Hawaii. Special Publication 13: 249–264.

——— (1980)."Expressive Phonology and Prosaic Phonology of Mon-Khmer." In Theraphan Thongkum et al., eds., *Studies in Mon-Khmer and Thai Phonology* and *Phonetics in Honor of E. Henderson*. Bangkok: Chulalonghorn University Press. pp. 49–59.

Dimock, Edward C. (1957). "Symbolic forms in Bengali." Taraporewala Memorial Volume. Bulletin of the Deccan College Research Institute 18: 22–29.

Dombrovszky, József (1963). "Les notions de l'espace et du temps dans la formation du systeme aspecto-temporel de l'Indo-Europeen." *Studia Slavica (Hungarica)* 9: 179–191.

DuBois, John (1985). "Competing Motivations." In John Haiman, ed., *Iconicity in Syntax*. Amsterdam: John Benjamins. pp. 343–365.

Durbin, Marshall (1973). "Sound Symbolism in the Maya Language Family." In Munro Edmunson, ed., *Meaning in Mayan Languages: Ethnolinguistic Studies*. Janua Lingauarum: Series Practica no. 158. The Hague: Mouton. pp. 23–49.

Emeneau, Murray (1969). "Onomatopoeics in the Indian Linguistic Area." *Language* 45(a): 274–299.

Feld, Steven (1982). *Sound and Sentiment*. Philadelphia: University of Pennsylvania Press.

Fernandez, James (1991). *Beyond Metaphor*. Stanford, Calif.: Stanford University Press.

Frei, Henri (1970). "Cinquante Onomatopees Japonaises." In David Cohen, ed., *Melange Marcel Cohen*. Janua Linguaraum: Series Major no. 27. The Hague: Mouton. pp. 359–367.

Friedrich, Paul (1974). "On Aspect Theory and Homeric Aspect." *International Journal* of *American Linguistics* (Memoir 28).

——— (1979). "The Symbol and Its Relative Non-arbitrariness." In Anwar Dil, ed., *Language, Context, and the Imagination: Essays by Paul Friedrich*. Stanford, Calif.: Stanford University Press. pp. 1–61.

——— (1986). *The Language Parallax: Linguistic Relativism and Poetic Indeterminacy*. Austin: University of Texas Press.

——— (1991). "Polytropy." In James Fernandez, ed., *Beyond Metaphor*. Stanford, Calif.: Stanford University Press. pp. 17–55.

Gellner, Ernest (1988). *Plough, Sword, and Books: The Structure of Human History*. Chicago: University of Chicago Press.

Goffman, Erving (1979). "Footing." *Semiotica* 25(1/2): 1–29.

Goody, Jack (1977). *The Domestication of the Savage Mind*. New York: Cambridge University Press.

Haiman, John, ed. (1985). *Iconicity in Syntax*. Amsterdam: John Benjamins.

Harrison, Regina (1989). *Signs, Songs, and Memory in the Andes*. Austin: University of Texas Press.

Hartmann, Roswith (1979). "Quechuismo preincaico en el Ecuador?" *Ibero-Amerikanisches Archiv* 5(3): 267–299.

Heath, Shirley B. (1983). *Ways with Words*. New York: Cambridge University Press.

Henderson, Eugenie J. A. (1965). Final -k in Khasi: A Secondary Phonological Pattern." *Lingua* 14: 459–466.

Hockett, Charles (1957). "Two Models of Grammatical Description." In Martin Joos, ed., *Readings in Linguistics I*. Chicago: University of Chicago Press. pp. 386–399.

Hopper, Paul (1979). "Aspect and Foregrounding in Discourse." In Talmy Givon, ed., *Syntax and Semantics*.Vol. 12: *Discourse and Syntax*. New York: Academic Press. pp. 213–241.

Hopper, Paul and Thompson, Sandra (1980). "Transitivity in Grammar and Discourse." *Language* 56(2): 251–299.

Householder, Fred (1946). "On the Problem of Sound and Meaning, an English Phonestheme." *Word* 2: 83–84.

Howes, David, ed. (1991). *The Varieties of Sensory Experience: A Sourcebook in the Anthropology of the Senses*. Toronto: University of Toronto Press.

Hjelmslev, Louis (1928). *Principes de Grammaire Generale*. Copenhagen.

Hymes, Dell (1974). "Ways of Speaking." In Richard Bauman and Joel Sherzer, eds., *Explorations in the Ethnography of Speaking*. New York: Cambridge University Press. pp. 443–451.

——— (1975). "Breakthrough into Performance." In Kenneth S. Goldstein and Dan Ben-Amos, eds., *Folklore: Performance and Communication*. The Hague: Mouton. pp.11–74.

——— (1981). "Discovering Oral Performance and Measured Verse in American Indian Narrative." In D. Hymes, ed., *"In Vain I Tried to Tell You": Essays in Native American Ethnopoetics*. Philadelphia: University of Pennsylvania Press. pp. 309–341.

Jakobson, Roman (1960). "Closing Statement: Linguistics and Poetics." In Thomas Sebeok, ed., *Style in Language*. Cambridge, Mass.: MIT Press. pp. 350–377.

——— (1968). "Poetry of Grammar and Grammar of Poetry." *Lingua* 21: 597–609.

——— (1971a). "On the Relation between Visual and Auditory Signs." In *Roman Jakobson Selected Writings*. Vol. 2: *Word and Language*. The Hague: Mouton. pp. 338–344.

——— (1971b). "Relationship between Russian Stem Suffixes and Verbal Aspects." In *Roman Jakobson Selected Writings*. Vol. 2: *Word and Language*. The Hague, Mounton. pp. 198–202.

——— (1971c). "Shifters, Verbal Categories, and the Russian Verb." In *Roman Jakobson Selected Writings*. Vol. 2: *Word and Language*. The Hague, Mouton. pp. 130–147.

——— (1985). "Two Poems by Pushkin." In Krystyna Pomorska and Stephen Rudy, eds., *Verbal Art, Verbal Sign, Verbal Time*. Minneapolis: University of Minnesota Press. pp. 47–58.

Jaramillo Alvaredo, Pio (1954). *El indio ecuatoriano*. Quito: Casa de la Cultura Ecuatoriana.

Johnson, Mark (1987). *The Body in the Mind*. Chicago: University of Chicago Press.

Kay, Paul (1977). "Language Evolution and Speech Style" In Ben G. Blount and Mary Sanches, eds., *Sociocultural Dimensions of Language Change*. New York: Academic Press. pp. 21–33.

Kean, Mary-Louise (1992). "Markedness." In William Bright, ed., *International Encyclopedia of Linguistics*. Vol. 2. New York: Oxford University Press. pp. 390–391.

Koehn, Edward and Koehn, Sally (1986). "Apalai." In Desmond C. Derbyshire and Geoffrey Pullum, eds., *Handbook of Amazonian Languages*, Vol. 1. Berlin: Mouton de Gruyter. pp. 33–127.

Kristeva, Julia (1989). *Language the Unknown*. New York: Columbia University Press.

Labov, William (1972). *Language in the Inner City*. Philadelphia: University of Pennyslvania Press.

Lakoff, George (1987). *Women, Fire and Dangerous Things: What Categories Reveal about the Mind.* Chicago: University of Chicago Press.

Lakoff, George and Johnson, Mark (1980). *Metaphors We Live By.* Chicago: University of Chicago Press.

Langacker, Ronald (1991). *Concept, Image and Symbol.* Berlin: Mouton de Gruyter.

León, Augustin M., ed. [1950?] n.d. *Gramatica de quichua.* Unpublished manuscript of Fray Agustin M. Leon, O. P., Dominican mission, Puyo, Ecuador.

Longacre, Robert (1985). "Sentences as Combinations of Clauses." In Timothy Shopen, ed., *Language Typology and Syntactic Description.* Vol 2: *Complex Constructions.* Cambridge: Cambridge University Press. pp. 235–286.

Lyons, John (1983). *Semantics*, vol. 2. Cambridge: Cambridge University Press.

Mannheim, Bruce (1986). "Popular Song and Popular Grammar: Poetry and Metalanguage." *Word* 37: 45–75

——— (1988). "The Sound Must Seem an Echo to the Sense: Some Cultural Determinants of Language Change in Southern Peruvian Quechua." *Michigan Discussions in Anthropology,* no. 8: 175–195.

——— (1991). *The Language of the Inka since the European Invasion.* Austin: University of Texas Press.

Markel, Norman and Hamp, Eric (1960–1961). "Connotative Meanings of Certain Phoneme Sequences." *Studies in Linguistics* 15: 47–61.

Moravcsik, Edith (1978). "Reduplicative Constructions." In Joseph Greenberg, ed., *Universals of Human Language.* Stanford, Calif.: Stanford University Press. pp. 299–334.

Newman, Paul (1968). "Ideophones from a Syntactic Point of View." *Journal of West African Languages* 2: 107–117.

Newman, Stanley (1933). "Further Experiments in Phonetic Symbolism," *American Journal of Psychology* 45: 53–75.

——— (1944). *Yokuts Language of California.* New York: Viking Fund.

Nichols, Johanna (1971). "Diminutive Consonant Symbolism in Western North America." *Language* 47: 826–848.

Nuckolls, Janis (1993). "The Semantics of Certainty in Quechua and Its Implications for a Cultural Epistemology." *Language in Society* 22: 235–255.

Orr, Carolyn (1962). "Ecuador Quichua Phonology." In Benjamin Elson, ed., *Ecuadorean Indian Languages I.* Norman: Summer Institute of Linguistics, University of Oklahoma. Linguistic Series no. 7, pp. 60–77.

——— (1978). *Dialectos Quichuas del Ecuador.* Quito: Instituto Lingüistico de Verano.

Orr, Carolyn and Wrisley, Betsy (1981). *Vocabulario Quichua del Oriente.* 2d Ed. Quito: Instituto Lingüistico de Verano and Ministerio de Educación y Cultura.

Parker, Gary (1969). "Comparative Quechua Phonology and Grammar IV: The Evolution of Quechua A." Honolulu: University of Hawaii. Working Papers in Linguistics 1 (9): 49–204.

——— (1971). "Comparative Quechua Phonology and Grammar V: The Evolution of Quechua B." Honolulu: University of Hawaii. Working Papers in Linguistics 3 (3): 45–109.

Peirce, Charles (1955). "Logic as Semiotic: The Theory of Signs." In Justus Buchler, ed., *Philosophical Writings of Peirce.* New York: Dover. pp. 98–119.

Popjes, Jack and Popjes, Jo (1986). "Canela-Krahô." In Desmond C. Derbyshire and Geoffrey Pullum, eds., *Handbook of Amazonian Languages*, vol. 1. Berlin: Mouton de Gruyter. pp. 28–199.

Ross, Ellen (1979). *Introduction to Ecuador Highland Quechua.* Madison, Wisc.: Foundation for Inter-Andean Development.

Salomon, Frank and Urioste, George (1991). *The Huarochirí Manuscript*. Austin: University of Texas Press.

Samarin, William (1971). "Survey of Bantu Ideophones." *African Language Studies* 12: 130–168.

Sapir, Edward (1921). *Language*. New York: Harcourt, Brace, and World.

——— (1929). "A Study in Phonetic Symbolism." In David Mandelbaum, ed., *Selected Writings of Edward Sapir*. Berkeley: University of California Press. pp. 61–72.

——— (1994). *The Psychology of Culture*. Lecture notes reconstructed and edited by Judith Irvine. New York: Mouton de Gruyter.

Saussure, Ferdinand de (1959). *Course in General Linguistics*. New York: Philosophical Library.

Schachter, Paul (1985). "Parts-of-Speech-Systems." In Timothy Shopen, ed., *Language Typology and Syntactic Description I: Clause Structure*. Cambridge: Cambridge University Press. pp. 3–61.

Schiffrin, Deborah (1984). "Jewish Argument as Sociability." *Language in Society* 13: 311–335.

Sharon, Douglas (1978). *Wizard of the Four Winds*. New York: Free Press.

Sherzer, Joel (1983). *Kuna Ways of Speaking*. Austin: University of Texas Press.

——— (1987). "A Discourse Centered Approach to Language and Culture." *American Anthropologist* 89: 295–309.

——— (1990). "On Play, Joking and Humor among the Kuna." In E. Basso, ed., *Native Latin American Cultures through their Discourse*. Bloomington: Folklore Institute, Indiana University. pp. 85–114.

Silverstein, Michael (1976). "Shifters, Linguistic Categories, and Cultural Description." In Keith Basso and Henry Selby, eds., *Meaning in Anthropology*. Albuquerque: University of New Mexico Press. pp. 11–55.

Slobin, Dan and Aksu, Ayhan (1982). "Tense, Aspect, and Modality in the Use of the Turkish Evidential." In Paul Hopper, ed., *Tense-Aspect: Between Semantics and Pragmatics*. Amsterdam: John Benjamins. pp. 185–200.

Stankiewicz, Edward (1964). "Problems of Emotive Language." In Thomas Sebeok, Alfred Hayes, and Mary Bateson, eds., *Approaches to Semiotics*. London: Mouton. pp. 239–264.

Stark, Louisa (1985). "Indigenous Languages of Lowland Ecuador: History and Current Status." In Harriet Klein and Louisa Stark, eds., *South American Indian Languages, Retrospect and Prospect*. Austin: University of Texas Press. pp. 157–194.

Tannen, Deborah (1979). "The Analogical Tradition and the Emergence of a Dialogical Anthropology." *Journal of Anthropological Research* 41(2): 387–400.

——— (1980). "A Comparative Analysis of Oral Narrative Strategies: Athenian Greek and American English." In Wallace Chafe, ed., *The Pear Stories*. Norwood, N. J.: Ablex. pp. 51–87.

——— (1982a). "Oral and Literate Strategies in Spoken and Written Narratives." *Language* 58(1): 1–21.

——— (1982b). "The Oral/Literate Continuum in Discourse." In Deborah Tannen, ed., *Spoken and Written Language: Exploring Orality and Literacy*. Norwood, N. J.: Ablex. pp. 1–16.

——— (1983). *The Spoken Word and the Work of Interpretation*. Philadelphia: University of Pennsylvania Press.

——— (1984). *Conversational Style: Analyzing Talk among Friends*. Norwood, N. J.: Ablex.

——— (1989). *Talking Voices: Repetition, Dialogue, and Imagery in Conversational Discourse*. New York: Cambridge University Press.

Timberlake, Alan (1982). "Invariance and the Syntax of Russian Aspect." In Paul Hopper, ed., *Tense-Aspect: Between Semantics and Pragmatics*. Amsterdam: John Benjamins. pp. 305–331.

Torero, Alfredo (1974). *El Quechua y la historia social andina*. Lima: Universidad Ricardo Palma.

Urban, Greg (1985). "The Semiotics of Two Speech Styles in Shokleng." In Elizabeth Mertz and Richard Parmentier, ed., *Semiotic Mediation*. New York: Academic Press. pp. 311–329.

——— (1991). "Stylized Dialogicity and Interpretability." In *A Discourse Centered Approach to Culture*. Austin: University of Texas Press. pp. 123–147.

Waugh, Linda (forthcoming). "Iconicity in the Lexicon and Its Relevance for a Theory of Morphology." In Marge Landsberg, ed., *Syntactic Iconicity and Freezes: The Human Dimension*. Berlin: Mouton de Gruyter.

Weber, David (1989). *A Grammar of Huallaga (Huánuco) Quechua*. Berkeley: University of California Press.

Werner, Heinz (1948). *Comparative Psychology of Mental Development*. New York: International Universities Press.

Wescott, Roger (1976)."Allolinguistics: Exploring the Peripheries of Speech." In Peter Reich, ed., *The Second LACUS Forum*. Columbia, S. C.: Hornbeam Press. pp. 497–513.

Whitten, Norman (1976). *Sacha Runa*. Urbana: University of Illinois Press.

——— (1985). *Sicuanga Runa*. Urbana: University of Illinois Press.

Whorf, Benjamin (1956). "The Punctual and Segmentative Aspects of Verbs in Hopi." In John Carroll, ed., *Language, Thought, and Reality*. Cambridge, MA: MIT Press, pp. 51–56.

Wise, Mary Ruth (1985). Indigenous Languages of Lowland Peru: History and Current Status. In Harriet M. Klein and Louisa R. Stark, eds., *South American Indian Languages, Retrospect and Prospect*. Austin: University of Texas Press. pp. 194–223.

INDEX

Achuar: beliefs, 122
Adverbs: deictic, 103-4
Advertising: and image schemas, 280
Affricates: word-initial, 139-40
Aki, 143, 145, 165-67
Amarun, 82-93
Ang, 59, 142, 143, 204-6
Anthropology: and linguistics, 82
Apalai (Carib language), 138-39
Arbitrariness, 33-36
Aspect, 4, 30, 41-42, 142-44; and iconicity, 21-23, 29; perfective, and sound-symbolic adverbs, 58-60; performative, 62-63; periphrastic, 53-58; and poetic messages, 30. *See also* Point-line schema
Assertion: suffixal, 114
Atomism, 34
Awing, 128, 143, 208-10
Ayacucho Quechua, 138
Aymara, 37

Benveniste, Emile, 33
Binnick, Robert, 31-32
Bird sounds, 13, 79, 119-24
Bolinger, Dwight, 74-75
Brazil: and Carib language, 138-39

Canela Krahô (Ge language), 139
Canelos (Pastaza Quechua), 138
Carib language (Brazil), 138-39
Casson, Ronald, 12
Cerrón-Palomino, Rodolfo, 18
Chained verbs. *See* Coreference
Cham, 143, 240-42
Chatterjee, Ranjit, 32
Chinda, 143, 145, 175-77, 275
Chu, 12, 94, 96
Ch^{y}u, 143, 237-40
Chung, Sandra, 23-26, 40, 60
Cinema: and sound-symbolic utterances, 14, 77, 79, 104, 178-79, 280
Clauses: chaining structure of, 9-10, 55-60
Closure, 25-26; adverbs signaling, 142-43
Cognitive salience, 8-9
Cognitive structures, 278-79
Cole, Peter, 138
Coreference verbs, 9-10, 66; and *-sha*, 55-60
Cosmology: Quechua, 82, 120-22
Cuzco Quechua, 138
Czech, 32

DeReuse, Willem, 38
Death: narratives of, 122-29
Detachment: and involvement, 80-81
Dialects: in Peru, 17-20; Quechua, 138-39
Diffloth, Gerard, 140-41

Discourse: approach to language, 4
Durativity, 25-26, 40; and aspect, 55-58
Dzas, 142, 160, 252-55
Dzawn, 143, 148-50
Dzing, 107-8, 142, 250-52
Dzir, 142, 143, 189-94
Dziri, 183

Education: public, 286 n.2 ; in Puka yaku, 131-34. *See also* Literacy
English: and sound-symbolic words, 277-78, 283 n.2
Equivalences, 103
Event: process, and state, 42

Feld, Steven, 119
Foregrounding: intonational, 73-78, 104; syntactic, 71-73
Friedrich, Paul, 11, 28-30, 43

Ge language, 139
Grammar: as ecological system, 33. *See also* Aspect; Cognitive salience; Charles Hockett; Linda Waugh

Habituality, 25
Harrison, Regina, 82-83
Hausa, 277
Hockett, Charles, 31, 33-36
Hopi: and aspect, 27-28
Hopper, Paul, 32
Huallaga Quechua, 138
Humor, 118
Huy, 143, 145, 162-65, 166

Iconicity: and aspect, 21-23, 29, 32; and grammatical theory, 33-38; metaphorical and diagrammatic, 97-99; and Peirce, 81-82; as structural principle of language, 36-38
Ideophones: in Hausa, 277; and sound-symbolic adverbs, 138-39
Image schemas, 4, 73, 139, 142, 278; in Lakoff's work, 30-31; vs. logical, propositional structure, 12-13
Images: lexical, 96-97
Imbabura Quechua, 138
Indigenous peoples: rights of, 129-33
Ing, 106-7, 143, 206-8
Iterativity, 25

Jakobson, 12, 29, 30; and linguistic functions, 102-4; and theories of aspect, 22-23
Johnson, Mark, 11, 31

Kal^{y}a, 128, 143, 242-46
Kaluli, 13, 79, 119
Kant, Immanuel, 12
Ki, 143, 229-31
Koehn, Edward and Sally, 138
Kristeva, Julia, 3, 14, 280
Kuna: and humorous narrative, 118

Lakoff, George, 11, 30-33, 278; and cognitive salience, 9; and image schemas, 73, 139
Language: scientific representation of, 3, 6. *See also* English; Quechua; Russian; Spanish
Lengthening, 68-71
León, Augustin M.,138
Ling, 74, 143, 196-201
Linguistics: anthropological, 82
Literacy, 80-81, 102, 131-34
Longacre, Robert, 55
L^{y}u, 143, 167-70
L^{y}utarina, 141
L^{y}uw, 145
Lyons, John, 42

Magic, 106; death and, 120-25
Mannheim, Bruce, 36-38, 96, 138
Markedness, 5, 62, 102
Metaphors: and iconicity, 97-99
Modal/emotive function: and sound-symbolic adverbs, 115-19
Modernization: and sound-symbolic discourse, 102, 132
Mokilese, 26

Moravcsik, Edith, 63, 65
Morphology: Hockett's, 33-36
Multinational corporations: and indigenous land, 129-30
Myth: past-tense in, 51-53; and sound-symbolic utterances, 106

Narratives: of animals, 82-93; of death, 122-29; past-tense in, 51-53
Naturalness: conceptions of, 101, 121-22
Newman, Paul, 277
Newman, Stanley, 139

Objectivism, 11, 30-31
Onomatopoeia: in Quechua dialects, 138; Saussure's objections to, 7-8
OPIP, 129-30

Pa, 108-9
Pak, 10, 143, 222-26
Palay, 142, 143, 219-22
Papua New Guinea, 13, 79, 119
Parameters: aspect, 24-25
Patang, 7, 105, 142, 226-28
Peirce, Charles: and iconicity, 7, 81-82, 98
Perfective, 58-60
Ping, 73-74, 115, 142, 143, 215-20
Pitch rises, 73-78
Poetic: functions, 103-6; and humor, 118; messages, 30. *See also* Tropes
Point-line schema, 4, 14, 31-32, 144
Polang, 75, 98, 142, 145, 155-58; and intonational foregrounding, 104; and movements in water, 94-95, 96-97
Polo, 75-76, 143, 201-3
Predicates: and sound-symbolic adverbs, 142
Prepositional phrases: sound-symbolic adverbs as, 142
Process: event and state, 42
Pronunciation: of adverbs, 140
Puka yaku, 15-16; and Sara yaku, 102, 131-32

Quechua: classification of, 17-20; dialects, 138-39; as dynamicity language, 40; lowland Ecuadorean vs. Pastaza, 6, 15; Pastaza, 17-20; Southern Peruvian, 37-38, 96; verb roots, 102. *See also* Sound-symbolic adverbs; Verbs

Realism: experiential, 31
Reduplication, 63-65
Repetition, 65-68, 124, 143
Ross, Ellen, 138
Russian: and aspect, 22-23, 26, 32

Sa, 141, 143, 145-48
Sapir, 4, 139
Sara yaku: and Puka Yaku, 102
Saussure, Ferdinand de, 6-11, 33
Saw, 77, 143, 263-66
Schemas. *See* Image schemas
Semantics: sound-symbolic, 142-44, 145
Shaka, 126-28, 143, 246-49
Shaw, 143, 266-67
Sherzer, Joel, 4, 118
Signification, 33
Slavic, 29
Sociolinguistics, 81
Song: and magic, 120-22
Sound-symbolic adverbs: and perfective aspect, 42, 58-60; and verb endings, 139
Sound symbolism: and functions, 102-19; and physiology, 122; and women's speech, 132-33
Sounds: sound images of, 93-94
Spanish: verbs, in Quechua, 133
Speech event: vs. narrated event, 12, 22
Speech styles: as cultural indice, 5, 101-2; and markedness, 62
Spirits: and sound, 120-22
Stankiewicz, Edward, 11
Stark, Louisa, 18-19
Subjectivism, 11
Suffixes: of verbs, 43-53, 114

Syllable structure: and sound-symbolic adverbs, 139-40
Syntactic displacement, 72, 105
Syntactic foregrounding, 71-73
Syntactic isolation, 73

Tak, 78, 93, 99, 143, 178-86
Tʔak, 111, 113
Tʔam, 143, 145, 150-52
Tʔapi, 105-6, 141, 143, 186-89
Tarascan, 29
Tas, 128, 141, 271-75
Taw, 106-7, 143, 112-13, 213-15
Tay, 143, 255-59
Tense: and aspect, 22
Theory: descriptivist, 34; IP and IA, 34-35; linguistic, 6-11
Timberlake, Alan, 23-26, 40, 60
Toa, 141, 142, 143, 145, 153-55
Ton, 95, 143, 268-71
Transitivity, 42
Tropes: of death, 125; poetic, 11, 104-5
Tsak, 10, 59, 72, 143, 194-96
Tsapak: 97, 98
Tsuk, 59, 143, 232-34
Tsung, 143, 261-63
Tsuping, 76, 143, 259-61
Tsupu, 159-62
Tupu, 95, 98, 103, 142, 145
Tus, 142, 143, 210-12

Upglide, 74
Upjump, 75-77
Urban, Greg, 4-5, 62, 101-2

Verbs: and adverb relationship, 139, 141-42; and conjugation of *rina*, 281-82; and *karana*, 109; and *rikuna*, 99; roots, 27-28, 102; Spanish, in Quechua, 133; and stem, 43-53; and to be, in Quechua, 285 n.3. *See also* Coreference
Vowels: high and low, 140

Walʔang, 143, 145, 170-72
Waling, 76, 143, 234-37
Water: adverbs for movement in, 155-62; and underwater world, 286 nn. 2, 3
Waugh, Linda, 36-38
Weber, David, 138
Werner, Heinz, 283
Whorf, Benjamin, 27-28
Wikang, 143, 145, 172-75
Women's speech: and sound symbolism, 132-34